中国传统武术教程
汉英对照

Traditional Chinese Wushu

肖亚康　陈海英　主编

河南大学出版社
HENAN UNIVERSITY PRESS
·郑州·

图书在版编目（CIP）数据

中国传统武术教程：汉英对照 / 肖亚康，陈海英主编． -- 郑州：河南大学出版社，2022.12（2024.8重印）
ISBN 978-7-5649-5387-4

Ⅰ．①中… Ⅱ．①肖… ②陈… Ⅲ．①武术－中国－高等学校－教材－汉、英 Ⅳ．①G852

中国版本图书馆CIP数据核字（2022）第252495号

中国传统武术教程：汉英对照
ZHONGGUO CHUANTONG WUSHU JIAOCHENG：HAN-YING DUIZHAO

责任编辑	程若春
责任校对	林方丽
封面设计	郭　灿
出版发行	河南大学出版社
	地址：郑州市郑东新区商务外环中华大厦2401号
	邮编：450046　电话：0371-86059701（营销部）
	网址：hupress.henu.edu.cn
排　　版	河南大学出版社设计排版部
印　　刷	广东虎彩云印刷有限公司
版　　次	2022年12月第1版　　印　次　2024年8月第2次印刷
开　　本	787 mm×1092 mm 1/16　　印　张　27
字　　数	625千字　　　　　　　　定　价　60.00元

版权所有，侵权必究
本书如有印装质量问题，请与河南大学出版社营销部联系调换。

前　言

中华武术，源远流长，以其深远的中国文化基础和内部庞大的结构形成了独特完整的文化体系。武术不仅是一门技术，更是一门学问，是中国优秀文化的核心载体与代表，还是滋养人成长、健康、深邃、智达、修身的生存方式。本教程内容涉及武术概述、武术基本功和基本动作、传统武术经典拳术选编、传统器械组合选编、健身桩功选录、典型擒拿术、武术常用词汇汉英对照等七章。本教程最大的特点是以中国武术传承有序的经典传统武术为切入点，以武术文化、传统武术拳理技法、健身功法和擒拿术等构成教材内容，直观地彰显了中国武术"打、练、养、修"为一体的传承培养特色，使得整部教材的内容更加充实，也更富有新意，更好地认知和把握传统武术文化的内涵与功能。

本教程是黄淮学院规划教材，适用于普通高等院校体育专业武术选项教学、外国来华留学生、各类武术院馆校教学、涉外武术教学，同时也是国内外广大武术爱好者的参考资料。面对中华武术国际化推广进程和国际化教学发展需要，我们在借鉴、继承、探索中编写出版这本教材，由于水平有限，不妥之处在所难免，恳请广大读者批评指正，我们将不胜感谢。

编者

2022 年 11 月

Foreword

Chinese Wushu, with a long history, has formed a unique and complete cultural system with its profound Chinese cultural foundation and huge internal structural connotation. Wushu is not only a craft, but also knowledge. It is the core carrier and representative of Chinese culture, and a way of life that nourishes people's growth, health and self-cultivation. The contents of the textbook include the overview of Wushu, the basic skills and movements, the selection of traditional Quanshu, the typical combination of instruments, the health-keeping skills, self-defense techniques, and the bilingual Wushu terms. This textbook focuses on the orderly inheritance of Wushu culture illustrating the features of training Wushu talents by "fighting, practicing, developing and meditating". This book is more innovative and has richer contents which will help you grasp the essence and function of traditional culture and bring you better learning experiences.

As a textbook sponsored by Huanghuai University, this book is suitable for Wushu majors in various colleges or universities, foreign students in China, the students in Wushu schools and all the Wushu learners and players at home and abroad. Facing the rapid development of international education of Wushu, we compose this book by learning from the previous researches, inheriting the tradition and exploring the future. However, due to our limited ability, it is inevitable to make some mistakes in the writing. We are sincerely looking forward to your suggestions.

Xiao Yakang & Chen Haiying
November, 2022

目 录
Contents

第一章　中国武术概述 ·· 001
Chapter 1 Introduction to Chinese Wushu ··· 001
 第一节　武术的概念 ·· 001
 1.1 Concept of Wushu ··· 001
 第二节　武术的特点与作用 ·· 007
 1.2 Features and Functions of Wushu ·· 007
 第三节　武术的流派、形式与分类 ·· 013
 1.3 The Schools, Form and Classification of Wushu ····························· 013

第二章　武术基本动作与方法 ·· 027
Chapter 2 Basic Movements and Actions ·· 027

第三章　传统拳术选编 ·· 051
Chapter 3 Selections of Traditional Quanshu ··· 051
 第一节　红拳十三式 ·· 051
 3.1 Thirteen Moves of Hongquan ··· 051
 第二节　小红拳 ·· 067
 3.2 Xiao Hongquan ·· 067
 第三节　翻子拳 ·· 109
 3.3 Fanzi Quan ··· 109
 第四节　劈挂拳 ·· 144
 3.4 Pigua Quan ··· 144
 第五节　华　拳 ·· 184
 3.5 Hua Quan ··· 184

第四章　传统器械选编　226
Chapter 4 Selections of Traditional Instruments　226

第一节　盘龙棍　226
4.1 Dragon Club (Panlong Gun)　226

第二节　龙凤双刀　243
4.2 Dragon and Phoenix Double Blades　243

第三节　鞭杆　264
4.3 Biangan　264

第四节　三节棍　282
4.4 Three-Section Club　282

第五节　朴刀　292
4.5 Long-Hilt Broadsword (Pudao)　292

第六节　小连枷　324
4.6 Xiao Lianjia　324

第五章　武术桩功选编　342
Chapter 5 Selections of Wushu Zhuang Gong　342

第一节　武术桩功简介　342
5.1 Brief Introduction to Wushu Zhuang Gong　342

第二节　四段功　344
5.2 Siduan Gong　344

第三节　十三太保功　349
5.3 Shisantaibao Gong　349

第四节　开合功　355
5.4 Kaihe Gong　355

第六章　擒拿与解脱术　360
Chapter 6 Capture and Escape (Qinnashu)　360

第一节　擒拿术简介　360
6.1 Brief Introduction to Qinnashu　360

第二节　擒拿要害部位分类　366
6.2 The Key Parts of Qinna　366

第三节　擒拿解脱方法举要　376
6.3 The Ways to Get away from the Capture (Jietuo)　376

第七章 武术常用词汇汉英对照
Chapter 7 Chinese-English Wushu Terms
课程教学词汇汉英对照 392
Chinese-English Wushu Terms for Class Teaching 392
武术常用词汇汉英对照 394
Chinese-English Wushu Terms 394

主要参考文献 421
Bibliography 421

后　记 423
Acknowledgments 424

第一章　中国武术概述
Chapter 1 Introduction to Chinese Wushu

第一节　武术的概念
1.1 Concept of Wushu

一、武术的产生与发展 The Origin and Development of Wushu

武术是中华优秀传统文化的典型代表，在中华历史发展长河中延绵了数千年，形成了独特、鲜明的民族文化内涵与特色，成为中华民族传统体育项目的代表。武术产生于中国先民生产实践、军事战争搏斗技术与经验的总结，其内容丰富，结构体系庞大，文化思想意蕴深远，具有防身、健身、修性、竞技、娱乐等诸多价值功能，融汇了中华民族文化思想精髓，成为中华文化的结晶与缩影。

Wushu is a typical representative of Chinese excellent traditional culture, which has lasted for thousands of years with a unique and distinctive connotation and characteristics. Wushu originated from the absorption of the technologies or experience of Chinese ancestors in laboring and fighting. Being rich in content, huge in structure system and profound in cultural and ideological meaning, it has many value functions such as self-defense, fit-keep, cultivation, competition, entertainment, etc. It integrates the cultural and ideological essence of Chinese people from ancient times to the present, and becomes the crystallization and epitome of Chinese culture.

武术经历了数千年历史演进与发展，从人类早期与大自然共生中的简单防卫技能不断完善技术体系，石木兵器变为"五兵""五刃"，逐渐形成各种拳术与"十八般兵器"，由简单的射、砍、刺、击等发展为规范的刺、劈、崩、点、撩、挂、扎、斩、扫、缠、穿、架、踢、打、摔、跌等完备的技法思路，春秋战国时期演进成套路形式，明清之际武术发展到鼎盛时期，出现诸多武术专著和文献，各拳种、流派泾渭分明，形成了"打、练、养"为一体的武术技理体系。

Wushu has experienced thousands of years of evolution and development. At the very beginning, it only means simple self-defense skills for people to survive the rough living environment. Then, with the accomplishment of the skills, from the primitive society to the feudal society, the wood or stone-made weapons have become "eighteen kinds of weapons" in various styles of Quan. The moves in Wushu are also enriched from easy arrow-shooting, cutting, stabbing, striking to more standard acts, such as splitting, breaking, covering, hanging, beating and so on. During the Warring States period (770BC-221BC), Wushu developed into a complete set system. It came to its peak in the Ming and Qing Dynasties (1368-1644) along with the various styles of Quan and references as well as all kinds of schools. A cultural and technical system integrating "fight, practice and cultivation" has come into being.

1927年在南京创立"中央国术馆"，1928年和1933年举行了两次国术国考。1936年组队赴柏林参加第十一届奥林匹克运动会进行武术表演并惊艳世界。中华人民共和国成立后，武术成为新中国体育事业的重要组成部分，1955年国家体委设立武术研究室，将武术列为体育院、系专业课，1956年成立中国武术协会，1957年武术列为体育竞赛项目，1960年和1974年组建武术代表团出访亚洲和欧洲诸多国家，至上世纪80年代，通过武术团出访、国际武术邀请赛、世界武术锦标赛、国际武术推广等活动与世界诸多国家和地区进行友好往来，武术一度成为英语国家民众认知中国的文化符号。武术以中国古老东方哲学思想形成了"和合""尚武崇德""师法自然""性命双修"的练养原则，受到全世界追求健康人们的青睐，武术也不断为全世界爱健康、爱和平的人民服务。

Nanjing established the "National Martial Arts Museum" in 1927. In 1928 and 1933, it held two national examinations on Wushu. In 1936, the martial arts performance was displayed before the world in the 11th Olympic Games in Berlin. After the founding of the People's Republic of China, Wushu has become an important part of sports in New China. In 1955, the National Sports Commission set up a Wushu Research Office, and listed Wushu as a professional course in the Physical Education Institutes or departments. In 1956, the Chinese Wushu Association was established. In 1957, Wushu was listed as a sports competition item. In 1960 and 1974, a Wushu delegation was set up to visit many countries in Asia and Europe.

In the 1980s, Wushu once became a symbol for people in other countries to recognize China through the overseas-visiting of Wushu delegations and International Wushu Games. It is favored by people all over the world who pursue physical or mental health.

二、武术的技击本质 The fighting nature of Wushu

武术从起源产生、发展都离不开其技击核心本质与特征。在不同的历史时期对武术呈现不同的称谓，它的内涵与外延是随着社会历史发展和武术本身的文化演进而变化，如角力、手搏、角觗、技击、短兵、拳、武舞、武艺、国术等称谓，多着眼于武术技击本质的总结，具有搏斗内涵的称谓还有"角力""手搏""相扑""击剑""较棒""刺枪"等。以舞练形式和格斗运动还有"戈舞""矛舞""刀舞""剑舞""双剑舞"等等都蕴含对技击的概括与理解。

The origin and development of Wushu are inseparable from its core and nature. In different historical periods, there are different names for Wushu. Its connotation and extension change with the development of social history and its own evolution. It was once called wrestling, hand wrestling, fighting, Duanbing, Quan, martial dance or martial techniques. These names are focused on the summary of fighting skills. Besides, the names such as Stab Dancing, Spear Dancing, and Sword Dancing connot the fighting nature.

从历史发展来看，有不少归属武术类的名称，春秋战国时称"技击"兵技巧一类，汉代出现了"武艺"一词，并延用至明末，清初又借用南朝《文选》中"偃闭武术"（当时泛指军事）的"武术"一词，民国时称"国术"，新中国成立后仍沿用"武术"一词，在海外，很多华人华侨称做功夫。

Historically, there are many names belonging to Wushu. In the Han Dynasty, the term "Wuyi" was used until the end of Ming Dynasty. In the early Qing Dynasty, the term "Wushu" came into being. In the Republic of China, it was called "Guoshu". After the year 1949, the term "Wushu" was still used. Many overseas Chinese tend to call it "Kung Fu".

武术是从古代军事战争中总结出来的技击搏杀术，有丰富的技术法则与训练方法以及选拔考试制度。这些技术散落流传于民间和社会各个阶层，成为民间、宫廷、社会追捧的风尚，进一步丰富了武术的内涵与形式，武术技击方法也更加丰富多变，包括踢、打、摔、拿、击、刺以及身体躯干挤、撞、抖、靠等进攻技法，摔法、拿法也更为灵巧多变，孕育出多种风格独异的拳种技法与广博的器械类别，形成诸多拳种流派独到的技击方法与风格内涵，构成了中国武术丰富多彩、气象万千的庞大技术体系。

在运动形式上，既有对抗形式的搏斗运动，又有势势相承的套路运动和养生救护的功法内容。

As a kind of fighting skill born in ancient fighting fields, Wushu has rich technical training methods and examination systems. These techniques spread to all levels of the folk and society, and become the social fashion. The techniques are becoming more flexible and changeable. There are not only fighting movements but also the set-up routines and the function of health preservation and rescue.

三、武术的文化体系与哲学思想 The cultural system and philosophy of Wushu

武术不仅是以技击为核心的人体文化，更是一门中华文化现象，在其长期发展演进过程中，经历不同时代的洗礼，汲取了传统哲学、伦理学、养生学、兵学、中医学、美学等多种传统文化思想和观念，凝聚着中国哲学的智慧、美学的意境、艺术学的神韵、兵学的谋略、中医学的救护、文化学的自强，形成了特有的思维方式、民族性格和伦理道德。

In its long-term evolution, Wushu has been nourished by ancient philosophy, ethics, self-preservation, warring laws, traditional Chinese medicine, aesthetics, etc., and condensed the unique thinking mode, national character and ethics.

武术以尚武崇德树立了文化结构基础，以儒家仁爱观念构筑武术伦理思想核心，以道家"道论"建立了武术认识与方法论，以法家变革为武术塑造秩序意识，深厚的中华民族传统文化为武术提供了思想理论框架。道家老子就从《道德经》揭示了武之道，讲"柔弱"胜"刚强"，"无为"而"有为"的"武之道"思想。儒家孔子对"武术"认识更深，他告诫学生"有文事者必有武备，安能以小道末艺视武者乎？"还有阴阳家对立统一、墨家尚力兼爱、兵家虚实谋略等等诸多哲学思想对武术文化与思想体系奠定了强大基础。

The cultural structure of Wushu is built on the Confucian benevolence, Taoist methodology and the Legalist transformation. Lao Tzu revealed the way of Wushu from *Tao Te Ching*, "softness is better than hardness" and "lack of advancement is better than advancement". Confucius told his students that "those who are of letters must learn Wushu too". The philosophical ideas of Yin-Yang School, Mohism (emphasizing strength and loving all), and the Art of War (strategic warfare) laid a solid foundation for the system of Chinese

Wushu.

中国传统文化不仅提高和发展了武术理论，而且决定着武术的运动技术、技法功能特征与价值取向，是促进武术健康发展的内在动力源泉，不断丰富和完善了中华武术文化的形态与体系。武术的一切活动和思维皆源于中华传统文化思想，并表现出强烈的体悟过程，以技击为载体在实践对抗中取得获胜和生存的本质特性决定了这种身体技巧由武技进入技艺层面，再由技艺上升为"道"的境界。武术的拳技、法理和养生修身诸多方面不仅以外练强壮，更以培养元气提升内在的养护和强实，达到内、外修炼有法，养气、炼气顺应"天人合一"，形成了武术内涵丰富、寓意深刻、注重内外兼修、德艺兼备的文化与思想体系，从而使中华武术成为世界民族文化的奇葩瑰宝。

Chinese traditional culture not only improves but also determines the functional characteristics and technical skills of Wushu. It is the internal power source to promote healthy development. All the activities of Wushu show a strong process of appreciation. The essential characteristics of winning and surviving in the practical confrontations determine that this physical skill enters the technical level and then rises from the technical level to the realm of "Tao". Wushu not only makes the body strong, but also refines the inner Qi to conform to the "unity of man and nature", forming a cultural system and ideological theory.

四、武术的概念与属性 The concept and attributes of Wushu

发展到今天，武术的基本定义可概括为：以中华传统文化为理论基础，以徒手和器械的踢、打、摔、拿、击、刺、劈、扎等攻防技击为主要技术内容，以套路演练、搏斗对抗、功法锻炼为主要运动形式，注重内外兼修的民族传统体育项目。武术历史悠久，源远流长，具有民族性、文化性、艺术性、体育性、健身性、竞技性、娱乐性等多种综合属性特点。武术所展现给人们的是一种最为朴素、简练、实用、美观的身体活动形式，它以人体内在精神气质为基础，强调手、眼、身法、步、精神、气、力、功高度协调配合，体现了中国传统体育项目注重阴阳平衡、天人合一、身心和谐、形神兼备、内外双修的修持理念。

Today, the basic definition of Wushu can be summarized as follows: A traditional sport based on traditional culture, with unarmed or armed kicking, hitting, stabbing, pricking and so on as the main technical contents, focusing on both internal and external cultivation. It is characterized by nationality, culture, art, sports, fitness, competition, entertainment and other comprehensive attributes. It shows the simplest, most concise, and beautiful form of physical activities. It emphasizes the balance of Yin and Yang, the unity of heaven and man, the harmony of body and mind, the combination of body and spirit, and the cultivation of both inside and outside.

新中国成立以后，确立武术为正式体育运动项目之一，属于民族传统体育类。武术的体育归属开辟了武术更多新形式，武术学校教育和竞技比赛得到广泛开展，武术健身与竞技功能获得了空前发展，开拓了以西方体育思想指导下追求人体运动能力为最高目标的现代竞技武术，同时，兼顾继承发展传统武术。传统武术简单概括是产生于古代农耕文明并长期受传统文化滋养，以攻防技击动作为本质，注重内外兼修，融中国特色文化内涵为一体，发展历史流传有序的各种自成体系拳种的总称。

Since 1949, Wushu has been established as one of the formal sports, which belongs to the category of national traditional sports. Wushu education and competitions have been widely carried out, and the functions of its keeping fit have been given unprecedented attention. Under the guidance of western sports thoughts, it has developed modern competitive Wushu with the highest goal of human body sports ability.

现代竞技武术以传统武术为根源，与传统武术共同推进国内外传承和创新发展。中国武术与奥林匹克体育既有东西方文化基因上的根本区别又同时存在相同的进取精神和道德价值观，中国武术文化与奥林匹克文化的融合将成为世界体育文化发展的必然趋势。因此，武术的基本属性是它所具有体育和文化的双重特性，武术是中华民族的一种宝贵文化遗产，武术源于中国，属于世界。

Modern competitive Wushu takes traditional Wushu as its root, and promotes new development at home and abroad together with traditional Wushu. Wushu and Olympic sports not only have the fundamental differences in the eastern and Western cultural genes, but also have the same moral value system, enterprising spirit and values. The integration of Wushu and Olympic culture will become the inevitable trend of the development of world sports culture. Wushu comes from China and belongs to the world.

第二节 武术的特点与作用
1.2 Features and Functions of Wushu

一、武术的特点 Wushu's Features

(一)技击特点 The art of attack and defense

武术产生于古代军事战争,赋予了武术技击本质特点。武术动作具有攻防技击性,无论是武术特有的套路练习形式还是搏斗对抗练习形式,都是以技击实践决定动作基本依据和相关的训练方法。在实践运用中,其目的在于杀伤、制服对方,它常常以最有效的技击方法,迫使对方失去反抗能力,这些技击术至今仍在军队、公安中被采用。

Wushu is originated from ancient military fighting which endows it with essential features of attack and defense. The acts of Wushu is mainly based on the military training or the actual fighting ways in the battle fields. The purpose of these training or the fighting ways is to kill or subdue the enemy effectively or efficiently. These attacking and defending skills which can force the opposite lose his chance to fight back or attacks are still used in the present soldier or police training.

武术作为体育运动,技术上仍不失攻防技击的特性,武术技击以"攻、守"辩证关系奠定了技术的演变规律,成为武术拳术、器械和搏斗以及功法共同追求的价值理念。搏斗运动集中体现了武术攻防格斗的特点,但是从体育的观念出发,它受到竞赛规则制约,以不伤害对方为原则。套路运动是中国武术特有的表现形式,不少动作在技术规格、运动幅度等方面与技击意图有所变化,但是动作方法上仍然保留了技击的特性,随着武术与文化属性的发展,武术的技击本质特点,仍将作为武术技术的最基本特点而长期存在。

However, as a sport game now, Wushu is now restricted by the rules of competition and required not to hurt the others in the fighting. Technically, attacking and defending are two laws of Wushu. Whether it is a style of Quan or a kind of Wushu apparatus, the practices of them all follow the laws of attacking and defending. With the involvement of Wushu in the modern competitive sports, some of its acts or moves may be changed, but the basic features will exist for a long time as an identity of Wushu.

（二）内外合一，形神兼备的民族风格 The national style of internal and external integration

武术讲究形体规范，又追求精神传意、内外合一的整体观。所谓内，指心、神、意等心志活动和气息的运行；外，即手眼身步等外在形体活动。内外合一是形神兼备的具体表现，内与外、形与神是相互联系的统一整体。

Wushu emphasizes both the standard form and spiritual resemblance. It pursues the internal and external integration. The internal refers to mental activities and breath movement while the external refers to the physical activities. The unity of inner and outer is the concrete expression of both form and spirit.

武术"内外合一，形神兼备"的特点主要通过武术功法和技法来体现。"内练精气神，外练筋骨皮"是各拳种流派练功的准则，如太极拳主张身心合修，要求"以心行气，以气运身"，形意拳讲究"内三合与外三合"，少林拳也要求"精、力、气、骨、神"内外兼修。拳谚有"内练一口气，外练筋骨皮"，强调外练，又要内练，强调外练是注重形体外在的肌肉、关节、骨骼的锻炼，注重由这些运动系统所完成的各种外在动作的能力要求，强调内练就是对人体内脏、神经系统"精、气、神"的锻炼。

The unity of both form and spirit are mainly realized by Wushu skills and techniques. "Internal training for energy, Qi and spirit, external training for muscles, bones and skin" is the main principle of various schools of Wushu. For example, Taijiquan advocates the combination of body and mind. Xingyiquan stresses the combination of "three internals and three externals". Shaolinquan also requires the combination of Qi and bones. This combination emphasizes the training on the internal organs and nervous system as well as human body.

武术内家拳和外家拳虽在练神修气的方法上有所区别，但对内练与外练的特性上是一致的。太极拳把手眼身法步的协调动作同导引吐纳结合起来，使意识、呼吸和动作三者密切结合，成为内外合一的内功拳术。少林五祖拳拳理以内练五脏，颐气养神，练气化神，树立了五祖拳的练拳宗旨。内练与外练是武术修持的特性，内练是注重生命修养，是对外练的内在支配，内炼不仅是精气神的修炼，还包含道德情操的修养，通过精气神与道德情操的内练和完善引领外练的精湛才能达到形神的高度统一。

There are some differences in the methods of cultivating spirit and Qi for Neijiaquan and Waijiaquan Schools. Taijiquan combines the coordinated movements of hands, eyes, legs, arms, and feet with breath so that consciousness, breath and movement are closely combined. Shaolin Wuzuquan tends to practice five internal organs to cultivate Qi and spirit. Internal training is not only the cultivation of essence and spirit, but also the cultivation of moral sentiment. Only through the internal training and perfection of essence and spirit and moral sentiment, can we achieve the high unity of form and spirit.

(三) 广泛的适应性 Wide adaptability

武术的练习形式、内容丰富多样,有竞技对抗性的搏斗运动,如散手、推手、短兵、长兵,有适应演练的各种拳术、器械和对练,还有与其相适应的各种练功养护方法。不同的拳种和器械有不同的动作结构、技术要求与运动风格,分别适应人们不同年龄、性别、体质的需要进行选择练习。同时,武术对场地、器材的要求较低,拳谚有"拳打卧牛之地",武术练习可以根据场地大小变化练习内容和方式,受时间、季节限制小,较之其他体育运动项目,具有更为广泛的适应性。

There are various forms and contents of Wushu, including competitive and antagonistic fighting sports, such as Sanshou, Pushing hand, short weapon, long weapon and all kinds of training methods adapted to it. Different kinds of Quan and instruments have different structures, requirements and styles, which can meet the needs of different ages, genders and physiques. At the same time, it has low requirements for sites and equipment. Wushu practice can change the content and method of practice according to the size of the practicing places. Compared with other sports, it has a more extensive adaptability.

武术强调文化习得和对个人修身养性的关注,武术以德养性、以技修身,是通过技术体验道德并追求人生哲学的学问。武术文化的深邃内涵与精神更适应、更贴近人的健身修身需要,武术能在民间历久不衰,受到全世界健身爱好者青睐与这一特点不无关系,这一特点为现代大众健身活动提供方便,武术运动社会化也不断得到发展。

Wushu emphasizes cultural acquisition and personal cultivation. The profundity, connotation and spirit of Wushu culture are more suitable and closer to people's health and self-cultivation needs. Wushu has been popular among fitness enthusiasts all over the world for a long time, which is not unrelated to this feature. This feature provides convenience for modern public physical training activities, and the socialization of Wushu sports are also developing.

二、武术的作用 Functions of Wushu

(一) 防身自卫作用 Self-defense

武术本质上是一种技击术,进行武术练习一方面可以全面提高人的身体素质,逐渐提高人进行技击对抗的能力;另一方面学习与掌握各种踢打摔拿击刺等技击方法,可以提高身体的灵活性和反应能力。武术练习,持之以恒的练功,还能增长劲力,提高练习者进行技击对抗的水平,具备防身自卫的能力。

Wushu practice can comprehensively improve one's physical quality and gradually improve his ability to self-defense. Learning and mastering various techniques such as kicking, throwing, holding, stabbing, etc. can improve the flexibility and reaction ability of the body.

现代竞技体育下的武术竞赛套路运动技击价值虽然已不是那么突出,但这些技术中仍包含着原来实战技击技术的主要攻防环节,所以在掌握了这些技术以后,再经过必要的训练,就可以使之还原成原来的生死搏斗中的实战技术。同时在其训练过程中,加强必要的专项身体素质训练,进一步提高防身自卫和应变意外情况的能力。

In modern competitive sports, the techniques still contain the main attacking and defensing. Therefore, after necessary training, one can strengthen the special physical fitness training, and further improve the ability of self-defense and contingency.

(二) 健身养生作用 Fitness and Health Preservation

武术不仅追求打和练,更追求修和养。武术不仅强调形体上的锻炼,而且更关注人体身心全面的锻炼与养护,对外能利关节、强筋骨、壮体魄,对内能理脏腑、通经脉、调精神,尤其是武术许多功法注重调息行气和意念活动,对调节体内环境的平衡、调养气血、改善人体机能,增强体质是十分有益的。

Wushu not only emphasizes the physical exercise, but also pays more attention to the comprehensive physical and mental exercise and maintenance of the human body. It can regulate the internal energy, the viscera, the channels, and the spirit. It is very beneficial to adjust the balance of the internal environment, regulate the Qi and blood, improve the human body function, and strengthen the physique.

中国人历来重视生命养生之道,武术发展的过程中和道家养生术、导引、气功相互融合,形成了丰富的练养方法和养生保健手段。武术练习围绕人体四肢以及内部脏器、经络活动运化来实现技击目的和养生保健,一切武术活动都关切人体生命修性是否顺遂自然，是否"精气神"统一，能否"性命双修"。武术动作练习讲求配合呼吸，以气息运行带动劲力释放和调适内脏器官的运化，武术桩功、气功以及各种配合中医药物的练习手段，都是对人的力量、耐力、速度、柔韧和内部脏器等的锻炼。例如太极拳，以其轻柔缓慢的运动方式受到海内外人群的青睐，它松静自然、气沉丹田，运动强度适中，不仅对心血管、呼吸系统有良好的影响，而且有利于调节神经系统、陶冶性情、缓解压力，很好地发挥了武术运动益寿延年、养生保健的目的。

Chinese people have always attached great importance to the ways of life and health care. In the process of Wushu development, Taoism health care, Daoyin (guide the Qi to go through the body properly) and Qigong are integrated with each other, forming a wealth of training and health care methods. All Wushu activities are concerned about the cooperation of one's organs and breath movement. Wushu sets, Qigong and various training methods with traditional Chinese medicine are all exercises for human strength, endurance, speed, flexibility and internal organs' health. Taijiquan, for example, is favored by people at home and abroad for its gentle and slow movement. It is loose and natural, with deep breath, and moderate exercise intensity. It not only has a good impact on the cardiovascular and respiratory system, but also is conducive to regulating the nervous system, cultivating temperament, relieving pressure, and greatly satisfying the purpose of martial arts to prolong life and health care.

（三）教化育人作用 The role of education

武术是学校教育的主要内容，中国古代教育就提倡"通五经贯六艺"。《周礼·保氏》六艺礼、乐、射、御、书、数与古代军事武艺关系密切，孔子开私学就主张文武兼修的教育思想。武术教育可以树立人真善美价值观，塑造做人处事冷静干练的性格，培养处乱不惊的勇气和冷静果敢的气质，建立对正义的认识观，培养吃苦耐劳和做事持之以恒的品质。

Wushu is the content of school education. Ancient Chinese education advocated "Five Classics and six arts". The six arts of rites, music, archery, cart driving, calligraphy and numbers are closely related to the ancient art and Wushu. Wushu education can set up the values of the truth, the good and the beautiful, shape the cool and capable character of people, cultivate the courage of being calm and resolute, the understanding of justice, and cultivate the quality of hard work and perseverance.

学习武术对人还有武德的教育作用。武德可以理解为掌握武技的人所应具备的道德素养，武德不仅是对习武者的规范与约束，更是从文化、哲学、技术体系对参与者的教化与修行的手段。"未曾学艺先学礼，未曾习武先习德"，礼德为先是我们尊师重道的传统秩序，谦卑虚心的态度是武术学习的基本素养要求，成为习武的开端。

Learning Wushu also has an educational effect on people's morality. Military morality can be understood as the moral quality that the people who master the martial arts should possess. It is not only the norm and restriction to the Wushu practitioners, but also the means to educate and cultivate the participants from the culture, philosophy and technology system.

武术学校教育可以使学生认识更为理性，眼光变得敏锐，思维更加活跃，引领学生树立正确的认识观与价值观，通过教学过程中礼节和人际交往、处事来培育人的品质。因此，武术不仅是一门技术，更是一门文化，是滋养人成长、健康、深邃、智达、修身的生存方式。

Wushu teaching can make students understand more rationally, sharpen their eyes and think more actively, and lead them to establish correct understanding and values. Therefore, Wushu is not only a technology, but also a culture. It is a way of life that nourishes people's growth, health, profundity, wisdom and self-cultivation.

（四）观赏交流作用 Appreciation and communication

武术可供观赏以丰富人们的文化生活。所有的体育活动都有运动员表演和观众观赏的过程，武术是人的身体活动，赛场上无论是两人斗智较勇的对抗性搏斗，还是显现武术功力与技巧的套路演练，都会引人入胜，给人以美的享受，丰富人们的文化生活，展示浓郁的观赏价值。

Wushu can enrich people's cultural life. All sports activities have the process of athletes' performance and audience's watching each other. Wushu is a kind of physical activity of people. In the competition field, two people fight bravely, or show martial arts' skill, which is fascinating, and gives people a beautiful enjoyment, and enriches people's cultural life, and shows rich viewing value.

武术的群众性活动，可以成为人们切磋技艺、交流思想、增进友谊的良好形式。随着武术在世界广泛传播，武术发挥了巨大的文化公共外交功能，团结各国武术爱好者共同交流学习，营造追求健康、和平的文化氛围。可以看出，武术运动在健身、娱乐观赏以及传播中国传统文化方面都发挥具大的作用。

The public Wushu activities can become a good form for people to learn skills, exchange ideas and enhance friendship. With the wide spread of Wushu in the world, it has played a great role in cultural public diplomacy, uniting Wushu lovers from all countries to exchange and study together, and pursuing a healthy and peaceful cultural atmosphere.

第三节 武术的流派、形式与分类
1.3 The Schools, Form and Classification of Wushu

一、武术的流派 Wushu Schools

武术流派是早期人们对武术的归类,是将一些技法特征相同或相近的拳种归为一类,形成较大的拳派或者拳种支系繁衍发展新拳派。武术发展演进中不同的技术特点和风格形成了不同流派,武术流派对于传承延续技艺起到一定的积极作用。中国武术门类繁多,武术流派依据地域、传承与起源、功法、技法风格特点等进行分类与命名。

Wushu school is an early classification of the different types of Quan or Gongfu with similar features. In the development and evolution of Wushu, various schools came into being by branching or innovating. Wushu schools play a positive role in inheriting and continuing traditional Wushu skills. They are usually classified or named according to the origination, inheritance and technical styles.

(一)"长拳"与"短打"类 Chang Quan and Duan Da

明代戚继光在《纪效新书》中论述了当时流行的拳法有"长拳""短打"的分类,记载了宋太祖三十二式长拳以及"张伯敬之打""李半天之腿"和"鹰爪王之拿"等不同流派。明代程宗猷《耕余剩技·问答篇》记载"长拳有太祖温家之类,短打有绵张任家之类"。唐顺之的《武编》、何良臣的《阵记》也均有记载。长拳多为大开大合、松长舒展的拳术;将动作幅度较小、短促多变、贴身近战之类拳术归为短打类。

Qi Jiguang of Ming Dynasty discussed the classification of Chang Quan and Duan Da in his military book. There were 32 types of Chang Quan inherited from the first Emperor in the Song Dynasty. Duan Da can also be found in some historical records in the Ming Dynasty. Generally speaking, Chang Quan means the acting range is long and loose, the arms or the legs of the doers tend to stretch out straightly or close tightly in practicing. Duan Da means the range of any acts is very short and the acts are changeable and quick, which is more convenient for the hand-to-hand fighting.

（二）"南派"与"北派"之分 "Southern School" and "Northern School"

按照武术拳种流传地域、地理环境等进行的广义划分，南北地域形成两种技法特点与风格。南方流传的武术拳种拳法多，腿法较少，动作紧凑，劲力充沛；北方流传的武术拳种腿法丰富，动作起伏明显，快速有力，故有"南拳北腿"之称。民国陆师通《北拳汇编》等书使用"南派""北派"的分法。

This is a division according to the spreading area and geographical environment. Southern School focuses on the hand acts which are featured as quick, tight and hard. That is the reason why there are so many various Quan (fist) in Southern School. However, Northern School is rich in leg acts, with obvious ups and downs, fast and powerful. So it is called "Nan Quan (south fist) Bei Tui(north leg)".

（三）"内家"与"外家"之说 Nei Jia(Inner School) and Wai Jia(Outer School)

清初黄宗羲所作《王征南墓志铭》："少林以拳勇名天下，然主于搏人，人亦得以乘之。有所谓内家者，以静制动，犯者应手即仆，故别于少林为外家。"较为详细记述了内家拳历史传承、技法名称等。到民国期间发展成"凡主于搏人""亦足以通利关节"者，概称"外家拳"；凡注重"以静制动""得于导引者为多"，概称为"内家拳"，后来有把太极、形意、八卦归为内家拳的说法。

In *The Epitaph of Wang Zhengnan* written by Huang Zongxi in the early Qing Dynasty, it is said that Shaolin is famous for its powerful Quan acts in winning the fighting while there are so-called Nei Jia Quan which depends on inner Qi to overcome the rivals. So Shaolin Quan belongs to Wai Jia Quan. And Taiji, Xingyi and Bagua belong to Nei Jia Quan.

内家拳主要以道家文化为基础，讲究"内气功"炼养，实现力法上的"刚柔相济"，技法上讲究"以弱胜强"，并注重打法的理念、法则、方法的拳派。外家拳以少林为代表，讲究修心悟性，力法上多倾向于主动搏人，技法上兼顾刚柔并蓄，兼有内功练习的拳法。"内家"与"外家"都是以传统文化为修持理论基础，都有各自练外与修内的理念和方法。因此，"内家"与"外家"之说不能概全而论，是口头上对一些拳术的划分，从文化发展和学术视角已经较少使用了。

Nei Jia Quan is mainly based on Taoist culture. It stresses the cultivation of Qi or spirit or inner energy to help adjust the body moves to beat the rivals by combining the hardness with softness. Wai Jia Quan, represented by Shaolin, stresses mental and physical cultivation. It tends to fight actively and directively. Both Nei Jia Quan and Wai Jia Quan are based on traditional culture, and they have their own ideas and methods in external and internal practicing or cultivation. Therefore, this kind of division is gradually discredited.

（四）现代武术与传统武术之分 Modern Wushu and Traditional Wushu

现代武术是新中国成立后国家武术研究院为武术事业发展与体育竞赛推广，组织相关武术专家对流传面广、颇具影响力的拳种进行创编的系列拳术，包括 20 世纪 50 年代甲、乙组、初级拳套路，以后又有"少年拳""青年长拳"等，随着武术发展与推向世界的需要，又创编出系列国际武术竞赛套路。

Modern Wushu is a series of Quan types communicated and spread by the National Academy of Wushu for the development and promotion of Wushu and sports competitions after the founding of New China. It is composed of A and B series and primary Quan types in the 1950s. Later, there are "Juvenile Quan" and "Youth Chang Quan". To meet the needs of the international spread, a series of International Wushu competition routines have been created.

传统武术是固有的主要依托于民间习武群落流传有序的各种自成体系拳种，现代武术与传统武术之间是一脉相承的，传统武术是现代武术的活水源头，现代武术吸取传统武术的技法结构，并在此基础上发展，在价值取向上发生了很大的变异，现代武术的竞技价值和健身价值显得更为突出，正在向多元化发展。

Traditional Wushu is the general term of all kinds of folk Quan. Modern Wushu and traditional Wushu are in the same line. Traditional Wushu is the source of modern Wushu. Modern Wushu absorbs the benefits of the traditional Wushu and grows on with great changes in the value orientation. The competitive value and fitness value of modern Wushu are getting more prominent and its development tends to be more plural.

二、武术的形式、分类 Wushu form and classification

武术内容丰富多彩，按其运动形式可分：套路运动、搏斗运动、武术功法。

The content of Wushu is rich and colorful. According to its movement form, it can be divided as routine, bear-handed fighting and meditation.

（一）套路运动 Taolu (Routines)

套路运动是以技击动作为素材，以攻防进退、动静疾徐、刚柔虚实等矛盾运动规律编成的整套练习形式。主要内容包括拳术、器械、对练、集体表演。

It is a set of exercises composed of the regular and stable movements such as advancing, attacking, defending and retreating. The main contents of routines include Quan, appliances, double event and collective event.

1. 拳术 Quanshu

拳术是徒手练习的套路运动。它的种类很多，主要有长拳、太极拳、南拳、形意拳、八卦掌、劈挂拳、少林拳、戳脚、地躺拳、象形拳等。

It is a kind of bare-handed practice including Chang Quan, Taiji Quan, Nan Quan, Xingyi Quan, Bagua Zhang, Pigua Quan, Shaolin Quan, Chuo Jiao, Ditang Quan and Xiangxing Quan.

（1）长拳 Chang Quan

长拳是一种姿势舒展、动作灵活、快速有力、节奏分明，并有蹿蹦跳跃、闪展腾挪、起伏转折和跌扑滚翻等动作与技术的拳术。主要包括拳、掌、勾三种手型，弓、马、仆、虚、歇五种步型，一定数量的拳法、掌法、肘法和屈伸、直摆、扫转等不同组别的腿法，以及平衡、跳跃、跌扑、滚翻动作。长拳套路主要包括适应普及的初级套路、中级套路，以及适应竞赛的规定套路和自选套路。长拳运动特点是撑拔舒展、长击顺劲、快速有力、灵活多变、蹿蹦跳跃、节奏鲜明、气势磅礴。

The style of long-extending, fast and flexible moves with quick jump, roll and fall is a characteristic of Chang Quan. It mainly includes three kinds of hand pose: fist, palm and hook and five step poses: bowing, horse-riding, crawling, empty, and squat. Chang Quan routine mainly includes the primary, middle, competitive and self-selected routines.

（2）太极拳 Taiji Quan

太极拳是一种柔和、缓慢、轻灵的拳术。它以掤、捋、挤、按、采、挒、肘、靠、进、退、顾、盼、定等为基本方法。传统的太极拳有陈式、杨式、吴式、孙式和武式等。各式太极拳均要求：第一，静心用意，以意识引导动作，动作与呼吸紧密配合，呼吸平稳，深匀自然。第二，中正安舒，柔和缓慢，身体保持舒松自然，不偏不倚，动作绵绵不断，轻柔自然。第三，动作弧形，圆活不滞，以腰为轴，上下相随，周身形成整体。第四，连贯协调，虚实分明，动作之间衔接和顺，处处分清虚实，重心保持稳定。第五，轻灵沉着，刚柔相济，动作不浮不僵，外柔内刚，发劲完整。国家体委（国家体育总局）

先后整理出版了简化太极拳、48式太极拳及各式太极拳竞赛套路。太极拳运动特点是心静体松、呼吸自然、轻灵沉着、圆活连贯、上下相随、虚实分明、柔中寓刚。

Taiji Quan is soft, slow and light. Its basic moves are blow, smooth, push, press, pick, lean, elbow and so on with the eyes' on a certain direction. Traditional Taiji Quan includes Chen, Yang, Wu, Sun and Wu styles. However they all have the same requirements for the practicing such as: 1) Calm down. Keep the body moves with the pace of breathing; 2) Stand relaxed. Make your body stand naturally; 3) Curve move. Move around the waist: 4) Alternate empty with real moves; and 5) Mingle hardness and softness. The General Administration of Sport has released simplified Taiji Quan, 48-move Taiji Quan and Taiji Quan routines for competition.

（3）南拳 Nan Quan

南拳是流传于中国南方各地诸拳种的统称。拳种流派颇多，广东有洪、刘、蔡、李、莫等家，福建有咏春、五祖等派。南拳运动特点是拳势刚烈、步法稳固，多桥法，擅标手，动作紧俏、常以发声吐气发力助拳势。

It is a general name for the Quan spreading in southern China. There are many branches of Nan Quan, including Hong's, Liu's, Cai's, Li's and Mo's Quan which are all named after their initiator family names. Yongchun Quan and Wuzu Quan in Fujian Province also have long-lasting influences. Nan Quan is famous for its tough Shi (inner energy) and stable steps and the uttering of some sounds with each move.

（4）形意拳 Xingyi Quan

形意拳以三体式为基本桩法，以五行拳(劈、崩、钻、炮、横五拳)和十二形拳(龙、虎、猴、马、鼍、鸡、鹞、燕、蛇、鮐、鹰、熊十二种动物形象击法)为基本拳法组成的拳术。其运动特点是动作整齐简练、严密紧凑、动静分明、手脚合顺、身正步稳、发力沉着、朴实明快。

Xingyi Quan mainly imitates the fighting or defending skills of animals or birds. Its basic Quan style includes Wuxing Quan and Shierxing Quan (dragon, tiger, monkey, horse, rooster, swallow, altogether 12 animals and birds). Its characteristic is that the moves are unity of hands and feet, arms and legs, and the force is generated very quickly.

（5）八卦掌 Bagua Zhang

八卦掌是一种将攻防技术融合于绕圈走转之中的拳术。以站桩和行步为基本功，以绕圈走转为基本运动形式，步法变换以摆扣步为主，并包括推、托、带、领、扳、拦、截、扣等技法。基本八掌包括单换掌、双换掌、顺势掌、转身掌、磨身掌、双劈掌、背身掌、翻身掌等。其运动特点是沿圆走转、身捷步灵、势势相连、随走随变、纵横交错、协调圆活、劲力沉实、刚柔相间。

This is a kind of Quan that integrates attack and defense techniques into the circle walking. The basic training of this Quan is standing in proper pose and walking in a certain circle. The steps are various. The basic Zhang includes Danhuan Zhang, Shuanghuan Zhang, Shunshi Zhang, Zhuanshen Zhang, Moshen Zhang, Shuangpi Zhang, Beishen Zhang and Fanshen Zhang. Its features are changeable hands with changeable steps and smooth movement.

（6）通背拳 Tongbei Quan

通背拳以"腰背发力，放长击远，通肩达臂"，故称通背拳。其手法以摔、拍、穿、劈、钻为主，讲求圈揽勾劫、削摩拨扇八法运用。其运动特点是出手为掌、击手成拳、腰背发力、放长击远、甩膀抖腕、立抡成圆、大开密合、击拍响亮、发力冷弹脆快。

Tongbei Quan is called Tongbei (reach the back and shoulder) because the force is generated from the wrist and goes to the back and shoulder. The hands are required to be flexible to different changes. Arms and shoulders stretch out and close tightly. Each burst move goes along with a hard and sharp clapping.

（7）八极拳 Baji Quan

八极拳是一种以挨、傍、挤、靠等贴身近攻为主要内容的拳术。其套路结构短小精悍，发力刚脆，步法以震脚闯步为主。八极拳具有节短势险、刚猛暴烈、猛起硬落、逼身紧攻的短打类型拳术特点。

It is a kind of Quan focusing on close attack. Its moves are short and light. The force is generated from the inner side sharply. Its step techniques tend to be hard and quick stepping on the ground. This Quan is suitable for close fighting or defending.

（8）翻子拳 Fanzi Quan

翻子拳是一种短促灵便、严密紧凑、拳法密集、出手脆快的拳术。主要拳法有冲、崩、挑、托、滚、劈、叉、刁、裹、扣、搂、封、锁、盖、压等。其运动特点是步疾手密、连珠炮动、上下翻转、闪摆取势、迅猛遒劲、双拳交替快捷、全套一气呵成。有"双拳密如雨，脆快一挂鞭"之称。

This Quan is featured in the quick and frequent moves of fists. The main techniques are punch, crack, pick, hold, roll, split, fork, buckle, hug, seal, lock, cover, etc. Its characteristic is the quick and close pace with hands going up and down, just like the old saying:"the moving fists are like pouring rain and the sound of the practicing is just like firecrackers".

（9）劈挂拳 Pigua Quan

劈挂拳是一种以猛劈硬挂为主、长击快打、兼容短手的拳术。基本方法有滚、勒、劈、挂、斩、卸、剪、采、掠、擯、伸、收、摸、探、弹、砸、擂、猛十八字诀。练习时要求拧腰切胯，溜臂合腕，讲究滚勒劲、吞吐劲、劈挂劲、翻扯劲和辘轳劲等劲法。其运动特点是大开密合、猛起硬落、冷抽长击、迅猛剽悍、双臂交劈、斜拦横击、吞吐含放、翻滚不息。

Pigua Quan is mainly based on long and fast strike. The basic moves are rolling, clipping, chopping, hanging, cutting, unloading, picking, mining, shoveling, stretching, touching, probing, flicking, smashing, beating all eighteen characters tips together. In practicing, it requires to twist the waist and big movements of legs or arms.

（10）华拳 Hua Quan

华拳是以精、气、神"三华贯一"得名的拳术。其动作姿势舒展、工整，要求力贯股肱，动作强劲有力。华拳运动节奏要求"动如奔獭"之急，"静如潜鱼"之悠，"心肃则神凝"，"心凝则精劲"，"心正而后身正"。其运动特点是动迅静定、势正招圆、结构严谨、动紧身整、一气贯通、进疾退速，刚柔相济，心动形随、意发神传。

Hua Quan claims the trinity of energy, Qi and spirit. The practice of Hua Quan focuses on setting all the steps in a smooth series. One has to have an upright heart and body before practicing this Quan.

（11）少林拳 Shaolin Quan

少林拳是少林武术的总称，因嵩山少林寺而得名。少林拳套路结构短小精悍，严密紧凑，巧妙而多变，注重技击，立足实战。动作起、落、进、退多为直来直往，手法要求出拳、出掌"曲而不直，直而不曲"。身法在定势中要正，运动中进退和顺，起落自然，变换灵活，步法要求轻灵敏捷。其运动特点是沉实稳固，劲力主刚，讲究刚健有力、勇猛快捷。

Shaolin Quan is named after the Shaolin temple on Songshan Mountain. The actions in Shaolin Quan are quick and strong. The leg or hand moves are required to go or come back in a short second with a very straight posture.

（12）地躺拳 Ditang Quan

地躺拳是以跌、扑、滚、翻等地趟摔法和地趟腿法技术为主要内容的拳术。拳术技巧性较强，动作难度较高，常出现的动作有抢背、盘腿跌、摔剪、乌龙绞柱、虎扑、栽碑、扑地蹦、鲤鱼打挺及勾、剪、扫、绞等腿法。其运动特点是顺势而跌、旋即而起、卧地而击、高翻低滚、起伏闪避、一气呵成。

The acts in this Quan are mainly falling down or rolling on the ground. It is a little bit hard to practice such actions. Its features are both the falling down and getting up are done in a short moment. The actions are coherent and finished very quickly.

（13）象形拳 Xiangxing Quan

象形拳是模仿各种动物的技能、特长和形态，或模拟某些特定人物的搏斗动作形态，结合攻防技法创编的拳术。象形拳取法自然，分象形、取意两种。象形是以模仿动物和人物的形态为主，取意则以取意动物的博击特长充实技击动作的内容。流传较广有醉拳、猴拳、螳螂拳、鹰爪、蛇拳以及武松脱铐等拳术。象形拳具有以形取势、以意传神的特点，不仅重其形，而且更重其意、心动形随，形象生动活泼、技巧性强、风格独特。

Xiangxing Quan also relies on the imitation of the animals. By putting the animals' acts into its own practicing system, Xiangxing Quan is vivid and unique. The popular imitation animals in Xiangxing Quan are monkey, mantis, eagle, snake and tiger.

（14）红拳 Hong Quan

红拳是流传于陕西关中的古老拳种，以红火、艳美、吉祥之意命名，其内容丰富，套路繁多，技法全面，以"撑补为母，勾挂为能，化身为奇，刁打为法"尽八法之变，形成了盘、法、势、理俱全的拳理与打手体系。红拳招势古朴、拳架工整、劲力饱满、姿态优美，外柔内刚，突出一个"巧"字。其运动特点是势轻劲柔、气顺招圆、心意为根、以步制人、刁打巧击、劲道柔中寓刚。

Hong Quan is an ancient Quan popular in Shaanxi. Hong means gorgeous beauty and auspiciousness. Hong Quan has difficult and changeable moves. It stresses an all-rounded technique in practical fighting.

2. 器械 The appliances

器械是手持武术兵器的练习套路形式。器械的种类很多，分为长器械、短器械、双器械和软器械。刀、枪、剑、棍是长、短器械的代表。目前在武术竞赛中刀、枪、剑、棍也是重点竞赛项目。短器械主要有刀、剑、匕首等，长器械主要有枪、棍、大刀等，双器械主要有双刀、双剑、双钩、双枪、双鞭等，软器械主要有三节棍、九节鞭、绳镖和流星锤等。

The appliances are the weapons used in Wushu. They can be divided as long, short, soft and couple ones. Broadsword, spear, sword and stick are the representatives of long and short apparatus and the key items in the competitions. Couple apparatus includes double broadsword, double sword, double hook, double spear, and double whip. Soft apparatus includes three-section-club, nine-section-whip, and rope dart.

（1）剑术 Sword

剑是短器械中的一种。由刃、背、锋、护手、柄等部分组成，长度以直臂垂肘反手持剑的姿势为准，剑尖不低于本人的耳上端。剑术主要以刺、点、撩、截、崩、挑等剑法，配合步型、步法等构成套路。其运动特点是轻快敏捷、潇洒飘逸、灵活多变、刚柔相济、富有韵律。

Sword is composed of blade, back, front, hand guard, handle and other parts. The length is subject to the posture of holding the sword with straight arm and elbow, and the point of the sword is not lower than the upper ear of the holder. Sword playing is light, flexible and elegant.

（2）刀术 Knife

刀是短器械中的一种。是由刃、背、尖、护手盘和刀柄等构成，刀的长度是以直臂垂肘抱刀姿势为准，刀尖不得低于本人的耳上端。刀术主要以劈、砍、斩、撩、扎、挂、刺等基本刀法为主，并配合各种步型、步法、跳跃等动作构成套路。其运动特点是勇猛快速、激烈奔腾、气势逼人、紧密缠身、刚劲有力、雄健剽悍。

It's one of the short instruments. It is composed of blade, back, point, guard plate and hilt, etc. The knife should be held in hand with straight arm and elbow and the tip of the knife must not be lower than the upper end of the ear. Knife playing reflects the strength and courage of the player.

（3）枪术 Spear

枪是长器械中的一种。由枪头、枪缨和枪杆组成。枪术主要以拦、拿、扎、崩、点、穿、挑、云、劈等枪法，配合各种步型、步法、跳跃构成套路。其运动特点是力贯枪尖、走势开展、上下翻飞、变幻莫测。

It's one of the long instruments. It is composed of spear head, spear tassel and spear stem. Its movement characteristic is that the force goes through the spear, the trend is capricious with big ups and downs.

（4）棍术 Stick

棍是长器械中的一种。棍的长度同本人的身高。棍术主要以抡、劈、扫、挂、戳、崩、点、云、拨、绞、挑等棍法，配合步型、步法、身法等构成套路。其运动特点是勇猛泼辣、横打一片、密集如雨、气势磅礴。

It is one of the long instruments.The length of the stick is the same as the height of the player. Its movement is characterized by the forceful and dense beating as well as large sweeping space.

（5）大刀 Broadsword

长器械的一种。以劈、砍、斩等刀法为主，结合舞花、掌花、背花等动作构成套路。在演练中都是双手握持，以腰力发劲，一动一静表现出雄浑威武、勇敢果断的气势。"大刀看顶手"，握在刀盘下面的右手运用刀法始终顶住刀盘，虎口对准刀背。大刀的特点是劈刀递攮、大劈大砍、雄伟泼辣、气势轩昂。

It is one of the long instruments. It should be held with both hands. The right hand should press tightly on the plate. The characteristics of broadsword are the big scope of movements and powerful heroic momentum.

（6）双刀 Double knife

双器械的一种。以劈、斩、撩、绞等刀法结合双手左右缠头、左右腕花、交互抡劈等变化构成套路练习。拳谚讲"双刀看走"，两手持刀舞动时，步法必须与刀法上下相随，对上下肢的协调要求较高。双刀的运动特点是刀法密集、贴身严谨、左右兼顾、边走边打。

It is a kind of double weapons. When playing double knife, one has to keep his step pace with the hands moving and interactions with each knife in his hand. This sport needs higher coordination of arms and legs. Its characteristics are intensive acts, close linking of left and right as well as upside and downside.

（7）双剑 Double sword

双器械的一种。主要以穿、挂、云、刺等剑法为主，结合身法、步法，双手交替变换而构成套路。讲求剑法、身法、步法三者合一，其运动特点是身随剑动、步随身移、潇洒奔放、矫捷优美。

It is a kind of double weapons. It emphasizes the combination of sword, body and feet moves. Usually the body will go following the sword, the feet also move after the body. Double sword playing is typed of grace and flexibility.

（8）双钩 Double hook

双器械的一种。主要以勾、搂、锁、挂等方法构成套路。其运动特点是钩走浪势、身随钩走、钩随身活、身灵步轻、造型洒脱多变。

It is a kind of double weapons. To hook, rake and hang are the main acts in the routine. Its characteristics are changeability and flexibility.

（9）九节鞭 The nine-section whip

软器械的一种。主要以抡、扫、缠、挂及各种舞花动作组成套路。主要动作有手花、腕花、缠臂、绕脖、扫鞭、背鞭等。其运动特点是鞭走顺劲、抡舞如轮、横飞竖打、势势相连；常以"抡起似车轮，舞起似钢棍""收回一团，放走一片"来形容九节鞭的运动风格。

It is a kind of soft weapon. It can be used to blow, sweep, twine and includes many other variety movements. It is played like a wheel as well as an iron stick. It can be a useful thing when it is pulled back and it can be a shield when it is released.

（10）三节棍 Three-section-stick

软器械的一种。主要以抡、扫、劈、戳及舞花等构成套路。其运动特点是轻巧灵便、能长能短、可伸可缩、软硬变换、勇猛泼辣、势如破竹。

It is a kind of soft weapon. It can be stretched out long and shrank short depending on the situation.

（11）绳镖、流星锤 Rope dart and Rope hammer

软器械的一种。以绳索缠绕着身体各部而变化出各种击法和技巧构成套路。主要动作有踢球、拐线、缠膝、绕脖、十字披红、胸前挂印等。练习时须用巧劲，一根长索在身前、身后、腿部、肘部、颈部缠绕收放，出击自如，变幻莫测，是技巧性较强的项目。

It is a kind of soft weapon. With the rope around the various body parts, the player can kick, turn or wrap the rope to display various movements. This kind of practice needs crafty skills to make good control of the rope and the dart or hammer.

3. 对练 Pair practice

对练是在单练基础上，两人或两人以上，按照预定的程序进行的攻防练习套路。包括徒手对练、器械对练、徒手与器械对练。

Two or more than two players, according to the predetermined procedures, practice attack and defense including bear-handed practice, armed practice, and bear-handed vs. armed practice.

(1) 徒手对练 Unarmed pair practice

运用踢、打、摔、拿等方法，按照攻防格斗运动规律编成的拳术对练套路。有对打拳、对擒拿、南拳对练、跑拳打手、八极对接、形意拳对练等。

By kicking, hitting, throwing, catching, locking or unlocking, in accordance with the rules of combating routine, the players try to beat down their rivals. There are boxing, locking and unlocking.

(2) 器械对练 Armed pair practice

以器械的劈、砍、击、刺等技击方法组成的对练套路，如单刀进枪、三节棍进棍、双匕首进枪、对刺剑等。

The players need to use the weapons in their hands such as spear, stick or sword to slap, hit or probe each other.

(3) 徒手与器械对练 Unarmed vs. Armed pair practice

这是一方徒手，另一方持器械进行的攻防对练套路，如空手夺刀、空手夺棍、空手进双枪等。

The bear-handed player tries to catch the armed one's weapons by using certain attacking and defending skills.

4. 集体演练 Group practice

集体演练是集体进行的徒手、器械或徒手与器械的演练。集体表演通常是以六人以上的徒手或器械集体演练，可变换队形与图案和采用音乐伴奏，要求队形整齐，动作协调一致。

Group practice means a kind of collective performance usually composed of more than six players. It is required that the moving or changing of the whole group should keep a certain form and pattern with the background music.

(二) 搏斗运动 Fighting games

搏斗运动是两人在一定条件下，按照一定的规则进行斗智较力的对抗练习形式。目前武术竞赛开展的有散手、推手、短兵等。

Fighting games are two players fighting against each other to win the game according to certain rules. At present, Wushu fighting games are San Shou, Tui Shou and Duan Bing.

1. 散手 San Shou (boxing)

散手是两人按照一定的规则，使用踢、打、摔等方法制胜对方的竞技项目。

It is like a kind of boxing in which punching, throwing and kicking are allowed to use to beat down the other.

2. 推手 Tui Shou (hand-pushing)

推手是两人遵照一定的规则，使用掤、捋、挤、按、采、挒、肘、靠等太极拳劲力手法，双方粘连黏随，通过肌肉的感觉来判断对方的用劲，然后借力发劲将对手推出，以此决定胜负的竞技项目。

The players take advantages of hands, arms and shoulders to move, blow, push, sway, squeeze or elbow to make the other one out of the circle field. This game needs one to feel the rival's energy and take good use of it to push him or her out of the circle.

3. 短兵 Duan Bing (Short weapon)

短兵是中国武术短兵器的总称，是两人手持一种用藤、皮、棉制作的短棒似的器械，在场地内按照一定的规则，使用短兵器劈、砍、刺、崩、点、斩等方法进行决胜负的竞技项目。

Duan Bing is the general term for all the short weapons in Wushu. It is a competitive game in which two players holding the short kind of sticks made of cane, leather and cotton fight against each other for winning according to certain rules.

（三）功法练习 Training of Gong Fa

功法练习是通过简单动作或特定的姿势，以精神内敛，调节意、气运行，从而使体力、气力充沛，达到健体或增强身体某方面机能的运动。按其形式和功能可分为内功、外功、轻功和柔功。

Gong Fa means the certain practices or standing poses done by the Wushu player to regulate his Qi and energy and improve the health condition. According to its form and function, Gong Fa is usually divided into four categories: internal, external, light and flexible Gong.

思考题：Questions for consideration

1. 武术与传统文化之间的关系？

1. What is the relationship between Wushu and Chinese traditional culture?

2. 武术的价值有哪些方面？

2. What are the values of Wushu?

3. 传统武术的概念？

3. The concept of traditional Wushu?

4. 武术的功能是什么？传统的十二型？

4. What is the function of Wushu? What are the twelve types?

5. 武术器械的分类有哪些？试举例。

5. What are the categories of Wushu weapons? Give some examples.

第二章 武术基本动作与方法
Chapter 2 Basic Movements and Actions

一、基本手型及手法 Basic hand forms and moves

（一）手型 Hand forms

1. 拳 Quan (fist)

四指并拢卷握，拇指紧扣食指和中指第二指节。（图 2-1）

Close the four fingers into a fist with the thumb over the forefinger and the middle finger (Fig. 2-1)

图Fig 2-1

动作要点：拳握紧，拳面平，直腕。

Key points: tightly clenched, flat face of fist, and wrist straight.

2. 掌 Palm

四指并拢伸直，拇指弯曲紧扣于虎口处。（图 2-2）

Stretch the four fingers and draw them close together while bending the thumb and placing its second phalange over the palm (Fig. 2-2)

图Fig 2-2

动作要点：掌面绷平，大拇指扣紧。

Key points: flatten the palm face and tighten the thumb.

3. 勾 Hook

五指第一指节捏拢在一起，屈腕。（图 2-3）

Bunch the finger and thumb tips and bend the wrist (Fig. 2-3)

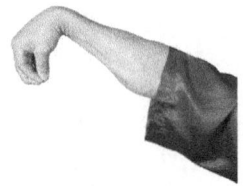

图 Fig 2-3

（二）手法 Hand moves

1. 冲拳 Chong Quan (thrust fist)

两拳抱于腰间，拳心向上，肘尖向后，挺胸、收腹、直腰。（图 2-4）右拳从腰间向前猛力冲出，转腰、顺肩，在肘关节过腰后，前臂内旋，力达拳面，臂伸直，高与肩平。拳心向下为平拳。（图 2-5）拳眼向上为立拳。（图 2-6）

Two fists are held at the waist, the elbow tips backward, the chest straight, the belly flat, and the waist straight. (Fig. 2-4) The right fist thrusts forward from the waist; the waist turns and makes it and the shoulder in a line. After the elbow joint passes the waist, the forearm rotates inward; the force reaches the fist face with the arm straight and the height as the shoulder. The heart of the fist down is horizontal, (Fig. 2-5) the fist eye up is vertical. (Fig. 2-6)

图 Fig 2-4　　　　图 Fig 2-5　　　　图 Fig 2-6

动作要点：出拳快速有力，拧腰、顺肩、急旋前臂，具有爆发力。

Key points: thrust should be powerful and fast, twisting, giving shoulder and twist the forearm with explosive force.

2. 架拳 Jia Quan (uphold fist)

预备姿势；与冲拳同。Ready position: the same as thrusting.

右拳由下向左、向上经头前向右上方画弧架起，拳眼向下，目视左方。(图 2-7) 左架拳动作相同，方向相反。

Draw an arc with the right fist downward, leftward and upward through the front of the head and rightward and upward, with the fist eye downward and eyes to the left side. (Fig. 2-7) The same movements of the left fist and the direction is opposite.

动作要点：松肩，肘微屈，前臂内旋。

Key points: loosen shoulders, bend the elbow slightly, and the forearm rotates inwards.

3. 推掌 Tui Zhang (Pushing palm)

两掌收于腰间，掌心向上，肘尖向后，挺胸、收腹、直腰，右掌从腰间向前猛力冲出，转腰、顺肩，前臂内旋，力达掌根（或掌外侧），臂伸直，高与肩平，掌尖向上。(图 2-8)

Two palms set closely to the waist, palm hearts up, elbow tips backward, chest straighten. Right palm rushes out from the waist forward with force, turn the waist left, with the right shoulder stretching forward with the right arm, forearm turn left side making the force reach the palm. The arms should be straight, and horizontally high as the shoulder level. Palm tip up. (Fig. 2-8)

图Fig 2-7　　　　图Fig 2-8

动作要点：快速有力，拧腰、顺肩、急旋前臂。

Key points: fast and powerful, waist twisting, shoulder going with the pushing arm and forearm turning.

4. 架掌 Jia Zhang (uphold plam)

右掌向下、向左、向上经头前向右上方画弧架起,拇指侧向下,掌心朝外,目视左方。(图 2-9) 左架掌动作相同,方向相反。

The right palm draws an arc downward, leftward and upward through the front of the head to the right and upward, with the thumb side down, the palm heart outward, and eyes to the left. (Fig. 2-9) The left palm has the same action and opposite direction.

图Fig 2-9

动作要点:松肩,肘微屈,前臂内旋。

Key points: shoulder loose, elbow bent slightly, forearm rotates inward.

二、基本步型及步法 Basic foot forms and acts

(一) 步型 Foot forms

1. 马步 Ma Bu (Horse-ride step)

两脚平行开立(约为本人脚长3倍左右),脚尖正对前方,屈膝半蹲,膝部不超过脚尖,大腿接近水平,全脚着地,身体重心落于两腿之间,两手抱拳于腰间,拳心向上。(图2-10)

The feet are parallel (about 3 times the length of one's feet), the toes are facing the front, the knees are half bent, the knees do not surpass the toes, the thighs are parallel to the ground, and the gravity of the body lies between the legs. Two hands clasped at the waist, fist eyes up. (Fig. 2-10)

图Fig 2-10

动作要点：挺胸、塌腰、脚跟外蹬，膝部外撑。

Key points: chest uphold, waist loose, knees outward holding

2. 弓步 Gong Bu (bow step)

右脚向前跨一大步，右腿屈膝半蹲（大腿水平），膝与脚尖垂直，左腿挺膝伸直，脚尖内扣（斜向前方），两脚全脚着地，上体正对前方，目视正前方。两手抱拳于腰间，拳心向上。弓右腿为右弓步，（图2-11）弓左腿为左弓步。（图2-12）

Take a big step forward with the right foot, the right leg squat (thigh horizontal), the knee is vertical to the toe; straighten the left leg and tiptoe oblique to the front. Two hands clasped at the waist, fists eyes up. (Fig. 2-11) The left bow step is the same but in the opposite direction. (Fig. 2-12)

图Fig 2-11　　　　图Fig 2-12

动作要点：前腿弓，后腿绷；挺胸、塌腰、沉髋，两脚前后成一直线。

Key points: bow the front leg and stretch the back leg; straighten the chest, down the waist and the hip and the front foot is in line with the back foot.

3. 仆步 Pu Bu (crouch step)

两脚左右开立，右腿屈膝全蹲，臀部接近小腿，右脚全脚着地，脚尖和膝关节外展；左腿挺直平仆，脚尖里扣，全脚着地，两手抱拳于腰间，拳心向上，目视左方。仆左

腿为左仆步，（图 2-13）仆右腿为右仆步。（图 2-14）

Stand upright with feet apart. Make a full squat with the right leg, the right thigh resting on the calf and the right foot and knee turn outward while the left leg is stretched sideways, the toe pointing inward. The hands are clenched into fists and placed on the wrist. Crouching the left leg is the left crouch step, (Fig. 2-13) vice versa. (Fig. 2-14)

图Fig 2-13　　　　　　图Fig 2-14

动作要点：挺胸、塌腰、沉髋。

Key points: chest uphold, waist and hip down

4. 虚步 Xu Bu (empty step)

两脚前后开立，右脚外展 45°，屈膝半蹲；左脚脚面绷平，脚尖稍内扣，虚点地面，左膝微屈，重心落在右腿上，两手抱拳于腰间，拳心向上。左脚在前为左虚步，（图 2-15）右脚在前为右虚步。（图 2-16）

Stand upright with feet apart vertically with the left foot in front of the right. Turn the right foot 45 degrees outward and bend the right knee for a half squat while raising the left heel with toes turning slightly inward and the left leg slightly bend at knee. Hands are clenched into fists on the wrist. Eyes straight forward, (Fig. 2-15) the right empty step is opposite. (Fig. 2-16)

图Fig 2-15　　　　　　图Fig 2-16

动作要点：挺胸、塌腰、虚实分明。

Key points: chest uphold, waist down, definite the empty and actual moves

5. 歇步 Xie Bu (seated step)

两腿交叉靠拢全蹲，右（左）脚全脚掌着地，脚尖外展；左（右）脚前脚掌着地，膝部贴近左（右）脚跟处，两手抱拳于腰间，拳心向上。左腿在前为左歇步，（图2-17）右腿在前为右歇步。（图2-18）

Cross legs and drop to a full squat with the left thigh resting on the right thigh and the right buttock on the raised right heel, while the left foot is placed flat on the ground with toes turned leftward. Hands are clenched into fists on the wrist. Eyes left-ward,(Fig. 2-17) the right seated step is opposite. (Fig. 2-18)

图Fig 2-17　　　　图Fig 2-18

动作要点：挺胸、塌腰、两腿交叉并贴紧。

Key points: chest uphold, waist down, legs crossed closely

（二）步法 Step moves

1. 上步 Shang Bu (Step forward)

双脚前后站立，前脚向前进一步或后脚向前进步。

Stand with feet back and forth, step forward with the front foot or back foot.

2. 侧闪步 Ceshan Bu (Step sideway)

双脚前后站立，后脚向侧方上步，前脚跟随。

Stand with feet back and forth, the back foot step sideway, and the front foot follows up.

3. 击步 Ji Bu（Beat step）

两脚前后站立，左脚在前，右脚在后，两手掌前后插掌，大拇指侧向上。（图2-19）

Stand with left foot back and right foot forth, stretch out arms with palm hearts outside

(Fig. 2-19)

上体前倾，右脚离地提起，左脚随即蹬地踏跳，在空中时右脚向前碰击左脚，右脚先落，左脚后落，目视正前方。(图 2-20)

Lean forward, lift the right foot off the ground, the left foot immediately jump, when in the air, the right foot strikes the left foot forward, lower the right foot first, and the left foot later. Look ahead.(Fig. 2-20)

图Fig 2-19　　　　　　　图Fig 2-20

动作要点：跳起时上体正直并侧对前方。

Key points: keep trunk upright and one shoulder forward in flight

4. 垫步 Dian Bu (skipping step)

两脚前后站立，(图 2-21) 后脚离地提起，脚掌向前脚处落步，前脚立即以脚掌蹬地向前上提起，将位置让与后脚，然后屈膝提腿向前落步，目视前方。(图 2-22)

Stand with feet back and forth, (Fig. 2-21) lift the back foot off the ground, and skip forward the front foot. Then, the front foot gives way to the back foot quickly, then bend the front knees and lift the leg to skip forward. Look ahead. (Fig. 2-22)

图Fig 2-21　　　　　　　图Fig 2-22

5. 弧形步 Huxing Bu (curved step)

两脚前后站立，两腿微屈，两脚迅速连续向侧前方行步，每步大小略比肩宽，走弧形路线，目视前方。

Stand with feet back and forth, with legs slightly bent. Walk quickly and continuously in a half circular outward. Each step is slightly wider than the shoulder. Look ahead.

动作要点：挺胸、塌腰，保持微蹲姿势，身体重心移动平稳，注意转腰。

Key points: chest up and waist down, keep a slight squat position, stabilize the body gravity, and turn waist.

6. 震步 Zhen Bu (stamping step)

一脚支撑，另一脚提膝下落，全脚重踏地面，同时屈腿下蹲替换支撑脚。

Lift one bending leg on the other one and stamp on the ground while bending down to replace the supporting foot.

动作要点：挺胸、收腹，重心下沉，铿锵有力。

Key points: chest up, tight belly, gravity down, stamp heavily

三、基本腿法 Basic leg forms and acts

（一）直摆腿法 Straight leg swing

1. 正踢腿 Zhengti Tui (Right kick)

图Fig 2-23　　　　　　图Fig 2-24

预备姿势；两脚并步站立，两手立掌或握拳，两臂侧平举。（图2-23）

左脚向前上半步，左腿支撑，右脚脚尖勾起向前额处摆踢，目视正前方。（图2-24）练习时左右腿交替进行。

Preparation posture: stand with feet together, stand with hands or clench hands, and lift arms horizontally. (Fig. 2-23)

Action description: take the left foot half step forward, support the left leg, and swing the right toe forward, and look straight ahead, (Fig. 2-24) the left and right legs alternate during the exercise.

动作要点：挺胸、直腰、收腹、踢腿时勾脚尖，踢腿要有寸劲。

Action points: chest, waist, abdomen, when kicking hook toe, kick to have sudden strength.

2. 侧踢腿 Ceti Tui (Side kick)

预备姿势：与正踢腿同。Ready position: the same as kicking.

左脚向前上半步，脚尖外展，右脚脚跟稍提起，身体微左转，右掌向前推掌，左掌向后推掌，掌尖均向上。(图 2-25) 接着，右脚勾脚尖向右耳侧摆踢，同时左臂上举架掌，左掌心向上，右臂屈肘，右掌收于左肩前，目视正前方。(图 2-26) 踢右腿为右侧踢，左侧踢动作相同，左右相反。

Step the left foot forward for the first half, extend the toe, slightly lift the heel of the right foot, turn the body slightly to the left, push the palm forward with the right palm, push the palm backward with the left palm, and all the palm tips are upward . (Fig. 2-25) Then, swing the toe of the right foot to the right ear side, and lift the palm on the left hip elbow, with the center of the left palm upward, the right arm elbow, and the right palm in front of the left shoulder, and look straight ahead. (Fig. 2-26) the right kick is the right kick, and the left kick is the same with the opposite direction.

图Fig 2-25

图Fig 2-26

动作要点：挺胸、直腰、开髋、侧身、收腹。

Action points: chest, waist, hip, side, abdomen.

3. 里合腿 Lihe Tui (Adduct leg)

预备姿势；与正踢腿同。Ready position: the same as kicking.

左脚向左前方上半步，右脚脚尖勾起里扣并向右上方摆踢，经面部前向左侧上方直腿摆动，下落收于左脚后，左手掌可在左侧上方迎击右脚掌。目视正前方。(图 2-27) 练习时，左右腿交替进行。

Step the left foot forward to the left, hook up the toe of the right foot and swing it to the right and up, then swing the upper straight leg to the left through the face, fall to the left foot, and the left palm can hit the right palm at the top of the left. Look straight ahead. (Fig. 2-27) In practice, the left and right legs alternate.

图Fig 2-27

动作要点：挺胸、直腰、松髋、合髋，摆腿成扇形，幅度要大。

Action points: straighten the chest, waist, loosen the hip, close the hip, swing the legs into a fan, with a large range.

4. 外摆腿 Waibai Tui (Outer swing leg)

图Fig 2-28

预备姿势；与正踢腿同。Ready position: the same as kicking.

左脚向左前方上半步，右脚向左侧上方踢起，经面前向右侧上方摆动，直腿落于在左脚内侧。双掌或右掌可在上方击拍右脚背，目视正前方。(图 2-28) 练习时左右腿交替进行。

Take the left foot to the left and the front half step, the right foot tip is hooked up and kicked up to the upper left side, then swing to the upper right side through the front, and the straight leg falls on the inner side of the left foot. Double or right palms can tap the back of the right foot on the top, and look straight ahead. (Fig. 2-28) The left and right legs alternate during the exercise.

动作要点：挺胸、塌腰、松髋、展髋，摆腿成扇形，幅度要大。

Action points: chest, waist, loose hip, hip, leg into a fan-shaped, large range.

（二）屈伸腿法 Leg flexion and extension

1. 弹腿 Tan Tui (Spring Leg)

两脚并立，双手握拳抱于腰间，(图 2-29) 左腿上步，右腿屈膝提起，右脚绷直，(图 2-30) 小腿以膝关节为轴向前摆踢，猛力挺膝，力达脚尖，右腿弹踢伸直，高度过腰，左腿伸直或微屈支撑，目视正前方。(图 2-31)

Stand with both feet together, clench hands and hold them at the waist, (Fig. 2-29) Step up the left leg, bend the right leg and lift it up, straighten the right leg, (Fig. 2-30) Swing the leg forward with the knee joint as the axis, hold the knee with strong force, reach the toe, stretch the right leg with elastic kick, and stretch it straight, with the height over the waist, straighten or slightly bend the left leg for support, and look straight ahead. (Fig. 2-31)

图Fig 2-29

图Fig 2-30

图Fig 2-31

动作要点：挺胸、直腰、脚面绷直、收髋，弹踢有寸劲。

Action points: chest straight, waist straight, feet straight, hip close, play and kick with inch strength.

2. 蹬腿 Deng Tui (Kick leg)

两脚并立，双手握拳抱于腰间，左腿上步，右腿屈膝提起，右脚勾脚尖，(图 2-32) 小腿以膝关节为轴向前蹬踏，猛力挺膝，力达脚跟，右腿弹踢伸直，高度过腰，左腿伸直或微屈支撑，目视正前方。(图 2-33)

Stand with your feet together, hold your hands to your waist, step up on your left leg, bend your right leg and lift it up, hook your toes on your right foot. (Fig. 2-32) Step forward on your lower leg with the knee joint as the axis, firmly hold your knees, reach your heels, stretch your right leg with a spring kick, and reach your waist, straighten or slightly bend your left leg, and look straight ahead. (Fig. 2-33)

图Fig 2-32

图Fig 2-33

动作要点：挺胸、直腰、脚面勾起、收髋。

Action points: chest, waist, feet, hip.

3. 侧踹腿 Cechuai Tui (Side kick)

两脚并步站立，两掌收在腰间，右脚上步，脚尖外展，两腿交叉，稍屈膝，两掌收至胸前交叉，(图 2-34) 随即右腿伸直支撑，左腿屈膝提起，左脚内扣，脚跟用力向左侧上方踹出，上体向右侧倾，两掌随之推掌，目视左脚。(图 2-35) 练习时可左右交替进行。

Stand with your feet together, put your hands between your waist, step on your right foot, extend your toes, cross your legs, bend your knees a little, put your hands in front of your chest, (Fig. 2-34) Then straighten and support your right leg, lift your left leg with your knees bent, buckle your left foot, and kick your heels out to the top of your left side, lean your upper body to the right, and then push your hands, and look at your left foot. (Fig.2-35) Practice alternately from left to right.

图Fig 2-34

图Fig 2-35

动作要点：挺膝、开髋、脚外侧朝上，力达脚跟。

Action points: straighten the knee, open the hip, turn the outside of the foot upward, and reach the heel.

（三）击拍腿法 Clap leg technique

单拍脚 Danpai Jiao (single beat foot)

图Fig 2-36

图Fig 2-37

两脚并步站立，两掌收于腰间，左脚向前上一步，左掌向前穿掌，掌心向上，左臂内旋使掌心朝下，左臂上举，掌尖朝上，掌心向前，右掌下落贴右腿向上立圆摆起，右手背迎击左手掌；(图 2-36) 同时重心前移左脚，左腿支撑，右脚脚背绷直向前额处摆踢，右手迎击右脚面，左掌从上向后下落，掌心朝下，目视前方。(图 2-37)

Stand with two feet together, two palms close to the waist, one step forward for the left foot, one step forward for the left hand, one step upward for the palm center, one step inward for the left arm, one step upward for the left arm, one step upward for the palm tip, one step forward for the palm center, one step upward for the right foot, one step upward for the right hand, and one step forward for the right hand; (Fig. 2-36) Move the center of gravity forward for the left foot, one step forward for the left leg. On the right foot, lower the left palm from top to back, with the palm center facing down, and look ahead. (Fig. 2-37)

动作要点：挺胸、直腰、收腹，击响动作连续、准确、响亮。

Key points of action: chest, waist, abdomen, continuous, accurate and loud percussion.

（四）扫转腿法 Sweeping leg technique

1. 前扫腿 Qian Saotui (Front leg sweep)

两脚并立，右冲拳，左掌立掌于右胸前。（图 2-38）左脚向左侧跨步，上体左后转180°，重心移至左脚，左腿全蹲，左脚跟提起，左前脚掌碾转，右腿直腿平铺，脚尖内扣，脚掌着地，两手变掌收至胸前交叉，初期练习也可双手体前扶地，增加稳定性，（图 2-39）随重心下压继续左转，右脚贴地直腿向前扫转一周后两脚踏实成右仆步，左掌向上变横掌架于头上方，右掌下落向身后变勾手，勾尖向上。（图 2-40）

Two feet stand side by side, right punch, left palm standing on the right chest. (Fig. 2-38) Step left foot to the left, turn left back 180°, for upper body, move weight to the left foot, squat the left leg completely, lift the left heel, roll left front paw, lay the right leg straight and flat, buckle the toe inside, touch the ground, turn hands into palms to cross chest, and hold the ground in front of hands for initial practice to increase stability. (Fig. 2-39) Continue to turn left with the weight down, and sweep the right foot to the ground and straight the leg forward for a circle. Two feet change firmly into the right footstep, the left palm upward change horizontal palm frame in the top of the head, the right palm down behind change hook, hook pointing up. (Fig. 2-40)

图Fig 2-38　　　　　图Fig 2-39　　　　　图Fig 2-40

动作要点：头部上顶，上体正直，扫转时保持右仆步姿势，保持身体重心平衡，右膝挺直。

Action points: head on top, upper body straight, keep right step position when sweeping, keep balance of body center of gravity, right knee straight.

2. 后扫腿 Hou Saotui (Back leg sweep)

两腿并立，两掌收抱于腰间，左脚上步，左腿屈膝半蹲，右腿挺膝伸直成左弓步，两掌从两腰侧向前平直推掌，掌指朝上，掌心向前。(图2-41)左脚尖内扣，左腿屈膝全蹲，成右仆步姿势；同时上体右转前俯，两掌随身体右转在右腿内侧扶地，随着上体向右后拧转，以左脚前掌为轴，右脚贴地向后扫转一周，(图2-42)重心上提成左弓步，右掌向前撩掌，再立圆从上向后变勾手，左掌从下向前挑掌成立掌，掌尖向上，目视左掌。(图2-43)

Two legs stand side by side, two palms are folded at the waist, the left foot is stepped up, the left leg is bent and half squatted, the right leg is straightened and extended into the left bow step, at the same time, two palms are pushed forward from both waist sides, palms and fingers are facing up, palms are facing forward. (Fig. 2-41) Buckle the left foot tip, bend the left leg to the knees, and squat to the right. At the same time, turn the upper body to the right and lean forward. Turn the two palms to the inside of the right leg to hold the ground with the body turning right. Turn the upper body to the right and back. Take the left forefoot as the axis, and sweep the right foot to the ground and turn backward for a circle, (Fig. 2-42) Lift the left bow step on the center of gravity, lift the right palm forward, and then turn the vertical circle from the top to the back to the hook, and lift the left palm from the bottom to the front palm tip up, look at the left palm. (Fig. 2-43)

图Fig 2-41　　　　　图Fig 2-42　　　　　图Fig 2-43

动作要点：转体、俯身、撑地用力紧凑连贯、一气呵成。

Key points of action: turn, lean and support the ground tightly and coherently.

四、基本跳跃、平衡练习 Jumping Exercises

（一）跳跃练习 Jumping practice

1. **腾空飞脚** Tengkong Feijiao (Flying feet)

右脚上步，左腿向前、向上摆踢，(图2-44) 右脚蹬地跃起，身体腾空，两臂由下向前、向头上摆起，右手背迎击左手掌。在空中，右腿向前上方弹踢，脚背绷直，右手迎击右脚面；同时左腿屈膝，左脚收于右腿侧，脚背绷直，脚尖向下。左手在击响的同时摆至左侧上方成勾手，上体微前倾，目视前方。(图2-45)

Step up with your right foot, swing your left leg forward and up, (Fig. 2-44) jump up with your right foot, lift your body into the air, swing your arms forward from below and head up, and hit your left palm with your right back. In the air, the right leg bounces and kicks forward and upward, the instep is taut and straight, and the right hand hits the right foot; at the same time, the left leg bends, the left foot closes to the right leg side, the instep is taut and straight, and the toe is downward. The left hand swings to the top of the left hand to form a hook when it strikes. The upper body leans forward slightly and looks forward. (Fig. 2-45)

图Fig 2-44

图Fig 2-45

动作要点：右腿摆踢高度过腰，击响动作连续、准确、响亮；腾空上体正直微前倾，忌坐臀。

Action points: the right leg kicks over the waist, and the action is continuous, accurate and loud; the upper body is upright and slightly forward in the air, and it is forbidden to sit on the hip.

2. **旋风脚** Xuanfeng Jiao (Whirlwind feet)

并步站立，右脚向左前方盖步，推左掌，掌尖朝上，右拳抱于腰间，目视左掌。(图2-46) 左脚向左上步，身体随之左转，右拳变掌，右臂伸直向后、向下摆动，右腿随即上步，脚尖内扣，左臂向下摆动并屈肘收至右胸前，右臂向上、向前抡摆，上体向左旋转前俯。（图2-47）重心右移，右腿屈膝蹬地踏跳，左腿提起向左上方摆动，上体向左上方翻转，同时两臂向下、向左上方抡摆，身体向左旋转一周，右腿在空中完成里合腿，左手在面前迎击右脚掌，左腿自然下垂。（图2-48）

Stand in parallel, cover the right foot to the left and front, push the left palm, with the tip of the palm facing up, hold the right fist at the waist, and look at the left palm. (Fig. 2-46) The left foot moves up to the left, the body turns to the left, the right fist turns to the palm, the right arm stretches straight and swings backward and downward, the right leg moves up, the toe is buckled inside, the left arm swings down and bends the elbow to the right chest, the right arm swings up and forward, and the upper body turns to the left and bends forward. (Fig. 2-47) Move the center of gravity to the right, step and jump with the right leg bent and pedaled, lift the left leg and swing it to the left and up, turn the upper body to the left and up, swing both arms down and to the left and up, rotate the body to the left for one circle, close the right leg in the air, hit the right foot palm with the left hand in front of you, and the left leg will drop naturally. (Fig. 2-48)

图Fig 2-46　　　　　　图Fig 2-47　　　　　　图Fig 2-48

动作要点：①右腿摆腿时贴近身体，膝挺直，摆腿成扇形；②击响点要靠近面部，抡臂、踏跳、转体、里合右腿要协调一致，身体的旋转不少于270°。

Action points: ① the right leg is close to the body when swinging, the knee is straight, and the leg is fan-shaped; ② the hit point should be close to the face, and the links such as arm swing, step jump, body rotation and inner closing of the right leg should be consistent, and the rotation of the body should not be less than 270°.

（二）平衡练习 Balance exercise

1. 提膝平衡 Balance with one knee raised

右腿直立支撑，左腿屈膝提起（过腰），脚背绷直，垂扣于右腿前侧，目视左侧。(图 2-49)

The right leg is upright and supported, the left leg is bent and lifted (over the waist), the instep is stretched and straight, and it is buckled at the front of the right leg, and look left. (Fig. 2-49)

图Fig 2-49

动作要点：平衡站稳，提膝过腰，脚内扣。

Action points: stand steadily, lift the knee over the waist, and inner the foot.

2. 侧身平衡 Side balance

支撑腿直立站稳，上体侧身前俯成水平，另一腿挺膝伸直举于体后，高于水平，脚面绷平或脚尖勾起。双臂分别向前下方和后上方展出。(图 2-50)

The supporting leg stands upright, the upper body is bent horizontally in front of the body, the other leg is straight and lifted behind the body, higher than the level, and the feet are flat or the toes are raised. The arms are displayed in front and back. (Fig. 2-50)

图Fig 2-50

动作要点：支撑腿站稳，上体与上举腿之间不要有角度，抬头。

Action points: stand firmly on the supporting leg, do not have an angle between the upper body and the lifting leg, and look up.

五、基本组合练习 Basic combination exercise

五步拳 Five-step-Quan (Wubu Quan)

1. 并步抱拳 Bingbu Baoquan (ready) (图 2-51) (Fig. 2-51)

图Fig 2-51

2. 弓步冲拳 Gongbu Chongquan (bow step + thrust fist)

左脚向左跨一步屈膝半蹲成左弓步；同时左手向左平搂并收回腰间抱拳，拳心向上，右拳向前冲拳，拳心向下，目视前方。(图 2-52)

Step the left foot to the left, bend your knees and squat to form a left lunge step. At the same time, hold the left hand to the left and draw back the waist fist. The heart of the fist is upward, and the right fist is forward. The heart of the fist is downward. Look ahead. (Fig. 2-52)

图Fig 2-52

3. 弹踢冲拳 Tanti Chongquan (spring kick + thrust fist)

重心前移左腿，右腿向前弹踢，脚背绷直；同时左拳由腰间向前冲拳，拳心向下，右拳收回腰间。(图 2-53)

The center of gravity moves forward the left leg, the right leg bounces forward and kicks, the instep is taut and straight, at the same time, the left fist punches forward from the waist, the heart of the fist is down, and the right fist retracts from the waist. (Fig. 2-53)

图Fig 2-53

4. 马步架打 Mabu Jiada (horse-ride step+ uphold fist)

右脚向前落步，脚内扣，身体左转体90°，两腿下蹲成马步；同时左拳变掌，屈臂上架，掌心向上，右拳由腰间向右冲拳，拳眼向上，头部右转，目视右拳。(图2-54)

Step forward with the right foot, buckle the foot, turn the body 90° to the left, squat down with both legs into a horse stance; at the same time, turn the left fist to the palm, bend the arm to the upper frame, palm center up, right fist to the right from the waist, fist eye up, head right turn, Look at the right fist. (Fig. 2-54)

图Fig 2-54

5. 歇步盖打 Xiebu Gaida (seated step +downward fist)

左脚向右脚后插步，两腿交叉，身体左转90°；同时右拳变掌经头上向左下盖，掌心向前，左掌收回腰间抱拳，拳心向上，目视右掌。(图2-55) 接上动，两腿屈膝全蹲成右歇步，左拳向前冲拳，拳心向下，右掌变拳收回腰间，拳心向上，目视左拳。(图2-56)

Step backward with the left foot to the right foot, cross two legs, turn left 90°, at the same time, change the palm of the right fist and cover it with head up, left and down, palm forward, take back the waist fist of the left palm, fist heart up, and look at the right palm. (Fig. 2-55)

Take up the movement, squat with both legs bent to the right rest step, punch forward with the left fist, with the heart of the fist downward, with the right palm changing to the waist, with the heart of the fist upward, and look at the left fist. (Fig. 2-56)

图Fig 2-55　　　　　　图Fig 2-56

6. 仆步穿掌 Pubu Chuanzhang (crouch step + shuttle palm)

重心上提，两腿起立，身体左转，两脚贴地拧转，左拳变掌，掌心向下，右拳变掌，掌心向上，（图2-57）右掌经左掌背向右上穿出，同时左腿提膝，左掌下收至右肩前，目视右掌。（图2-58）左脚向左落地成左仆步，左手掌指朝前沿左腿内侧向前穿掌，右掌大拇指侧朝上，目视左掌。（图2-59）

Lift the weight up, stand up with two legs, turn the body to the left, turn the feet close to the ground, turn the left fist to the palm, turn the palm downward, turn the right fist to the palm, turn the palm upward. (Fig. 2-57) Put the right palm through the back of the left palm, lift the knee of the left leg, turn the left palm to the front of the right shoulder, and look at the right palm. (Fig. 2-58) Shovel the left foot to the left and land into a left footstep, put the left palm finger forward to the inside of the left leg in the front, put the right palm thumb side up, and look at the left palm. (Fig. 2-59)

图Fig 2-57　　　　　　图Fig 2-58　　　　　　图Fig 2-59

7. 虚步挑掌 Xubu Tiaozhang (Empty step + pick palm)

重心前移左腿屈膝前弓，右脚蹬地向前上半步，脚尖点地成右虚步；同时左掌向上、向后立圆成勾手，略高于肩，勾尖向下，右手由后向下、向前顺右腿外侧向上挑掌，掌指向上，高与肩平，目视前方。（图 2-60）

Move forward the weight of the left leg, bend the knee and bow forward, step up and step forward with the right foot, and form the right virtual step with the toe point. At the same time, the left palm is upward and backward to form a hook, slightly higher than the shoulder, with the hook point downward. The right hand is downward and forward to pick up the palm along the outside of the right leg, with the palm pointing upward, with the height level with the shoulder, and Look ahead. (Fig. 2-60)

收势；左脚向右脚并步，双手变拳抱于腰间。（图 2-61）五步拳可左右练习，另一侧动作相同，方向相反。

Ending: step the left foot to the right foot; turn your hands to your waist. (Fig. 2-61) Five step boxing can be practiced left and right, the other side has the same movement and opposite direction.

图Fig 2-60　　　　图Fig 2-61

思考题：Questions for consideration

1. 马步的基本要求有哪些？

1. What are the basic requirements of horse-ride step?

2. 下肢柔韧练习方法有哪些?

2. What are the methods of softening the legs?

3. 弹腿的动作要点是什么?

3. What are the main points of the action of the spring leg?

4. 击响腿法的要求有哪些?

4. What are the requirements of kicking?

5. 武术腿法的分类有哪些? 试举例。

5. What is the classification of Wushu leg techniques? Give some examples.

第三章 传统拳术选编
Chapter 3 Selections of Traditional Quanshu

第一节 红拳十三式
3.1 Thirteen Moves of Hongquan

一、红拳十三式简介 Introduction

"红拳十三式"是国家级非物质文化遗产——红拳项目管理单位陕西红拳文化研究会组织红拳诸多专家创编推广普及的红拳小套路。红拳十三式选用红拳技法中古朴、经典的十三个动作组合而成,在不失红拳风格、劲力及技击打法风格的前提下,呈现了红拳基本"揭、抹、捅、斩"等技法特点,突出了红拳的健身、养生、技击功能,而且易学、易懂、易练、易用。

"Thirteen Moves of Hongquan" is created by Shaanxi Hongquan Culture Research Association, an official unit in charge of Hongquan (National Intangible Cultural Heritage). It is composed of thirteen simple and classic moves and easy to learn, practice and communicate. So it is very popular and becomes the set-moves for practice or competition. The moves present the basic technical characteristics of Hongquan such as "uncovering, wiping, stabbing and chopping" and highlight the functions of body-building, health preservation and fighting.

"红拳十三式"可根据不同的年龄分为快慢两种练习方法,初学由慢到快,长期习练会增强人体的协调性、灵活性,柔韧性,对强身健体延长运动生命有着不可估量的功能,尤其对青少年骨骼发育、身体协调发展有重要的功效。

"Thirteen Moves of Hongquan" can be divided into fast and slow exercise methods according to different ages. Beginners should learn from slow ones and long-term practice will enhance the coordination and flexibility of human body, especially for the bone and muscle development of young people.

二、红拳十三式技术特点 Technical characteristics

红拳十三式技法以红拳盘、势、法、理内涵体系构建技术思路，表现出以下特点：

The following features are highlighted in "Thirteen Moves of Hongquan":

1. 突出红拳技法风格 Hongquan Style

十三式尽显"撑补为母、勾挂为能、化身为奇、刁打为法"的红拳技击法则，以撑补斩为基，勾挂缠粘为能，侧身换膀和刁打贯穿始终，紧密相连，技法运用变换妙无穷。

It fully shows Hongquan Style of "supporting and holding as main moves with quick and various changes of body limbs".

2. 动作严谨，方法清晰，内容丰富 Rigorous moves

动作简练，内容丰富，拳架工整、劲力饱满，涵盖多种步型、步法和身法。动作创编既有古典红拳招式，又蕴含丰富势法变化，以势行法简单明快，变化灵活尽显红拳八法之变。

The moves are concise and have a full covering a variety of steps, which not only include the classical Hongquan moves, but also the flexible modern changes. All the moves are clear and logically related.

3. 突出红拳健身、养生功能 Health-keeping

红拳十三式动作刚柔相济，高低起伏多变，动作开展幅度可大可小，速度可快可慢，老少皆宜，对强身健体延长运动生命有显著效果，对于活动身心和研磨技法都有极强的价值，突出彰显红拳健身、养生功效。

The thirteen moves combine the firms and softs, ups and downs. The range of the movements can be large or small and the playing speed can be fast or slow, suitable for all ages. They have significant effect on strengthening body and prolonging life span. They also have great value for physical and mental health.

十三式歌（谱）诀

简易红拳十三式，非遗红拳新创编；

十字开势有传承，撑补捅捶威力大；

双扎接连裙拦势，拳经尽显雀地龙；

单片吊手面贴金，卸手抱头五连捶；

拦斩揭膀抹捅捶，魁星提斗换打虎；

狮子抖毛风摆肩，新拳老架传遍天。

三、红拳十三式动作图解 Illustration

第一段 The first section

预备式 Ready

自然站立，两脚并拢，两手成掌型自然下垂贴于身体两侧，抬头挺胸，下颌微收，两眼平视前方。（图 3-1-1）

Stand naturally, feet close together, hands in palm shape on both sides of the body naturally, head up and chest up, lower jaw slightly retracted, looking straight ahead. (Fig. 3-1-1)

双手抱拳迅速上提至腰间，两臂夹肘，拳心向上，目视前方。（图 3-1-2）

Quickly lift the two hands to the waist, clamp the elbows with two arms, with the heart of the fist upward, and look ahead. (Fig. 3-1-2)

图Fig 3-1-1　　　　图Fig 3-1-2

1. 海底捞月鹦哥架（十字手）Parrot frame (cross hands)

（1）双拳变掌，两臂向下伸直，双腿挺直，俯身弯腰，双掌贴腿下伸至指尖接近地面，掌心向前，双臂伸直，目随手动。（图 3-1-3-1、图 3-1-3-2）

(1) Turn fists into palms, extend arms downward, legs straight, bend over, extend palms close to legs until fingertips are close to the ground, palms inside forward, arms straight, eyes

follow the hand moving. (Fig. 3-1-3-1, Fig. 3-1-3-2)

图Fig 3-1-3-1　　　　　　　　　　图Fig 3-1-3-2

（2）接上式起身，两臂伸直上抬至与肩同高，双臂微屈双掌交叉回收胸前，右掌在左掌上，双掌内旋成立掌，掌腕相交，左掌在外、右掌在内，两掌向前推出，交叉成"十"字状，与肩同高，目视左侧。（图 3-1-4-1、图 3-1-4-2）

(2) Get up, straighten and lift the arms to the same height as the shoulder, slightly bend the arms and cross the palms to recover the chest, put the right palm on the left palm, rotate the palms inward to form the palm, intersect the palms and wrists, put the left palm outside and the right palm inside, push the two palms forward, cross into the shape of "十", the same height as the shoulder, and look in the left direction. (Fig. 3-1-4-1, Fig. 3-1-4-2)

图Fig 3-1-4-1　　　　　　　　　　图Fig 3-1-4-2

（3）双臂打开至两侧伸直，与肩同高，目视左掌；（图 3-1-5）两掌外旋至掌心向上；虎口朝后，转头目视右掌方向；（图 3-1-6）双手握拳迅速收回腰间，拳心向上，转头目视左侧，下颌微收。（图 3-1-7）

(3) Stretch arms to both sides and straighten them to the same height as your shoulders, and look at your left palm; (Fig. 3-1-5) turn your hands outward until the palm is facing up and turn your head to look at the right palm; (Fig. 3-1-6) quickly close your fists at your waist, with the fist center facing up, turn your head to look at your left side, and slightly close your jaw. (Fig. 3-1-7)

图Fig 3-1-5　　　　　　图Fig 3-1-6　　　　　图Fig 3-1-7

动作要点:"十字手"撑架有力,双臂含圆,双掌外旋缠腕有力。

Key points: "cross hand" bracket is powerful, with round arms, two palms are powerful.

2. 撑补势 Propping up

(1) 左拳由腰间向前向上提起,使小臂与大臂成90°,拳面朝上,拳心朝内,拳面与眼同高,目视左侧,同时提左膝,脚背绷直,左脚尖扣于右膝前方。(图 3-1-8)

(1) The left fist is lifted forward from the waist to form 90° between the forearm and upper arm, with the fist face upward, the fist heart inward, and the fist face at the same height as the eyes. Look at the left side, lift the left knee at the same time, with the back of the foot stretched straight, and the left foot pointed in front of the right knee. (Fig. 3-1-8)

图Fig 3-1-8

(2)仆步冲拳:左脚向前落步成左仆步,左拳打开下压,拳心向上,拳面朝前,左拳与小臂紧贴左大腿内侧向前探至左脚面,目视左拳;(图 3-1-9)重心前移至左腿成左弓步,左拳继续前冲出,左臂旋转滚动向上撑架,右拳由腰间向前冲拳,冲拳过程中右臂内旋,拳眼向上,右拳与肩同高,目视右拳方向。(图 3-1-10)

(2) Fist Pushing with Crouch step: crouch the left foot, the left fist is opened and pressed,

the heart of the fist is upward, the face of the fist is forward, the left fist and the forearm are close to the inner thigh, and the left fist is pushed forward to the left foot, and the left fist is seen; (Fig. 3-1-9) the center of gravity is moved forward to the left leg, and the left fist continues to rush forward, the left arm rotates and rolls to the upper bracket, the right fist is pushed forward from the waist, and the right arm is rotated inward, the eye of the fist is upward, and the right fist is punched during the punching process at shoulder height, look in the direction of the right fist. (Fig. 3-1-10)

图Fig 3-1-9　　　　　　　　　　图Fig 3-1-10

动作要点：仆步时下伏上体，左拳前冲与左弓步协调一致。

Key points: step down to the upper body, left punch forward and left bow step in harmony.

3. 双扎手 Shuangzhashou

（1）右拳变掌收于腰间，左拳变掌从头顶下按至胸前，（图 3-1-11) 右掌迅速经左掌上向前插出，掌尖与颈部同高，目视右掌方向。(图 3-1-12)

(1) The right fist changes its palm to close at the waist, and the left fist changes its palm from the top of the head down to the front of the chest, (Fig. 3-1-11) the right palm is quickly inserted forward through the left palm, the palm tip is the same height as the neck, and the right palm direction is observed. (Fig. 3-1-12)

图Fig 3-1-11　　　　　　　　　　图Fig 3-1-12

（2）右大臂不动，右掌由外向内、由上向下按至胸前，（图 3-1-13) 左掌迅速经右

掌上向前插出，掌尖与颈部同高，目视前方。(图 3-1-14)

(2) Connect the right big arm, press the right palm from the outside to the inside, from the top to the bottom and from the front to the chest, (Fig. 3-1-13) quickly insert the left palm through the right palm forward, with the palm tip as high as the neck, and look forward. (Fig. 3-1-14)

图Fig 3-1-13

图Fig 3-1-14

动作要点：插掌有力，双臂盖压穿插掌配合协调迅速。

Action points: insert the palms powerfully and cooperate with both arms quickly.

4. 裙拦势 Qunlan form

（1）重心上提，两脚开立，左掌变勾手向斜后方挂出，左臂伸直，勾尖向上。(图 3-1-15) 身体微右转, 左腿直立, 右腿屈膝上提; 同时右臂贴右腿向后分掌打开, 目视右侧。(图 3-1-16)

(1) Lift your gravity, separate your feet, change the left palm into a hook, extend the left arm, hook point is upward, (Fig. 3-1-15) turn the body slightly to the right, keep the left leg upright, bend the right leg and lift it up, at the same time, open the right arm against the right leg and divide the palm backward, and look in the right direction. (Fig. 3-1-16)

图Fig 3-1-15

图Fig 3-1-16

（2）右腿落步，重心移至右腿，左腿屈膝上提，身体左转 90°，右臂由后向头上架掌，右臂微屈成弧形，掌心向上，架右掌的同时迅速摆头，左臂伸直，左勾手不变，目视左侧，

（图 3-1-17）右腿屈膝半蹲，左脚回收，左脚尖点于右脚内侧，左腿紧贴右腿内侧成丁步，收臀挺胸，竖腰，目视左侧。（图 3-1-18-1、图 3-1-18-2）

(2) Step down the right leg, move the gravity to the right leg, bend the left leg and lift it up, turn the body 90° left, put the palm on the right arm from the back to the head, bend the right arm slightly into an arc, with the palm center upward, swing the head quickly while erecting the right palm, stretch the left arm straight, keep the left hook unchanged, and look at the left side, (Fig. 3-1-17) bend the right leg and squat, recover the left foot, point the left foot on the inside of the right foot, and keep the left leg close to the inside of the right leg for a long time. Hips, chest, waist, left side. (Fig. 3-1-18-1, Fig. 3-1-18-2)

图Fig 3-1-17　　　　图Fig 3-1-18-1　　　　图Fig 3-1-18-2

动作要点：丁步重心要低，上体尽力左转，双臂大开。

Key points: keep the gravity lower with T step, turn left as far as one can, and open arms as wide as possible.

5. 雀地龙 Quedilong

（1）挎腿按掌：接上式，重心上提，左腿伸直开立，右掌收于腰间，左勾手变掌由腰间向右方下按，左掌与肩同高，目视左掌。（图 3-1-19）

(1) Lift the gravity, open the left leg straight, turn the right palm into a fist and close it at the waist, turn the left hook into a palm and press it from the waist to the right, keep the left palm at the same height with the shoulder, and look at the left palm. (Fig. 3-1-19)

（2）插掌穿喉：重心移至右腿，左腿屈膝上提，左脚面绷直，右掌由腰间向右穿掌，左掌收于右肩前，目视右侧。（图 3-1-20）

(2) Insert the palm and pierce the throat: move the gravity to the right leg, lift the left

knee, straighten the left foot, pierce the right palm from the waist to the right, recover the left palm in front of the right shoulder, and look at the right side. (Fig. 3-1-20)

（3）仆步穿掌：右掌内旋变勾手，勾尖向上，身体左转，重心下蹲，左脚向左平伸成左仆步，左掌由右肩向前穿掌，前伸出左脚面，左掌和左臂紧贴大腿内侧，目视前方。(图 3-1-21)

(3) Turn the right palm into the hook, point up, turn left, squat down, extend the left foot to the left to form a left step, put the left palm forward from the right shoulder, extend the foot forward, keep the left palm and left arm close to the inner thigh, and look ahead. (Fig. 3-1-21)

图Fig 3-1-19　　　　图Fig 3-1-20　　　　图Fig 3-1-21

动作要点：穿掌力点在掌尖，掌尖微上翘，上体左转挺胸。

Key points: put the force on the tip of the palm, slightly raise the tip of the palm, and turn the upper body to the left to straighten out the chest.

6. 吊手单片 Diaoshoudanpian

接上式不停，左掌向前撑起，重心前移，竖腰成左弓步，(图 3-1-22) 右掌自下而上，由后向前抡起，与左掌击响于头上方，(图 3-1-23) 接着左掌变拳收于腰间，右掌由头顶向右耳侧屈肘格挡，右腿迅速向上摆踢，右脚面绷平，右掌由耳侧向前迎拍右脚面，目视前方。(图 3-1-24)

The left palm is propped up forward, the center of gravity is moved forward, and the waist is erected into a left bow step. (Fig. 3-1-22) The right palm is swung from the bottom to the top and swung forward from the back, and the left palm is hit on the top of the head, (Fig. 3-1-23) then the left palm turns to the waist, the right palm is bent from the top of the head to the right ear side, the elbow is blocked, the right leg is stretched flat and the foot is quickly swung up, and the right palm is swung forward from the ear side to shoot the right foot, and then look forward. (Fig. 3-1-24)

图Fig 3-1-22　　　　　　图Fig 3-1-23　　　　　　图Fig 3-1-24

动作要点：踢腿要高，拍脚脆快有力。

Key points: kick high, clap fast and powerfully.

7. 抹手贴金 Mashoutiejin(Wipe hands to gild)

（1）抹手：右脚向前落步，左脚再向前上步成左弓步，右臂伸直，左拳变掌由腰间斜向前伸出，两臂伸直，与额头同高，（图 3-1-25）右手先下自然击打右大腿面，左掌前探下劈击打左腿面，目视前方。（图 3-1-26）

(1) Wipe hands: step forward with the right foot, then step forward with the left foot to form a left bow step, with the right arm extended straight, the left fist palm extended from the waist obliquely forward, with the two arms extended straight, at the same height as the eyes, (Fig. 3-1-25) first hit the right thigh with the right hand, then hit the left leg with the left palm, and then look ahead. (Fig. 3-1-26)

图Fig 3-1-25　　　　　　　　　　　　图Fig 3-1-26

（2）贴金：左臂屈臂下压掌，掌心向下，右掌从左掌上向前推出，掌尖向上，左掌贴于右臂外侧，目视前方。（图 3-1-27）

(2) Gilding: press the palm with the left arm bent down, the palm center down, the right palm pushed forward from the left palm, the palm tip up, the left palm pasted on the outside of the right arm, and look forward. (Fig. 3-1-27)

图Fig 3-1-27

动作要点：抹手推掌要上步相随，左掌配合右臂相护。

Key points: wipe hands and push palms to follow each other in the upper step and protect each other with the left palm.

第二段 The second section

8. 卸手抱头 Remove the hand and hold the head

左掌顺右臂向前卸手，左臂伸直，掌心朝外，右手回抽握拳，向右侧打开至与右髋同高，右拳向左侧抢拳贯打，左手立掌垂肘迎击，同时右脚向左脚并步，立正站立，目视右侧。(图 3-1-28)

The left palm goes forward along the right arm, the left arm is extended with palm center outward.The right hand draws back and clenches the fist, opens to the right side to the same height as the right hip. The right fist swings to the left side and hits, the left hand pushes the right foot moves to the left foot. Stand upright and look in the right direction. (Fig. 3-1-28)

图Fig 3-1-28

动作要点：右拳贯打与左掌迎击准确。

Key points: right fist and left palm should be hit accurately.

9. 连五捶 Lianwuchui

图Fig 3-1-29　　　　图Fig 3-1-30　　　　图Fig 3-1-31

图Fig 3-1-32　　　　图Fig 3-1-33

右脚向前迈半步，脚尖点地成右虚步；同时右拳由左耳侧向下抡砸，左掌变拳收于腰间，拳心向上。(图 3-1-29) 重心前移至右脚，左腿屈膝上提，左拳由腰间提起向下、向前抡砸，(图 3-1-30) 左脚前落成左弓步，左拳向前冲拳，拳眼向上，(图 3-1-31) 左拳回收至腰间，右拳向前冲拳，拳眼向上，拳与肩同高，左弓步不变，(图 3-1-32) 右臂迅速回收滚架于头顶，左拳由腰间冲出，拳眼向上，拳与肩同高，身体微右转，左弓步变马步，目视左拳。(图 3-1-33)

Take a half step forward with your right foot, and make a right empty step at the toe of your foot. At the same time, swing your right fist sideways from your left ear to the bottom, turn your left palm into a fist and close it at your waist, with the heart of your fist facing up, (Fig. 3-1-29) move the center of gravity forward to the right foot, bend the left leg and lift it up, lift the left fist from the waist and swing it down and forward, (Fig. 3-1-30) In front of the left foot, a left lunge is formed, with the left fist punching forward and the fist eye upward, (Fig. 3-1-31) the left fist is recovered to the waist, while the right fist punching forward, the fist eye upward, the fist is the same height as the shoulder, and the left lunge does not change, (Fig. 3-1-32) the right arm is quickly recovered and rolled on the top of the head, the left fist is rushed out from the waist, the fist eye upward, the fist is the same height as the shoulder, the body turns slightly to the right, the left lunge changes to the horse stance, and the left fist is visually viewed. (Fig. 3-1-33)

动作要点：五拳连贯快速，弓步变马步时转胯发力，步法与冲拳协调配合。

Key points: The five fists-hitings should be coherent and fast. Step changes need the crotch to generate strength. The footsteps and fists should be coordinated.

10. 拦斩揭膀 Lanzhanjiebang

（1）身体微右转，重心移至右腿，右拳下落至左肩，左臂随转身内旋裹肩，左脚收回半步，(图3-1-34) 身体左转，左脚向前上步；同时左臂提起，左掌向前下按，左掌侧由上向下拦，右掌提起向下抢劈，左掌上挂于右肩，右臂下斩的同时，屈左腿，提右膝，使右脚贴于左腿膝窝处，目视前方。(图3-1-35)

(1) Turn the body slightly to the right, move the center of gravity to the right leg, drop the right fist to the left shoulder, turn the left arm inward to wrap the shoulder with the turn, and withdraw the left foot for half a step, (Fig. 3-1-34) turn the body left, step the left foot forward, lift the left arm at the same time, press the left palm forward and down, block it up and down with the external cause of the palm, lift the right palm and swing it downward, hang the left palm on the right shoulder, and at the same time, bend the left leg and lift the right knee to make the right foot Stick it to the knee socket of the left leg and look ahead. (Fig. 3-1-35)

图Fig 3-1-34　　　　　　　　图Fig 3-1-35

（2）揭膀：右腿提膝向前落右脚成右弓步；同时两臂伸直，右臂由下向前向上揭起，左臂向下向后揭膀，左掌掌心朝外，虎口向下，两膀放松，目视前方。(图3-1-36)

(2) Arm lifting: lift the right leg and knee forward. Straighten both arms, lift the right arm

from the bottom to the front, lift the left arm from the bottom to the back, lift the left palm to the outside, with the left thumb down, relax both arms, and look ahead. (Fig. 3-1-36)

图Fig 3-1-36

动作要点：左右臂拦斩要迅猛有力，两臂揭膀幅度要大，双肩大开。

Key points: the right and left arms should go quickly and powerfully, the arms should be lifted by a large margin, and the shoulders should be wide open.

11. 抹手捅 Mashoutong

图Fig 3-1-37　　　　　图Fig 3-1-38　　　　　图Fig 3-1-39

（1）抹手：左脚向前上步成左弓步，右臂下落至面部时，左掌由腰间向前插穿，（图3-1-37）右手向下抹，右手下落自然击打右腿面，左手向前拓，下抹击打左腿面。(图3-1-38)

(1) Wipe hands: step the left foot forward to form a left bow step. When the right arm falls to the face, insert the left palm forward from the waist, (Fig. 3-1-37) wipe down with the right hand, when the right hand falls, hit the right leg naturally, stretch forward with the left hand, and hit the left leg with the down wipe. (Fig. 3-1-38)

（2）上步捅捶：上右步成弓步；同时右掌变拳向前捅捶（冲拳），拳眼向上，拳与肩同高，左手立掌护于右大臂内侧，目视前方。（图3-1-39）

(2) Step up and punch: step the right foot forward to form a right bow step. and at the same time, change the right palm to fist and punch forward. The fist eye is upward, the fist is the same height as the shoulder, and the left hand stands on the inner side of the right big arm to protect, and look forward. (Fig. 3-1-39)

动作要点：抹手、上步、捅捶一气呵成。

Key points: wipe hands, step up, poke and beat together.

12. 魁星提斗打虎势 Kuixingtidou Dahushi

（1）魁星提斗：重心后移，身体左转90°，右脚向回收半步震脚，左腿后撩上翘，两手握拳，两臂打开，右臂伸直，左臂微屈上架，目视右拳。(图 3-1-40)

(1)Kuixingtidou: Move your weight backward, turn your body 90° left, and shake your feet with your right foot half step back. Lift your left leg up, clench your hands, open your arms, straighten your right arm, slightly bend your left arm up to the shelf, and look at your right fist. (Fig. 3-1-40)

（2）打虎势：身体左转90°，左脚向前落成左弓步，左拳面朝下栽于左膝上，左肘顶起肘尖向上，拳心朝外，右拳由后向头顶上打出，打至头顶正上方，拳面朝前，目视左肘方向。(图 3-1-41)

(2) Tiger fighting(Dahushi): turn your body 90° to the left, put your left foot forward into a left lunge, and plant your left fist face down on your left knee. Lift your left elbow up, with your fist heart facing out, with your left shoulder tightened. Hit your right fist from the back to the top of your head, with your fist face facing forward, directly above your head. Look in the direction of your left elbow. (Fig. 3-1-41)

图Fig 3-1-40　　　　　　　　图Fig 3-1-41

动作要点：魁星提斗腰胯配合身体转向，左脚后撩与两臂立圆抡劈协调顺畅。

Key points: The waist and crotch are lifted to match the body's turn, and the left foot is lifted back to coordinate with the two arms standing and swinging smoothly.

13. 狮子抖毛 Lion's rock

右臂打开向后抡，左臂打开向上抡，同时身体右转，重心移至右腿成右弓步，目视右拳方向，(图 3-1-42) 两臂继续向上抡，抡至两臂打开与肩同高，(图 3-1-43) 身体微左转，重心下蹲成马步，两大臂不动，小臂同时向内、向下栽拳于膝盖上，两肘外撑，拳心朝外，目视左方。(图 3-1-44)

Swing back with the right arm open, swing up with the left arm open, and turn your body right at the same time, move your weight to the right leg to form a right lunge, and look at the direction of the right fist, (Fig. 3-1-42) continue to swing up with both arms open to the same height as the shoulder, (Fig. 3-1-43) turn your body slightly to the left, squat down with the center of gravity into a horse stance, keep the two arms still, and drop the small arm into the knee at the same time, support the two elbows outwards, with the center of the fist outwards, and look left. (Fig. 3-1-44)

图Fig 3-1-42

图Fig 3-1-43

图Fig 3-1-44

动作要点：马步下栽拳配合双肩抖动，起到放松作用。

Key points: the horse step download, the shoulders shake and relax.

收势 Ending up

（1）身体直立，左脚向右脚并步成立正姿势；同时双拳收于腰间，拳心向上，目视左侧。(图 3-1-45)

(1) The body is upright, the left foot goes to the right foot and establish a straight posture, at the same time, the two fists are recycled in the waist, the heart of the fist is upward, and look in the left direction. (Fig. 3-1-45)

（2）双拳变掌自然垂下，身体放松，目视正前方。(图 3-1-46)

(2) The two fists become palms and naturally lowered; the body is relaxed, and look straight ahead. (Fig. 3-1-46)

图Fig 3-1-45

图Fig 3-1-46

第二节 小红拳
3.2 Xiao Hongquan

一、小红拳简介 Brief introduction

红拳是流传于关中的古老拳种，其内容丰富，套路繁多，技法全面，以撑补为母，勾挂为能，刁打为法，化身为奇，钻身贴靠，腿法凌厉著称。红拳取名兴盛、红火、吉祥、鲜艳、绝好之意。《史记·张仪传》记载："秦人秦声舞琴舞击缶弹筝，击膊拊髀"，这与近代红拳技法属于同样的表现形式。明代，红拳也称为"西家拳"，明代王圻《续文献通考》中惯用的拳势名称雀地龙、裙拦等均出自关中方言，戚继光《纪效新书·拳经捷要篇》所录三十二势也有所记载。

Hongquan is an old type of Wushu popular in Guanzhong (Northwest China). It has rich contents, various routines and comprehensive techniques. It is famous for various techniques of beating, kicking and other body moves. Hongquan means being prosperous, auspicious, bright and excellent. According to the *Biography of Zhang Yi* in *The Historical Records*, "Qin people dance and play Qin, Fou and Zheng (the ancient mucical instruments) with exaggerated moves of every part of the body", which has close relationship with Hongquan techniques. In the Ming Dynasty, Hongquan was also called "Xijia Quan"(Western Quan). According to the general examination of continuous documents by Wang Qi in the Ming Dynasty, the commonly used Quan names at that time, such as Quedilong and Qunlan, were all from

Guanzhong Dialect. Qi Jiguang's thirty-two movements recorded in *Ji Xiao's New Book* also recorded Hongquan.

道光、咸丰年间，关中红拳不断吸取其他拳种的实战招式，使红拳发展到一个鼎盛时期，代表人物以关中四杰为显，即三原"鹞子"高三（高占魁）、临潼"黑虎"邢三（邢福科）、潼关"饿虎"苏三（苏海潮）、临潼"通背"李四，四人皆精于红拳，并在红拳原有套路的基础上，形成了盘、法、势、理俱全的红拳套路与完整的打手体系。至今，红拳广泛流传于陕、甘、宁、新、豫、晋、蜀、皖、滇等地。小红拳是红拳七大拳系的基础拳术，习练红拳都以小红拳为入门的开始。

In the years of Daoguang and Xianfeng(1820-1861), Hongquan in Guanzhong continuously absorbed the practical moves of other kinds of Quan, which led to the development of Hongquan to a hot period. The four outstanding figures in Guanzhong were Gao Zhankui, Xing Fuke, Su Haichao and Lisi. All four of them were proficient in Hongquan. On the basis of this, a complete system of Hongquan routine and a complete system of hitters have been formed. Up to now, Hongquan has been widely spread in Shaanxi, Gansu, Ningxia, Xinjiang, Henan, Shanxi, Sichuan, Anhui, Yunnan and other places. Xiao Hongquan is the basic form of the seven major schools of Hongquan. The practice of Hongquan begins with Xiao Hongquan.

二、小红拳技术特点 Technical characteristics of Xiao Hongquan

（1）突出拳理技法特点 Highlight the fighting techniques

尽显"撑补为母、勾挂为能、化身为奇、刁打为法"八法技击法则，以撑补撑斩为基，勾挂缠粘为能，侧身换膀化身，刁打贯穿始终，动作紧密相连，技法运用变换无穷。

The eight attack rules based on supporting and chopping, hooking and sticking. The actions are closely connected, and techniques are used infinitely.

（2）动作内容丰富、方法清晰 Rich action contents and clear methods

整套拳术内容丰富，动作简练，拳架工整，劲力饱满，涵盖多种步型、步法和身法。动作富有古典招式，蕴含丰富势法变化，体现出化身闪绽之妙，刁打巧击之法。

The whole set of fighting is rich in content, simple in action, neat in frame and full in strength, covering a variety of steps, footwork and body method. The movement is rich in classical moves, rich in potential changes, reflecting the brilliance of the incarnation and the skill of tricky attack.

（3）拳套舒展巧美，劲道柔中寓刚 The moves combine softness and strength.

小红拳以柔为主，外柔内刚，以轻巧见长，拧腰捩胯，侧身换膀，运动方向多走直线，势势相承，舒展巧美、连贯自然。动作注重内三合、外三合，强调形神相合，内外合一，构成拳术节奏鲜明、势柔劲刚、拳架大方的拳种演练风格。

Xiao Hongquan is mainly soft outside and strong inside. It is light and skilful. Its moves are in a straight line with the combination of the skillful and natural moves. The movement focuses on the combination of internal and external, emphasizes the combination of form and spirit.

小红拳歌（谱）诀

抱拳十字开势妙，海底捞月鹦鸽架；
裙拦托掌雀地龙，踩步云手打法高；
单片坐盘双撑补，抱头打虎称英雄；
倒插盖脚快如风，二起抹手华山摇；
丁门收势变化奇，小红快拳敌难逃。

三、小红拳基本动作与方法 Basic movements and methods of Xiao Hongquan

（一）手法 Hand moves

1. 卸手：掌向前、向外推出，虎口向上，拆卸对方的手。

1.Xieshou (Remove the hand): push the palm forward and outward, with the fist eye upward, and remove the opponent's hand.

2. 叫拳：拳心向内，由下向上打击对方下颌或面部。

2.Jiaoquan: strike the opponent's jaw or face from the bottom to the top with the heart of the fist inward.

3. 捋手：手型成掌，掌心向前，指尖向上，由上向下用肘带动，用力坐腕。

3.Lvshou: the hands are formed into palms, the palms are forward, the fingertips are up, and the wrist is driven by elbows from up to down.

4. 抹手：手经体前由上向下劈抹，虎口朝前，掌心向下。

4.Mashou: the hands are split and wiped from top to bottom in front of the body, with the tiger mouth facing forward and the palm of the hand facing down.

5. 塌手：手型成掌，掌沿向前，指尖向上，向前推按。

5.Tashou: form a palm with the palm edge forward, fingertips up, and push the palm forward.

6. 捺手：拳向内翻转向前推出，拳心向前，拳眼向下。

6. Nashou: turn the fist inward and push it forward, with the heart forward and the eyes downward.

7. 贯耳捶：拳经体侧向外屈肘划弧，至肩部向内摆击，拳心向下，拳眼向内。

7. Guanerchui: bend the elbow outwards through the body side of the fist and make an arc until the shoulder blows inwards. The center of the fist is downward and the eye of the fist is inwards.

（二）步法 Step

1. 退步：两脚前后站立，后脚向后退步或前脚向后退步。

1. Step back: stand back and forth with both feet, step back with the back foot or step back with the front foot.

2. 上步：两脚前后站立，前脚向前上步或后脚向前上步。

2. Step up: stand back and forth with your feet, step forward with your front feet or step forward with your back feet.

3. 震步：一脚支撑，另一脚提膝下落，全脚重踏地面或脚后跟重踏地。

3. Shake step: one foot is supported, the other foot is lifted to the knee, and the whole foot is stepped on the ground or the heel is stepped on the ground again.

四、小红拳动作图解 Illustration of Xiao Hongquan

第一段 Part I

抱拳势 Fist hold

（1）两脚并步站立，两手自然垂于身体两侧，两手成掌型，掌心朝内，悬头竖项，自然呼吸，目视前方。（图 3-2-1）

(1) Stand with two feet together, two hands naturally hanging on both sides of the body, two hands in palm shape, palm inward, hanging head and standing up, breathe naturally, and look ahead. (Fig. 3-2-1)

（2）两脚不动，两掌变拳，抱拳于腰间，拳心向上，目视前方。(图 3-2-2)

(2) Keep your feet still, turn your hands into fists, hold your fists at your waist, keep your heart up, and look ahead. (Fig. 3-2-2)

图Fig 3-2-1　　　　图Fig 3-2-2

动作要点：抬头、挺胸、收腹、敛臀；抱拳动作迅速。

Key points: head up, chest up, abdomen in, buttocks in; move quickly.

1. **十字手开势** Cross hand opening

图Fig 3-2-3　　　　图Fig 3-2-4　　　　图Fig 3-2-5

（1）两脚不动，两腿挺直，双拳变掌，掌心向上，上体俯身弯腰，双臂伸直，双掌贴腿下伸至指尖接近地面，(图 3-2-3) 两掌交叉，(图 3-2-4) 两臂伸直上抬至与肩同高，双臂微屈双掌交叉回收胸前，左掌在右掌外侧，双掌内旋成立掌，(图 3-2-5) 两腕相交，直臂前撑，成"十"字状，目视左侧。(图 3-2-6-1、图 3-2-6-2)

(1) Keep your feet still, keep your legs straight, turn your fists into palms, turn your palms upward, bend your upper body over, straighten your arms, extend your palms to your

fingertips and close to the ground, (Fig. 3-2-3) cross your palms, (Fig. 3-2-4) straighten your arms and lift them up to the same height as your shoulders, slightly bend your palms to recover your chest, turn your left palms outside the right palms, and form palms inside, (Fig. 3-2-5) cross your wrists, straighten your arms forward, and form a palm " 十 " shape. Look left. (Fig. 3-2-6-1, Fig. 3-2-6-2)

图Fig 3-2-6-1　　　　　图Fig 3-2-6-2

（2）双臂打开至两侧伸直，与肩同高，目视左掌，（图 3-2-7) 两掌外旋，掌心向上，虎口朝后，转头目视右掌方向，（图 3-2-8) 双掌握拳迅速收至腰间，拳心向上，转头目视左侧。(图 3-2-9)

(2) Open your arms to both sides and straighten them to the same height as your shoulders. Look at your left palm. (Fig. 3-2-7) Rotate your two palms outwards, with the palm facing up and the tiger's mouth facing back. Turn your head to look at the direction of your right palm, (Fig. 3-2-8) rotate your two palms inwards until the palm is facing down, with your hands clenched quickly at your waist, with the fist facing up, and turn your head to look at the left side. (Fig. 3-2-9)

图Fig 3-2-7　　　　　图Fig 3-2-8　　　　　图Fig 3-2-9

动作要点：①身体前下俯身与上肢撩掌动作要协调，双腿并拢，手法清楚。②"十字手"撑架有力，双臂含圆立直前推，双掌外旋缠腕有力。

Key points: ① the front of the body and the upper limbs should be coordinated, the legs should be close together, and the technique should be clear. ② The "cross hand" bracket is powerful, the arms are round, and the palms are powerful to wrap around the wrist.

2. 弓步冲拳 Bow step punch

身体左转，左脚向右后侧撤步，右腿屈膝半蹲成右弓步，左脚跟提起；同时左拳向前冲拳，拳眼向上，右拳收至腰间，目视前方。(图 3-2-10)

Turn your body to the left, move your left foot to the right, bend your right leg and half squat into a right bow step, lift your left heel, punch forward at the same time with your left fist, keep your right fist up to your waist, and look ahead. (Fig. 3-2-10)

图Fig 3-2-10

动作要点：左腿插步要远，重心下蹲，冲拳手臂前伸。

Key points: the left foot should be far, the weight should be squatted, and the punching arm should be extended.

3. 合拳弹踢 Hequantanti

（1）右拳向前冲拳，左拳回收合于右拳背，(图3-2-11)双手外旋向后划弧回收于腰间，右拳心向上，目视前方。(图 3-2-12)

(1) The right fist is hurtled forward, the left fist is recovered on the back of the right fist, (Fig. 3-2-11) the two hands are turned outward and arc backward to recover on the waist, the right fist is centered upward, and look ahead. (Fig. 3-2-12)

（2）接上式，重心前移至右腿，左脚向前蹬踢，力达脚跟。(图 3-2-13)

(2) Shift the gravity to the right leg, and kick the left foot. (Fig. 3-2-13)

动作要点：合拳旋腕快速，回收腰间时夹臂，弹踢动作清晰。

Key points: close the fist and rotate the wrist quickly, and play and kick clearly.

图Fig 3-2-11　　　　　图Fig 3-2-12　　　　　图Fig 3-2-13

4. 撑补势 Propping up

图Fig 3-2-14　　　　　图Fig 3-2-15　　　　　图Fig 3-2-16

（1）双手不动，右腿挺膝直立，左腿屈膝收回，（图 3-2-14）右腿全蹲，左脚向左铲出平铺成左仆步，左拳心向上，贴左腿向前冲拳，右拳心向上收于腰间，目视左前方。（图 3-2-15）

(1) Keep your hands still, keep your right leg upright, bend your left leg back, (Fig. 3-2-14) squat your right leg completely, shovel out your left foot to the left and spread it into a left footstep, with your left fist facing up, punch forward with your left leg, close your right fist at your waist, and look at the left front. (Fig. 3-2-15)

（2）重心前移，左腿屈膝成左弓步，左拳内旋腕上架于头上方，拳心向上；同时，右拳向前冲拳，拳眼向上，与肩同高，目视前方。（图 3-2-16）

(2) Move the gravity forward, bend the left leg to form a left lunge step, rotate the left fist to the top of the head, and the fist heart is upward; the right fist rushes forward, the fist eye is upward, the same height as the shoulder, and look forward. (Fig. 3-2-16)

动作要点：撑架时力贯小臂，左拳旋腕上架与冲右拳协调快速。

Key points: when supporting, the force passes through the forearm, and the left fist and the right fist are coordinated quickly.

5. 铁匠三拳 Blacksmith's three punches

左拳变掌下落拍击右前臂上方,(图3-2-17)右拳变掌,向后拍击右大腿面,(图3-2-18)左掌下落拍击左大腿面,(图3-2-19)左掌随即外旋掌心向上,右手经腰间向后、向上立圆划弧过头后向下斩拳,拳眼向上,前臂贴于左掌心上。(图3-2-20)

Turn the left fist into palm and pat the upper part of the right forearm. (Fig. 3-2-17) Turn the right fist into palm and pat the right thigh, (Fig. 3-2-18) the left palm falls and taps the left thigh, (Fig. 3-2-19) the left palm immediately turns the palm upward, and the right hand goes though the waist and upward the vertical arc over the head becoming the fist and strike downward. The fist eye is upward, and the forearm is attached to the left palm center. (Fig. 3-2-20)

图Fig 3-2-17　　　　　　　　图Fig 3-2-18

图Fig 3-2-19　　　　　　　　图Fig 3-2-20

动作要点：拍击快速、准确、清脆，右拳立圆劈斩。

Key points: to pat fast, accurately and crisply; to chop down in vertical circle with right fist.

6. 左右盘头花 Left and Right Pantouhua

图Fig 3-2-21　　　　　　图Fig 3-2-22

图Fig 3-2-23　　　　　　图Fig 3-2-24

（1）左右盘头花：双脚不动，右手向左、向后水平顺时针划弧至腰间，左手配合经胸前向左、向上划弧再向下按掌，左掌心向下，目视前方。（图3-2-21）

(1) Left and right Pantouhua: keep your feet still, turn your right hand to the left and back horizontally and clockwise to the waist, turn your left hand to the left and up through your chest and press your palm downward, with the center of your left palm downward, and look ahead. (Fig. 3-2-21)

（2）扎手：双脚不动，右掌经左掌上向前插出，掌尖与颈部同高，掌心向上，目视右掌方向。(图3-2-22) 右大臂不动，右掌由外向内、由上向下从面前下按至胸前，左掌收至腰间，(图3-2-23) 左掌迅速经右掌上向前插出，掌尖与颈部同高，掌心向上，目视前方。(图3-2-24)

(2) Zhashou: keep your feet still, insert the right palm forward through the left palm, keep the tip of the palm at the same height as the neck, with the center of the palm upward, and observe the direction of the right palm, (Fig. 3-2-22) the right big arm does not move, the right palm is pressed from the front to the chest from the outside to the inside, from the top to the bottom, and the left palm is retracted to the waist, (Fig. 3-2-23) the left palm is quickly inserted forward through the right palm, the palm tip is the same height as the neck, the palm center is upward, and look ahead. (Fig. 3-2-24)

动作要点：双手盘头花平圆绕转，线路清晰，插掌有力，双臂配合迅速。

Key points: the two hands are flat and round, the lines are clear, the palms are powerful, and the two arms cooperate quickly.

7. 裙拦势 Qunlanshi

（1）左右卸手：左臂屈臂回收，左臂伸直，左掌变勾手向斜后方挂出，勾尖向上，（图 3-2-25）身体微右转，左腿直立，右腿屈膝上提，同时右臂贴右腿向后卸手，目视右侧。（图 3-2-26）

(1) Left and right Xieshou: the left arm bends back and extends. The left hook stretches out behind. The hook point is upward, (Fig. 3-2-25) the body turns slightly to the right; the left leg is upright. The right leg is bent and lifted up. The right arm pastes against the right leg. Watch the right side. (Fig. 3-2-26)

图Fig 3-2-25 图Fig 3-2-26

（2）裙拦势：右脚落步，重心移至右腿，左腿屈膝上提，身体左转90°，右臂由后向头上架掌，右臂微屈成弧形，掌心向上，架右掌的同时迅速摆头，左臂伸直，左勾手不变，目视左侧，(图 3-2-27) 右腿屈膝半蹲，左脚尖点于右脚内侧成丁步，左腿紧贴右腿，左腿屈膝下蹲使左腿面与地面平行，收臀挺胸，竖腰，目视左方。(图 3-2-28-1、图 3-2-28-2)

(2) Qunlanshi: Stand on the right leg, lift the left leg bending and turn 90° to the left.The right arm stretches from the back to the head into an arc with palm center up. Swing the head and stretch the left arm with a left hook hand and watch the left side. (Fig. 3-2-27) Half squat on the right leg, form a T step with the left foot tip, the left leg and the right leg are close and the tap be parallel to the ground. (Fig. 3-2-28-1, Fig. 3-2-28-2)

图Fig 3-2-27　　　　图Fig 3-2-28-1　　　　图Fig 3-2-28-2

动作要点：丁步要低，上体尽力左转，双臂大开。

Key points: T-step should be low, turn left as far as you can, and open the arms widely.

8. 雀地龙 Quedilong

（1）挎腿按掌：接上式，重心上提，左腿伸直开立，右掌变拳收于腰间，左拳变掌向右方下按，左掌与肩同高，目视左掌。(图 3-2-29)

(1) Stride and push: lift the gravity, strech the left leg straight, turn the right palm into a fist and close it at the waist, turn the left fist into a palm and press it down to the right, the left palm is the same height as the shoulder, and look at the left palm. (Fig. 3-2-29)

（2）插掌穿喉：重心移至右腿，提左膝，左脚面绷直，右掌由腰间向右上穿掌，左掌回收于右肩前，目视右侧。(图 3-2-30)

(2) Insert the palm in front of the throat: move the gravity to the right leg, lift the left knee, straighten the left foot, put the right palm into the palm from the waist to the right,

recover the left palm in front of the right shoulder, and look at the right side. (Fig. 3-2-30)

（3）仆步穿掌：右掌内旋变勾手，勾尖向上，身体左转，重心下蹲，迅速摆头，左脚向左前平铺成左仆步，左掌由右肩向前穿掌，目视前方。(图 3-2-31)

(3) Pubuchuanzhang: turn the hook inside the right palm, point up, turn left, squat down, swing your head quickly, spread the left foot to the left and forward to form a left step, and put the left palm forward from the right shoulder, and look ahead. (Fig. 3-2-31)

图Fig 3-2-29　　　　图Fig 3-2-30　　　　图Fig 3-2-31

动作要点：仆步要低，穿掌力在掌尖，掌尖微上翘，上体左转挺胸。

Key points: lower the steps, put the force on the tip of the palm, slightly raise the tip of the palm, and turn the upper body to the left to straighten out the chest.

9. 虚步刁手 Xubudiaoshou

重心前移，起身直立，右脚上半步成右虚步，左、右臂直臂向上、向后经体侧立圆抡摆，(图 3-2-32) 当右臂由后划至体侧时向上提手变勾手至头上方，力达勾顶，勾尖朝下，左手变拳抱于腰间，拳心向上，目视前方。(图 3-2-33)

Move the gravity forward, stand upright, the upper half of the right foot steps into the right virtual step, the left and right arms are straight up and backward through the side of the body, and a circle swing is erected. (Fig. 3-2-32) When the right arm is drawn from the back to the side of the body, the hands are lifted up to the top of the head, the force reaches the hook top, the hook tip is downward, the left hand is changed to hold the fist at the waist, the fist heart is up, and look ahead. (Fig. 3-2-33)

图Fig 3-2-32　　　　　　　　　图Fig 3-2-33

动作要点：两臂立圆，动作连贯，两脚虚实分明，上下肢配合协调。

Key points: arms go along the vertical cycle; one foot is empty and the other is solid; arms and legs go smoothly and cooperatively.

10. 搂膝塌掌 Louxitazhang

重心前移右腿，左脚向前上步，上体右转，重心前移左脚，右腿提膝，脚尖绷直，右手变掌向后搂手，(图3-2-34)右掌变拳回收至腰间，拳心向上，右脚向右落步成右弓步；同时，左手经腰间向右塌掌，掌沿向前，力达掌根，目视左掌。(图3-2-35)

Move the weight of the left leg forward, turn the upper body to the right, lift the knee of the right leg, straighten the toe, and turn the right palm to hug the hand back, (Fig. 3-2-34) turn the right palm to the waist, turn the heart of the fist upward, and turn the right foot to the right to form the right lunge; at the same time, collapse the left hand to the right through the waist, move the palm edge forward, reach the root of the palm, and look at the left palm. (Fig. 3-2-35)

图Fig 3-2-34　　　　　　　　　图Fig 3-2-35

动作要点：两臂线路清晰协调，塌掌发力干脆。

Key points: the routine of the two arms are clear and coordinated, and the power of the palm collapse is short and powerful.

11. 叶子手 Yezishou

（1）左撩阴掌：重心移至右腿，右腿直立，身体左转，左腿屈膝上提，左掌下落至右肩前，（图 3-2-36）左脚向斜前方上步成左弓步，左手经体前向前向上撩掌并向上架掌，掌心向上，同时右手紧随左掌向斜下方提撩，掌心向前，指尖斜向下，力达掌根，目视撩掌。（图 3-2-37）

(1) Left Yin palm: Move the gravity to the right leg, turn left, bent the left leg and lift up, the left palm goes to the front of the right shoulder, (Fig. 3-2-36) the left foot is tilted forward to form a left bow step. The left hand is lifted forward through the front of the body and lifted up to the upper palm, the palm is up, and the right hand following the left palm syncline, the palm is forward. (Fig. 3-2-37)

图Fig 3-2-36　　　　　　　图Fig 3-2-37

（2）右撩阴掌：接上式，右脚向斜前方上步屈膝半蹲成右弓步，右手经体前向前向上撩掌并翻架掌，掌心向上，同时左手紧随右掌向斜下方提撩，掌心向前，指尖斜向下，力达掌根，目视撩掌。（图 3-2-38）

(2) Right Yin palm: the right foot is tilted forward, the knee is bent and half squatted, the right hand is tilted forward through the front of the body, the palm is lifted forward and turned over, the palm center is upward, and the left hand is lifted below the right palm syncline, the palm center is forward, the fingertip is tilted downward. (Fig. 3-2-38)

（3）左撩阴掌：左腿继续向左前上步成左弓步，左掌上撩架掌，右掌下方提撩，力达掌根。（图 3-2-39）

(3) Left Yin palm: move the left leg forward to form a left bow step, lift the frame palm on the left palm, and lift the lower part of the right palm to reach the end of the palm. (Fig. 3-2-39)

图Fig 3-2-38   图Fig 3-2-39

动作要点：上下肢动动作连贯、协调；步法稳健，撩掌手法清楚，力达掌根。

Key points: the arms and legs are consistent and coordinated; the footstep steady, the hand lifting technique powerful.

12. **虚步塌掌** Xubutazhang

重心后移至右腿，左脚回收，左脚尖点地成左虚步，左掌屈臂下压，掌心向下，指尖向右，右掌收至腰间，目视左掌。（图 3-2-40）

The gravity back to the right leg, the left foot tip points into a left virtual step. The left palm flexes the arm to press down, the palm center downward, the fingertip right, the right palm is retracted to the waist, and look at the left palm. (Fig. 3-2-40)

图Fig 3-2-40

动作要点：塌掌与重心协同一致，动作有力。

Key points: the palm collapse and the gravity are coordinated, and the action is powerful.

13. 卸手 Xieshou

左脚向前上步成左弓步，右掌经左掌上向前推掌，掌尖向上，左掌贴于右臂下方，(图 3-2-41) 紧接着，重心后移至右腿，左脚回收于右脚前点地成左虚步，左掌贴右臂向前卸手塌掌，掌心向下，力达掌侧，右掌收至腰间，目视左掌。(图 3-2-42)

The left foot moves forward to form a left bow step, the right palm pushes forward through the left palm, the palm tip upward, the left palm is pasted under the right arm, (Fig. 3-2-41) then, the gravity is moved back to the right leg, the left foot is recycled in front of the right foot to form a left virtual step, the left palm pastes the right arm to push the palm forward, the palm center is downward, the force reaches the palm side, the right palm is retracted to the waist. Look at the left palm. (Fig. 3-2-42)

图Fig 3-2-41　　　　　　　　图Fig 3-2-42

动作要点：左掌贴右臂向前挑卸，与右臂回收快速有力。

Key points: the left palm is attached to the right arm and lifted forward, which is fast and powerful with the coming back of the right arm.

14. 歇步叫手 Xiebujiaoshou

重心上提，右掌直臂向前撩掌划弧，右掌背迎击左掌，(图 3-2-43) 右掌继续向后立圆划弧至右肩上，左脚向外拧转，重心下蹲，两腿交叉下蹲成歇步，右掌下落右肩上托掌，左掌收至腰间，目视前方。(图 3-2-44)

The straight arm goes forward to draw an arc, the back of the right palm hits the left palm and continues to draw an arc backward and vertically to the right shoulder, (Fig. 3-2-43) The left foot turns outward, the weight squats down and the legs cross down to form a rest step, the right palm falls to the right shoulder, the left palm is to the waist, and look ahead. (Fig. 3-2-44)

图Fig 3-2-43　　　　　　　图Fig 3-2-44

动作要点：击掌响亮，右掌立圆抡摆快速。

Action points: Clap loudly, and the right palm stands round and swings quickly.

15. 单片提膝连斩 Danpiantixilianzhan

重心上提前移左腿，右腿向上弹踢，右手拍击右脚面，左拳收于腰间，拳心向上，（图 3-2-45）接着，右腿屈膝下落回收，脚尖绷直，右手变拳顺势向下屈肘劈斩至腹前，拳心向上，目视右拳。（图 3-2-46）

Move the gravity to the left leg, lift the right leg and kick, right hand clap on the right foot, left fist close to the waist, fist heart up. (Fig. 3-2-45) Then, bend the right leg to the knee, straighten the toe, turn the right hand to the elbow and chop to the front of the abdomen, fist heart up, and look at the right fist. (Fig. 3-2-46)

图Fig 3-2-45　　　　　　　图Fig 3-2-46

动作要点：弹踢有力，击拍脚面清脆响亮；斩拳动作力达拳背。

Key points: lift and kick powerfully, hit and clap the foot loudly; chop fast and with whole force of the fist.

16. 坐盘架打 Zuopanjiada

右脚向前外展落步，身体右转，左脚跟步，重心下蹲成坐盘，右腿在前；同时，右拳向前冲拳并向上外旋架于头上右侧，拳心向上，左拳向前冲出，拳眼向上，目视前方。(图 3-2-47)

Step forward with the right foot, turn to the right, following the left foot, squat with the right leg in front; swing the right fist forward and outward on the right side of head, with fist heart up, and then rush out with the left fist forward, and look ahead. (Fig. 3-2-47)

图Fig 3-2-47

动作要点：左右拳协调一致、动作连贯。

Key points: the left and right fists are coordinated and the action is consistent.

第二段 The second part

17. 猴子望镜 Monkey watch

坐盘不动，左拳经体前逆时针划弧向上至右额前内旋撑架，拳心向下，拳眼向前，右拳体侧划弧收至腰间抱拳，目视前方。(图 3-2-48)

Sit still, turn the left fist anticlockwise to the front of the body and turn it up to the front of the right forehead. Turn the center of the fist downward and look forward. Turn the right fist sideways to the waist and look ahead. (Fig. 3-2-48)

图Fig 3-2-48

动作要点：团身要紧，似猴子反手遮日，神形相似。

Key points: curl up the body closely; like a monkey watch from a height with its hand blocking the sun

18. 背剑腿 Beijiantui

（1）起身搂斩：重心上提直立，左拳变掌由上向下劈斩，右拳由下向上抢劈，目视前方。（图 3-2-49）

(1) Get up and cut: lift the gravity up and stand upright, change the left palm into fist to chop from top to bottom, blow with right fist from bottom to top, and look ahead. (Fig. 3-2-49)

（2）背剑腿：左掌拦击右拳后收至右腋下，左腿直腿向上勾脚侧踢，右拳向上划弧抖腕亮拳，目视前方。（图 3-2-50）

(2) BeiJianTui: block the right fist with the left palm and back to the right armpit. Kick with the left leg straight to the side of the upper hook foot. Swing the right fist upward and shake the wrist. Look ahead. (Fig. 3-2-50)

图Fig 3-2-49　　　　　图Fig 3-2-50

动作要点：侧踢快速、有力，两腿均不能弯曲。

Key points: side kick is fast and powerful, and both legs cannot be bent.

19. 转身搂膝塌掌 Zhuanshenlouxitazhang

左脚落地支撑，身体右转，右腿提膝，脚尖绷直，右手经体侧向后搂手，左掌收至腰间，（图 3-2-51）右腿落地，重心移至右腿，提左膝，左脚面绷直，右掌由腰间向右穿掌，左掌回收于右肩前，目视右侧。（图 3-2-52）

The left foot as support, turn right, raise the right leg to the knee, the toe taut and straight, the right hand backward through the body side, the left palm is to the waist. (Fig. 3-2-51) Move the gravity to the right leg, raise the left knee, the left foot taut and straight, the right palm passes through the waist to the right, the left palm recovered in front of the right shoulder, and watch the right side. (Fig. 3-2-52)

图Fig 3-2-51　　　　　图Fig 3-2-52

动作要点：搂手与塌掌协调，塌掌发力干脆。

Key points: hand and palm go coordinately and simply.

20. 雀地龙 Quedilong

右掌内旋变勾手，勾尖向上，身体左转，重心全蹲，左脚向左铲出成左仆步，左掌由右肩向前穿掌，前伸出脚面，目视前方。（图 3-2-53）

Turn the right palm into the hook, point up, turn left, squat fully, shovel the left foot to the left to form a left footstep, put the left palm forward from the right shoulder, extend the foot forward, and look ahead. (Fig. 3-2-53)

动作要点：仆步要低，穿掌力在掌尖，掌尖微上翘，上体左转挺胸。

Key points: lower the steps, put the force on the tip of the palm, slightly raise the tip of the palm, and turn the upper body to the left to straighten out the chest.

图Fig 3-2-53

21. 击步二起脚 Jibuerqijiao

图Fig 3-2-54　　　　　　　图Fig 3-2-55

图Fig 3-2-56　　　　　　　图Fig 3-2-57

重心上提前移，左腿前弓，双手变掌，(图 3-2-54) 双脚起跳腾空，右脚碰击左脚，(图 3-2-55) 右脚先落地，左脚向前落地，右脚再上步蹬地踏跳，左腿屈膝向上摆动，(图 3-2-56) 右腿直腿向上弹踢；同时，左掌由下向前向上摆起，右掌向上，左掌拍击右手背，在跳起腾空的瞬间分手，右手向下拍击右脚面。(图 3-2-57)

Move the gravity forward, bow the left leg forward, and change both hands into palms. (Fig. 3-2-54) Hit the left foot with the right foot, (Fig. 3-2-55) land the right foot first, step up with the right foot and the left leg bent up to lift the knee. (Fig. 3-2-56) Kick with the right leg straight up; swing with the left palm up from the bottom, and hit the right back with the left palm, and then jump up.The right hand taps on the right foot. (Fig. 3-2-57)

动作要点：击步两腿伸直，脚背绷直，起跳摆腿击拍响亮。

Key points of action: stretch the legs in the strike step, straighten the instep, jumping, swing and claping should be loud and clear.

22. 揭膀抹手 Jiebangmashou

（1）揭膀：腾空落地，右脚向前上步，两臂伸直，右臂由下向前向上揭起，左臂向下向后揭膀，左掌掌心朝外，虎口向下，两膀放松，目视前方。（图 3-2-58）

(1) Jiebang: Jump in the air, step forward with right foot, straighten arms, lift right arm from the bottom to the top, lift left arm from the bottom to the back, lift left palm outward, thumb downward, and look ahead. (Fig. 3-2-58)

（2）弓步抹手：左脚上步屈膝半蹲成左弓步，双掌经体前由上向下抹，虎口朝前，掌心向下，双手抹至腰间抱拳，拳心向上，目视前方。（图 3-2-59）

(2) Gongbumashou: bent the left foot to form a left bow step, the palms go down in front of the body, with thumbs forward. The palm center is down, the hands are to the waist, the heart of the fist is up, and watch the front. (Fig. 3-2-59)

图Fig 3-2-58　　　　　　图Fig 3-2-59

动作要点：两膀放松，双肩打开；抹手动作连贯，上下肢配合协调。

Key points: relax your arms and open your shoulders; wipe your hands in a consistent way and coordinate your upper and lower limbs.

23. 捅捶 Tongchui

双脚不动，右手从腰间向前冲拳，拳眼向上，(图3-2-60)身体右转，弓步变马步，左手从腰间向前冲拳，拳眼向上，右拳向上撑架头上方，拳心向上，目视左拳方向。(图3-2-61)

Keep your feet still, punch forward from the waist with your right hand, with your fist eye up, (Fig. 3-2-60) turn your body to the right, change bow step to horse stance, punch forward from the waist with your left hand, with your fist eye up, right fist up above the head of the bracket, with your fist heart up, and look at your left fist. (Fig. 3-2-61)

图Fig 3-2-60   图Fig 3-2-61

动作要点：弓、马步转换快速与冲、架拳配合协调。

Key points of action: fast transition of bow and horse stance, coordination with punching and boxing.

24. 侧闪搂斩 Ceshanlouzhan

身体右转，右脚向右侧上步，左脚跟步；同时，双手变掌随右转裹肩下带，右掌收至左肩，(图3-2-62)身体迅速左转180°，右掌变拳向上抡举，(图3-2-63)重心前移左脚，右拳向下劈斩至左胯外侧，力达拳轮，左手划弧上挂右肩前，目视前方。(图3-2-64)

Turn your body to the right, move your right foot up to the right, and follow your left foot. At the same time, wrap your hands around your shoulders with your right hand, and put your right hand back to your left shoulder, (Fig. 3-2-62) turn your body 180° quickly to the left, and swing your right hand up to your right fist, (Fig. 3-2-63) move your weight forward to your left foot, and chop your right fist downward to reach the fist wheel. Hang your left hand on your right shoulder and look ahead. (Fig. 3-2-64)

图Fig 3-2-62　　　　　图Fig 3-2-63　　　　　图Fig 3-2-64

动作要点：侧身迅速，两臂抡臂搂斩快速、有力。

Key points: Two arms swing and cut quickly and powerfully.

25. 弹腿捅捶 Kicking and punching

图Fig 3-2-65　　　　　　　　图Fig 3-2-66

左腿直立，右腿向前蹬腿，勾脚尖，力达脚跟，（图3-2-65）右脚快速屈膝收回，右拳向身前沉肘，右拳心向上，（图3-2-66）重心下蹲，右脚向前铲出成右仆步，右拳贴右腿向前冲出，左拳抱于腰间，（图3-2-67-1、图3-2-67-2）重心快速前移，仆步成右弓步，右拳、左拳依次快速向前冲拳，拳眼向上，（图3-2-68）身体左转成马步，左拳冲拳后上架头上方，右拳继续向前冲拳，拳眼向上，目视右拳。（图3-2-69）

The left leg stands upright, the right leg kicks forward, hooks the toe.(Fig. 3-2-65) The right foot bends back quickly, the right fist sinks the elbow forward, the right fist moves upward, (Fig. 3-2-66) the center of gravity down, the right foot shoves forward to form a right footstep, the right fist pushes forward against the right leg, the left fist holds the waist, (Fig. 3-2-67-1, Fig. 3-2-67-2) the center of gravity moves forward rapidly, the footstep forms a right bow step, and the right fist and the left fist move in turn quickly forward, (Fig. 3-2-68) turn left into a horse stance, punch left and right, and look at the right fist. (Fig. 3-2-69)

图Fig 3-2-67-1　　　　　　　　图Fig 3-2-67-2

图Fig 3-2-68　　　　　　　　图Fig 3-2-69

动作要点：弹腿回收下蹲快速；两拳连环快速冲、架拳配合协调。

Key points: fast squatting with kicks over; fast punching with two fists in a row.

第三段 The third part

26. 槛子腿 Kanzitui

重心上提，身体左转90°，两脚拧转，重心移至左脚，右脚向前拦踢槛子腿，与腰同高；同时，右拳向前撩拳，拳心向上，左掌收于右肩，目视前方。（图3-2-70）

Lift the gravity up, turn the body 90° to the left, turn the two feet, move the weight to the left foot, kick with the right foot at the same height as the waist; lift the right fist forward, with the heart of the fist upward, close the left palm to the right shoulder, and look ahead. (Fig. 3-2-70)

图Fig 3-2-70

动作要点：槛子腿时勾脚尖，力达脚跟。

Key points: hook the toe of the foot with the force reaching to the heel.

27. 仆步括腿 Pubukuotui

右脚震脚落步，左腿向前挺膝仆腿平伸，右腿全蹲成左仆步；同时，左拳由前向后括腿，拳眼向上，右拳抱腰，目视左手。（图 3-2-71）

The right foot stamps the ground, the left leg stretches forward, the right leg squats to the left, and the left fist embraces the leg from the front to the back, the eye of the fist is up, the right fist embraces the waist and looks at the left hand. (Fig. 3-2-71)

图Fig 3-2-71

动作要点：震脚有力，左拳括腿力达拳轮。

Key points : stamp hard, the left fist expanding force reaching to the arm.

28. 卸手抱头 Xieshoubaotou

（1）戳拳：重心前移，左腿屈膝成左弓步，身体稍向前倾，右拳由腰间反手向斜前上贯拳，拳眼向上，左拳收至腰间，目视右拳。(图 3-2-72)

(1) Chuoquan: move the gravity forward, bend the left leg to form a left bow step, lean forward slightly, and the right fist goes from the waist upward, with the first eye upward and the left fist close to the waist, and watch the right fist. (Fig. 3-2-72)

（2）卸手抱头：身体右转，右脚向左脚并步直立，右拳回收经腰间再向左上冲拳，拳心向下，左拳变掌拦击右拳，目视右侧。(图 3-2-73)

(2) Xieshoubaotou: turn right and stand upright, pull right fist back and punch left and upward through waist, with the heart of fist downward, turn left fist to palm and block right fist, and look at the right side. (Fig. 3-2-73)

图Fig 3-2-72　　　　　　　　图Fig 3-2-73

动作要点：戳拳有力，力达拳面。

Key points: powerful punch.

29. 打虎势 Tiger-beating

身体快速右转 90°，同时左脚起跳，右脚震脚落步，右腿直立，左腿屈膝上提，右手随转身向后摆拳，(图 3-2-74)左腿向前上一大步屈腿半蹲成左弓步，左手经体前顺时针画弧栽拳于左大腿面上，拳面向下，右拳经后向上架于头上，拳心向上，目视前方。(图 3-2-75)

Turn the body fast 90° to the right, take off the left foot, shake the right foot, stand up with the right leg, bend the left leg and lift it up, swing the fist backward with the right hand turning around, (Fig. 3-2-74) bend the left leg forward with a big step and half squat to form a left bow step, draw the arc of the left hand clockwise in front of the body and drop the fist on the left thigh face, the fist face down, the right fist back and up on the head, the fist heart up, and look ahead. (Fig. 3-2-75)

图Fig 3-2-74　　　　　　　　图Fig 3-2-75

动作要点：转身震脚摆臂立圆自然，上下配合协调。

Key points: turn around, shake your feet, swing your arms, naturally, and coordinate with the upper and lower parts.

30. 雀地龙 Quedilong

右脚向前上步，右腿微屈，身体左转，左拳变掌向前上立圆盖掌，右掌收至腰间，（图 3-2-76）重心移至右腿，右腿直立，左腿屈膝上提；同时，右掌向右上斜穿掌，左手收于右肩，掌尖向上，（图 3-2-77）身体左转，右腿全蹲变左仆步，右掌内旋成勾手，勾尖向上，左掌由右肩前向左前插掌，左掌和左臂紧贴大腿内侧，目视左方。（图 3-2-78）

The right foot moves forward with the right leg bend slightly. Turn left, change the left fist to the palm forward, and the right palm back to the waist.(Fig. 3-2-76) The center of gravity is moved to the right leg, lift the right leg to the knee, the right palm goes up to the right, the left hand is closed to the right shoulder, and the palm tip is upward, (Fig. 3-2-77) turn left, the right leg is fully squatted, the right palm is turned into a hook with the tip upward, and the left palm goes to the left in front of the right shoulder, keep the left palm and arm close to the inner thigh, and look to the left. (Fig. 3-2-78)

图Fig 3-2-76　　　　　图Fig 3-2-77　　　　　图Fig 3-2-78

动作要点：左穿掌和右手内旋勾手快速一致，上体左转挺胸。

Key points: the left palm and the right hand go consistent, the upper left turn with chest upright.

31. 撑补势 Chengbushi

重心前移成左弓步，左掌前穿变拳内旋腕上架头上方，右勾手变拳经腰间向前冲拳，目视右拳。(图 3-2-79)

Move the gravity forward, make the left bow step, put the left palm through the variable fist, rotate the wrist over the head of the upper frame, and punch forward through the waist with the right hook fist, and watch the right fist. (Fig. 3-2-79)

图Fig 3-2-79

动作要点：撑架时力贯小臂，旋腕上架左拳与冲右拳协调快速。

Key points: when supporting, the force passes through the forearm, and the left fist and the right fist are coordinated quickly.

32. 双扎手 Shuangzhashou

两腿不动，左拳变掌下按，右拳变掌向前穿掌，右掌心向上，（图 3-2-80）右臂屈臂回旋向内、由上向下按至胸前，左掌迅速经右掌上向前插出，左掌心向上，目视前方。（图 3-2-81）

Stand still, press down the left palm and, penetrate forward with the right palm heart upward, (Fig. 3-2-80) bend the right arm and rotate inward and press down to the chest from top to bottom, quickly insert the left palm forward through the right palm, the left palm heart upward, and look ahead. (Fig. 3-2-81)

图Fig 3-2-80　　　　　　　　图Fig 3-2-81

动作要点：插掌线路清晰有力，双臂配合迅速。

Key points: the line of inserting palms is clear and powerful, and the two arms cooperate quickly.

33. 裙拦势 Qunlanshi

（1）左右卸手：左掌变勾手向斜后方挂出，左臂伸直，勾尖向上，右掌收至左肩，（图 3-2-82），左腿直立，右腿屈膝上提，同时右臂贴右腿向后分掌卸手打开，目视右侧。（图 3-2-83）

(1) Left and right Xieshou: the left hook goes to the back in a syncline with the left arm extended straight, the hook point upward, the right hand retracted to the left shoulder. (Fig. 3-2-82) The left leg upright, the right leg is raised by bending the knee. The right arm is close to the right leg and watch the right side. (Fig. 3-2-83)

（2）裙拦势：右腿落步，重心移至右腿，左脚回收，左脚尖点于右脚内侧，左腿紧贴右腿内侧，右腿屈膝半蹲成丁步，同时右手向上架掌至头顶上方，右臂微弧形，掌心向上，指尖向左，架右掌的同时迅速摆头，左臂伸直，左手勾手不变，目视左侧。

(图 3-2-84)

(2) Qunlanshi: step down the right leg, move the center of gravity to the right leg, recover the left foot, point the left foot on the inside of the right foot, keep the left leg close to the inside of the right leg, bend the right leg to squat into a small step, at the same time, put the right hand up to the top of the head, slightly arc the right arm, palm up, fingertip to the left, quickly swing the head while holding the right palm, straighten the left arm, keep the left hook unchanged, and look at the left side (Fig. 3-2-84)

图Fig 3-2-82　　　　　　　图Fig 3-2-83　　　　　　　图Fig 3-2-84

动作要点：左右手贴腿向后卸手勾挂；裙拦势丁步要低，上体尽力左转，双臂大开。

Key points: the left and right hands are close to the legs and the hand hook is removed backward; the skirt block should be low, the upper body should turn left as far as possible, and the arms should be wide open.

34. 歇步亮掌 Xiebuliangzhang

图Fig 3-2-85

左脚脚尖外展上步，身体左转180°重心下蹲成左歇步，右手由上向下摆动变勾手，

勾尖向上，左手由下向上摆动抖腕亮掌，头向右转，目视前方。（图3-2-85）

Step up with the tip of the left foot outstretched, turn the body 180° to the left and squat down, swing the right hand up to down with the tip of the hook up, swing the left hand down to up, shake the wrist and show the palm, turn the head to the right, and look ahead. (Fig. 3-2-85)

动作要点：身体拧转与两臂配合协调，抬头挺胸。

Key points: body twisting coordinates with two arms, head and chest up.

35. 左右挎剑腿 Left and Right Kuajiantui

（1）右挎剑腿：双手不动，左腿支撑，右脚屈膝向前侧踹，脚尖内扣，目视前方。（图3-2-86）

(1) Right Kuajiantui: hands are still, left leg is supported, right foot is kneeling forward and side kicking, toe is buckled inside, and look ahead. (Fig. 3-2-86)

（2）左挎剑腿：右脚下落，脚尖外展，身体右转，重心移至右脚，左掌向右挂掌，（图3-2-87）左掌经右侧向下摆动变勾手，勾尖向上，右臂经体前由下向上摆动抖腕亮掌，左腿屈膝向前侧踹，脚尖内扣，头向左转，目视前方。（图3-2-88）

(2) Left Kuajiantui: turn the right, move the gravity to the right foot, move the left palm to the right, (Fig. 3-2-87) swing the left palm down through the right side into the hook, swing the right arm up through the front of the body to shake the wrist and show the palm, bend the left leg to the front and kick forward, buckle the toe inside, turn the head to the left, and look ahead. (Fig. 3-2-88)

图Fig 3-2-86　　　　图Fig 3-2-87　　　　图Fig 3-2-88

动作要点：踹腿要有高度，力达脚外沿。

Key points: kick to a height and reach the maximum force.

36. 包脚（旋风脚）Whirlwind feet

左腿屈腿微下落，（图 3-2-89）右脚蹬地踏跳，以腰为轴跃起腾空，左腿向外摆动，右腿直腿向左成里合腿摆动，两臂向左上方摆动，左手拍击右脚，身体左旋转 180°。（图 3-2-90）

Bent down the left leg, (Fig. 3-2-89) life the right leg and jump, swing outward the left leg, the right leg straight to the left.The two arms are swinging upward to the left, the left hand tapping the right foot, and rotate the body 180° to the left. (Fig. 3-2-90)

图Fig 3-2-89　　　　　　　　　　图Fig 3-2-90

动作要点：蹬地踏跳有力，击拍快速响亮。

Key points: step on the ground and jump powerfully, tap quickly and loudly.

37. 燕子噙泥 Swallow holding mud

左脚先落地，右脚再向右落步，身体右转，左掌随转身右上挂，（图 3-2-91）右腿屈膝全蹲，左腿平铺成仆步，脚尖回扣，右臂直臂向外立圆挂臂，抡至身体外侧时向内翻转成勾手，勾尖向上，左臂直臂向左后挂出成勾手，勾尖向上，身体以左肩先导、右肩随之，重心移至左脚成左弓步，目视前方。（图 3-2-92、图 3-2-93）

Standing on the left foot, turn to the right, the left palm goes right. (Fig. 3-2-91) The right leg squats completely, the left leg is into a footstep with the toe kickback, the right arm is straight and swings to the outside into a hook with the hook point upward.The gravity is to the left foot forming a left bow step and look ahead. (Fig. 3-2-92, Fig. 3-2-93)

图Fig 3-2-91　　　　　　图Fig 3-2-92　　　　　　图Fig 3-2-93

动作要点：动作连贯，抡臂协调快速，噙泥动作尽量贴地而行。

Key points: be consistent, the swing is coordinated quickly, and the action of holding mud is as close to the ground as possible.

38. 抹手捅捶 Mashoutongchui

图Fig 3-2-94　　　　　　图Fig 3-2-95　　　　　　图Fig 3-2-96

身体右转180°，右脚随转身外展震脚落地，左脚向前上步成左弓步，双勾手变掌向前上穿出，掌心向下。（图3-2-94）两掌依次由上向下抹，虎口朝前，右掌下抹于右腿，左掌下抹左膝盖。（图3-2-95）右拳向前冲拳，拳眼向上，左掌收至右胸前，掌尖向上，目视右拳。（图3-2-96)

Turn the body 180 ° to the right, standing on the right foot, step forward to form a left bow step. The palms go up and out with the palm center down.(Fig. 3-2-94) The two palms press down with thumbs forward, the right palm presses on the right leg, and the left palm on the left knee.(Fig. 3-2-95)Punch forward with the right fist, pull back the left palm to the right chest, and look at the right fist.(Fig. 3-2-96)

动作要点：转身迅速，抹手和冲拳动作连贯。

Key points: turn around quickly, wipe hands and punch continuously.

39. 肋里塞足 Xielisaizu

上右步，再急上左步，同时右拳立圆由上向下劈斩，左掌在身前拦接右臂，(图3-2-97)接着，右腿向前弹踢，左掌向上架掌，右拳向下向后抡摆，目视前方。(图3-2-98)

Step up the right foot, and then step up the left. Cut the vertical circle of the right fist from top to bottom. Block the right arm in front of the body with the left palm. (Fig. 3-2-97) Then, spring and kick the right leg forward, put the left palm up and swing the right fist downward and backward. Look ahead (Fig. 3-2-98)

图Fig 3-2-97

图Fig 3-2-98

动作要点：上步快速连环，劈斩有力。

Key points of action: step up quickly, chop powerfully.

40. 海底炮 Gun from the bottom of the sea

右脚向前落步，左脚跟步，重心微下蹲，右拳向前撩摆拳，左手合击于右前臂。(图3-2-99) 重心后移左脚，右脚虚点地，两臂向上屈臂回收，(图3-2-100) 右脚向前上步，重心前移右脚，右腿屈膝半蹲，左脚向右脚跟步下蹲，右拳内旋翻转向前冲拳，拳眼向下，左掌扶于右拳背，目视右拳。(图3-2-101)

Step forward with the right foot, following the left foot, squat slightly with the center of gravity, lift and swing the right fist forward, and click the left hand together in the right forearm. (Fig. 3-2-99) Move the center of gravity backward to the left foot, empty the right foot, and bend the arms upward to recover, (Fig. 3-2-100) Move the weight forward to the right foot, bend the right leg and squat, move the left foot to the right foot and squat, turn the right fist inward and punch forward, with the eyes down, hold the left palm on the back of the right fist, and look at the right fist. (Fig. 3-2-101)

第三章 传统拳术选编 103

图Fig 3-2-99　　　　　　图Fig 3-2-100　　　　　　图Fig 3-2-101

动作要点：右拳回旋身体协调跟进。

Key points: right hand swings with body.

第四段 The fourth part

41. 撑补捶 Chengbuchui

图Fig 3-2-102　　　　　　图Fig 3-2-103　　　　　　图Fig 3-2-104

（1）独立拐肘：身体左转90°，右腿直立，左腿屈膝上提，右拳抱腰，左臂屈臂上抄拳，目视左侧。(图 3-2-102)

(1) Elbow: turn 90° to the left, right leg upright, left leg knee bending and lifting, right fist embracing waist, left arm bending and arm copying, and look at the left side. (Fig. 3-2-102)

（2）撑补捶：右腿全蹲，左脚向前铲出成左仆步，右拳抱腰，左拳贴左腿向前冲拳，(图 3-2-103) 重心前移成左弓步，左拳冲拳后内旋腕上架于头上方，右拳经腰间向前冲

拳，目视右拳。(图 3-2-104)

(2) Chengbuchui: squat the right leg, the left foot forward, hold the waist with the right fist, and punch forward with the left fist against the left leg, (Fig. 3-2-103) move the center of gravity forward to form a left bow step, turn the left fist to punch and then put the wrist on the upper part of the head, punch forward with the right fist through the waist, and watch the right fist. (Fig. 3-2-104)

动作要点：仆步冲左拳贴近地面，旋腕上架左拳与冲右拳顺达协调。

Key points: the left fist is close to the ground, and the left fist and the right fist are coordinated smoothly.

42. 铁匠三拳 Blacksmith's three punches

左拳变掌下落拍击右前臂上方，(图 3-2-105) 右拳变掌向后拍击右大腿面，左掌下落拍击左大腿面，(图 3-2-106) 左掌随即外旋向上，右手向后、向上立圆划弧过头后向下斩拳，拳眼向上，前臂贴于左掌心，目视右拳。（图 3-2-107）

The left fist changing palm taps the upper part of the right forearm, (Fig. 3-2-105) the right fist changing palm taps the right thigh side backward, and the left palm taps the left thigh side, (Fig. 3-2-106) the left palm immediately turns upward, and the right hand stands back and up to make a circle and then cuts the fist downward, the fist eye is upward, the forearm is closed to the center of the left palm, and watch the right fist. (Fig. 3-2-107)

图Fig 3-2-105

图Fig 3-2-106

图Fig 3-2-107

动作要点：拍击快速、准确、清脆。

Action points: Clap quickly, accurately and crisply.

43. 盘头花 Pantouhua

（1）盘头花：双脚不动，两手变掌体前顺时针盘舞花手，右掌收至腰间，左掌配合右掌经左向前下按掌，与肩同高，目视前方。(图 3-2-108)

(1) Pantouhua: keep your feet still, turn your right hand to the left and back horizontally and clockwise to the waist, turn your left hand to the left and up through your chest and press your palm downward, with the center of your left palm downward, and look ahead. (Fig. 3-2-108)

（2）双扎手：双脚不动，右掌经左掌上向前插出，掌尖与颈部同高，目视右掌。(图 3-2-109) 右大臂不动，右掌由外向内、由上向下从面前下按至胸前，左掌迅速经右掌上向前插出，掌尖与颈部同高，目视左掌。(图 3-2-110)

(2) Double Zhashou: keep your feet still, insert the right palm forward through the left palm, keep the palm tip as high as the neck, and look at the right palm. (Fig. 3-2-109) The right big arm does not move, the right palm is pressed from the front to the chest from the outside to the inside, from the top to the bottom, the left palm is quickly inserted forward through the right palm, the palm tip is the same height as the neck, and look at the left palm. (Fig. 3-2-110)

图Fig 3-2-108　　　　　图Fig 3-2-109　　　　　图Fig 3-2-110

动作要点：双手盘头花平圆，线路清晰，插掌有力，双臂配合迅速。

Key points: the two hands are flat while rotating.The lines clear, the palms powerful, and the two arms cooperate quickly.

44. 裙拦势 Qunlanshi

（1）左右卸手：重心上提，左掌变勾手向斜后方挂出，左臂伸直，勾尖向上，(图 3-2-111) 身体微右转，左腿直立，右腿屈膝上提；同时右臂贴右腿向后分掌卸手打开，目视右侧。(图 3-2-112)

(1) Left and right Xieshou: lift up the center of gravity, hook behind the left palm, extend the left arm, (Fig. 3-2-111) turn the body slightly to the right, keep the left leg upright, and lift

the right leg with the knee bent; the right arm goes to the right leg by palming backward, and watch the right side. (Fig. 3-2-112)

（2）裙拦势：右腿落步，左腿屈膝上提，身体左转90°，右臂由后向头上架掌，左臂伸直，左勾手不变，目视左侧，（图3-2-113）右腿屈膝半蹲，左脚尖点于右脚内侧成丁步，目视左方。(图3-2-114)

(2) Qunlanshi: the right leg falls, the left leg bends and lifts, the body turns 90 ° to the left, the right arm stretches from the back to the head, the left arm stretches straight, the left hook remains unchanged, and the left side is visualized, (Fig. 3-2-113) the right leg bends and squats, the left foot tip points on the inner side of the right foot for a small step, and look at the left side. (Fig. 3-2-114)

图Fig 3-2-111   图Fig 3-2-112

图Fig 3-2-113   图Fig 3-2-114

动作要点：同前。

Key points: same as the above.

45. 连三捶 Liansanchui

重心上提，右腿直立，左腿屈膝上提，右拳抱腰，左臂屈臂上抄拳，目视左侧。(图

3-2-115)左脚向左跨步成左仆步，左拳贴左腿向前冲拳，(图3-2-116)重心前移成左弓步，左拳冲出后，接连再冲右拳，(图3-2-117)再冲左拳，连环冲三拳，三拳都是立拳，目视左拳。(图3-2-118)

Lift the gravity up with right leg upright, bend the left leg and lift the knee, right fist embracing waist, bend the left arm and lift up; look at the left side. (Fig. 3-2-115) Step left with left footstep, and punch forward with left fist against left leg, (Fig. 3-2-116) move forward with gravity on left, and then punch right after the left fist rushes out, (Fig. 3-2-117) punch left again, and punch three times in a row. All three punches are vertical and watch the left fist. (Fig. 3-2-118)

图Fig 3-2-115

图Fig 3-2-116

图Fig 3-2-117

图Fig 3-2-118

动作要点：左右拳动作连贯、协调。

Key points: left and right fist movements are coherent and coordinated.

46. 双捧拳 Shuangpengquan

重心后移右脚，左脚回收半步成左虚步，双拳由两侧向下向体前合拢，再向上双捧拳，拳心均向上，目视左拳。(图3-2-119)

Move the gravity back to the right foot, the left foot empty, close the fists from both sides downward to the front, then hold the fists upward, with the heart of the fists upward, and look at the left fist. (Fig. 3-2-119)

图Fig 3-2-119

动作要点：收左脚时，重心上下协调平稳，体现精、气、神。

Action points: when retracting the left foot, keep balanced and stable

47. 收势 Ending up

左脚向右脚并步逐渐直立，双拳变掌经两侧向上再向下按掌于体侧，掌心向下，转头目视左方。(图3-2-120、图3-2-121)

The left foot goes gradually back to the right foot, and change the two fists into palms and press up and down to the side of the body, with the palms down, turn and look to the left. (Fig. 3-2-120, Fig. 3-2-121)

图Fig 3-2-120　　图Fig 3-2-121

动作要点：立圆按掌时目随手动；抬头、项直、挺胸、收腹、敛臀。

Key points: while pressing palm, the eyes follow the moves; when looking up, the neck and the chest straight, the abdomen tight.

第三节　翻子拳
3.3 Fanzi Quan

一、翻子拳简介 Introduction

翻子拳是一种短小精悍、严密紧凑，劲道脆、快、硬、弹的拳术。翻子拳原名八闪番，也称番拳，属于武术短打类的拳术，拳法密聚多变，技法迅速连环。明代戚继光所著《纪效新书》卷十四《拳经捷要篇》中记载："……八闪番、十二短，此亦善之善者也"。"闪"，即言其快，意为闪摆收势如电掣雷动。翻子拳，其名有用"翻""番"，两字各有侧重，"番"为次数，即翻生不息。徐哲东《国技论略》中写道："八番，即明代八闪番之旧称而加简文，番子，则后起之名也"。说明番子拳在明代就有完整、系统的技术套路。

Fanzi Quan is a kind of short, tight and compact Quan with crisp, fast, and elastic techniques. Fanzi Quan, formerly known as "Eight Shanfan", also known as "Fan Quan", means fast beating, defending and reaction in the fighting. The techniques are dense and changeable. In Volume 14 of *Ji Xiao Xin Shu·Quan Jing*, Qi Jiguang of the Ming Dynasty wrote, "…Eight flashes, twelve short, this is what the professionals are good at". "Flash", that is to say, very fast, like lightning. The name of Fanzi Quan also means this Quan will develop endlessly. In Xu Zhedong's *A Brief Introduction to Wushu*, he pointed out, "Bafan (Eight Changes) is the old name of eight flashes in the Ming Dynasty". It shows that Fanzi Quan had a complete and systematic technical routine in the Ming Dynasty.

清代以来，翻子拳流传于我国北方各省，形成了以河北、东北和西北地区为主要传承流域。西北地区的翻子拳套路中融入劈挂、戳脚、螳螂、八极等拳种之长，丰富了拳术技法内容，完善了健宗翻、萃八翻、站桩翻、掳手翻等套路，发展成兼具截脚灵活多变的腿法，螳螂拳敏捷的手法和劈挂拳劲力贯穿的身法，并贯以通备武艺劲道使其成为中华武苑的一朵奇葩，形成了传域更广、具有西北风格特点的一大拳种。

Since the Qing Dynasty, Fanzi Quan has spreaded in the northern provinces of China, forming Hebei, northeast and northwest regions as the main inheritance region. In the northwest area, there are many kinds of boxing, such as splitting and hanging, poking foot, praying mantis, eight pole boxing, which enrich the content of boxing techniques, improve the boxing techniques, such as standing Jianzong turning, extracting eight turning, standing pile turning, abducting and handspring turning, and develop into a leg technique with flexible and changeable cutting foot. The quick hand technique of praying mantis boxing and the body technique with splitting and hanging power run through, and make it a wonderful flower in the Wushu garden.

二、翻子拳技术特点 Technical characteristics of Fanzi Quan

翻子拳出势一律是"旗鼓势",这是分辨是否是翻子拳的标记。翻子拳技术短促多变,讲究近战快打,技法特点可归纳为以下四点:

All the moves of Fanzi Quan start from "Qigushi", which distinguishes from other Quan. The technique of Fanzi Quan is quick fighting and changeable combat ways. The characteristics of the technique can be summarized as follows:

(1) 一势多法,一法多用,技法合用 Multiple ways to play one movement

翻子拳每一势蕴含多种技法,如"抹打挑打"出手进攻是招,缩手防守还是招。另外,一种方法有多种用途,多种技法相互交融,上翻下转连环使用,技法变化莫测,动作迅猛遒劲。

Every move of Fanzi Quan contains many ways to play. For example, in the move "Madatiaoda", attack or defenes can be the way to play. In addition, one method can be used for many purposes. Many techniques blend with each other. Turning and flapping are used in a chain. The techniques are unpredictable and the movements are swift and powerful.

(2) 连环强攻,势如破竹 A series of strong attacks

翻子拳双拳密如雨、硬起硬落、快而不乱、攻防兼施、脆快一挂鞭的动态下运使各种技法,讲究脆、快、硬、弹等技法快捷配合。"脆"是发拳明确,用招果断敏捷,拳诀曰:攻则有法,守之有方。"快"是对技艺的速度要求,拳诀曰:出招似流星,运动如闪电。"硬"是功力的体现,也是运动中技法动作的着力点和准确性,拳诀曰:出招必准,中者必损。"弹"是发拳要有弹力、崩劲,蓄发得体,如出弓之箭,拳诀曰:冷弹疾发,发不及觉。

The moves of Fanzi Quan are as dense as pouring rain. All the acts are fast but not random. Both attack and defense are crispy and quick. "Crispness" is to make the fist clear and use the move decisively and nimbly. The chant of Fanzi Quan says: to attack like a meteor and to move like lightning. "Hardness" is not only the embodiment of the power, but also the focus and accuracy of the skills in the movement. The chant of Fanzi Quan says: the attack must be accurate, and the object must be damaged once attacted. "Elasticness" is to make a punch elastic, like the arrow out of the bow.

（3）结构严谨、往返连环，步疾手快 Rigorous structure

套路短小精悍，结构严谨连环，步法稳、身法灵，姿势端正，四面见线，简捷实用。翻子拳双拳忽而直出直进，忽而上提下滚，手法如暴风骤雨，步法往返连环，衔接迅疾，以步法的快捷配合手法的密集也是一大特点。

The routine set is short, precise and continuous in structure, stable in footwork, smart in body moves, simple and practical. The fist moves of Fanzi Quan are suddenly straight out and in, up and down, like a storm. The footstep is linked up and down. The fast matching technique of footwork is also a major feature.

（4）以腰发力，浑厚一气 Strength from the waist

西北流传的翻子拳受吞吐发力、辘辘翻扯、搅靠劈重的劲力染化，形成了以腰发力，发力迅猛遒劲，架势俯伏闪动，气势浑厚的特点。

Fanzi Quan is influenced by the breath move in some northwest Quan techniques. The force usually is generated from the waist. The strength is fast and strong and the posture is stable and heavy.

萃八翻歌（谱）诀

开门起鼓势如山，滚劈三拳步连环；
麻打挑打贯上下，斜身进步豁崩拳；
左闪八翻右相连，滚架上步阴阳拳；
双闯跺子顺手展，左右圈锤似闪电；
进步直发开门炮，缩身进步铁翻杆；
三盘连发连环拳，翻拳用法速为先。

三、翻子拳基本动作与方法 Basic movements and skills

（一）手型 Hand type

1.瓦棱拳：四指并拢卷屈，食指紧扣于虎口内侧，其余三指依次微凸起，拇指紧扣于食指第二指节上。（图3-3-1）

1.Walengquan: four fingers are folded and bent together, the index finger is tightly fastened to the inside, the other three fingers are slightly raised in turn, and the thumb is tightly fastened to the second knuckle of the index finger. (Fig. 3-3-1)

2.八字掌：四指自然伸直，拇指与食指自然分开，掌心内凹。（图3-3-2）

2.Bazizhang: the four fingers are naturally stretched straight, the thumb and the index finger are naturally separated, and the palm center is concave. (Fig. 3-3-2)

3.螳螂手：拇指、食指、中指轻合拢，其余二指屈于手心。（图3-3-3）

3. Mantis hand: the thumb, index finger and medium finger are slightly closed, and the other two fingers are bent on the palm. (Fig. 3-3-3)

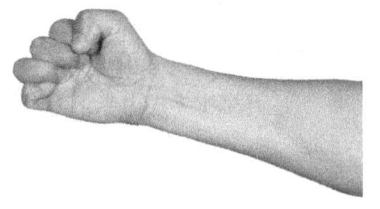 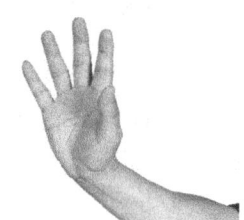 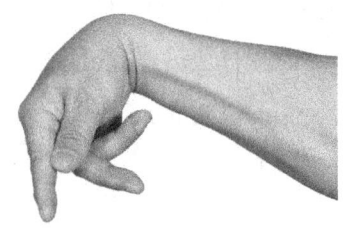

图Fig 3-3-1　　　　　图Fig 3-3-2　　　　　图Fig 3-3-3

（二）步型 Steps

1.半马步：两脚左右开立，两脚距离同马步，前脚尖向外，后脚尖与膝内扣。（图3-3-4）

1. Half horse-ride step: open left and right feet, the distance between the two feet is the same as that of a horse step, the front toe is outward, the back toe and knee buckle. (Fig. 3-3-4)

2.麒麟步：前腿屈膝，大腿成水平，脚尖内扣；后腿屈膝落其后，前脚掌着地，身体重心落于两腿之间。（图3-3-5）

2. Qilinbu: bend the front leg to the knees, level the thighs, and buckle the toes inside; the front foot on the ground, and the center of gravity of the body falls between the

two legs. (Fig. 3-3-5)

图Fig 3-3-4　　　　　　　　　　图Fig 3-3-5

（三）手法 Hand Techniques

1. 弹拳：由腰、肩、肘及腕部发出弹力，使拳向前或向右弹击，力达拳面。

1. Tanquan: spring from the waist, shoulder, elbow and wrist to make the fist move forward or to the right and reach the fist face.

2. 崩拳：右拳由左侧向右侧横击，力达拳背。

2. Bengquan: strike the right fist horizontally from left to right, reaching the back of the fist.

3. 劈拳：拳由上向下或向斜下方向迅猛劈击，力达拳轮。

3. Piquan: the fist is rapidly split from up to down or syncline to the fist wheel.

四、翻子拳动作图解 Illustration of Fanzi Quan

第一段 Part I

1. 开门势 Start

（1）两脚并步站立，两臂自然垂于身体两侧，两手成掌型，掌心向内，悬头竖项，自然呼吸，目视前方。（图 3-3-6）

(1) Stand on two feet, two arms naturally hanging on both sides of the body, two hands in palm shape, palm inward, head erect, breathe naturally, and look ahead. (Fig. 3-3-6)

（2）两臂外旋，快速提掌收至腰间，掌心向上，目视左方。（图 3-3-7）重心下蹲，两臂伸直沿身体两侧由下向左前上撩掌，肘部微屈，目视右掌。（图 3-3-8）

(2) Rotate arms outward, palm up, and look to the left. (Fig. 3-3-7) Squat with the center of gravity, stretch the arms straight along both sides of your body, lift your palms from bottom to left, bend the elbows slightly, and look at the right palm. (Fig. 3-3-8)

图Fig 3-3-6　　　　　图Fig 3-3-7　　　　　图Fig 3-3-8

（3）两掌外旋，掌心向上，两掌回收下落，两掌掌背分别拍击两大腿面后向两侧撩掌，右掌向右后，左掌向左前撩掌，目视右掌。（图3-3-9）

(3) Turn two palms outward, palm center up, slap the back of two thighs, right palm to the right, left palm to the left to lift the palms forward, and look at the right palm. (Fig. 3-3-9)

（4）屈膝半蹲，两掌向上摆掌，掌心相对，目视右掌。（图3-3-10）重心上提直立，两掌向两侧按掌，目视左方。（图3-3-11）

(4) Bend your knees and squat, put your palms up, palms facing each other, and look at the right palm, (Fig. 3-3-10) lift the center of gravity vertically, press the palms to both sides, and look to the left. (Fig. 3-3-11)

图Fig 3-3-9　　　　　图Fig 3-3-10　　　　　图Fig 3-3-11

动作要点：含胸收腹、顶头、精神集中，动作稳、慢。

Action points: head up and move steady and slow.

2. 旗鼓势 Qigu posture

（1）上步托掌：右脚向左前上步，双掌外旋向左上方托掌，掌心向上，臂微屈，目视左掌。（图 3-3-12）两小臂内旋，立圆向上向右摆掌，掌心朝下，目视右掌。（图 3-3-13）

(1) Step up and palm up: step up the right foot to the left, turn the two palms outward to the left, slightly bend the arm, and look at the left palm. (Fig. 3-3-12) Rotate the two arms inward, and swing them upward and to the right with the palms facing down, and look at the right palms. (Fig. 3-3-13)

（2）点腿穿掌：双掌外旋向左上方穿掌，掌心向上；同时左腿屈膝上提，左脚尖绷直向左上点出，力达脚尖，目视点腿方向。（图 3-3-14）

(2) The palms rotate outwards to the left and top, palm center up; bend the left leg and lift it up, point the left foot straight to the left and up, and watch the leg. (Fig. 3-3-14)

图Fig 3-3-12　　　　图Fig 3-3-13　　　　图Fig 3-3-14

（3）旗鼓势：左腿屈膝收回至右腿膝窝处，双掌向上向右侧（顺时针）摆掌，（图 3-3-15）双掌变拳，双臂外旋，从右腋下经胸前向左侧冲出，拳心斜向上，右拳在左肘内侧处；同时，左脚向左侧落步，重心下蹲稍前移成半马步，目视左拳。（图 3-3-16）

(3) Qigu posture: bend the left leg to the knee socket of the right leg, swing the palms upward to the right (clockwise), (Fig. 3-3-15) turn the palms into fists, turn the arms outward, and rush out from the right armpit to the left through the chest front, with the fist heart inclined upward, and the right fist is at the inner side of the left elbow; step the left foot to the left, squat slightly forward as Qilin step, and look at the left fist. (Fig. 3-3-16)

图Fig 3-3-15　　　　　　　　图Fig 3-3-16

动作要点：点腿挺胯，双掌右摆含胸；半马步重心前移，双拳外旋直冲。

Key points: the legs pointing, chest close.

3. 马步按掌 Mabuanzhang

（1）展打：右拳收于腹前，拳心向上，重心上提移至右腿，右腿站直，左脚收回至右脚后点地待动；左拳变掌贴身下落向后经头顶上方向前下盖掌，掌心向前，掌尖向右，与肩同高，（图3-3-17）右拳变掌，经左掌上方向前展打，掌背向前迎打，右掌掌腕弯屈，掌心向后，左掌贴右臂下落至右腋下，目视右掌。（图3-3-18）

(1) Zhanda: Move the right fist to the abdomen, lift the center of gravity up to the right leg, stand straight on the right leg, and withdraw the left foot to the back of the right foot to wait for movement; change the palm of the left fist to fall close to the body and cover the palm forward and down through the top of the head, with the palm forward, the tip of the palm to the right, at the same height as the shoulder, (Fig. 3-3-17) change the palm of the right fist, spread forward through the upper direction of the left palm, hit the back of the palm forward, bend the palm and wrist of the right palm, palm center Backward, left palm pastes right arm to fall to the right armpit, and look at the right palm. (Fig. 3-3-18)

（2）马步按掌：身体左转90°，左脚向左侧跨一步下蹲成马步，左掌向左上方格挡上撑，掌尖朝上，掌心向右，右掌经上向左向下，再向右弧线向外按掌，与腰同高，右臂微屈，力达掌侧，掌心向下，目视右掌方向。（图3-3-19）

(2) Mabuanzhang: turn the body 90° to the left, step the left foot to the left and squat into a horse stance. Hold the left palm to the upper left and block it up. The palm tip is up, the palm center is right, the right palm is up to the left and down, and then press the palm outwards in an arc to the right, the same height as the waist, the right arm is slightly bent, the force reaches

the palm side, the palm center is down, and look at the right palm. (Fig. 3-3-19)

图Fig 3-3-17　　　　　　图Fig 3-3-18　　　　　　图Fig 3-3-19

动作要点：左掌下盖迅猛，右掌展打掌面绷平、绷紧。

Key points: the left palm is covered rapidly, and the right palm is stretched flat and tight.

4. 并步劈拳 Bingbupiquan

左脚不动，右脚向左脚并步直立；同时，右掌握拳随右腿向左向上抡摆至于左肩同高时，左掌下压扣握右拳腕，（图 3-3-20）右拳继续经左向上至右上方时迅速向右下劈拳，然后上收腰间，目视右前方。（图 3-3-21、图 3-3-22）

The left foot still, and the right foot moves to the left foot and stands upright; at the same time, swing the right fist with the right leg to the left and up to the same height as the left shoulder, press the left palm to hold the right wrist, (Fig. 3-3-20) when the right fist continues to move from the left to the upper right, split quickly to the right and down, then close up the waist and look at the right front. (Fig. 3-3-21, Fig. 3-3-22)

图Fig 3-3-20　　　　　　图Fig 3-3-21　　　　　　图Fig 3-3-22

动作要点：右拳抡摆成顺时针方向，从按掌 3 点钟方向顺时针抡摆至 1 点钟方向下劈，下劈迅猛，上收轻盈。

Key points: swing the right fist in a clockwise direction, swing it from 3 o'clock to 1 o'clock, and chop it down quickly.

5. 骑龙步冲拳 Qilongbu Punch

（1）右脚向右前方上一步，左脚向右前跟半步，重心前移右腿，两腿微屈，左掌仍扣握右拳腕，右拳向前冲拳，与额头同高，目视右拳。（图 3-3-23）

(1) Step up the right foot to the right and forward, follow the left foot for half a step, move the weight forward to the right leg, slightly bend the two legs, hold the right wrist with the left palm, and punch forward with the right fist, which is the same height as the forehead, and look at the right fist. (Fig. 3-3-23)

（2）右脚向右前方上一大步，左脚向前跟一小步，重心前移右腿，重心下蹲，同时右拳下压收回再向前冲拳，左掌仍扣握右拳腕，右拳与鼻同高，目视右拳。（图 3-3-24、图 3-3-25）

(2) Step forward to the right with the left foot following, the center of gravity is on the right leg, the right fist is pressed back to punch forward, the left palm is still clasped to hold the right fist wrist, the right fist is the same height as the nose, and watch the right fist. (Fig. 3-3-24, Fig. 3-3-25)

图Fig 3-3-23　　　　图Fig 3-3-24　　　　图Fig 3-3-25

（3）右脚再向前方上一大步，左脚跟一小步，重心仍至右腿，重心半蹲，右大腿面平行地面，左脚前脚掌踩实地面，同时右拳下压收回再向前冲拳，左掌仍扣握右拳腕，右拳与肩同高，目视右拳。（图 3-3-26、图 3-3-27）

(3) Take a big step forward with the right foot, and take a small step with the left heel. The center of gravity is still on the right leg. The right thigh is parallel to the ground. The front

foot of the left foot firmly steps on the ground. At the same time, press down the right fist and take it back, and then punch forward. The left palm still clasps the right fist wrist. The right fist is the same height as the shoulder. Look at the right fist. (Fig. 3-3-26, Fig. 3-3-27)

图Fig 3-3-26　　　　　　　　图Fig 3-3-27

动作要点：收拳、冲崩拳与上步一致。

Key points: fist and step go consistently.

6. 麻打挑打 Madatiaoda

右拳与左掌下压收回右腰间，（图 3-3-28）左掌向前下推压掌，与肩同高，同时右脚上半步，左脚紧跟半步，（图 3-3-29）右拳从左掌背向前冲拳，左掌贴右臂收至右腋下，（图 3-3-30）紧接着左掌迅速从右臂外侧向前推掌，右拳同时收至腰间，（图 3-3-31）右拳再向前快速冲拳，左掌贴右臂内侧收至右肩前，（图 3-3-32）继而左拳与右拳连环冲拳至右冲拳时，左拳收至腹前，拳心朝上，重心半蹲，目视冲拳方向。（图 3-3-33、图 3-3-34）

The right fist and the left palm are pressed down to the right waist, (Fig. 3-3-28) the left palm is pushed forward and pressed down to the same height as the shoulder, while the right foot is in the upper half of the step, and the left foot is closely followed, (Fig. 3-3-29) the right fist is punched forward from the back of the left palm, and the left palm is pressed close to the right arm, (Fig. 3-3-30) the left palm is pushed forward quickly from the outside of the right arm, and the right fist is pushed back to the waist, (Fig. 3-3-31) the right fist is moved forward, put the left palm close to the inner side of the right arm and close to the front of the right shoulder. (Fig. 3-3-32) Then, when the left fist and the right fist are linked to punch to the right, the left fist is closed to the front of the abdomen, the center of the fist is upward. (Fig. 3-3-33, Fig. 3-3-34)

图Fig 3-3-28 　　　　图Fig 3-3-29

图Fig 3-3-30 　　　　图Fig 3-3-31 　　　　图Fig 3-3-32

图Fig 3-3-33 　　　　图Fig 3-3-34

动作要点：左拳与右拳交替并与右脚上步协调一致，连环冲拳探肩击远，借助转腰发力。

Key points: left fist and right fist alternate and coordinate with the right foot step up, the ring punch is used to probe shoulder and strike far, and the power is generated by turning waist.

7. 中盘顿肘 Zhongpandunzhou

左转身，左掌贴身向后上撩掌，右拳屈臂向上格挡，（图 3-3-35）继而右拳外旋下砸，左掌拦接，右拳力达拳背，右腿屈膝上提，右脚扣于左膝窝，（图 3-3-36-1、图 3-3-36-2）迅速右转身，右脚向右前落步，左脚跟步成麒麟步，随转身右臂屈肘向前顶肘，左掌推顶右拳面，目视顶肘方向。（图 3-3-37-1、图 3-3-37-2）

Turn left, lift left palm close to your body, bend arm of right fist to block upward, (Fig. 3-3-35) then turn right fist downward and smash, block with left palm, reach back of fist, bend knee of right leg to lift up, buckle right foot to left knee socket, (Fig. 3-3-36-1, Fig. 3-3-36-2) turn right quickly, lower right foot forward, follow left foot to form Qilin step, bend elbow of right arm to push elbow forward, push right fist with left palm, and watch the elbow direction. (Fig. 3-3-37-1，Fig. 3-3-37-2)

图Fig 3-3-35　　　　图Fig 3-3-36-1　　　　图Fig 3-3-36-2

图Fig 3-3-37-1　　　　图Fig 3-3-37-2

动作要点：转身顶肘、上步迅速统一。

Key points of action: turn around, push your elbow, and step up quickly.

8. 连环崩拳 Lianhuanbengquan

两脚不动，右拳向前冲崩拳，（图 3-3-38）接着左拳、右拳连环冲崩拳，两拳在体

前立圆夹肘向前冲崩，重心逐渐上提，目视前方。（图 3-3-39、图 3-3-40）

Keep your feet still, and punch forward with your right fist. (Fig. 3-3-38) Then punch left and right fist in a chain. Stand in front of your body and press your elbows forward. Gradually lift your center of gravity and look ahead. (Fig. 3-3-39, Fig. 3-3-40)

图Fig 3-3-38　　　　　图Fig 3-3-39　　　　　图Fig 3-3-40

动作要点：两臂小臂贴近向前冲崩拳。

Key points: the forearms close to the front.

9. 并步崩拳 Bingbubengquan

身体左转，两脚拧转，左拳下落随转身挑拳，（图3-3-41）右脚上步，右拳贴右腿立圆上挑，左拳屈臂举拳于左肩上，左拳眼向下，左脚再向前上步，（图3-3-42），右转身180°，（图3-3-43）右脚向左脚并步，脚跟并拢，前脚掌分开，脚跟提起，重心下伏全蹲、团身，左拳向前下崩拳，右拳后撩，两拳拳腕外屈，两拳眼均向下，目视前方。（图3-3-44）

Turn your body to the left, turn your feet around, and lift your left fist, (Fig. 3-3-41) step up with your right foot, put your right fist against your right leg, and turn your left fist to your left shoulder, with fist eye down, and then step up with your left foot forward, (Fig. 3-3-42) turn to right 180°, (Fig. 3-3-43) move your right foot to your left foot, keep your heels together, separate your front feet, lift your heels, and squat. The left fist goes forward, the right fist goes back, and look ahead. (Fig. 3-3-44)

图Fig 3-3-41   图Fig 3-3-42

图Fig 3-3-43   图Fig 3-3-44

动作要点：两臂立圆抡举，直线崩拳。

Key points: two arms rotate in a vertical circle and push in a straight line.

10. 展身崩打 Zhanshenbengda

（1）重心迅速上提，左脚向前上步，（图 3-3-45）右腿屈膝迅速向后撩摆，同时，左拳变掌从胸前向下、向前推出并向前上架掌拉开，右拳变掌随右腿后摆向后拉开，目视前方。（图 3-3-46）

(1) Lift the gravity, the left foot is stepped forward, (Fig. 3-3-45) the right leg is pulled back quickly with knees bent. The left palm is pushed down from the chest, pushed forward and upward. The right palm is pulled back with the back swing of right leg, and watch the front. (Fig. 3-3-46)

（2）重心迅速前移下压，右腿向前落步，左脚跟步成麒麟步，右掌随重心向前挑打，左掌下挂搭在右腕处，目视右掌方向。（图 3-3-47-1、图 3-3-47-2）

(2) Move the gravity forward and down, with the right leg following the left foot as a Qilin step. Turn the right palm into fist and smash forward. Hang the left palm on the right wrist and watch the direction of the right fist. (Fig. 3-3-47-1, Fig. 3-3-47-2)

图Fig 3-3-45　　　　　图Fig 3-3-46

图Fig 3-3-47-1　　　　图Fig 3-3-47-2

动作要点：展身时拉开背弓，崩挑落步要远。

Key points of action: unfold the back open, and take a long step when punch

11. 连环抄拳 Lianhuanchaoquan

（1）连环抄拳：重心前倾上提；同时左拳向前抄拳，拳心向后，右拳收至左臂上，（图3-3-48）右拳再向前抄拳，拳心向后，左拳收至右臂上，（图3-3-49）再上左脚，左拳向前抄拳，拳心向后，右拳收至左臂上。（图3-3-50）

(1) lean forward and lift the gravity; at the same time, cut forward with the left fist, with the heart of the fist backward and the right fist closed to the left arm, (Fig. 3-3-48) cut forward with the right fist, with the heart of the fist backward and the left fist closed to the right arm, (Fig. 3-3-49) cut forward with the left fist, with the heart of the fist backward and the right fist closed to the left arm. (Fig. 3-3-50)

（2）上崩下翻：右脚上步，身体左转，右腿直立，左腿屈膝上提，身体右倾，左拳变掌下按，右拳从左掌上向前崩拳，（图3-3-51）左脚向后落步成马步，右拳屈臂向内旋腕经左臂内向前下方摆拳，右拳眼向下，拳心向后，左掌收于右肩，目视右拳，（图 3-3-52）重心前移右脚，右腿直立，左腿屈膝扣至右膝后，右拳从左掌上向前上崩拳，左掌收于右肩下，目视右拳。（图 3-3-53）

(2) Step up with the right foot, turn left, stand up with the right leg, bend the knee and lift the left leg up, lean right, turn the left fist to the palm and press down, and turn the right fist forward from the left palm, (Fig. 3-3-51) step backward with the left foot into a horse stance, turn the right fist to the inside and swing the wrist forward and down through the left arm, turn the right fist eye downward, turn the heart backward, and close the left palm to the right shoulder, and look at the right fist. (Fig. 3-3-52) Move center of gravity the right foot forward, keep the right leg upright, bend the left leg and buckle it to the right knee, then the right fist will break forward from the left palm, and the left palm will close under the right shoulder. Watch the right fist. (Fig. 3-3-53)

图Fig 3-3-48　　　　图Fig 3-3-49　　　　图Fig 3-3-50

图Fig 3-3-51　　　　图Fig 3-3-52　　　　图Fig 3-3-53

动作要点：两拳抄拳含胸团身，上崩下翻身体舒展。

Key points: stretch out the body with limb movements.

12. 甩袖披挂 Shuaixiupigua

图Fig 3-3-54　　　　　图Fig 3-3-55　　　　　图Fig 3-3-56

图Fig 3-3-57　　　　　图Fig 3-3-58

　　左脚扣膝不动，右脚拧转，身体迅速右后转身，上体团身含胸，右拳随转身下落，拳心向上，左掌收于右腋下，（图3-3-54）两腿不动，左掌向前横抽打，掌心向下，右拳收至腰间，（图3-3-55）左脚向前落步，右脚再上步，右拳变掌向前横抽打，掌心向上，左掌收至腹前，（图3-3-56）左脚向前插步，左掌贴右臂向前卸手，（图3-3-57）右脚向前上步成马步，左掌卸手前挂掌再向身体左侧横挂，右掌八字掌向前推掌，两掌虎口向上，目视前方。（图3-3-58）

　　Bend the left knee inward, twist the right foot, turn the body quickly right and back, and bent the upper body. The right fist falls with the turning, with the heart of the fist upward. The left palm is closed under the right armpit.(Fig.3-3-54)The two legs are still, the left palm goes forward and horizontally with the heart of the fist downward, and the right fist is closed to the waist.(Fig.3-3-55)The left foot goes forward and followed by the right foot. The right palm goes horizontally forward with the palm-heart upward and the left palm back to the abdomen.

(Fig.3-3-56)The left foot goes forward in a cross step, and the left palm against the right arm and punches forward.(Fig.3-3-57)The right foot goes forward into a horse step.The left palm goes forward and leftward, the right palm goes forward in Bagua Palm with the thumbs up and look ahead.(Fig.3-3-58)

动作要点：拧转团身含胸，卸手贴紧右臂前穿。

Key points: twist the body with upper part close, the hand goes forward close to the right arm.

13. 左舞花展打 Zuowuhuazhanda

两掌收至左胸前，右掌心朝内，左掌心朝外，两掌腕相对贴合，（图3-3-59）左脚起跳，右脚跟随，身体腾起向右后转身180°落地成半马步，同时，双掌腕旋转180°，（图3-3-60）左掌向前展打，力达掌背，屈掌腕，掌心朝内，右掌回拉至右肩前，目视左掌方向。（图3-3-61）

Two palms are folded to the front of the left chest, the right palm is facing in, the left palm is facing out, and the two palms and wrists are relatively close, (Fig. 3-3-59) the left foot takes off, the right foot follows, the body takes off and turns 180° to the right and lands in a half horse stance, at the same time, the two palms and wrists rotate 180°, (Fig. 3-3-60) the left palm is stretched forward, the force reaches the back of the palm, the palms and wrists are bent, the palms are facing in, the right palm is pulled back to the front of the right shoulder, and look in the left palm direction. (Fig. 3-3-61)

图Fig 3-3-59　　　　　图Fig 3-3-60　　　　　图Fig 3-3-61

动作要点：起跳落步轻盈，舞花手迅速，左掌展打与右掌后拉成扩拉开合劲。

Key points: the take-off and landing steps are light, the hand dancing is fast.

14. 右舞花展打 Youwuhuazhanda

两掌收至右胸前，左掌心朝内，掌右心朝外，掌腕相对贴合，（图 3-3-62）两手掌上举并旋腕 180°，身体左转，左脚上步，（图 3-3-63）右脚上步，左脚迅速再向前插步，右掌向前展打，力达掌背，屈掌腕，掌心朝内，左掌回拉至左肩前，目视右掌方向。（图 3-3-64-1、图 3-3-64-2）

Two palms are retracted to the right chest, the left palm is inward, the right palm is outward, and the palms and wrists are relatively close, (Fig. 3-3-62) two palms are raised to rotate the wrist 180°, the body is turned left, the left foot is stepped up, (Fig. 3-3-63) the right foot is stepped up, the left foot is quickly moved forward and then crossed, the right palm is stretched forward to reach the back of the palm, the palms and wrists are bent, the palms are inward, the left palm is pulled back to the left shoulder, and watch the right palm direction. (Fig. 3-3-64-1, Fig. 3-3-64-2)

图Fig 3-3-62　　　　　　图Fig 3-3-63

图Fig 3-3-64-1　　　　　图Fig 3-3-64-2

动作要点：上步轻盈快速，舞花手迅速，右掌展打与左掌后拉成扩拉开合劲。

Key points: the take-off and landing steps are light, the hand is fast.

15. 拐肘搬打 Guaizhoubanda

右脚向右跨步，身体左转，右拳向左臂外侧抄拳，右小臂裹紧左大臂，（图3-3-65）两脚拧转，身体右转180°，（图3-3-66）左拳向前冲拳，拳眼向上，右拳拉至身体右后方，（图3-3-67）重心前倾，右拳内旋向前冲拳，拳眼向下，左拳收至腰间，目视右拳。（图3-3-68）

Step right with the right foot, turn left with the right fist to the outside of the left arm, wrap the right small arm around the left big arm, (Fig. 3-3-65) twist the two feet, turn right180°, (Fig. 3-3-66) punch forward with the left fist, with the eye up, pull the right fist to the right rear of the body, (Fig. 3-3-67) lean forward with the center of gravity, punch forward with the right fist turning inward, with the eye down, close the left fist to the waist, and look at the right fist. (Fig. 3-3-68)

图Fig 3-3-65　　　　图Fig 3-3-66

图Fig 3-3-67　　　　图Fig 3-3-68

动作要点：抄拳裹臂要紧，双臂与身体协调拧转。

Key points: wrap and twist your arms in coordination with your body.

16. 铁翻杆 Tiefangan

（1）架崩拳：右脚向左脚并步；同时右拳向左抡砸拳，左掌拦接，（图 3-3-69-1、图 3-3-69-2）身体右转，右脚向前上一大步，左脚跟步，左脚跟提起，右拳向上旋腕架拳，拳心向上，左拳向前冲拳，拳眼向上。（图 3-3-70）

(1) Step right foot to left foot; swing right fist to the left at the same time, and block it with left palm. (Fig. 3-3-69-1, Fig. 3-3-69-2) Turn right, step right foot forward, step left foot, lift heel, turn right fist to wrist frame fist upward, fist heart up, left fist forward, fist eye up. (Fig. 3-3-70)

图Fig 3-3-69-1　　　图Fig 3-3-69-2　　　图Fig 3-3-70

（2）铁翻杆：身体左转，左拳立圆向左抡劈收于腰间，右拳随转身屈腕向左抡劈下压，（图 3-3-71）左脚向后插步，身体前倾下伏，左拳向前冲拳，右拳收至腰间，目视左拳。（图 3-3-72）

图Fig 3-3-71　　　图Fig 3-3-72

(2) Tiefangan: turn left, swing left fist to the left and close to the waist, bend your wrist to the left with the right fist, (Fig. 3-3-71) step backward with the left foot, lean forward and lean down, punch forward with the left fist, close the right fist to the waist, and look at the left fist. (Fig. 3-3-72)

动作要点：翻转身时两臂立圆迅速翻肩。

Key points: turn your arms round and turn your shoulders quickly.

第二段 Part II

17. 滚劈手 Gunpishou

重心移至右脚，右腿半蹲支撑，左腿向前弹踢，左掌向前穿掌，掌心向上，右掌向后穿掌，（图 3-3-73）右脚掌为轴，迅速右转体 180°，带动左腿屈膝随转，左脚扣于右膝窝，左臂内旋裹肩，左勾手向上，右掌挂至左肩，（图 3-3-74）右脚向左后垫跳一步，随即左脚向后落步，成右弓步，再迅速左转身 180°，左臂向前抡劈收至腰间，右掌随左臂向下抡劈下压掌，与肩同高，掌尖向上，目视右掌。（图 3-3-75）

Shift the gravity to the right foot, the right leg is squatted, the left leg is bounced forward, the left palm goes forward, the palm center upward, and the right palm goes backward. (Fig. 3-3-73)Turn 180° to the right, the left leg bend.The left arm is rotated inward, the left hook upward, and the right palm is to the left shoulder. (Fig. 3-3-74) The right foot is padded to the left and then the left foot falls backward in a right bow step, turn 180° left, swing the left arm forward to the waist, swing the right palm down and look at the right palm. (Fig. 3-3-75)

图Fig 3-3-73　　　　　　图Fig 3-3-74　　　　　　图Fig 3-3-75

动作要点：左裹肩团身要紧，反劈立圆送肩。

Key points: The left shoulder turns around with close upper body, the split should be in a vertical circle.

18. 麻打挑打 Madatiaoda

两脚不动，左拳从右掌背向前冲拳，右掌贴左臂收至左腋下，（图 3-3-76）紧接着右掌迅速从左臂外侧向前推掌，左拳同时收至腰间，（图3-3-77）左拳再向前快速冲拳，右掌贴左臂内侧收至左肩前，（图3-3-78）继而右拳与左拳连环冲拳至左冲拳时，左臂屈肘向右挑格肘，右拳收至腰间，目视挑肘方向。（图3-3-79、图3-3-80）

Punch left fist forward from the back of the right palm, the right palm goes with the left arm and to the left armpit, (Fig. 3-3-76) the right palm goes forward from the outside of the left arm and close the left fist to the waist, (Fig. 3-3-77) punch left fist forward and close the right palm to the inside of the left arm and close it to the front of the left shoulder, (Fig. 3-3-78) then punch right fist and left fist, bend the elbow of the left arm and put the right fist to the waist, and watch the elbow direction. (Fig. 3-3-79, Fig. 3-3-80)

图Fig 3-3-76　　　　　　　图Fig 3-3-77

图Fig 3-3-78　　　图Fig 3-3-79　　　图Fig 3-3-80

动作要点：右掌与左拳贴紧卸手冲拳，左拳与右拳连环冲拳送肩击远，借助转腰发力。

Key points: the right palm is close to the left fist, the left fist is close to the right fist.

19. 展身撩打 Zhanshenliaoda

左臂向后撩挂，左腿屈膝迅速向后撩摆，右掌向前上架掌拉开，目视前方。（图

3-3-81）重心迅速前移下压，左腿向前落步，右脚跟步成麒麟步，左掌随重心向前提打，力达左手虎口，右掌下挂搭在左腕处，目视左掌。（图 3-3-82）

Left arm backward, bend the left leg and quickly lift and swing backward, pull the right palm forward and look ahead. (Fig. 3-3-81) Move the gravity forward quickly and press down. Step forward with the left leg, and follow the right foot as a Qilin step.Look at the left palm. (Fig. 3-3-82)

图Fig 3-3-81　　　　图Fig 3-3-82

动作要点：展身时拉开背弓，提打抖腕。

Key points: stretch the back when open the body and shake the wrists when attack.

20. **挫手点腿** Cuoshoudiantui

重心上提，两手变掌由两侧向后分掌，（图 3-3-83）左腿直立支撑身体，右腿向前上点腿，力达脚前掌，右掌向前穿掌，掌心向上，目视右掌。（图 3-3-84）

Gravity up, the palms backward from both sides. (Fig. 3-3-83) The left leg is upright to support the body, the right leg is forward, the palm center is upward, and watch the right palm. (Fig. 3-3-84)

图Fig 3-3-83　　　　图Fig 3-3-84

动作要点：点腿前上穿高度过肩，上体微后挺身。

Key points: leg kicking, with the height over the shoulder.

21. 横挂拳 Hengguaquan

图Fig 3-3-85　　　　图Fig 3-3-86　　　　图Fig 3-3-87

图Fig 3-3-88　　　　图Fig 3-3-89

左脚拧转，身体迅速左后转180°，转身后右脚向前落步，重心前移右脚，左脚跟提起，上体前倾，冲右拳，拳眼向上，左掌变拳收于腰间，目视右拳。（图3-3-85）两脚拧转，身体迅速左转180°，右臂直臂随转身向左挂拳，拳眼向下，（图3-3-86）两脚不动，左拳向前抄拳，裹右臂回带至左肩，重心后移，（图3-3-87）重心前移成左弓步，冲右拳，左拳收于腰间，（图3-3-88）身体微右转成马步，冲左拳，右拳收于腰间，目视左拳。（图3-3-89）

Turn 180° to left back, right foot forward, lift the left heel, lean the upper body forward, punch with the right fist, the left palm to the waist, and watch the right fist. (Fig. 3-3-85) Turn 180° to the left, turn your right arm straight to the left, and hang the fist to the left with fist eye down, (Fig. 3-3-86) left fist forward, right arm back to the left shoulder. (Fig. 3-3-87) Punch with the right fist, and put the left fist to the waist, (Fig. 3-3-88) turn slightly right into a horse stance, punch with left fist, right fist to the waist, look at the left fist. (Fig. 3-3-89)

动作要点：转身横挂迅速直臂，上体前倾。

Key points: turn quickly and the upper body should lean forward.

22. 圈捶 Quanchui

图Fig 3-3-90　　　　　图Fig 3-3-91　　　　　图Fig 3-3-92

重心前移，左脚踏实，右脚向前勾踢，右脚跟落地，右拳瓦楞拳向前挑打，左掌拦至右臂，（图3-3-90）右脚踏实，左脚向右脚后插步，左掌从右腋下穿出向左前横摆，右拳收于腰间，（图3-3-91）右脚迅速上步成马步；同时，右拳向前横贯崩拳，拳腕外屈，拳眼向下，与肩同高，左掌摆至右肩前，重心微蹲，目视右拳。（图3-3-92）

Move the gravity forward, with the left foot standing firm, the right foot is hooked and kicked forward, the right heel is on the ground, the right fist is corrugated and punched forward, the left palm is blocked to the right arm, (Fig. 3-3-90) the right foot is firm, the left foot is crossed to the back of the right foot, the left palm passes through the right armpit and swings forward to the left, and the right fist is closed at the waist, (Fig. 3-3-91) the right foot quickly steps up into a horse stance; at the same time, the right fist crosses the smashing fist forward, the fist wrist is bent outward, and the fist eye is downward , at the same height as the shoulder, put the left palm to the front of the right shoulder, squat slightly with the center of gravity, and watch the right fist. (Fig. 3-3-92)

动作要点：右圈捶向前横向贯打与马步拧腰转胯协调发力。

Key points: the horizontal penetration and the waist twisting should be coordinated.

23. 千斤坠 Qianjinzhui

身体左后转身，右臂屈肘回穿，右拳经胸前向左前穿出，左拳随右拳跟穿，（图3-3-93）身体迅速再右后转，右脚外旋震脚落步，两腿交叉，两臂屈肘随震脚向腹前沉肘，（图3-3-94）左脚向前上步，重心前移左脚，双肘随重心前移反腕摆掌，（图3-3-95）重心迅速后移右脚并下沉坠，左脚随重心勾脚尖，双掌（九宫掌）向后下沉拽，右腿微屈，目视双掌。（图3-3-96-1、图3-3-96-2）

The body turns left and back, the right elbow bends back, the right fist passes through the chest to the left and goes forward, the left fist follows the right fist, (Fig. 3-3-93) the body turns right and back quickly, the right foot rotates outward and shakes the foot to fall, the two legs cross, the two elbow bends forward and sinks the elbow to the abdomen with the shaken foot, (Fig. 3-3-94) the left foot moves forward, the center of gravity moves forward and the left foot, the elbows move forward with the center of gravity and the wrist swings the palm, (Fig. 3-3-95) the center of gravity moves back quickly The right foot sinks and falls, the left foot hooks the toe with the center of gravity, the double palms (Jiugong palms) sink backward and pull, the right leg slightly bends, and the eyes are on the double palms. (Fig. 3-3-96-1, Fig. 3-3-96-2)

图Fig 3-3-93　　　　图Fig 3-3-94　　　　图Fig 3-3-95

图Fig 3-3-96-1　　　　图Fig 3-3-96-2

动作要点：左右拳穿出时，身体随势转而微团上身、缩肩，重心前移与后拽同双臂协调一致。

Key points: when the left and right fists are pierced, the body will turn to the upper body and shrink the shoulders, and the center of gravity will move forward and backward in coordination with the arms.

24. 右撩挂起脚 Youliaoguaqijiao

重心前移左脚，右拳向左前撩拳，拳眼向上，与胸同高，左掌下挂右肘内侧，同时，右脚向左前勾踢，目视勾踢方向。（图 3-3-97）

Move the gravity forward to the left foot, and lift the right fist to the left, with the fist eye upward and at the same height as the chest. Hang the right elbow under the left palm. At the same time, hook and kick the right foot to the left and forward to look in the direction of hook and kick. (Fig. 3-3-97)

图Fig 3-3-97

动作要点：勾踢力达脚跟，与右拳劲力一致。

Key points: the force of the kick should reach to the heel, consistent with the power of right fist.

25. 回身埋伏 Huishenmaifu

左脚拧转，身体迅速左转身180°，左腿半屈，右脚内旋向下挂踢，右拳变掌随转身立圆下落，（图 3-3-98）右脚下踢落地，脚跟提起，右掌随转身向前立圆一圈向前反抡劈掌，力达掌背，左掌向左上穿掌，双掌心均向上，目视右掌。（图 3-3-99）

Turn the left foot, turn the body 180° to the left quickly, half bend the left leg, turn the right foot inward and hang the kick downward, turn the right fist to the palm and fall in a vertical circle, (Fig. 3-3-98) kick the right foot to the ground, lift the heel, and swing the right palm forward with the turn to reach the back of the palm, put the left palm on the left and upward, both palms are upward, and look at the right palm. (Fig. 3-3-99)

图Fig 3-3-98   图Fig 3-3-99

动作要点：转身迅速，团身紧缩，右掌立圆一周反抡劈，双臂顺肩。

Key points: turn around quickly, tighten the body, stand on the right palm for a circle.

26. 甩袖披挂 Shuaixiupigua

后撤左脚，身体左转180°成马步，左掌向前横抽，掌心向下，右掌收于腰间，（图3-3-100）右脚向前上步，身体左转180°成马步；同时，右掌向前横抽，掌心向上，左掌收于腰间，（图3-3-101）左脚向前插步，左掌贴右臂向前卸手，（图3-3-102）右脚向前上步成马步，左掌卸手挂掌后向身体左侧横挂，右掌八字掌向前推掌，两掌虎口向上，目视前方。（图3-3-103）

Withdraw the left foot, turn the body 180° to the left to form a horse stance, draw the left palm forward horizontally, with the palm center downward and the right palm closed at the waist, (Fig. 3-3-100) step the right foot forward and turn the body 180° to form a horse stance; at the same time, draw the right palm forward horizontally, with the palm center upward and the left palm closed at the waist, (Fig. 3-3-101) step the left foot forward and fork, with the left palm close to the right arm and unload the hand forward, (Fig. 3-3-102) step the right foot forward to form a horse stance, with the left palm closed at the right arm Before removing the palm, hang it horizontally to the left side of the body, push the right palm forward with the splayed palm, and look ahead with the two palms facing up. (Fig. 3-3-103)

图Fig 3-3-100   图Fig 3-3-101

图Fig 3-3-102　　　　　　图Fig 3-3-103

动作要点：拧转团身含胸，卸手贴紧右臂前穿，两臂平圆横劈打。

Key points: twist the body with chest closed, and split the arms horizontally.

27. 芍手冲崩 Shaoshouchongbeng

两脚拧转，身体左转180°，右臂直臂随转身向左挂拳，拳眼向下，左拳收于腰间，（图3-3-104）两脚不动，左拳向前抄拳，裹右臂回带至左肩，重心前移成左弓步，冲右拳，左拳收于腰间，（图3-3-105）身体微右转成马步，冲左拳，右拳收于腰间，目视左拳。（图3-3-106）

Turn your body 180° to the left, with the right arm turning to the left, with the fist eyes down, and close the left fist to the waist, (Fig. 3-3-104) keep your feet still, punch the left fist forward, bring the right arm back to the left shoulder, move the gravity forward to the left lunge step, punch the right fist, close the left fist to the waist, (Fig. 3-3-105) turn your body slightly to the horse stance, punch the left fist, close the right fist to the waist, and watch the left fist. (Fig. 3-3-106)

图Fig 3-3-104　　　　　图Fig 3-3-105　　　　　图Fig 3-3-106

动作要点：转身横挂迅速直臂，上体前倾。

Key points: turn and hang your arms straight and lean your upper body forward.

28. 右勾踢横打 Yougoutihengda

重心上提，左脚外展，重心前移左脚，右脚向左前勾踢，脚跟落地；同时，右掌从左腋下向左前穿插并向右横切，左臂屈肘向后拉顶，目视右掌。（图 3-3-107、图 3-3-108）

Lift the gravity up, extend the left foot, move the center of gravity forward to the left foot, hook and kick the right foot forward to the left, and the heel lands; at the same time, insert the right palm from the left armpit forward to the left and crosscut it to the right, bend the elbow of the left arm to pull the top backward, and look at the right palm. (Fig. 3-3-107, Fig. 3-3-108)

图Fig 3-3-107　　　　图Fig 3-3-108

动作要点：左右臂成拉弓姿势，借助开拉劲向前横切打。

Key points: draw the left and right arms into a bow position, and use the pull force to cut forward.

29. 左勾踢横打 Zuogoutihengda

右脚向右前外展落步，重心前移右脚，身体右转，左脚向右前勾踢，脚跟落地；同时，左掌从右腋下向右前穿插并向左横切打，右臂屈肘向后拉顶，目视左掌。（图 3-3-109、图 3-3-110）

The right foot moves forward and outward, the center of gravity moves forward and the right foot, the body turns right, the left foot hooks and kicks right and forward, and the heel lands; at the same time, the left palm penetrates right and forward from the right armpit and cuts to the left, the right arm bends the elbow and pulls back to pull the top, and look at the left palm. (Fig. 3-3-109, Fig. 3-3-110)

图Fig 3-3-109　　　　图Fig 3-3-110

动作要点：左右臂成拉弓姿势，借助开拉劲向前横切打。

Key points: draw the left and right arms into a bow position, and use the pull force to cut forward.

30. 右勾踢横打 Yougoutihengda

图Fig 3-3-111

左脚向左前外展落步，重心前移左脚，右脚向左前勾踢，脚跟落地；同时，右掌从左腋下向左前穿插并向右横切打，左臂屈肘向后拉顶，目视右掌。（图 3-3-111）

The left foot stretches to the left and falls forward, the center of gravity moves forward to the left foot, the right foot hooks and kicks left and forward, and the heel lands; at the same time, the right palm penetrates from the left armpit to the left and cuts to the right, the left arm bends the elbow to pull back and top, and watch the right palm. (Fig. 3-3-111)

动作要点：同上。

Key points: the same as above.

31. 翻身叉打 Fanshenchada

重心上提，右脚外撇震脚落地，右转身90°，右掌随转身从上向前下反劈打，并收至腰间，左掌屈腕向前下压至胸前，（图 3-3-112）左脚向前上步成左弓步，右掌从左掌上向前插掌，左掌收至右腋下，目视右掌方向。（图 3-3-113）两脚不动，上体右转，重心下蹲成半马步，右掌回拉身体右侧，左掌向左前插掌，目视左掌方向。（图 3-3-114）

Lift the gravity, shake the right foot to the ground, turn 90° to the right, and then swing the right palm from the top to the bottom, bend the left palm and press the wrist forward and down to the chest, (Fig. 3-3-112) step the left foot forward to form a left bow step, insert the right palm forward from the left palm, and close the left palm to the right armpit, and look at the right palm direction. (Fig. 3-3-113) Keep your feet still, turn your upper body to the right, squat down into a half horse stance, pull back the right side of your body with the right palm, insert the left palm to the left and forward, and look in the direction of the left palm. (Fig. 3-3-114)

图Fig 3-3-112　　　　　图Fig 3-3-113　　　　　图Fig 3-3-114

动作要点：右臂反劈打伸肩击远，插掌力达掌背，外撑发劲。

Key points: right arm back stroke, shoulder extension, far stroke, palm thrust up to the back of the palm, external support.

32. **旗鼓势** Qigushi

（1）提膝穿掌：右脚向左前方上步，右腿直立，左腿屈膝上提，上体微左倾，双掌向左上穿掌，掌心斜朝上，目视左掌。（图 3-3-115）

(1)Tixichuanzhang: step up the right foot to the left, with the right leg upright, the left leg bent to the knee, the upper body leaning slightly to the left, put the two palms on the left, with the palm center inclined upward, and look at the left palm. (Fig. 3-3-115)

（2）下伏旗鼓：双掌经上向右摆掌，（图 3-3-116）左脚向左前落地，重心下蹲稍前移成半马步；同时，双掌握拳，从右腋下经胸前向左侧冲出，拳心斜向上，双臂均外旋，

右拳在左肘内侧处；目视冲拳方向。（图 3-3-117）

(2)Xiafuqigu: swing the palms to the right through the upper part of the two palms. (Fig. 3-3-116) Land the left foot to the left, squat down slightly and move forward to the Kirin step. At the same time, clench the fist with both palms, and rush out from the right armpit to the left through the chest front, with the fist heart inclined upward, both arms turned outward, and the right fist is at the inner part of the left elbow. Look in the punching direction. (Fig. 3-3-117)

图Fig 3-3-115　　　　　图Fig 3-3-116　　　　　图Fig 3-3-117

动作要点：双掌右摆含胸，半马步重心前移，双拳外旋。

Key points: palms swing right with chest bent, move forward the gravity with the fists outward.

33. 收势 Ending up

左脚向右脚并拢，双拳变掌向下、由两侧向上分掌，掌心均向上，目视右掌，（图 3-3-118）两掌由两侧向上再向下按掌至腹前，重心上提至立正姿势，掌心向下，目视左侧，（图 3-3-119）双手自然下放身体两侧，目视正前方。（图 3-3-120）

With the left foot close to the right foot, turn the hands of the two fists downward and divide the palms from both sides upward. The palms are all upward. Look at the right palms, (Fig. 3-3-118) press the palms upward and downward from both sides to the front of the abdomen. Lift the center of gravity up to the upright position, and look down the palms to the left, (Fig. 3-3-119) lower the hands naturally on both sides of the body and look straight ahead. (Fig. 3-3-120)

图Fig 3-3-118　　　　　　图Fig 3-3-119　　　　　　图Fig 3-3-120

动作要点：收势时，肢体要放松、圆滑，动作稳慢，眼要有神。

Key points: the limbs should be relaxed, smooth, steady and slow, and the eyes should be alert.

第四节　劈挂拳
3.4 Pigua Quan

一、劈挂拳简介 Brief introduction

劈挂拳，亦称披挂掌，是一种以猛劈硬挂为主，长击快打，兼容短手，比较古老的拳术。明代武术文献中已有记载，至少在明代中晚期，劈挂已经是一个比较成熟的拳种了。明代戚继光《纪效新书·拳经捷要篇》编选三十二势中有取自劈挂拳的内容。清代以来，劈挂拳主要流传于河北盐山、沧县、南皮县等地，清道光、咸丰年间潘文学主持盐山书院时，设文武科教授学生，传承劈挂拳，以李云标、肖和成为代表传承人，之后，黄林彪、于保麟是劈挂拳的主要传习者，黄林彪后传至马凤图。1928年中央国术馆也将劈挂拳列入教材。劈挂拳在发展传承中经马凤图、马英图钻研施教，并与翻子、八极、戳脚诸拳兼而习之，形成了通备拳流派，通备劈挂拳以"理象会通、体用具备、通神达化、备万贯一"为拳理宗旨，充实和完善了所属拳械理论技术体系。

Pigua Quan, also known as the Pigua Zhang, is a kind of Quan which is mainly used for fierce split and hard hanging, with long strike and quick hit, compatible with short hand, and relatively old. It has been recorded in the Wushu literature of the Ming Dynasty. At least in the middle and late Ming Dynasty, it had become a relatively mature kind of Quan. In Qi Jiguang's "Ji Xiao's New Book", Pigua Quan was selected and recorded. Since the Qing Dynasty, Pigua Quan mainly spread in Yanshan, Cangxian, Nanpi Counties and other places in Hebei Province. During Daoguang and Xianfeng regimes in the Qing Dynasty, Pan Wenxue was in charge of Yanshan School in which Wushu was one of the teaching contents and there were many Pigua Quan learners, among whom Li Yunbiao and Xiao Hecheng became the representative inheritors. Later, Huang Linbiao and Yu Baolin were the main inheritors of Pigua Quan, which was later passed on to Ma Fengtu. In 1928, Pigua Quan was also included in the teaching materials of the Central Wushu Institute. Ma Fengtu and Ma Yingtu, combining Pigua Quan with Fanzi Quan, Baji Quan and other types of Quan, formed Tongbei Quan, a new school, enriching and expanding the types of Quan.

劈挂拳主要流传在河北、北京、甘肃、陕西、青海、新疆、宁夏、山东、广东、东北等地。在甘肃、陕西一带广泛传承通备劈挂拳术的套路有一路抹面、二路青龙、三路飞虎、四路太淑和大架子，一路劈挂拳传播较广，是习练通备拳术的启蒙教材之一。劈挂拳源流有序、拳理明晰、风格独特、自成体系，发展至今被列为重点开展拳种。

It is mainly spread in Hebei, Beijing, Gansu, Shaanxi, Qinghai, Xinjiang, Ningxia, Shandong, Guangdong, and other northeast places. In Gansu and Shaanxi, there are a wide range of it.The first is Mamian, the second is Qinglong, the third is Feihu, the fourth is Taishu and Dajiazi. The first one is widely spread and is one of the enlightening teaching materials for practicing. It has been listed as a key type by the state for its orderly origin, clear principle, unique style and self-made system.

二、劈挂拳技法特点 Technical characteristics

劈挂拳属于典型的长拳类，拳术练习注重内外兼修和轻重、缓急、动静、虚实、刚柔间的转化。演练追求正、顺、合、活、快、力、精、巧、妙、绝十字要诀，练拳讲究慢拉架子，快打拳，急打招，在格斗中以上擎下取，下擎则上取。

劈挂拳风格表现为：起落钻伏、不招不架、猛劈硬挂、迅猛彪悍、气势贯通；劲力通达、刚柔有度、意气贯通、翻滚不息、闪展腾挪；随势进招、发力饱满、速攻快打、兼容短打。

Pigua Quan belongs to the typical Chang Quan. Its practice focuses on the combination of internal and external and the transformation of gravity, priority, movement and stillness, hardness and softness. Drill to pursue the key points of correct, smooth, harmonious, flexible, fast, powerful, precise, ingenious, wonderful and absolute cross. When practising, one should be slow in posture and quick in fighting.

劈挂拳技法特点：大开大合、长刀冷抽、步法多变、身法灵活、长击短打相兼，藏锋鹰目、气势逼人。拳诀曰：藏锋十路埋伏，透形周身示弱。

The characteristics of Pigua Quan techniques: big opening and closing, changeable footwork, flexible body moves, long hitting and short fighting.

三、劈挂拳基本动作与方法 Basic movements and methods of Pigua Quan

（一）手型 Hand form

1.瓦棱拳：四指并拢卷曲，食指紧扣于虎口内侧，其余三指依次微屈突起，拇指紧扣于食指第二关节上。（图3-4-1）

1.Walengquan: four fingers are closed and curled together, the index finger is tightly connected to the inside of the tiger mouth, the other three fingers are slightly bent and protruded in turn, and the thumb is tightly connected to the second joint of the index finger. (Fig. 3-4-1)

2.瓦面掌：四指并拢，大拇指第二指节扣屈，紧贴于虎口。（图3-4-2）

2. Wamianzhang: four fingers close together, the second knuckle of the thumb buckles and bends, clinging to the mouth of the tiger. (Fig. 3-4-2)

3.凤眼勾：拇指与食指指端撮拢，其余三指卷曲，腕关节紧屈。（图3-4-3）

3. Fengyangou: the thumb and index finger are closed, the other three fingers are curled, and the wrist joint is tightly bent. (Fig. 3-4-3)

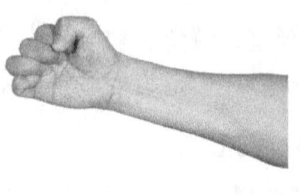
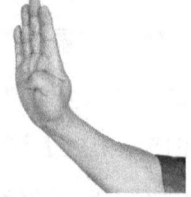
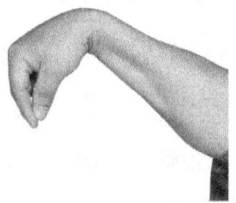

图Fig 3-4-1　　　　　　图Fig 3-4-2　　　　　　图Fig 3-4-3

4. 九宫掌：五指分开，自然伸直，掌心空起，手腕上翘，力点用在掌跟。（图 3-4-4）

4. Jiugongzhang: the thumb and fingers are separated, naturally straightened, the palm center is empty, the wrist is up, and the point of force is used in the heel of the palm. (Fig. 3-4-4)

5. 八字掌：四指伸直并拢，大拇指与四指分开。（图 3-4-5）

5. Bazizhang: the four fingers are extended and close together, and the thumb is separated from the four fingers. (Fig. 3-4-5)

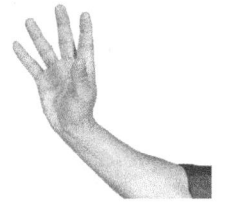

图Fig 3-4-4　　　　　图Fig 3-4-5

（二）步型 Step form

1. 半马步：两脚左右开立，距离同马步，前脚尖向外，后脚尖与膝内扣。（图 3-4-6）

1. Half horse-ride step: open the left and right feet, the distance is the same as horse stance, the front toe outward, the back toe and knee buckle inward. (Fig. 3-4-6)

2. 跪膝步：前腿屈膝全蹲，后膝跪落于前脚内侧，但不触及地面，脚跟提起，前脚掌着地。左脚在前为左跪膝步，右脚在前为右跪膝步。（图 3-4-7）

2. Guixibu: the front leg is bent down, the back knee is kneeling on the inside of the front foot, but does not touch the ground, the heel is raised, and the front foot is on the ground. The left foot in front is the left kneeling step, and the right foot in front is the right kneeling step. (Fig. 3-4-7)

3. 掰弓步：前腿屈膝半蹲，后腿伸膝蹬直，脚跟提起，前脚掌着地，两脚相距与弓步相同，上体正对前方。（图 3-4-8）

3.Baigongbu: the front leg is bent and half squatted, the back leg is extended and straight, the heel is lifted, the front foot is on the ground, the distance between the two feet is the same as the lunge, and the upper body is facing the front. (Fig. 3-4-8)

图Fig 3-4-6　　　　　　　　图Fig 3-4-7　　　　　　　　图Fig 3-4-8

（三）手法 Hand Techniques

1. 反滚臂：两臂在滚旋中反手伸臂挥劈。（图 3-4-9）

1. Fangunbi: the two arms extend and swing during rolling. (Fig. 3-4-9)

2. 扑挂掌：两臂腹前交叉，伸臂伸肘经头上向两侧反手劈下，两手背击于两臀侧。（图 3-4-10）

2. Puguazhang: cross your arms in front of your abdomen, extend your arms and elbows, split them from your head up to both sides of your backhand, and hit your hands on your hips. (Fig. 3-4-10)

3. 斩拳：以拳轮为力点，以前臂为半径，由上向下成斜面斩击。向内侧斩击为内斩拳，向外侧斩击为外斩拳。（图 3-4-11）

3.Zhanquan: take the fist wheel as the force point, the forearm as the radius, and cut from the top to the bottom. (Fig. 3-4-11)

4. 缠额手：手臂由腰间向后向上经同侧颈部再向前推击，伸臂成瓦面掌横击。（图 3-4-12）

4.Chan-e-shou: push the arm back and up from the waist through the neck on the same side, then push forward, extend the arm to form tile face palm and strike horizontally. (Fig. 3-4-12)

5. 横掌：掌心向下，手臂由内向外拦腰横击。（图 3-4-13）

5. Hengzhang: the palm center is downward, and blow the arm horizontally from inside to outside. (Fig. 3-4-13)

6. 合子掌：两手掌相叠，掌指相对，掌心相合，由后向前撞击。上体吞胸拔背，收腹坐髋；前手合腕，掌背朝前，后手推击，力达前手掌背。（图 3-4-14）

6.Hezizhang: the two palms are overlapped, and go from back to front. The upper body tight; the front hand closes the wrist, the back of the hand faces forward, and the back hand pushes and hits, reaching the back of the front hand. (Fig. 3-4-14)

7. 戳指掌：掌心朝上，掌指朝前，一手经腰间从另手臂内旁出，力达掌指。（图 3-4-15）

7.Chuozhizhang: the palms are up, the fingers facing forward, one hand comes out from the other arm through the waist. (Fig. 3-4-15)

图Fig 3-4-9 　　　　　图Fig 3-4-10 　　　　　图Fig 3-4-11

图Fig 3-4-12 　　　　　图Fig 3-4-13 　　　　　图Fig 3-4-14

图Fig 3-4-15

（四）步法 Foot Techniques

1. 提步：进步时经屈膝上提，然后落地。

1.Tibu: bend the knees and lift, then land on the ground.

2. 撤步：后脚向后撤一步，前脚向后移半步。

2.Chebu: step backward.

3. 交错步：两脚前后开立，原地两脚前后交换。

3.Jiaocuobu: stand with feet front and back, then exchange.

4. 纵跳步：一脚提起，另一脚蹬地前跳落地。

4. Zongtiaobu: lift one foot and jump to the ground with the other foot.

5. 卸步：两脚前后开立，后脚贴地面向后撤一步，前脚随之后撤，落于后脚内侧，足尖点地。

5.Xiebu: stand with feet front and back, the back foot backward one step, with the front foot backward into the back foot.

6. 跨步：左脚先进一步，右脚随之向前跨一大步，屈膝坐胯，足尖内扣，重心前移，左脚顺势跟进半步。有大跨步、小跨步之分，小跨步步幅略小。

6.Kuabu: the left foot steps one step forward with the right foot following, sit on the hip with knees bent, move the gravity forward, and the left foot half a step forward.

四、劈挂拳（一路抹面拳）动作图解 Illustration

第一段 Part I

1. 开门立势 Start

（1）预备式：并步直立，两臂垂于体侧，两手成掌型，掌心向内，贴于腿侧，凝气聚神，目视前方。（图 3-4-16）

(1) Ready: stand upright in parallel steps, with arms hanging on the side of the body, hands in palm shape, palms inward, close to the leg side, and look ahead. (Fig. 3-4-16)

图Fig 3-4-16　　　图Fig 3-4-17　　　图Fig 3-4-18

图Fig 3-4-19　　　　　图Fig 3-4-20

（2）开拳：两脚拧转，身体右转45°站立，稍定。（图3-4-17）两肘外撑上提，摆头目视左侧，（图3-4-18）身体微右转，右脚向右后方撤一小步，屈膝半蹲，双掌心朝下向小腹前交叉插出，目视双掌，（图3-4-19）双掌分开向两侧做燕尾状划开收握拳至身体两侧，两肘向外撑，成倒三角，左脚向右脚并步，目视左侧。（图3-4-20）

(2) Start: twist your feet, turn right 45° and stand, slightly fixed. (Fig. 3-4-17) Lift the elbows up, swing your head to the left, (Fig. 3-4-18) turn your body slightly to the right, take a small step to the right and back of your right foot, bend your knees and squat, insert your palms downward to the front of your abdomen, and then look at your palms, (Fig. 3-4-19) separate your palms to the two sides in a swallow tail shape, open and hold your fists to both sides of your body, support your elbows outward to form an inverted triangle, and step left foot to the right foot. Look left. (Fig. 3-4-20)

（3）开门立势：右脚经左脚向前盖步，同时双拳变掌右上左下开展，（图3-4-21）重心前移全蹲成右歇步，右掌向左下劈，左掌上挂右耳外侧,（图3-4-22）重心前移到右脚，右腿直立，左腿屈膝上抬，脚背绷直，双掌向右上、左下两侧开肩打开，目视前方。（图3-4-23）

(3)Kaimenlishi: move the right foot forward through the left foot, and turn the fists into palms at the same time, (Fig. 3-4-21) squat into a right Xiebu, the right palm splits left and down, the left palm is near the right ear. (Fig. 3-4-22) Move the weight forward to the right foot, the right leg upright, bend the left leg to the knee, straighten the back of the foot, open the shoulders and look forward. (Fig. 3-4-23)

图Fig 3-4-21　　　　　　图Fig 3-4-22　　　　　　图Fig 3-4-23

（4）虚步按掌：左脚向前下方铲出，重心下蹲成左仆步，（图3-4-24）重心前移，仆步变左弓步，双掌由两侧向正前方划弧合掌，掌心向下，（图3-4-25）重心后移右腿，左脚微后收成左虚步，双掌后收并向身体两侧按掌，目视左方。（图3-4-26）

(4) Xubuanzhang: left foot shovels forward and lower, squat to form a left footstep, (Fig. 3-4-24) move the weight forward, change the footstep to a left bow step, arc the palms from both sides to the front, with the palm center downward, (Fig. 3-4-25) move the weight back to the right leg, slightly retract the left foot to form a left empty step, and then press the palms back to both sides of the body, slightly curve the arms, and look at the left side. (Fig. 3-4-26)

（5）并步按掌：接上动，左脚向右前方盖步，双掌外旋掌心朝上向左前方穿掌，（图3-4-27）右脚向右前方跨步成马步，双掌向下、经两侧向上托至头上方，目视右掌，（图3-4-28）左脚向右脚并步，两掌屈腕下按至小腹前，掌心向下，两臂微屈，肘外翻，目视左方。（图3-4-29）

(5) Bingbuanzhang: move up, turn the palms outwards and pass through the palms to the left and front, (Fig. 3-4-27) step the right foot to the right and front, hold the palms downward and upward to the top of the head, and look at the right palm, (Fig. 3-4-28) step the left foot to the right foot in parallel, bend the arms slightly, press the palms to the front of the abdomen, turn the palms downward, bend the arms slightly, turn the elbows outwards, look to the left. (Fig. 3-4-29)

图Fig 3-4-24　　　　　　图Fig 3-4-25　　　　　　图Fig 3-4-26

图Fig 3-4-27　　　　　　图Fig 3-4-28　　　　　　图Fig 3-4-29

动作要点：含胸收腹、顶头、精神集中，动作稳、慢；身体重心随掌下按逐渐上提直立。

Key points: the center of gravity is gradually raised.

2. 滚臂单劈手 Gunbidanpishou

（1）单劈下压：双臂侧平举，掌心均向上，（图3-4-30）右脚向右跨一大步，左脚紧跟半步，身体右转下压，左膝内合成跪膝步，左臂内旋裹肩下劈至左后侧，右掌屈肘回收上挂至左耳侧，重心全蹲，目视左方。（图3-4-31）

(1) Single press down: both arms are lifted horizontally, palms are all up, (Fig. 3-4-30) right foot takes a big step to the right, left foot closely follows half step, turn right and press down, kneeling, left arm is rotated and wrapped inside shoulder and then split to the left rear side, right palm bends elbow and recovers and to the left ear side, look at the left side. (Fig. 3-4-31)

（2）左单劈手：左脚向后撤一大步，左臂向前、上向后抡劈，紧接着上体左后转成左弓步，右臂随左臂向上向左侧下抡劈至左膝外侧，左臂屈肘上挂至右耳侧，指尖向上，目视右劈手方向。（图3-4-32）

(2) Zuodanpishou: take a big step backward with the left foot, swing the left arm forward, up and back, then turn the left back of the upper body to form the left bow step, swing the right arm up and left down with the left arm to the outside of the left knee, bend the elbow of the left arm to the right ear side, and swing the fingertip up, and watch the direction of the right hand. (Fig. 3-4-32)

图Fig 3-4-30　　　　　　图Fig 3-4-31　　　　　　图Fig 3-4-32

（3）右单劈手：右臂向前、上向后抢劈，（图3-4-33）紧接着上体右后转成右弓步，左臂随右臂向上向右侧下抢劈至右膝外侧，右臂上挂至左耳侧，指尖向上，目视左劈手方向。（图3-4-34）

(3) Youdanpishou: swing the right arm forward, up and back, (Fig. 3-4-33) turn to right bow step, swing the left arm up and right down with the right arm to the outside of the right knee, the right arm up to the left ear side, and watch the left hand. (Fig. 3-4-34)

（4）左单劈手：左臂再次向前、上向后抢劈，紧接着上体再次左后转成左弓步，右臂随左臂向上向左侧下抢劈至左膝外侧，左臂屈肘上挂至右耳侧，指尖向上，目视右劈手方向。（同上左单劈手）

(4) Zuodanpishou: swing the left arm forward, up and back again, and then turn the upper body into a left bow step, swing the right arm up and left to the outside of the left knee with the left arm, the left arm elbow up to the right ear side, with the fingertip up, and watch the right hand. (The same as the left split)

图Fig 3-4-33　　　　　图Fig 3-4-34

动作要点：①身体下压快速，旋臂裹肩，拧腰抢臂一致。②抢臂收腹含胸，力达掌侧和前臂，上下连贯。③转身带臂与蹬转协调，身体由开到合。

Key points: ① press the body down quickly and tightly, and swing the arms in the same way. ② blowing with the chest and belly closed. ③ Arms turning and legs kicking should be coordinated.

3. 提膝穿掌 Tixichuanzhang

（1）插步盖掌：身体上提右转，右臂向上、右抢劈，（图3-4-35）右掌收至腰间，左掌向右上方抢盖掌；同时，右脚向左脚后插步，目视左手方向。（图3-4-36）

(1)Chabugaizhang: body up and turn right, swing the right arm up and right. (Fig. 3-4-35)

Put the right palm to the waist, swing the left palm to cover the palm above the right; the right foot back to the left foot, and look at the left hand. (Fig. 3-4-36)

（2）提膝穿掌：重心移至右脚，左腿提膝，右掌从腰间向右上穿出，大拇指侧向上；同时左掌收至右肩，掌尖向上，目视穿掌方向。（图 3-4-37）

(2) Tixichuanzhang: move the weight to the right foot, knee lifting of the left leg, right palm from the waist to the right, thumb side up; put the left palm to the right shoulder, palm tip up, and watch the direction of the front palm. (Fig. 3-4-37)

动作要点：转身、右掌抡劈和左掌盖掌快速有力，上下协调，动作连贯。

Key points: turning, swing and pressing quickly and powerfully.

图Fig 3-4-35

图Fig 3-4-36

图Fig 3-4-37

4. 马步插掌 Mabuchazhang

（1）仆步穿掌：右腿下蹲，左脚向左前方落步成左仆步；同时左掌向左脚前穿出，虎口朝上，右臂斜举身体右侧，目视左掌方向。（图 3-4-38）

(1) Pubuchuanzhang: squat down on the right leg, and step left forward with the left foot; at the same time, put the left palm out in front of the left foot, and lift the right arm to the right side, and look at the left palm. (Fig. 3-4-38)

（2）垫步前插掌：身体重心前移至左脚并向前垫跳一大步；同时右腿屈膝上提，左掌变勾手上提，右掌收至腰间，（图 3-4-39）右脚向前落步成马步，左勾手变掌外旋向上架掌，右掌成九宫掌向前推出，目视右掌方向。（图 3-4-40-1、图 3-4-40-2）

(2) Dianbuqianchazhang: move the weight forward to the left foot and take a big step forward; at the same time, bend the right leg and lift, turn the left palm to the hook and lift, and turn the right palm to the waist, (Fig. 3-4-39) step the right foot forward into a horse step, turn the left hook outside of the palm, turn the right palm into the Jiugongzhang and push forward, and look at the right palm. (Fig. 3-4-40-1, Fig. 3-4-40-2)

动作要点：仆步下压要快，左掌前穿要远，垫步高而远，马步推掌力随腰发。

Key points: step down quickly; left palm goes forward as far as possible, pushing power should be generated from the waist.

图Fig 3-4-38   图Fig 3-4-39

图Fig 3-4-40-1   图Fig 3-4-40-2

5. 垫步左插掌 Dianbuzuochazhang

（1）云手劈掌：上体稍左转，右掌向左上云掌划弧，（图3-4-41）重心移至左脚，团身下压，右掌向左上云掌划弧经右上斜下劈至左胯侧，掌心朝外，力达掌侧，左掌配合右掌划弧屈肘回收上挂至右耳侧，掌尖朝上，目视右劈手方向。（图3-4-42-1、图3-4-42-2）

(1) Yunshoupizhang: turn the upper body slightly to the left, right palm goes to the left and in an arc. (Fig. 3-4-41) Move the center of gravity to the left foot, press the right palm to the left, right palm goes to the left and make an arc, palm center outside, left palm and right palm to make an arc and bend elbow back to the right ear, palm tip up, and look at the right hand. (Fig. 3-4-42-1, Fig. 3-4-42-2)

图Fig 3-4-41　　　　　　图Fig 3-4-42-1　　　　　　图Fig 3-4-42-2

（2）转身插掌：重心迅速上提右转，右腿屈膝上提，左脚黏地拧转；同时右臂微屈肘向右上震顶肘，左掌配合向左胯侧按掌，（图3-4-43）右脚向右前落步并向右前垫跳一大步，右脚先落步，左脚向前落步成马步，左掌上提经腰间向前插出；同时右掌外旋向上架掌，目视左掌方向。（图3-4-44）

(2) Turn around and insert the palm: quickly lift the gravity and turn right, bend the right leg to the knee and lift it up, and turn the left foot. At the same time, slightly bend the elbow of the right arm and shake the top to the right, and press the palm on the left with the left palm, (Fig. 3-4-43) the right foot falls forward and a big step to the right, the right foot falls first, the left foot falls forward into a horse step, and the left palm is lifted and inserted forward through the waist; at the same time, turn the right palm outward. Look at the left palm. (Fig. 3-4-44)

图Fig 3-4-43　　　　　　图Fig 3-4-44

动作要点：团身下压由开胸到紧缩含胸，右肘震顶以腰转带劲；转身垫步高快远。

Key points: press the body down from chest opening to chest compression, shake the right elbow and turn to waist with strength; step high and fast.

第二段 Part II

6. 左右鹞子穿林 Left and Right Hawks fly

（1）左鹞子穿林：①左、右脚同时向右碾转，上体急右转 90°成虚步，右掌外旋上托，左掌收至腰间，（图 3-4-45）重心移至右脚，左脚经右脚向右前方上步，左掌向右经右掌上向前上穿出，掌心向上，右掌收至左腋下，目视穿掌方向。（图 3-4-46）

(1) Left-Hawk-fly: ① turn the left and right feet to the right at the same time, turn the upper body 90° to the right to form an empty step, turn the right palm outside to hold up, put the left palm to the waist, (Fig. 3-4-45) move the gravity to the right foot, step the left foot to the right through the right foot, put the left palm to the right through the right palm, palm up, put the right palm under the left armpit, and watch the palm. (Fig. 3-4-46)

②上体急速右后转 270°，右膝上提顶，右掌外旋向上架掌，左掌心朝上收至腰间。（图 3-4-47）

② Turn the upper body right 270° quickly, lift the top of the right knee, rotate the right palm outward to the upper palm, and close the left palm upward to the waist. (Fig. 3-4-47)

图Fig 3-4-45　　　　　图Fig 3-4-46　　　　　图Fig 3-4-47

图Fig 3-4-48　　　　　图Fig 3-4-49　　　　　图Fig 3-4-50

③右脚向右前方上步，左掌前穿，（图3-4-48）左脚继续向左方成弧形上步；同时左掌外旋向上架掌，掌心向上，弧形步至右脚在前时成半马步，右掌经腰间向前推掌（九宫掌），目视推掌方向。（图3-4-49、图3-4-50）

③Step right and forward with the right foot, put the left palm in front of you. (Fig. 3-4-48) Continue to step left in an arc. At the same time, turn the left palm outward to put the palm on the shelf, with the palm center upward. Step in an arc until the right foot forms a half horse step when it is in front. Push the right palm forward through the waist (Jiugong palm), and visually push the palm direction. (Fig. 3-4-49, Fig. 3-4-50)

（2）右鹞子穿林：动作相同左鹞子穿林，方向相反，左右相反。（图3-4-51、图3-4-52、图3-4-53、图3-4-54、图3-4-55、图3-4-56）

(2)Right-Hawk-fly: the action is the same as that of the Left-Hawk-fly, the direction is opposite, left and right are opposite. (Fig.3-4-51, Fig.3-4-52, Fig.3-4-53, Fig.3-4-54, Fig.3-4-55, Fig.3-4-56)

图Fig 3-4-51　　　　图Fig 3-4-52　　　　图Fig 3-4-53

图Fig 3-4-54　　　　图Fig 3-4-55　　　　图Fig 3-4-56

动作要点：①转身快而不乱，行步连贯，重心平稳，行走路线成一弧形。②穿掌连贯一气呵成，推掌随腰发力，目随势转。

Key points: ① turn quickly without random, walk in a coherent way, have a stable gravity, and walk in an arc. ② Put on the palms in a coherent way, push the palms to make force with the waist, and eyes follow the moves.

7. 滚臂跳搓掌 Gunbitiaocuozhang

（1）单劈下压：上体迅速右转下压，重心下蹲，左膝内合成跪膝步，左臂内旋裹肩下劈至左后侧，左掌随左臂内旋变勾手，勾尖向上，右掌屈肘上挂至左耳侧，目视左方。（图3-4-57）

(1) Danpixiaya: turn the upper body to the right and press it down quickly, squat down with the center of gravity, kneel step in the left knee, wrap the shoulder in the left arm and split it down to the rear left side, change the hook with the left arm turning inward, hook point up, bend the elbow in the right palm and hang it to the left ear side, and watch the left side. (Fig. 3-4-57)

图Fig 3-4-57　　　　图Fig 3-4-58

图Fig 3-4-59-1　　　　图Fig 3-4-59-2

（2）翻身搓掌：左臂直臂向下、向右上、向后抡劈，右臂随左臂向上向右划弧抡劈；同时身体以右脚掌为支撑轴向后转身蹬地起跳转身180°，（图3-4-58）落地下蹲成右仆步，右掌经胸前向下、向右脚前搓掌，掌心向下，左掌打开，掌心向上，目视搓掌方向。（图3-4-59-1、图3-4-59-2）

(2) Fanshencuozhang: swing the left arm straight downward, right upward and backward, and swing the right arm with the left arm upward and right; at the same time, turn the body backward with the right foot as the support axis to take off and turn 180°, (Fig. 3-4-58) squat on the ground into a right footstep, rub the right palm downward through the chest and right foot direction, palm downward, left palm open, palm upward, and watch palm rubbing direction. (Fig. 3-4-59-1, Fig. 3-4-59-2)

动作要点：滚背团身含胸，抡劈快速；翻身腾空轻快，贴近地面向前搓掌。

Key points: swing and chop quickly; turn over and take off quickly, and hands rub forward close to the ground.

8. 马步托闯 Mabutuochuang

（1）屈膝上托：重心上提，左腿直立，右腿屈膝上顶，左掌向右掌方向划弧与右掌心相对，双臂微屈，随重心上托提。（图 3-4-60）

(1) Quxishangtuo: gravity lift, keep the left leg upright, bend the right leg to the top of the knee, arc the left palm to the right palm opposite to the right palm, slightly bend the arms, and lift with the center of gravity. (Fig. 3-4-60)

（2）拧腰闯掌：身体右转 90°，右脚震脚落地，左脚向前落成马步；同时双掌向前插掌开闯，右臂内旋上架于头上，掌心向上，左掌八字掌向前推出，与肩同高，指尖向上，目视推掌方向。（图 3-4-61）

(2)Ningyaochuangzhang: turn the body 90° to the right, shake the right foot to the ground, and put the left foot forward to form a horse stance; at the same time, insert the two palms forward to break the palm, turn the right arm inward to stand on the head, palm center up, left palm splayed palm forward, shoulder height, fingertip up, and watch the palm direction. (Fig. 3-4-61)

图Fig 3-4-60　　　　　　图Fig 3-4-61

动作要点：双掌上托向前挤进，托掌拧腰转胯，送肘、发力完整。

Key points: push the two palms forward, twist the waist and turn the crotch with the palms, and send the elbow with complete force.

9. 横拦手 Henglanshou

两脚拧转成左弓步，右掌外旋向左横拦出，掌心向上；同时左掌迎击右小臂，（图3-4-62）紧接着，上体右转成马步，右臂内旋掌心朝下向右侧拦腰横击，左掌心向上收至腰间，目视右掌方向。（图3-4-63）

Turn the two feet into a left lunge step, turn the right palm outwards to block out to the left, and turn the palm upward; at the same time, turn the left palm to the right forearm. (Fig. 3-4-62) Next, turn the upper body right into a horse step, turn the right palm inwards and turn the palm downward to the right waist, turn the left palm upward to the waist, and look at the right palm direction. (Fig. 3-4-63)

图Fig 3-4-62   图Fig 3-4-63

动作要点：双臂迎击时含胸、沉肩，重心螺旋下压，力达前臂与掌侧。

Key points: when the two arms are attacking, the chest and shoulder are downward, and the center of gravity is spirally pressed down to reach the forearm and palm side.

第三段 Part III

10. 三环套月 Sanhuantaoyue

（1）团身抄手：左脚经右脚后向右插步，重心全蹲，上体含胸团身下伏，两掌从两侧屈腕相向穿掌，目视右掌。（图3-4-64-1、图3-4-64-2）

(1)Tuanshenchaoshou: the left foot is crossed to the right after the right foot, the upper body close and crouched down, the two palms are bent from both sides to penetrate, and watch the right palm. (Fig. 3-4-64-1, Fig. 3-4-64-2)

图Fig 3-4-64-1　　　　　图Fig 3-4-64-2

（2）展身劈掌：重心上提，右脚向右跨步成开立步，双臂随身体含胸后展身向两侧直臂下劈至胯侧，掌心朝外，力点在小指背侧，目视左侧。（图3-4-65）动作连续完成三次（图3-4-66、图3-4-67、图3-4-68）

(2)Zhanshenpizhang: Gravity up, step the right foot to the right to form an opening step, and then split the arms to the crotch side with the chest on both sides, with the palms facing out, the force point is on the back of the little finger, and look at the right direction. (Fig. 3-4-65) The action is completed three times continuously. (Fig. 3-4-66, Fig. 3-4-67, Fig. 3-4-68)

图Fig 3-4-65　　　图Fig 3-4-66　　　图Fig 3-4-67　　　图Fig 3-4-68

动作要点：动作紧密连贯，上下一致，两臂穿插含胸下伏，劈掌时挺胸开肩。

Key points: the action is close and coherent, the upper and lower parts are the same.

11. 滚臂劈手 Gunbipishou

（1）身体左转下压，重心移至左脚，左腿屈膝下蹲，右脚跟半步成跪膝步，右臂内旋下劈至右后侧，右手勾尖向上，左掌屈肘上挂至右耳侧，目视右侧。（图3-4-69）

(1) Turn to the left, bend the left leg and squat down, press the right foot tightly down, turn the right arm inward and split it to the right rear side, hook the right hand up, bend the left elbow to the right ear side, and look at the right side. (Fig. 3-4-69)

（2）右脚后撤落步并右转身；同时右臂经上向后抡劈，左臂紧跟其后抡劈，（图3-4-70）

(2) Step back with the right foot and turn right; at the same time, swing the right arm up and back, followed by the left arm, (Fig. 3-4-70)

（3）重心右移下蹲，上体下伏，左臂经右膝贴地面向左横摆，右臂紧跟其后，重心左移，身体左转，掌心均向下，目视左掌方向。（图3-4-71）

(3) Move the gravity to the right and squat down, lean the upper body down, swing the left arm to the left through the right knee, follow the right arm closely, move the gravity to the left, turn the body to the left, palm center all downward, and look at the left palm. (Fig. 3-4-71)

图Fig 3-4-69　　　　　　图Fig 3-4-70　　　　　　图Fig 3-4-71

动作要点：扣腿团身含胸锁肩，抡劈有力，身体从右至左要贴近地面。

Key points of action: The swing is powerful. The body should be close to the ground from right to left.

12. 右双撞掌 Right Shuangzhuangzhang

上动不停，重心移左腿，两掌体前穿掌，（图3-4-72）右腿提膝，左脚蹬地向前纵跳一大步，两掌从两侧屈腕相向穿掌，向上翻架直臂向两侧下劈，（图3-4-73）右脚向前落步成右弓步；同时两臂内旋，经两肋、耳侧向前推出，两臂微屈，左臂在上，右臂在下，虎口相对，掌心朝外，目视两掌之间。（图3-4-74）

Keep moving up, shift the weight to the left leg, palms front, (Fig. 3-4-72) lift the right knee, take a long step forward with the left foot, bend the wrists, turn the straight arms upward and split downward to both sides, (Fig. 3-4-73) step the right foot forward to form a right bow step; rotate the two arms inward, push forward through the ribs and ears, slightly bend the two arms, put the left arm up, put the right arm down, the palm is facing out, and look between the palms. (Fig. 3-4-74)

图Fig 3-4-72　　　　　　图Fig 3-4-73　　　　　　图Fig 3-4-74

动作要点：撞掌随转身发力，力达掌根，两臂间略呈圆形。

Key points: the force reaches the palm root. The arms form a slightly circular.

13. 叉步千斤坠 Chabuqianjinzhui

图Fig 3-4-75-1　　　　　　图Fig 3-4-75-2

上动稍停，右脚经左脚向后撤步；同时双臂外旋，两掌变爪直臂向左下用力拽劈，左肘向后上顶，左爪置于左肋，右爪拽劈至左跨外侧，目视前方。（图3-4-75-1、图3-4-75-2）

Move up and stop for a while, and then cross steps, rotate the arms outwards, and pull the straight arms to the left and lower down with force. Push the left elbow backward and top, and place the left claw in the left rib. Pull the right claw to the outside of the left span, and look ahead. (Fig. 3-4-75-1, Fig. 3-4-75-2)

动作要点：拧腰旋臂上下拧成整劲。

Action points: twist the waist and rotate the arm up and down by the whole force.

14. 左双撞掌 Left Shuangzhuangzhang

右脚向前上步，重心前移，身体右转，两掌体前穿掌，（图3-4-76）左腿提膝，右脚蹬地向前纵垫一大步，两掌向上翻架直臂向两侧下劈，（图3-4-77）左脚向前落步成左弓步；同时两臂内旋，两掌经两肋、耳侧向前推出，两臂微屈，右臂在上，左

臂在下，虎口相对，掌心向外，目视两掌之间。（图 3-4-78）

The right foot moves forward, the center of gravity moves forward, the body turns right, the palms are put in front of each other, (Fig. 3-4-76) the left leg lifts the knee, the right foot pedals forward for a long step, the two palms turn up, the straight arms are split to the two sides and down, (Fig. 3-4-77) the left foot moves forward to form a left bow step; at the same time, the two arms rotate inward, the two palms are pushed forward through the ribs and ears, the two arms are slightly bent, the right arm is on the top, the left arm is on the bottom, the palm is outward, and look between the two palms. (Fig. 3-4-78)

图Fig 3-4-76　　　　　　图Fig 3-4-77　　　　　　图Fig 3-4-78

动作要点：撞掌随转身发力，力达掌根，两臂略呈圆形。

Key points: the force reaches the palm root. The arms form a slightly circular.

15. 横拦手 Henglanshou

右掌外旋经右回旋向左侧挂出，掌心向上；同时左掌稍外旋迎击右小臂，（图 3-4-79）紧接着，上体右转成马步，右臂内旋掌心向下，向右侧拦腰横击，左掌心向上收至腰侧，目视右掌方向。（图 3-4-80）

The right palm rotates outward to the left, with the palm center upward; turn the left palm outward slightly and meet the right forearm. (Fig. 3-4-79) Then turn the upper body right into a horse stance, turn the right arm inward, with the left palm center upward to the waist side, and look at the right palm. (Fig. 3-4-80)

图Fig 3-4-79　　　　　　图Fig 3-4-80

动作要点：右臂回旋至右侧再向左挂出，迎击含胸、沉肩、重心螺旋下压。

Key points: turn the right arm to the right and then go out to the left, chest close, shoulders and the gravity down.

第四段 Part IV

16. 三环套月 Sanhuantaoyue

（1）团身抄手：左脚经右脚后向右插步，重心全蹲，上体含胸团身下伏，两掌从两侧屈腕相向穿掌，目视右掌。（图3-4-81）

(1) Tuanshenchaoshou: the left foot is crossed to the right after the right foot, the upper body crouched down, the two palms are bent from both sides to penetrate each other, and watch the right palm. (Fig. 3-4-81)

（2）展身劈掌：重心上提，右脚向右跨步成开立步，双臂随身体含胸后展身向两侧直臂下劈至胯侧，掌心朝外，力点在小指背侧，目视左侧方向。（图3-4-82）动作连续完成三次。（同动作10）

(2) Zhanshenpizhang: Gravity up, step the right foot to the right to form an open step, and then split the arms to the crotch side with the chest on both sides of the body, with the palms facing out, the force point is on the back of the little finger, and look at the left. (Fig. 3-4-82) The action is completed three times continuously. (The same as action 10)

图Fig 3-4-81　　　　图Fig 3-4-82

17. 滚臂提膝截掌 Gunbitixijiezhang

（1）滚臂下压：身体向左转下压，重心移至左脚，左腿屈膝下蹲，右膝紧扣左脚内侧，右臂内旋下劈至右后侧，左掌屈肘上挂至右耳侧。（图3-4-83）

(1) Gunbixiaya: turn to left, gravity on the left foot, bend the left leg and squat down, keep the right knee close to the inside, turn the right arm inward and split it to the back of right side, the left palm and elbow up to the right ear. (Fig. 3-4-83)

（2）翻腰：右脚向后落步并右转身；同时右臂向前经上向后抡劈，左臂紧跟其后抡劈，（图3-4-84）身体左转180°，右脚经左脚向前盖步，重心前移下蹲成右歇步，上体下伏，右掌左下劈至左胯，左掌上挂右耳侧，目视前方。（图3-4-85）

(2) Fanyao: the right foot falls backward and turns right; at the same time, the right arm swings forward, up and back, and the left arm follows the rear, (Fig. 3-4-84) the body turns 180° left, the right foot moves forward and covers the left foot, the center of gravity moves forward, the upper body falls down, the right palm splits left and down to the left hip, the left palm to the right ear side, and look ahead. (Fig. 3-4-85)

图Fig 3-4-83　　　　　图Fig 3-4-84　　　　　图Fig 3-4-85

（3）提膝截掌：重心前移到右脚，右腿直立，左腿屈膝上抬，脚背绷直；同时双掌向两侧截掌打开，右掌朝右上方，左掌朝左下方，掌心均朝前，目视前方。（图3-4-86）

(3) Tixijiezhang: move the weight forward to the right foot, keep the right leg upright, bend the left leg and lift, the two palms blow from both sides, the right palm to the upper right, the left palm to the lower left, and look ahead. (Fig. 3-4-86)

图Fig 3-4-86

动作要点：身体从右至左要贴近地面，劈掌团身含胸；提膝截掌动作稳、慢。

Key points: the body should be close to the ground from right to left; the movement of knee lifting and palm cutting should be stable and slow.

18. 撩阴掌 Liaoyinzhang

左脚向前落步成左弓步，右掌从下向前撩掌与肩平，左掌下盖迎击右小臂，目视右掌方向。（图 3-4-87）

The left foot falls forward to form a left bow step, the right palm lifts the palm from the bottom to the shoulder, the left palm hits the right forearm, and watch the right palm. (Fig. 3-4-87)

图Fig 3-4-87

动作要点：撩掌时重心下降要稳，撩掌要远。

Key points: when lifting the palm, the center of gravity down and the palm will be far away.

19. 托枪势 Tuoqiangshi

左脚回收与右脚并步，身体半蹲；同时右掌屈肘回收至身体右侧，左掌（八字掌）向前用力插出，虎口向上，目视左掌方向。（图 3-4-88）

Half squatted; at the same time, the right palm goes back to the right side, the left palm goes forward and watch the left palm.(Fig. 3-4-88)

图Fig 3-4-88

动作要点：右掌回收与左掌插出用力协调。

Key points: the forces of right palm left palm out should be in coordination.

20. 搓步插掌 Cuobuchazhang

双脚同时蹬地起跳向左转体180°震步落地，身体半蹲，同时；右掌从腰间向右用力推出，虎口向上，左掌经胸前向左侧打开，掌心朝上，目视右掌方向。（图3-4-89、图3-4-90）

Turn 180° to the left, half squat, push out the right palm from the waist to the right, the left palm goes to the left through the chest, with the palm center upward, and look at the right palm. (Fig.3-4-89,Fig.3-4-90)

图Fig 3-4-89　　　　　　　　图Fig 3-4-90

动作要点：身体跳转快速利落，右掌和左掌推收搓掌协调一致，拧腰推掌。

Key points: the body jumps quickly, the right palm and the left palm push back and forth coordinately.

第五段 Part V

21. 大跨步抄手起脚 Dakuabuchaoshouqijiao

（1）大跨步：身体微左转，右脚向左前上步，（图3-4-91）上身右转继续上左步，再上右脚；（图3-4-92）右脚向前跨一大步，左脚前脚掌催跟步，右臂立圆劈掌至身后，左臂向前下劈与肩同高，身体屈膝半蹲，力达左掌外侧，目视左掌方向。（图3-4-93）

(1) Dakuabu(big step): turn left slightly, step left and forward with the right foot, (Fig. 3-4-91) turn right the upper body, continue to step left and right; (Fig. 3-4-92) take a big step forward with the right foot, left foot following, right arm to the back, with the left arm forward and down at the same height as the shoulder, squat, and look at the left palm. (Fig. 3-4-93)

（2）抄手起脚：右脚上步并迅速起跳，左腿用力向前上摆起后屈膝，（图3-4-94）右脚向前上弹踢，脚尖勾起；同时，左掌回收再向前用掌背弹拍右脚面，目视右脚方向。

（图 3-4-95）

(2) Chaoshouqijiao: step on the right foot and take off quickly, swing the left leg forward and bend the knee. (Fig. 3-4-94) Bounce and kick the right foot forward and hook up the toe. At the same time, snap the right foot forward with the back of the left palm and watch the right foot. (Fig. 3-4-95)

图Fig 3-4-91　　　　　图Fig 3-4-92　　　　　图Fig 3-4-93

图Fig 3-4-94　　　　　图Fig 3-4-95

动作要点：①大跨步要连贯，左脚掌向前催跟步，左臂下劈并与身体屈膝半蹲一致。②起脚时，左脚上摆用力，右腿尽力屈膝上收，蹬腿有力，力达脚跟，掌背迎击脚面要准确清脆。

Key points: ① Long stride should be consistent, the left foot should be pushed forward to follow the step, the left arm should be split down and be consistent with the knee bending and half squatting. ② When starting, put the force on the left foot, bend the right leg as much as possible, kick the leg forcefully, and hit the foot with the back of the palm accurately and crisply.

22. 仆步拍掌 Pubupaizhang

左脚先落地，随后右腿向前落地内扣成右仆步，上体下压，左掌向后摆起，虎口向上，

右掌直臂向下拍地于右脚前，目视右掌方向。（图 3-4-96）

The left foot lands first, then the right leg lands forward into a right footstep, the upper body presses down, the left palm swings backward, the right palm straight in front of the right foot, and looks at the right palm. (Fig. 3-4-96)

图Fig 3-4-96

动作要点：落地成仆步时，上体迅速下压，拍掌下劈有力。

Key points: when landing into a footstep, the upper body should press down quickly, clap and chop powerfully.

23. 翻身单劈手 Fanshendanpishou

（1）翻身劈掌：上动不停，借助仆步拍掌顺势上弹，上体抬起，重心后移左脚，右脚屈膝上提，（图 3-4-97）以左脚掌为轴，身体向右后翻转180°，右脚落步，成开立步；同时，右掌随翻身向下劈打，左掌随之向下。（图 3-4-98）

(1) Fanshenpizhang: Spring up, move the center of gravity backward to the left foot, bend the right foot to the knee and lift up, (Fig. 3-4-97) take the left foot as the axis, turn backward 180° to the right, and then the right foot falls; the right palm chops down, and then the left palm follows. (Fig. 3-4-98)

图Fig 3-4-97　　　　图Fig 3-4-98

（2）单劈手：接上动，左掌向前立圆抡劈，右腿支撑，左腿向前弹踢，与腰同高，（图 3-4-99）以右脚掌为轴，右转体180°，带动左腿屈膝随转，左脚扣于右膝窝，左臂裹肩下收，左手勾尖向上，右掌收于左耳侧，（图 3-4-100）右脚向左后垫跳一步，随即左脚向后落步，紧接着上体左后转 180°成左弓步，右臂随转身抡劈至左膝外侧，左臂屈肘上挂至右耳侧，指尖向上，目视劈手方向。（图 3-4-101）

(2) Danpishou: The left palm chops in vertical round, the left leg forward with the same height as the waist, (Fig. 3-4-99) take the right foot as the axis, turn 180° to the right, the left leg bend follows the left arm around the shoulder and close the left hook tip up, and the right palm to the left ear side, (Fig. 3-4-100) the right foot jumps to the left and back, the left foot backward and turn the upper body back 180° to form a left bow step, swing the right arm to the outside of the left knee, bend the elbow of the left arm and to the right ear side, with the fingertip upward, and look at the left hand. (Fig. 3-4-101)

图Fig 3-4-99　　　　　图Fig 3-4-100　　　　　图Fig 3-4-101

动作要点：垫跳步小巧快速，垫跳与身体右转协调一致；抡臂要借用收腹含胸力量，力达掌和前臂。

Key points: jump in small and fast steps, coordinated with the right turn of the body; arm swing should use the strength of abdomen.

24. **进步扬掌** Jinbuyangzhang

（1）反手劈掌：重心上提，右后转身 180°，右脚随转身向左脚收回并步，右臂后抡劈掌收至腰间，左掌紧随下劈盖掌，虎口向下，目视左掌。（图 3-4-102）

(1) Fanshoupizhang: lift the center of gravity, turn 180° to the right back, take the right foot back to the left foot along with the turning, swing the right arm back to the waist, follow the left palm with the lower splitting, and look at the left palm. (Fig. 3-4-102)

（2）进步扬掌：右脚向前上步，左脚随即向右脚并步，身体半蹲，右掌向前推出，与肩同高，左掌屈肘收至右肩前，掌心朝右，目视右掌。（图 3-4-103-1、图 3-4-103-2）

(2) Jinbuyangzhang: the right foot moves forward, the left foot immediately moves to the

right foot, half squat, the right palm pushes forward, with the same height as the shoulder, the left palm bends, the elbow to the front of the right shoulder, the palm facing right, and look at the right palm. (Fig. 3-4-103-1, Fig. 3-4-103-2)

图Fig 3-4-102   图Fig 3-4-103-1   图Fig 3-4-103-2

动作要点：翻身以肩带臂抢劈，推掌紧随进步发力，力达掌根。

Key points: clip with shoulder driving the arm.

第六段 Part VI

25. 双滚臂劈手 Shuanggunbipishou

（1）右滚臂：重心上提，两臂向两侧平举，掌心向上，（图3-4-104）右脚右跨半步，上身右转下蹲成跪膝步，带动左臂直臂内旋并向下劈至左侧，右掌屈肘回收上挂左耳侧。（图3-4-105）

(1) Right Gunbi: lift the center of gravity, both arms horizontally to both sides, palm heart up, (Fig. 3-4-104) step the right foot right half step, turn the upper body right and squat down, the left arm rotates straight inside and splits down to the left, the right palm bends, the elbow to the left ear side. (Fig. 3-4-105)

图Fig 3-4-104   图Fig 3-4-105

（2）左滚臂劈掌：左脚向后撤步，身体左转180°，两臂随转身立圆向前抢劈，（图3-4-106）左腿支撑，右脚向前弹踢，（图3-4-107）身体急速左后转身，重心下压团身成裹肩滚臂，右脚扣于左膝窝，右臂内旋直臂下劈至右侧，左臂屈肘上挂贴于右耳侧，（图3-4-108）右脚向后落步，上体右转，两掌随转身立圆抢劈，（图3-4-109）重心前倾，左臂下抢劈至右膝外侧，右掌上挂至左耳侧，指尖朝上，目视劈手方向。（图3-4-110）

(2) Left Gunbipizhang: step backward with the left foot, turn left 180°, swing forward with the two arms in vertical circle, (Fig. 3-4-106) spring and kick with the right foot forward, (Fig. 3-4-107) turn left and back rapidly with the center of gravity down and roll the arm, the right foot to the left knee socket, turn the right arm inward and straight to the right, the left arm on the elbow and to the right ear, (Fig. 3-4-108) right foot backward, turn upper body to the right, turn palms around and make a circle swing. (Fig. 3-4-109) Lean forward, swing the left arm down to the outside of the right knee, right palm up to the left ear, and watch the direction of the splitting. (Fig. 3-4-110)

图Fig 3-4-106　　　图Fig 3-4-107　　　图Fig 3-4-108

图Fig 3-4-109　　　图Fig 3-4-110

动作要点：抢劈时身体要展开，提膝转身时右肩用力内扣，含胸收腹。

Key points: swinging with the body extended. When lifting the knee and turn around, the right shoulder and the chest should be closed.

26. 倒发五雷 Daofawulei

（1）右劈拳：重心上提，左后转身180°，左脚提起外展震脚落步，右脚向前勾踢，重心落于左脚，右脚跟落地，右掌变瓦楞拳立圆从上向左下砸劈至左胯外侧，左掌上挂贴于右耳侧，目视前方。（图3-4-111-1、图3-4-111-2）

(1) Right Piquan: gravity up, turn 180° left back, lift the left foot and step down, hook kick the right foot forward, the right foot heel falls to the ground, the right palm becomes the vertical circle, and smash and split from top to bottom outside the left hip, the left palm to the right ear side, and look ahead. (Fig. 3-4-111-1, Fig. 3-4-111-2)

图Fig 3-4-111-1　　　图Fig 3-4-111-2

（2）左劈拳：重心移至右脚，左脚向前上步，身体右后转180°，（图3-4-112）右脚提起外展拧转，左掌向上抡劈，（图3-4-113）右脚震脚落步，左脚向前勾踢，左脚跟落地，左掌变瓦楞拳向右胯侧下砸劈，右拳变掌上挂左耳侧，目视前方。（图3-4-114-1、图3-4-114-2）

(2) Left Piquan: move gravity to the right foot, step forward on the left foot, turn right back 180°, (Fig. 3-4-112) lift the right foot and twist it outwards, swing the left palm upward, (Fig. 3-4-113) shake the right foot and step down, hook kick the left foot forward, smash and chop the right side with the left palm to the left ear and look ahead. (Fig. 3-4-114-1, Fig. 3-4-114-2)

图Fig 3-4-112　　　图Fig 3-4-113

图Fig 3-4-114-1　　　图Fig 3-4-114-2

动作要点：步法要连贯快速，翻转身迅猛，震脚沉实，左拳下劈与右脚退步一致，同时含胸收腹，转胯发力，力达拳背小指侧。

Key points: the steps should be consistent, turning and shaking should be fast, stamping should be solid. The chest and abdomen should be enclosed, the crotch should be tight, and the force should reach the small finger side.

27. 眼望三见手 Yanwangsanxianshou

（1）勾踢抄拳：右掌变拳向右下落至右胯侧，重心前移左脚，右脚向前勾踢；同时，右拳向前上挑拳，与胸同高，左拳变掌下拦右臂，右拳拳眼向上。（图3-4-115）

(1) Goutichaoquan: the right fist falls to the right crotch side, the gravity moves forward to the left foot, and the right foot hook kick; at the same time, the right fist moves forward and up to the chest, the left palm and down to block the right arm, and the right fist eye upward. (Fig. 3-4-115)

图Fig 3-4-115

（2）马步连环手：重心前移右脚落步，左腿提膝，右拳变掌由下向前上掀掌，右掌心向下。（图3-4-116）紧接着左掌和右掌再次向前连环掀掌，掌心均朝下，（图3-4-117、图3-4-118）左脚向前落步，重心下蹲成半马步，右掌掀掌收至身体右侧，左掌向前推掌，与肩同高，力达掌根，目视前方。（图3-4-119）

(2) Mabulianhuanshou: move the weight forward, lift the left knee, lift the right fist from the bottom to the front, with the right palm downward. (Fig. 3-4-116) The left palm and the right palm push forward.(Fig. 3-4-117 and Fig. 3-4-118) The left foot forward, squatted into a half horse step, the right palm is lifted to the right side of the body, the left palm is pushed forward to the shoulder, and look ahead. (Fig. 3-4-119)

图Fig 3-4-116　　　　　图Fig 3-4-117　　　　　图Fig 3-4-118

图Fig 3-4-119

动作要点：右挑拳与右勾踢一致，两掌挑掀掌连环紧密；推掌拧腰送肘。

Key points: The right fist is the same as the right foot hook kick, and two palms moves are closely linked

28. 斜飞势 Xiefeishi

重心后移至右脚，右腿直立，左腿屈膝上提，左掌外旋向上震肩托掌，掌心向上，右掌向下劈按掌，目视左掌方向。（图 3-4-120）

Move the gravity back to the right foot, with the right leg standing upright, the left leg bending and lifting, the left palm turning outward to shake the shoulder, the palm center up, and the right palm splitting downward, and watch the left palm. (Fig. 3-4-120)

图Fig 3-4-120

动作要点：提膝迅猛，左托掌与右劈掌前后螺旋发力。

Key points: the knee is lifted rapidly, the left supporting palm and the right splitting palm are spiraling before and after.

29. 跳步拽拳 Tiaobuzhuaiquan

左脚向前落步同时踏跳，右脚向前落步，（图3-4-121）身体稍左转，左脚经右脚后插步下蹲成右歇步，右掌变拳从后经耳侧向前下内旋腕冲拳，拳眼向下，左臂屈肘上挂贴于右耳侧，目视右拳方向。（图3-4-122）

Step forward with the left foot and the right foot, (Fig. 3-4-121) turn slightly to the left, squat with the left foot behind the right foot to form a cross-legged crouch stance, turn the right palm into a fist from the back through the ear side, rotate the wrist forward and punch with the fist eye downward, the left elbow to the right ear side, and look at the right fist. (Fig. 3-4-122)

图Fig 3-4-121　　　图Fig 3-4-122

动作要点：左脚起跳腾空要远，歇步下沉要快，右拳翻腕冲出迅速。

Key points: take off as far as possible, squat quickly.

30. 扣腿刁手 Koutuidiaoshou

重心上提直立迅速左后转身180°，右拳变刁手随转体向向左上刁劈，左掌随转身上挂与右腕迎击；右腿屈膝紧扣在左膝窝，目视刁手方向。（图3-4-123）

Turn 180° left back quickly, the right hook hand goes up and left. The left palm hits the right wrist with the turn. The right leg is bent and tightly in the left knee socket, and watch the hook hand. (Fig. 3-4-123)

图Fig 3-4-123

动作要点：转体迅猛，刁手随转身立圆一圈从下向左上刁打，左掌迎击准确，含胸，重心左倾。

Key points: turn fast, hook hand turns around and makes a circle from bottom to top, with the left palm hitting accurately.

31. 双劈掌 Shuangpizhang

右脚右跨步成右弓步，双手变掌从上向两侧下劈，掌心朝上，力达掌背，劈至两大腿外侧，目视右侧方向。（图3-4-124）

Step the right foot into a right bow step, both palms chop from top to both sides, with palms hearts facing up, and look at the right side. (Fig. 3-4-124)

动作要点：右腿落步与双掌下劈同时，上下力量完整统一。

Key points: the right leg step and the two palms punch down at the same time.

图Fig 3-4-124

32. 仆步穿掌 Pubuchuanzhang

（1）扣腿刁手：重心移至左脚，左腿直立，右脚继续紧扣左膝窝，右掌变刁手再次随转体向左上刁劈与左掌迎击，目视刁手方向。（图 3-4-125）

(1) Koutuidiaoshou: move the center of gravity to the left foot, keep the left leg upright, keep the right foot close to the left knee socket, change the right palm to hook hand, turning body, split to the left and hit the left palm, and watch the hook hand. (Fig. 3-4-125)

（2）仆步穿掌：右脚向右铲出内扣，左腿下蹲成右仆步，右手变掌向右腿上穿出，左掌打开，目视右掌方向。（图 3-4-126）

(2) Pubuchuanzhang: shovel right the right foot, squat on the left leg to form a right bow step, the right palm passes through the right leg, and watch the right palm. (Fig. 3-4-126)

图Fig 3-4-125　　图Fig 3-4-126

动作要点：仆步穿掌下沉身体，上体前伏抬头。

Key points: Gravity is down. Upper body bows with head up.

33. 托枪势 Tuoqiangshi

右掌继续前穿，重心前移至右脚并右转身 90°，左脚向右脚并步震脚；同时右掌微屈肘回收至身体右侧，左掌向前插掌，虎口向上，与肩同高，目视左掌方向。（图 3-4-127）

The right palm goes forward with the gravity on the right foot, turn right 90°, move the left foot to the right and stamp; slightly bend the elbow of the right palm back to the right side of the body, insert the left palm forward, the same height as the shoulder, and look at the left palm. (Fig. 3-4-127)

图Fig 3-4-127

动作要点：右掌屈肘回收与左掌前插用力协调。

Key points: the right palm bending to the elbow and the left palm inserting in front are coordinate.

34. 虚步推掌 Xubutuizhang

左脚向左前上步，身体微左转，右臂向左平摆，掌心向下，左掌向右臂下穿掌，（图3-4-128）身体继续左转，右脚紧随转身向左落步内扣，两臂随转身向左平摆掌，右掌摆至左肩下落收于右腰间，左掌向左摆至脑后裹脑从右肩下落，（图3-4-129）身体继续左转，左脚向前落步并下蹲成左虚步，左掌收于腰间抱掌，掌心向上，右掌上提从右肩向前推掌，掌心朝外，目视左侧。（图3-4-130）

The left foot steps forward to the left, the body turns slightly to the left, the right arm swings to the left, the left palm passes under the right arm, (Fig. 3-4-128) the body turns left, the right foot follows the left step and snaps inward, the two arms follow the turn to the left, the right palm swings to the left shoulder back to the right waist, the left palm swings to the back of the head, (Fig. 3-4-129) the body continues to turn left, and the left foot moves forward and squat into a left empty step. The left palm to the waist, the right palm forward, look at the left side. (Fig. 3-4-130)

图Fig 3-4-128

图Fig 3-4-129

图Fig 3-4-130

动作要点：左转身一周，转身圆滑迅速，左右臂穿掌要协调，推掌力达掌侧。

Key points: the turning be smoothly and quickly, both left and right arms go coordinately.

35. 收势 Ending up

（1）盖步穿掌：上体微左转，左脚向右前盖步，右掌回收至腰间与左掌同时向前穿出，与肩同高，掌心向上，目视穿掌方向。（图3-4-131）

(1) Gaibuchuanzhang: turn the upper body slightly to the left, the left foot to step right

forward, the right palm back to the waist and goes forward with the left palm, with the same height as the shoulder, the palm center upward, and watch the palms. (Fig. 3-4-131)

图Fig 3-4-131

（2）并步按掌：右脚向右后撤步，两掌回收从两侧上举，（图3-4-132）左脚向右脚并步，重心半蹲，两掌掌心相对，（图3-4-133）两掌屈腕下按至腹前，重心徐徐上提直立，掌心向下，目视前方，还原立正姿势。（图3-4-134）

(2) Bingbuanzhang: the right foot moves backward to the right, and the two palms are lifted up from both sides, (Fig. 3-4-132) the left foot moves towards the right foot in parallel, half squatting, facing each other, (Fig. 3-4-133) the two palms bend down to the front of the abdomen, the center of gravity is slowly lifted up and upright, and restore to the upright posture. (Fig. 3-4-134)

图Fig 3-4-132　　　图Fig 3-4-133　　　图Fig 3-4-134

动作要点：肢体放松、圆滑、动作慢，眼要有神。

Key points: The limbs should be relaxed. The moves should be smooth and slow, and the eyes should be alert.

第五节 华 拳
3.5 Hua Quan

一、华拳简介 Introduction

华拳是中国传统拳术之一，属于长拳类拳种，讲究"三华贯一"，"三华"是指精、气、神，华拳因而得名。华拳的内容有徒手、器械、单练、对练，其动作姿势舒展、工整，要求力贯股肱，动作强劲有力。华拳的运动节奏表现为"动如奔獭"之急，"静如潜鱼"之悠，"心肃神凝"，"心凝精劲"，"心正而后身正"。近现代流行于山东、河南、河北、江苏、浙江、上海等地。1~12路华拳是其中具有代表性的拳术套路，以及刀、枪、剑、棍、对练套路，华拳既可单人习练，又能双人对练。

Hua Quan is one of the traditional Chinese Quan types, which belongs to the category of Chang Quan School. Hua means essence, Hua Quan means the unity of three essences (Jing, Qi and Shen, which are the inner spirits) in it. Its content includes unarmed, armed, single and double practices. Its moves or postures are open, neat, and powerful. The movement rhythm of Hua Quan is characterized by "dynamic like a running lion" and "static like a diving fish". It prefers the tranquility of the heart and the mind. It believes that the fair mind is the precondition of the strong body. Hua Quan is popular in Shandong, Henan, Hebei, Jiangsu, Zhejiang, Shanghai and other places. Among them, 1-12 sets of Hua Quan and some armed double fighting sets are typical.

二、华拳技术特点 Technical characteristics

（1）势正招圆，结构严谨 Vigorous posture

拳势要求左右对称，不歪不斜，不散不乱，拳势形体工整、匀称。

The posture should be symmetrical.

（2）动紧身整，一气贯通 Moves are connected by Qi.

华拳技术要求做到"招连招，势接势，步套步。""形断意连，势断气连"，技法运用内在的心志活动和眼神把前后动作的意向连接起来，使之势势相连，贯串一气。拳势运用"撑、拔、张、展、钩、扣、翘、相、蹦、顶、塌、收、沉"等表现"五体"

（躯干、上肢、下肢）的强壮，整体动作雄健浑厚，以"提、托、聚、沉"来调节呼吸，使之气顺劲整。

Hua Quan's techniques lie in the connecting of the moves by "Qi". It seems that the moves are separated but in fact they are the whole one with the continuous "Qi" as the soul and heart of the Quan. "Proping, pulling, stretching, unfolding, hooking, clasping, warping, pressing, jumping, topping, collapsing, retracting and sinking" are the main acts used to show the strength of the body. The whole movement is vigorous and thick. "Lifting, holding, gathering and sinking" are the actions to adjust breath and make the Qi smooth and vigorous.

（3）动迅静定，进疾退速 Dynamic and static moves

要求动则骤发，如风卷残云；静则突停，似平波镜湖；有招有势，"势为守，属阴，主静，招为攻，属阳，主动"。拳法要"进如风雨，退若山岳"，动迅静定，有节有序。

When it is required to move, it will suddenly appear, like the wind rolling residual clouds; when it is still, it will suddenly stop, like a flat lake; when it has a move, it has a potential,"when it has a move, it is defensive, it belongs to Yin, and when it is static, it belongs to attack, it belongs to Yang, and it is active". The fist technique should be "like wind and rain in advance, like mountains in retreat". It should move fast, be calm and orderly.

（4）刚柔相济，虚实分明 Hard and soft combination

行拳要求有刚有柔，能快能慢、伸缩张弛，抑扬顿挫均应在套路中合理运用。强调矛盾的双方要相辅相成，认为只有使"阴阳二气"协调起来，才能产生"神"的功用，在技法运动中十分注意对动静、虚实、刚柔、快慢、伸缩、张弛、抑扬、顿挫、轻重、起伏、内外、上下、正偏、左右等对立因素的掌握。

All the moves need to be rigid and soft, fast and slow, stretching and relaxation. It is emphasized that the two sides of the contradiction should complement each other. It is believed that only when the "Yin and Yang" are coordinated, can the function of "spirit" be produced. In the technical movement, great attention should be paid to the mastery of the opposite factors.

华拳歌（谱）诀

皓月当空双拆拳，丹凤朝阳展翅翩；
二郎担山赶日月，鱼跃龙门朝前穿；
二郎担山一条鞭，浪子蹴球踢下边；

白猿偷桃回头望，金丝裹腕翻身缠；
飞天卧佛落尘埃，万钧弩发飞天边；
铁椎击秦朝前打，托梁换柱弓步拳；
两手托印分左右，苍龙摆尾出海来；
行步云手飞双脚，叶底藏桃下压肘；
飞天卧佛落尘埃，倒卷银席贴地翻；
单风贯耳腮边击，鱼跃龙门纵身过；
连环炮打迎面拳，野马跳槽迎面打；
单掌推碑力无穷，二龙斗宝双戏珠；
风卷霹雳上九天，英雄打虎收招势。

三、华拳动作图解 Movement illustration

第一段 Part I

1. **虚步亮掌 Xubuliangzhang**

（1）预备式：并步直立，两臂垂于体侧，两手成掌型，掌心向内，贴于腿侧，凝气聚神，目视前方。（图 3-5-1）

(1) Ready: stand upright with arms hanging on the side of the body, palms close to the leg side, gather Qi and spirit, and look ahead. (Fig. 3-5-1)

图Fig 3-5-1　　　　　图Fig 3-5-2　　　　　图Fig 3-5-3

（2）虚步亮掌：右掌从右侧向上弧线直臂上举，（图3-5-2）右掌外旋，掌心向右，屈肘从左肩前下降,（图3-5-3）右掌落于左腋前，左掌经右臂上向上直臂穿掌，掌心向右，（图3-5-4）右手从左腋前向右下摆掌，（图3-5-5）右掌向上至头顶，屈肘屈腕架掌，掌心朝前，左手从左上向下、向身后直臂绕环，至身后时成勾手，勾尖向上；两腿屈

膝半蹲，右腿支撑，左脚向前伸半步脚尖点地，成左虚步，目视左侧。（图 3-5-6）

(2) Xubuliangzhang: raise the right palm from the right side upward in an arc,(Fig. 3-5-2) rotate the right palm outward, palm center to the right, bend elbow to lower down from the left shoulder, (Fig. 3-5-3) lower the right palm in front of the left armpit, the left palm through the right arm upward straight, palm center to the right, (Fig. 3-5-4) lower the right hand from the left armpit forward, palm center to the front, (Fig. 3-5-5) the left hand circles from the top left to the bottom and straight to the back. the left hand forms a hook, with the hook point upward; the two legs bend and squat on the right leg, the left foot extends forward half a step, and the foot points to the ground, forming a left empty step. Look at the left side. (Fig. 3-5-6)

图Fig 3-5-4

图Fig 3-5-5

图Fig 3-5-6

动作要点：①左右臂上下回环动作连贯，肩膀放松，协调一致。②双臂绕环动作中眼随右手而动；横亮掌时，甩腕抖掌。③虚步虚实分明，右腿半蹲，左脚绷平；挺胸、拔背、塌腰。

Key points: ① the left and right arms are consistent, the shoulders are relaxed and coordinated. ② The eyes move with the right hand in the circular movement of both arms; when the palm is horizontal, the wrist and shake the palm. ③ The empty steps are clear, the right leg is half squatted, the left foot is flat; the chest is straight.

2. 双勾手 Double hook hand

重心上提，右腿直立，左脚向右脚并步，左勾手不动，右掌变勾手向下、向身后反臂斜举，勾尖向上，目视左侧。(图 3-5-7)

Lift the gravity, keep the right leg upright, move the left foot to the right, keep the left hook still, turn the right palm to hook hand down, lift the back arm obliquely behind, hook tip up, and look at the left side. (Fig. 3-5-7)

动作要点：挺胸、拔背，直腰，两肩松沉后张，屈腕，肘直，两臂尽量向上反举。

Key points: chest and back up, waist straight, shoulders loose and backward, wrist bent, elbow straight, arms up and backward.

图Fig 3-5-7

3. 对握拳 Duiwoquan

两勾手变拳，从左右两侧向胸前屈肘环抱，肘平举，拳心向下，拳面相对，目视左侧。（图 3-5-8）

Turn two hook hands into fists, bend elbows from left and right sides to the chest, lift elbows horizontally, and look at the left side. (Fig. 3-5-8)

图Fig 3-5-8　　　　图Fig 3-5-9

动作要点：两拳握紧，拳腕平，两肩松沉，两脚并拢，膝挺直。

Key points: two fists are clenched tightly, the fist wrist is flat, the shoulders are loose and down, the feet are close together, and the knees are straight.

4. 左右撑拳 Left and Right Chengquan

两拳从胸前向左右冲崩伸直，拳眼向上，目视右拳。（图 3-5-9）

Two fists go from the chest to the left and right straight, fist eye up, and look at the right fist. (Fig. 3-5-9)

动作要点：两拳快而有力，肘、腕伸平，拳稍高过肩。

Key points: the two fists are fast and powerful, the elbows and wrists are extended flat, and the fist is slightly higher than the shoulder.

5. 左右双冲拳 Left and right Chongquan

（1）左弓步冲拳：右脚不动，左脚向左开步，两腿屈膝半蹲成马步，两拳从两侧收于腰间，拳心向上，（图 3-5-10）上体左转，左脚尖外展，右脚跟外转，左腿屈膝前弓成左弓步；同时，两拳向前冲拳，与肩同高、同宽，拳眼向上，目视两拳。（图 3-5-11）

(1) Left bow step Chongquan: the right foot does not move, the left foot moves to the left, the two legs bend to the knees and squat to form a horse stance, the two punches close to the waist from both sides, the heart of the punch is upward, (Fig. 3-5-10) the upper body turns left, the left foot tip extends outward, the right foot turns outward, and the left leg bends to form a left bow step; at the same time, and the eyes on the two punches. (Fig. 3-5-11)

（2）右弓步冲拳：上身右转，两腿屈膝半蹲成马步，两拳随转身收于腰间，拳心向上，紧接着右脚尖外展，左脚跟外转，右腿屈膝前弓成右弓步；同时，两拳向前平冲拳，与肩同高、同宽，拳眼向上，目视两拳。（图 3-5-12）

(2) Right bow step Chongquan: turn the upper body to the right, bend knees and half squat to form a horse stance, two palms to the waist, the right foot tip is abducted, the left foot is turned outward, and the right leg is bent to form a right bow step; the two palms are forward with the same height and width as the shoulder, and watch the two palms. (Fig. 3-5-12)

图Fig 3-5-10　　　　　图Fig 3-5-11　　　　　图Fig 3-5-12

动作要点：马步大腿要平，脚尖里扣，两膝外展，两肩松沉，两肘向后夹紧。

Key points: the legs should be flat, the toes should be inside, the knees should be outstretched, the shoulders should be loose, and the elbows should be tight.

6. 挑拳马步架打 Tiaoquanmabujiada

（1）弓步摆拳：左臂外旋，从前向下、向后直臂弧形绕环，至身后时左拳拳眼向上，目视右拳。(图 3-5-13)

(1) Gongbubaiquan: rotate the left arm outwards, straight the arm from the front to the back in an arc. The left fist eye is upward, and watch the right fist. (Fig. 3-5-13)

（2）挑拳马步架打：身体左转，重心移至左脚，左转成左弓步，左臂外旋屈肘收于右肩前，右拳同时从身后向下、向前直臂弧形撩摆拳，拳心向上，（图 3-5-14）紧接着，重心后移，上体右转，左脚尖里扣，两膝半蹲成马步，右臂内旋屈肘向上横架拳，左拳向左冲拳，拳眼向上，目视左拳。(图 3-5-15)

(2) Tiaoquanmabujiada: turn to the left, move gravity to the left foot to form the left bow stance, turn the left arm outward and bend the elbow in front of the right shoulder, swing the right fist downward and forward in an arc, (Fig. 3-5-14) move the gravity backward, turn the upper body to the right, left foot tip inward, squat in the horse stance, turn the right arm inward and bend the elbow to block, and punch the left fist to the left, watch the left fist. (Fig. 3-5-15)

图Fig 3-5-13　　　　　图Fig 3-5-14　　　　　图Fig 3-5-15

动作要点：马步屈膝坐平，脚尖里扣，两膝外展，挺胸、直背，左拳腕要直。

Key points: sit flat with knees bent in horse stance, outstretched knees, chest, back, left fist and wrist straight.

7. 虚步挑掌 Xubutiaozhang

（1）弓步挑掌：上身左转，重心前移成左弓步，同时左拳变掌向前平推，掌指向上，右拳变掌屈肘下落至左肘内侧，掌指向上，目视左掌。(图 3-5-16)

(1) Gongbutiaozhang: turn the upper body to the left, move the center of gravity forward to the left lunge, at the same time, change the palm of the left fist to push forward, change the

palm of the right fist to bend the elbow and fall to the inside of the left elbow, and look at the left palm. (Fig. 3-5-16)

（2）虚步挑掌：接上动，左脚跟微向外转，左腿全蹲，右腿伸直成右仆步，左臂内旋，掌指向下，右臂外旋，掌指侧斜向下，两掌同时从前向下、向右脚穿掌，（图3-5-17）至右脚上方时，两掌指向上，重心上提，右腿直立，左脚向右收半步，两掌继续向上绕环穿掌，（图3-5-18）右脚跟外展，上身左转，右腿屈膝半蹲，左腿屈膝半蹲脚尖虚点地成左虚步，两掌同时从上向身前绕环摆动，左掌刁手成勾手，与肩同高，右掌指向上成立掌屈肘附于左肘内侧，目视前方。（图3-5-19）

(2)Xubutiaozhang: turn the left heel outward slightly, squat the left leg, straighten the right leg, rotate the left arm inward, turn the finger downward, turn the right arm outward, and two palms go through from the front down to the right foot. (Fig. 3-5-17) Over the right foot, the two palms go upward, gravity lift, the right leg upright, the left foot goes half step to the right, and two palms swing upward, (Fig. 3-5-18) with the right heel outspread, the upper body turns left, the right leg bent and left leg half squatted, the two palms swing from the top to the front of the body, the two palms bent and the left hook as high as the shoulder, the right palm attaching to the inside of the left elbow, and watch forward. (Fig. 3-5-19)

图Fig 3-5-16　　　　　　图Fig 3-5-17

图Fig 3-5-18　　　　　　图Fig 3-5-19

动作要点：①两掌穿绕时肩关节放松，快速，身法与眼及两掌协调一致。②虚步分明，上身挺胸、拔背、塌腰。

Key points : ① The shoulder joints are relaxed and loose when the two palms are going through, and the eyes should go with the arms moving. ② The empty steps are clear, the upper body is straight, the back is pulled out, and the waist is loose.

8. 跃步双摆掌 Yuebushuangbaizhang

（1）独立挑掌：右腿直立，左腿屈膝上提，脚背绷直，两掌挑掌不变，目视左掌。（图 3-5-20）

(1) Single Tiaozhang: the right leg is upright, the left leg lifted with knee bent , the instep is straight, the two palms are the same, and watch the left palm. (Fig. 3-5-20)

（2）跃步双摆掌：左脚向前落步，重心前移，（图 3-5-21）左脚蹬地跳起，右脚向前跃进，左臂内旋，右臂外旋，两掌从前向下、由右后直臂弧形摆动，（图 3-5-22）右脚先落地，左脚随之向前落地，左腿屈膝半蹲成左弓步，两掌从后向上、向前直臂摆动，两掌屈腕成侧立掌，左掌与肩同高，右掌屈肘附于左肘内侧，目视左掌。（图 3-5-23）

(2) Yuebushuangbaizhang: step forward with the left foot and move the weight forward, (Fig. 3-5-21) The left foot kicks up, the right foot jumps forward, the left arm rotates inward, the right arm rotates outward, and the two palms swing in an arc from the front down to the right back, (Fig. 3-5-22) the right foot lands first, the left foot lands forward, the left leg bends the knee and squats half to form a left bow step, the two palms swing from the back up to the front, the two palms bend the wrist to form a side standing palm, the left palm is the same height as the shoulder, the right palm bends the elbow to attach to the inside of the left elbow, and watch the left palm.(Fig.3-5-23)

图Fig 3-5-20

图Fig 3-5-21

图Fig 3-5-22   图Fig 3-5-23

动作要点：提膝独立时右腿挺膝伸直，站立稳固；两臂绕环应与步法配合协调。

Key points: straighten the right leg and stand steadily when lifting the knee; the two arms' moving should be coordinated with the steps.

9. **弓步穿掌** Gongbuchuanzhang

图Fig 3-5-24   图Fig 3-5-25

接上动，左掌微向后移，右掌直腕由左掌背上向前穿出，掌指向前，拇指侧朝上，（图 3-5-24）左掌直腕从胸前向后方直臂平伸，拇指侧向上，目视右掌。（图 3-5-25）

Follow the above movement, move the left palm back slightly, put the right palm straight wrist forward from the left palm back, palm finger forward, (Fig. 3-5-24) the left palm straight wrist extends horizontally from the chest to the back, thumb up, and look at the right palm. (Fig. 3-5-25)

动作要点：两掌前后平穿同时完成，两掌微高过肩。

Key points: the two palms should go at the same time, and the two palms should be slightly higher than the shoulders.

10. **左右弓步架推掌** Left and right Gongbujiatuizhang

（1）独立架掌：重心后移至右腿，左腿屈膝上提，左脚向右绊踢，右臂内旋向左

胯前按掌，左臂内旋从身后直臂向下、屈肘向右前方弧形绕环上挑，指尖向上，目视左脚。（图 3-5-26）

(1) Single Jiazhang: move the gravity back to the right leg, bend the left leg and lift it up, move the left foot to the right, turn the right arm inward and press the palm before the left crotch, turn the left arm inward from behind and straight arm downward, bend the elbow to the right and front and circle it up, fingertip up, and look at the left foot. (Fig. 3-5-26)

图Fig 3-5-26　　　　　　图Fig 3-5-27　　　　　　图Fig 3-5-28

（2）右弓步推掌：左脚向右前方落步，右掌外旋从左胯向右下摆动，（图 3-5-27）身体左转，右掌立圆向左上弧形绕环摆动，左掌向下直臂弧形绕环屈肘收于左腰侧，掌心向上，左脚站立，右腿屈膝提起，（图 3-5-28）右脚向右前方落步，脚尖里扣，右腿伸直，左腿屈膝半蹲，上体左转，右掌从上向下按掌，掌心向下，目视右掌。（图 3-5-29）左掌向左上穿掌，上体右转，左腿屈膝全蹲成右仆步，右肘下垂，臂外旋掌心向上，从胸前向下、向右脚处直臂弧形绕环摆动，（图 3-5-30）右掌至右脚处外旋拇指外侧向上，上体前移，右腿屈膝半蹲，左腿蹬直成右弓步，右掌向上屈肘横架，掌心向上，左掌经左腰侧向前推掌，掌指向上，目视左掌。（图 3-5-31）

(2) Right Gongbutuizhang: the left foot goes forward to the right, the right palm rotates outwards from the left hip to the right and swings downward, (Fig. 3-5-27) the body turns left, the right palm stands round and swings upward to the left in an arc, the left palm is straight downward, the arm is curved and bent around the elbow to the left waist, the palm center is upward, the left foot stands, the right leg is bent and lifted to the left, (Fig.3-5-28) the right foot falls forward to the right, the toe is buttoned inside, the right leg is extended and the left heel is extended Turn in, bend your left leg and squat, turn your upper body left, press your right palm from top to bottom, palm center down, and look at your right palm. (Fig.3-5-29) Put the left palm on the left, turn the upper body to the right, squat the left knee to form a right

footstep, drop the right elbow, turn the palm out of the arm and swing it in an arc from the front of the chest to the right foot, (Fig.3-5-30) turn the right palm to the outside of the right thumb, move the upper body forward, bend the right knee to form a half squat, push the left leg to form a right lunge, turn the right palm up to form an elbow crossbar, turn the palm up, and turn the left palm through the left waist Push the palm forward, point it up, and look at the left palm. (Fig. 3-5-31)

图Fig 3-5-29　　　　　　图Fig 3-5-30　　　　　　图Fig 3-5-31

（3）独立架掌：重心后移至左腿，右掌向左前方弧形绕环上挑，指尖向上，左掌内旋向右胯前按掌，右腿屈膝，右脚向左前方摆踢落步，(图 3-5-32)，右脚向左前落步，重心前移，右腿直立，左腿屈膝提起，左掌直臂向上抄起，右掌向身后直臂绕环下收至腰间，掌心向上，目视前方。(图 3-5-33)

(3) Single Jiazhang: move the weight back to the left leg, turn the right palm to the left and forward in an arc, turn the fingertip upward, turn the left palm inward to the right and press the palm in front of the crotch, bend the right leg to the knee, and swing the right foot to the left and forward to kick and fall, (Fig. 3-5-32) move the right foot to the left and forward, move the weight forward, stand the right leg upright, bend the left leg to lift the knee, lift the left palm from the straight arm up, and turn the right palm to the straight arm behind and circle downward to the waist, look ahead. (Fig.3-5-33)

图Fig 3-5-32　　　　　　图Fig 3-5-33

（4）左弓步推掌：左脚向左前方落步，脚尖里扣，左腿伸直，右腿屈膝半蹲，上身同时右转，左掌从上向右上屈腕按掌，右掌收至腰间，目视左掌，(图 3-5-34) 右掌向右上穿掌，上体左转，右腿屈膝全蹲成左仆步，左肘下垂，臂外旋使掌心向上，从胸前向下、向左脚处直臂弧形绕环摆动，(图 3-5-35) 重心前移，左腿屈膝半蹲，右腿蹬直成左弓步，左掌向上屈肘横架，掌心向上，右掌经腰侧向前推掌，掌指向上，目视右掌。(图 3-5-36)

(4) Left Gongbutuizhang: step left forward, buckle in the toe, straighten the left leg, turn in the heel of the right foot, bend the knee and squat on the right leg, turn the upper body right at the same time, bend the left palm from the top to the right, press the wrist, and close the right palm to the waist, and look at the left palm, (Fig.3-5-34) put the right palm on the right side, turn the upper body to the left, squat the right knee to form a left footstep, with the left elbow drooping, rotate the arm outward to make the palm center upward, swing the straight arm arc around from the chest to the left foot, (Fig.3-5-35) move the center of gravity forward, bend the left leg to form a half squat, push the right leg to form a left bow step, bend the elbow crossbar upward, with the palm center upward, push the right palm forward through the waist, with the palm pointing upward, and look at the right palm. (Fig.3-5-36)

图Fig 3-5-34　　　　　图Fig 3-5-35　　　　　图Fig 3-5-36

动作要点：①各动连贯协调一致，两臂绕环快速，轻灵圆活，手眼身步配合一致。②上架前推，快而有力，上架掌腕关节抖腕侧屈，推掌时肩部下沉。③屈膝全蹲时防止撅臀、拔跟；左右脚屈膝踢摆脆快有力。

Key points of action: ① All movements are coherent and coordinated, the two arms are circling fast, light and flexible, and the eyes should follow the steps. ② Pushing should be fast and powerful. Shake the wrist and bend it laterally when the palms going upward. ③ Squat on the heels and the kick should be short and powerful.

11. 震脚下插掌 Zhenjiaoxiachazhang

（1）独立举掌：重心前移，右脚跟步，左掌从上向右上、向左再向下弧形摆动，右臂内旋向下、向右、向上直臂弧形绕环上举，右掌直腕，掌指向上，(图 3-5-37) 左脚不动，右腿屈膝上提，右脚绷直。(图 3-5-38)

(1) Single Juzhang: move the gravity forward, follow the step of the right foot, swing the left palm in an arc, and then downward, rotate the right arm inward, and upward straight,(Fig.3-5-37) left foot does not move, right leg bends and lifts up, right foot straight. (Fig.3-5-38)

图Fig 3-5-37　　　　　　　图Fig 3-5-38

（2）并步插掌：右掌随屈肘贴近右耳侧，左掌向前下摆，(图 3-5-39) 左腿屈膝，右脚在左脚内侧震脚并步；同时，右掌向前下方与左掌相搓直臂插伸，左掌屈肘收于右肩前，掌心向右，两腿屈膝半蹲，目视右掌。(图 3-5-40)

(2) Bingbuchazhang: the right palm is close to the right ear with the elbow bent, and the left palm is placed forward and downward, (Fig. 3-5-39) the left leg bends, and the right foot shakes in the inner side of the left foot. The right palm is kneaded with the left palm, and the left palm bends to the front of the right shoulder, and the palm center is to the right. The two legs bend and squat fully, and watch the right palm. (Fig.3-5-40)

图Fig 3-5-39　　　　　　　图Fig 3-5-40

动作要点：两掌绕环与提膝协调一致；下蹲插掌两脚两膝并拢靠紧，两肩下沉。

Key points: the two palms moving and knee lifting should be in coordination; when squat, the two feet should be close.

12. **提膝托掌** Tixituozhang

图Fig 3-5-41　　　　　　图Fig 3-5-42

重心上提，两腿直起，左臂外旋，掌心向上，由右肩处向前上方直臂伸出，右臂外旋，从下、向后直臂弧形绕环上举，（图 3-5-41）右腿直立，左腿屈膝上提，左脚面绷平，脚尖向下，左臂内旋提肘向右下按，左掌屈腕下按于左膝面，掌指向右，右掌向上屈腕抖手成横掌，掌指朝左，掌心向前，目视前方。（图 3-5-42）

Lift the gravity up, rotate the left arm outwards, extend the straight arm forward and upward from the right shoulder, rotate the right arm outward, and lift up from the lower and backward straight arc-shaped ring. (Fig.3-5-41) The right leg is upright, the left leg is bending and upward lifting, the left foot is flat, the toe is downward, the left arm is rotated inward and the elbow is downward, the left palm is wrist bending and downward on the left knee, the palm finger is to the right, and the right palm is wrist upward to shake horizontally, fingers to the left, palms center to the front, and watch ahead. (Fig.3-5-42)

动作要点：动作连贯，提膝、按掌、托掌迅速完成；右肘后张，左肩不能耸肩。

Key points: the movement is consistent, and the knee lifting, the palm pressing, and the palm holding should be done quickly; the right elbow is stretched backward, and the left shoulder keep level.

13. **上步高举腿** Shangbugaojutui

左脚向前落步，左掌直腕直肘从前向后直臂弧形绕环摆动，右掌直腕，臂外旋从上向前直臂绕环摆动，（图 3-5-43）右脚再向前上步，两臂立圆从后向前抡摆，右掌摆至向上绕环上举，至头顶上方时，屈腕抖手成横掌，屈肘横架，掌指朝左，右腿伸直，

左腿屈膝向前上方挺膝蹬伸，左掌屈肘按扶于左膝面，掌心向下，目视左脚。(图3-5-44)

The left foot falls forward, the left palm goes straight from front to back in an arc, the right palm turns from top to front with straight arm swings, (Fig.3-5-43) the right foot moves forward, the two arms swing from back to front, the right palm swing to the top of the head, the wrist is bent to shake the hand into a horizontal palm, the palm finger is facing left, the right leg is straight, the left leg is bent forward and stretch the left elbow bends on the left knee, palm center down, and look at the left foot. (Fig.3-5-44)

图Fig 3-5-43

图Fig 3-5-44

动作要点：①两臂向前立圆绕环时肩、肘、臂自然放松与步法配合协调。②上步时脚前掌挖地向后使脚底后翻，上身微向前顷，挺胸、直腰。③高蹬腿时脚尖勾紧，上身保持正直，站立稳固。

Key points: ① When the two arms go forward in a circle, the shoulders, elbows and arms are relaxed naturally and the footstep are coordinated. ② When step up, the upper body slightly forward, and the chest and waist are straight. ③ When kick high, the toes shall be hooked tightly, the upper body shall be kept upright and stand stably.

14. 跃步分掌 Yuebufenzhang

左脚向前上步，重心前移，右掌从上向右直臂下降成平举，(图3-5-45)左脚蹬地跳起，右脚向前跃进落步，两掌从两侧一起直臂向下、屈肘向身前弧形抄起交叉，右掌在下，左掌在上，两掌屈腕，掌指向上。(图3-5-46)左脚向前上步，右腿伸直，左腿屈膝成左弓步，两掌向上经额前向左右平摆，掌指仍向上，眼看右掌。(图3-5-47)

Step forward with the left foot, move forward the gravity, and lower the right palm from the top to the right into a flat lift. (Fig.3-5-45) Jump up on the left foot, jump forward on the right foot and step down, and cross the two palms with straight arms down from both sides, bending elbows to the front arc of the body, with the right palm at the bottom, the left palm at the top, and the palm fingers pointing up. (Fig.3-5-46) Step forward with the left foot, straighten the right leg, bend the left leg to form a left bow step, swing the palms up to the left and right through the forehead, keep the palms fingers up, and look at the right palm. (Fig.3-5-47)

图Fig 3-5-45　　　　图Fig 3-5-46　　　　图Fig 3-5-47

动作要点：跃步要远，落步要轻。

Key points: jump far and land light.

15. 弓步双冲拳 Gongbushuangchongquan

两掌变拳收于腰侧，拳心向上，目视前方。(图 3-5-48) 两脚不动，两拳向前冲出，拳心向下，目视两拳。(图 3-5-49)

Turn fists close at the waist side, with the heart of the fist upward, and look ahead. (Fig.3-5-48) Keep the feet still, run forward with two punches, with the hearts of the fists downward, and look at the fists. (Fig.3-5-49)

图Fig 3-5-48　　　　图Fig 3-5-49

动作要点：沉肩、紧拳、出拳迅速有力。

Key points: shoulders down, fists tight, quick and powerful.

第二段 Part II

16. 平搂扣腿夹抱 Pingloukoutuijiabao

身体右转，右腿屈膝，左腿挺膝，右拳向右、向后直臂弧形平搂，(图 3-5-50) 右拳向右腰侧揽回夹抱，拳心向上，重心移至左腿屈膝半蹲，右脚扣于左腿后，目视左拳。(图 3-5-51)

Turn your body to the right, bend your right leg to the knee, straighten your left leg to the knee, and straighten your right fist to the right and back to the straight arm in an arc, (Fig. 3-5-50) pull your right fist back to your waist, with the heart of your fist facing up, move your weight to your left leg to bend your knee and squat, bend your left leg to the knee, buckle your right foot behind your left leg, and look at your left fist. (Fig. 3-5-51)

图Fig 3-5-50　　　　图Fig 3-5-51

动作要点：平摆搂动作要快要柔，上身随之转动。

Key points: the flat swing and stroking should be soft, and the upper body should rotate accordingly.

17. 冲步抢手前搡 Chongbuqiangshouqiansang

右脚向右上一大步，脚尖里扣，两腿屈膝成马步，右拳向右平伸后收至腰间再向右冲拳，目视右拳。(图 3-5-52)

Take a big step to the right, toes inside, bend your legs to form a horse stance, extend your right fist to the right, then close it to your waist, then punch right, and watch your right fist. (Fig. 3-5-52)

202　中国传统武术教程：汉英对照

图Fig 3-5-52

动作要点：马步蹲平，扣脚，展膝，裆劲内收，挺胸，直背，塌腰。

Key points: squat flat, feet inward, knee straight, chest and back straight and waist loose.

18. 仆步穿掌 Pubuchuanzhang

两腿直起，身体右转，两臂依次向后抢摆，(图 3-5-53)两脚以前脚掌碾转，两腿交叉，右腿在前，(图 3-5-54)左脚向左后方伸出，左腿伸直，右腿屈膝半蹲；右臂向上向下弧形绕环后收至腰间，左掌向上弧形绕环至右上方时屈肘屈腕，右掌经左掌背向右穿掌，拇指侧朝上，左掌收于右腋下，(图 3-5-55)上身左转，右腿屈膝全蹲成左仆步，左臂外旋，左掌沿左腿内侧向左穿掌，拇指侧朝上，目视左掌。(图 3-5-56)

Turn right, the arms are swung backward in turn, (Fig. 3-5-53) the legs are crossed with the right leg front. (Fig. 3-5-54) Extend the left foot to the left and rear, straighten the left leg, bend the right leg and squat; bend the right arm upward and downward in an arc and then close it to the waist, bend the elbow and wrist when the left palm upward in an arc to the upper right, put the right palm through the back of the left palm to the right, thumb up, and put the left palm under the right armpit, (Fig. 3-5-55) turn the upper body to the left, squat on the right leg, turn the left arm outward, and put the left palm through the inside of the left leg to the left , thumb up, look at the left palm. (Fig. 3-5-56)

图Fig 3-5-53

图Fig 3-5-54

图Fig 3-5-55　　　　　　　　图Fig 3-5-56

动作要点：动作连贯，两臂回环要抡圆，仆腿防止撅臀、拱背、掀脚、拔跟。

Key points: the action should be consistent, the arms should be swung round, avoid pouting and hump backing.

19. 击步箭弹 Jibujiantan

上身前移，左掌向前抄起平举，左脚踏跳身体腾空，两腿伸直，右脚向左脚击步，（图 3-5-57）右脚落步，（图 3-5-58）左脚向左前方落步，右脚再向前上一步，（图 3-5-59）左掌变拳收抱至腰间，拳心向上，右掌变拳由右腰侧向前冲拳，拳眼向上；同时，左腿向前弹踢，脚背绷直，（图 3-5-60）右脚随即蹬地跳起，身体腾空，右脚向前踢出，脚面绷直，左脚趁势下垂落步，右拳回收腰侧，左拳向前冲拳，拳眼向上，目视右脚。（图 3-5-61）

Move the upper body forward, lift the left palm forward horizontally, the left foot in the air, straighten the legs, and hit the left foot with the right foot, (Fig. 3-5-57) step with the right foot, (Fig. 3-5-58) step with the left foot forward and step with the right foot forward, (Fig. 3-5-59) the left palm to the waist, with the heart of the fist up, and punch the right palm to the right waist, with the eyes of the fist up; spring and kick the left leg forward, (Fig. 3-5-60) jump up with the right foot, kick the right foot forward, the right fist on the waist side, punch forward with the left fist, and look at the right foot. (Fig. 3-5-61)

图Fig 3-5-57　　　　　　　　图Fig 3-5-58

图Fig 3-5-59　　　　　　　图Fig 3-5-60　　　　　　　图Fig 3-5-61

动作要点：纵跳提气，冲拳与踢腿同时，冲拳有力。

Key points: jump with breathing in, punching and kicking powerfully at the same.

20. 弓步指裆拳 Gongbuzhidangquan

右脚向前落地，右腿屈膝半蹲成右弓步，左拳变掌屈肘向上横架，掌心向上，右拳向前下方冲拳，拳眼向上；上身向前倾探，目视右拳。（图 3-5-62）

The right foot falls forward, the right leg is bent and half squatted into the right bow step, the left palm is upward, the right fist is forward and down, the fist eye is upward; the upper body is forward, and look at the right fist. (Fig. 3-5-62)

图Fig 3-5-62

动作要点：上体前倾与右拳下冲的动作协调一致。

Key points: the upper body forward and the right fist downward movement are in harmony.

21. 虚步磕肘 Xubukezhou

重心移至左脚屈膝半蹲，右脚屈膝提步收回，右脚尖点地成右虚步；同时，左掌变拳收于腰间，拳心向上，右臂屈肘从右向身前格挡，拳面向上，目视右拳。（图 3-5-63）

Shift the gravity to the left foot, half squat, the right knee bending with the right foot toe pointedly in the right empty step; the left fist is closed at the waist, the fist heart is upward, the right bent elbow blocking from the right to the front, the fist face up, and look at the right fist. (Fig. 3-5-63)

图Fig 3-5-63

动作要点：虚步半蹲，上身略前倾，挺胸、直背、塌腰，右肩向前牵引。

Key points: squat with empty steps, lean forward slightly, straighten your chest, back and waist, and pull your right shoulder forward.

22. 偷步撑拳 Toubuchengquan

上身稍起，右脚向右跨步，右腿伸直，左拳变掌向左弧形绕环，屈腕立掌，掌指向上，右掌摆向左肘处，(图3-5-64)左脚向右插步，两腿交叉，右掌变拳从左向右直臂弧形平摆，拳眼向下，左拳向右弧形平摆至右肩处，拳心向下，目视右拳。（图3-5-65）

The upper body slightly rises, the right foot strides to the right, the right leg straightens, the left palm rotates to the left, the wrist bends to stand the palm, the palm fingers up, the right palm swings to the left elbow, (Fig. 3-5-64) the left foot crosses to the right, the right fist swings from left to the right in an arc, the fist eye downward, the left fist swings to the right shoulder, the fist heart downward, and and look at the right fist. (Fig. 3-5-65)

图Fig 3-5-64　　　　　　　图Fig 3-5-65

动作要点：叉步摆拳协调一致。

Key points: step and fists are in coordination

23. 翻身二起脚 Fanshenerqijiao

上身前俯,左拳变掌反臂向左、向上弧形绕环抡摆,掌心反向上,目视左掌转动,(图 3-5-66)两脚掌碾转,上身从左向上、向后拧腰翻转,左掌和右拳随上身成车轮形抡摆翻转,翻身后上身立直,(图 3-5-67)左掌向下、向后绕环抡摆,右掌向上、向前绕环抡摆,右腿向上摆踢,左脚蹬地跳起,身体腾空,左腿向上直踢,脚面绷平,左掌从后向上、向前击拍左脚脚面,右拳收于腰间,拳心向上,目视左脚。(图 3-5-68)

The upper body leans forward, the left fist swings to the left and upward in an arc, turn the palm center down, and eyes following the left palm, (Fig. 3-5-66) turn the upper body from the left to the up and back, swing the left palm and the right fist into a wheel the upper body straight after turning over, (Fig. 3-5-67) swing the left palm downward and backward in a circle, swing the right palm upward and forward in a circle, and swing the right leg upward, jump up with the left foot, the left leg kicks straight up, the right fist to the waist, the heart of the fist is up, and look at the left foot. (Fig. 3-5-68)

图Fig 3-5-66　　　　　　图Fig 3-5-67　　　　　　图Fig 3-5-68

动作要点:叉步翻身前俯上身,两脚碾地拧转与两臂抡摆动作协调一致。

Key points: lean over the upper body before turning over with cross step, and feet turning to the ground to coordinate with the swing of the arms.

24. 弓步三拳 Gongbusanquan

右脚先落地,左脚向前落步,重心前移,左腿屈膝半蹲成左弓步,左掌变拳收于腰间,拳心向上,右拳向前冲拳,拳眼向上,(图 3-5-69)紧接着,再依次快速冲左拳和右拳,左拳收于左腰侧,拳心向上,目视右拳。(图 3-5-70、图 3-5-71)

The right foot first lands, the left foot moves forward, the center of gravity moves forward, the left leg bends to form a left bow step, the left fist close at the waist, the heart of the fist upward, the right fist rushes forward, the eye of the fist is upward, (Fig. 3-5-69) the left fist rushes and then the right fist, the left fist closes at the left waist side, the heart of the fist is upward, and look at the right fist. (Fig. 3-5-70, Fig. 3-5-71)

图Fig 3-5-69　　　　　　图Fig 3-5-70　　　　　　图Fig 3-5-71

动作要点：三次冲拳臂、肘伸直，肩部前送，右腿蹬直、右髋下沉。

Key points: three punches with elbow straight, shoulder forward, right leg straight and right hip down.

25. 马步架打 Horse-riding Stance Fight

右拳屈肘上架变横掌，小指侧朝上，掌指向左，左脚尖内扣，右脚跟内扣，身体右转，两腿屈膝成马步；左拳向前冲拳，拳心向下，目视左拳。(图 3-5-72)

The right fist bends and goes upward into the horizontal palm, fingers to left, the left foot tip snaps inward, the right foot heel turns inward, the body turns right, the two legs bend the knees to form a horse stance; the left fist rushes forward, the heart of the fist is down, and look at the left fist. (Fig. 3-5-72)

图Fig 3-5-72

动作要点：弓步变马步重心要稳，上身挺胸、拔背、塌腰，两肩松沉。

Key points: the upper body should be straight, the waist should be soft, and the shoulders should be loose.

第三段 Part III

26. 回身提膝按掌 Huishentixianzhang

重心上提移至左脚，身体同时右转 180°，右腿屈膝提起，右脚面绷平，脚尖向下，右掌变拳屈肘收于腰间，拳心向上，左拳变掌从左向上经头上向前直臂下按，掌心向下，掌指朝右，上身略前倾，目视左掌。（图 3-5-73）

The gravity is lifted to the left foot, the body is turned 180° at the same time, the right leg is lifted bending the knee, the right foot is stretched, and the toe is downward; the right fist is bent up to the waist, the heart of the fist is upward, the left palm pushes from the left to the top and forward, the fingers are to the right, the upper body is slightly forward, and look at the left palm. (Fig. 3-5-73)

图Fig 3-5-73

动作要点：转身、提膝、收拳、按掌动作同时完成。

Key points: turn around, lift the knee, and press the palm at the same time.

27. 弓步穿喉掌 Gongbuchuanhouzhang

右脚向前落地，右腿屈膝半蹲成右弓步，右拳变掌经左掌上向前平穿掌，掌心向上，左掌屈肘收右腋下，掌心向下，目视右掌。（图 3-5-74）

The right foot drops forward, the right leg is half squatted into a right bow step, the right palm passing through the left palm and goes forward, the palm hear upward, the left palm closed under the right armpit, the palm heart downward, and look at the right palm. (Fig. 3-5-74)

图Fig 3-5-74

动作要点：穿掌要快有力，两肩要平行。

Key points: the palms go quickly and forcefully, and keep the shoulders level.

28. 提膝上穿掌 Tixishangchuanzhang

重心上提前移至右脚，右转身90°，右臂内旋从前向上、向后直臂弧形绕环收于腰间，左臂外旋从右腋下向下、向前、向上绕环，(图3-5-75) 左腿屈膝上提，左脚面绷平；同时，右掌向上直臂冲出，掌指向上，左掌下收右腋，掌指向上，拇指侧靠身，目视左方。(图3-5-76)

Move the gravity to the right foot, turn 90° to the right, turn the right arm inwards, straight arm arc-shaped circles from the front up and back to the waist, turn the left arm outwards from the right armpit downward, forward and upward, (Fig. 3-5-75) bend the left leg and lift it up, the left foot flat; the right palm straight up and out, the left palm close to the right armpit, fingers pointing up, and look at the left side. (Fig. 3-5-76)

图Fig 3-5-75　　　　　　　　　图Fig 3-5-76

动作要点：穿掌、提膝与转头动作快速协调；提膝独立时，右臂向上拔肩。

Key points: palm penetrating and knee lifting coherently and quickly.

29. 弓步撩掌单鞭 Gongbuliaozhangdanbian

（1）仆步抄掌：右腿屈膝全蹲，左腿向前铺地成左仆步，右臂外旋屈肘向左肩立掌下压，掌指向上。(图3-5-77)

(1) Pubuchaozhang: squat down with the right leg bent, the left leg forward to form a left crouch stance, turn the right arm outward and bend the elbow to the left shoulder, and the fingers are pointing up. (Fig. 3-5-77)

（2）弓步撩掌单鞭：重心前移，左脚尖外展，左腿屈膝成左弓步，右掌向下、向身后挑掌，掌尖向上；左掌从右腋下向下、向前平撩，屈腕成侧立掌，掌指向上，小指侧向前，目视左掌。(图3-5-78)

(2) Gongbuliaozhangdanbian: move the gravity forward, extend the left toe, bend the knee of the left leg to form a left bow step, lift the right palm downward and backward, fingers upward; lift the left palm downward and forward from the right armpit, bend the wrist to form a side standing palm, point the palm upward, move the little finger forward, and look at the left palm. (Fig. 3-5-78)

图Fig 3-5-77　　　　　　　　　图Fig 3-5-78

动作要点：仆步左腿挺直，上身防止拱背、撅臀；弓步单鞭时两臂平行。

Key points: the upper body should not be arched or pouted; the two arms should be parallel.

30. 击步二起脚 Jibuerqijiao

重心前移，右脚离地直腿碰击左脚，(图 3-5-79) 右脚先落地，左脚向前落地，右脚再向前上一步，(图 3-5-80) 右脚上步蹬地踏跳，左腿屈膝向上摆动，右腿直腿向上弹踢，右掌从后下落向前上弧形甩臂上摆，左掌上举过头，在头顶上方迎击右掌背，右掌在额前击拍右脚面，左掌移向左侧变勾手，勾尖向下。目视右脚。(图 3-5-81)

Move the gravity forward, and hit the left foot by the right foot off the ground with straight leg, (Fig. 3-5-79) land the right foot and the left foot forward, and then move the right foot forward, (Fig. 3-5-80) the right foot jumps up, the left leg swings up, the right leg kicks up, the right palm swings forward from the back in an arc. Raise the left palm and hit the back of the right palm above the head; click the right palm in front of the forehead to pat the right foot, move the left palm to the left and change into a hook, with the hook point downward. Look at the right foot. (Fig. 3-5-81)

动作要点：二起脚摆腿和蹬脚快速、敏捷，一气呵成，拍脚击响准确、响亮。

Key points : swinging and kicking are fast, and the clapping and striking sound is loud.

图Fig 3-5-79　　　　　　图Fig 3-5-80　　　　　　图Fig 3-5-81

31. 旋风脚 Whirlwind feet

左脚落地，(图 3-5-82)左脚掌为轴碾地使上身向左转，右脚在右侧落地，两腿屈膝，上身前俯，(图 3-5-83)左脚提起，上身随之从左向上、向后翻转，右脚蹬地跳起，身体悬空，右脚随转身从右向上里合横腿，右掌变拳收至身体右侧，左勾手变掌迎击右脚底，目视右脚。(图 3-5-84)

Stand on the left foot, (Fig. 3-5-82) turn the upper body to the left, the right foot steps on the right side, knees are bent, and the upper body leans forward, (Fig. 3-5-83) the left foot lifted, the upper body is then turned from the left to the up and back, the right foot jumps, the right foot is turned from the right to the up horizontally, the right fist back to the right side, the left palm hits the bottom of the right foot, look at the right foot. (Fig. 3-5-84)

图Fig 3-5-82　　　　　　图Fig 3-5-83　　　　　　图Fig 3-5-84

动作要点：旋风脚翻转起跳时上身前倾，跳起上身直立，拍脚清脆响亮。

Key points: jump with the upper body leans forward, and the feet clapping are clear and loud.

32. 马步架打 Mabujiada

左脚、右脚相继落地，两腿屈膝，左掌伸向左侧，拇指侧向下，右手握拳收于腰间，目视左掌。(图 3-5-85) 左掌从左向下、向右直臂撩掌，掌心向上，上体随之右转 180°，左腿伸直成右弓步，(图 3-5-86) 左臂内旋，屈肘上架成横掌，两腿屈膝半蹲成马步，右拳向前冲拳，拳眼向上，目视右拳。(图 3-5-87)

The left foot and right foot step on the ground one after another, with the knees bent, the left palm extends to the left, the thumb side down, the right hand clenched and closed at the waist, and watch the left palm. (Fig. 3-5-85) The left palm is lifted from the left downward and right, the palm center upward, the upper body then turns right 180°, the left leg extends straight, (Fig. 3-5-86) the left arm rotates inward, the elbows bent, the legs half crouched into a horse stance, the right fist punches forward, and look at the right fist. (Fig. 3-5-87)

图Fig 3-5-85　　　　图Fig 3-5-86　　　　图Fig 3-5-87

动作要点：撩掌拧转马步冲拳协调一致，动作连贯。

Key points: the moves of palm and steps go harmoniously and move coherently.

33. 回身格挡下插掌 Huishengedangxiachazhang

右拳收于腰间，拳心向上，重心移至右腿，右腿直立，上身迅速向左拧转，左腿屈膝提起，脚面绷平，左掌从上经胸前向左侧平搂成勾手，搂至身体左侧，(图 3-5-88) 左脚向前落步，屈膝半蹲，右腿伸直成左弓步，目视左勾手，(图 3-5-89) 右拳变掌向右前插掌，掌心斜向上，目视右掌。(图 3-5-90)

The right fist is closed at the waist, the heart of the fist is upward, the center of gravity is shifted to the right leg, the right leg is upright, the upper body is quickly turned from the right and left, the left leg is bent and lifted, the foot is flat, the left palm is flat from the top to the front of the chest and left side to form a hook, (Fig. 3-5-88) step forward with the left foot, bend the knee and squat, straighten the right leg into a left bow step, and look at the left hook, (Fig. 3-5-89) change the palm of the right fist and insert the palm to the right, with the palm inclined upward, and look at the right palm. (Fig. 3-5-90)

图Fig 3-5-88　　　　图Fig 3-5-89　　　　图Fig 3-5-90

动作要点：上身向左转动平搂格挡以腰为轴；左勾手与右插掌成一斜直线，右肩下沉。

Key points: turn the upper body to the left and hold the block with the waist as the axis; form a diagonal line between the left hook and the right inserted palm, and sink the shoulder.

34. 摆莲腿 Bailiantui

图Fig 3-5-91　　　　图Fig 3-5-92

右臂内旋向左摆臂甩掌，左勾手变掌迎击右掌背，掌心向下，（图 3-5-91）两掌向上弧形绕环举起，掌心向前，重心前移左腿，左腿直立，右脚离地从身后向前外摆腿踢起，两掌先后击拍右脚面，目视手掌。（图 3-5-92）

Swing the right arm inward to the left and swing the palm. Turn the left hook to the back of the right palm and hit the back of the right palm with the palm downward, (Fig. 3-5-91) lift the two palms in an upward arc around the ring, with the palm forward and shift the gravity to the left leg. The left leg is upright, and the right foot kicks from behind and forward to the outside. The two palms successively pat the right foot and look at the palm. (Fig. 3-5-92)

动作要点：站立稳固，击拍准确、响亮，两腿挺膝伸直。

Key points: stand firmly, hit and clap accurately and loudly, straighten the legs and knees.

35. 提膝抄掌 Tixichaozhang

右腿向右方落地，脚尖里扣，右腿伸直，两掌从上向左弧形绕环，掌心向下，目视左掌，(图3-5-93)右掌从左向下、向右直臂反掌弧形绕环，掌心反向上，目随右掌转动，(图3-5-94)上身直起右转，右掌继续向上、向身后绕环，掌心向下，左掌从后向下、向前直臂弧形绕环，屈肘向上抄掌，掌指向前，重心前移右腿，左腿屈膝提起，左脚面绷平，脚尖向下，目视左掌。(图3-5-95)

Lift right leg rightward, turn the foot front inside, straighten the right leg, rotate the two palms from the top to the left with the palm center downward, and look at the left palm, (Fig. 3-5-93) rotate the right palm from the left to the right, straighten the right arm with the palm center upward, (Fig. 3-5-94) turn the upper body right, the lift the right and circle behind with the palm center downward, lift the left palm from the back to the down, go to the front in a circle, bend the elbow with the palm upward and fingers forward, bend the left leg and lift the knee, stretch the left foot with toes down, and look at the left palm. (Fig. 3-5-95)

图Fig 3-5-93　　　　　图Fig 3-5-94　　　　　图Fig 3-5-95

动作要点：独立步右手微高过肩，腕关节用力下屈；上身直，站立稳固。

Key points: the right hand is slightly higher than the shoulder, and the wrist is bent down with force; the upper body is straight, and the standing is stable.

第四段 Part IV

36. 环步提膝刁手 Huanbutixidiaoshou

（1）击步：左脚向前落地，重心前移，上身前冲，右掌变勾手，勾尖向下，左掌收至右肩，(图 3-5-96) 左脚起跳，身体腾空，右脚迅速向左脚击步。(图 3-5-97)

(1)Jibu: land the left foot forward, move the gravity forward, push the upper body, turn the right palm into the hook with the hook point downward, left left palm retracted to the right shoulder, (Fig. 3-5-96) jump off with the left foot, the right foot quickly following. (Fig. 3-5-97)

图Fig 3-5-96　　　　图Fig 3-5-97

（2）盖步：左脚向前方上一步，右脚从后向左脚左前方盖步，左掌向前弧形抄掌，右勾手变掌，拇指侧向上，目视左掌转动。(图 3-5-98)

(2) Gaibu: let the left palm forward, the right foot followed, the left palm goes to the front in an arch, turn the right hook hand into the palm, the thumb is up, and look at the left palm rotating. (Fig. 3-5-98)

图Fig 3-5-98

(3) 提膝刁手：左脚向左后斜方跨步，重心移向左后方，左掌向左后直臂弧形绕环举于身后，掌心向下，右掌从后向上、向前直臂弧形绕环，(图3-5-99)右腿屈膝提起，右脚面绷直，成独立步，右肘下垂，腕关节下屈，右掌拇指展开，其余四指并拢伸直向手背的一面翘张，右掌伸直向下、向后牵引，变成刁手龙爪，目视右掌。(图3-5-100)

(3) Tixidiaoshou: step left and backward, shift the gravity to the left and rear, lift the left palm to the left and around the back, palm heart down, right palm to the left and swing around, (Fig. 3-5-99) lift the right leg, straighten the right foot, with the right elbow drooping, wrist joint bending down, right thumb extending straight down and pulling backward, and other four fingers in parallel, straighten the back of the hand and turn it into a dragon claw. Look at the right palm. (Fig. 3-5-100)

图Fig 3-5-99　　　　　　图Fig 3-5-100

动作要点：①落步、击步、进步、迈步、移步等步法和两掌的绕环协调一致。②盖步以身体重心移动来带动步法转换。③刁手龙爪腕关节下屈，拇指外展向下、向后牵引，其它四指要并拢伸直向掌背翘张。

Key points: ① the steps of falling, striking, advancing, stepping and moving are in harmony with the ring-moving of two palms. ② the step moves with gravity shift. ③ the other four fingers should be extended to the back of the palm.

37. 歇步绞手掖掌 Xiebujiaoshouyezhang

右脚外展向前落步，两腿伸直，左臂外旋从后向前、向右直臂弧形摆动，右手变掌，直腕伸至左臂下方，掌心向下，(图3-5-101)身体微右转，两腿交叉，上身挺胸，左掌向右上方屈肘摆动下落左侧，右臂外旋，从左向前、向右直臂弧形平扫摆动；上臂成逆时针方向转动，(图3-5-102)左臂继续向右摆动，右掌由头顶上方屈肘向左弧形摆动，至左侧时肘下垂贴于左臂内侧，掌指向上，两腿屈膝全蹲成右歇步，目视左侧。(图3-5-103-1、图3-5-103-2)

Step forward with the right foot outspread, straight legs, swing the left arm outward from back to front and right straight arm arc, turn the right hand to palm, extend the straight wrist to the lower part of the left arm, palm center downward, (Fig. 3-5-101) turn the body slightly to the right, cross the two legs, hold the upper body straight chest, swing the left palm to the right and upper elbow to the left, turn the right arm outward, swing the right arm from left to front and right straight arm arc flat; turn the upper arm anticlockwise move, (Fig. 3-5-102) the left arm continues to swing to the right, and the right palm swings to the left by bending the elbow above the head. When it reaches the left, the elbow drops and pastes on the inner side of the left arm, the palm points upward, and the knees of both legs are bent to form a right rest step, and look at the left side. (Fig. 3-5-103-1, Fig. 3-5-103-2)

图Fig 3-5-101　　　　图Fig 3-5-102

图Fig 3-5-103-1　　　图Fig 3-5-103-2

动作要点：两掌绞花动作要柔和，肩、肘、腕均放松，歇步时两掌绞花动作刚脆。

Key points: the action of two palms wringing should be gentle, the shoulders, elbows and wrists should be relaxed, and the action of two palms wringing should be just and crisp when resting.

38. 分掌侧踹 Fenzhangcechuai

左臂内旋，掌心向下，与右掌经身前分开向左右两侧抄起分掌，拇指侧向下；同时，右腿直起，左脚向左上方侧踹，勾脚尖，目视左脚。（图3-5-104）

Turn the left arm inward, palm center down, separate the right palm from the right palm through the front of the body, turn the opposite arm to the left and right sides, and copy the palm, thumb side down; at the same time, straighten the right leg, kick the left foot to the left and upper side, hook the toe, and look at the left foot. (Fig. 3-5-104)

图Fig 3-5-104

动作要点：分掌和侧踹同时快速完成；侧踹脚跟用力，脚横平。

Key points: split and side kick at the same time; side kick needs the heel to generate the force, foot flat.

39. 击步撩掌 Jibuliaozhang

上身直起左转，左脚前落步，右脚跟离地，（图3-5-105）左脚踏跳，重心前移，右脚向左脚击步，（图3-5-106）右脚先落步，左脚向前上一大步屈膝半蹲成左弓步，右掌从后向下、向前撩掌，掌心向上，左掌屈肘按至右臂上，掌心向下，目视右掌。（图3-5-107）

Turn the upper body straight to the left, step forward with the left foot, and keep the right heel off the ground, (Fig.3-5-105) step forward with the left foot, move forward with the center of gravity, step forward with the right foot to the left foot, (Fig.3-5-106) step forward with the right foot, step forward with the left foot, step forward with the knee bent and half squatted into the left bow step with the left foot, lift the right palm from the back down and forward, palm center up, press the left palm to the right arm, palm center down, and look at the right palm. (Fig.3-5-107)

图Fig 3-5-105　　　　　　图Fig 3-5-106　　　　　　图Fig 3-5-107

动作要点：击步迅速，上身前冲带动步法，以身领步；左臂屈肘端平，两肩平行。

Key points: strike quickly, push forward the upper body to drive the footwork, lead the step with the body; bend the elbow of the left arm to level, and keep the shoulders parallel.

40. 抓手横掌弹踢 Zhuashouhengzhangtanti

右掌快速抓握拳，(图 3-5-108) 重心前移左腿，左手成横掌向前平推，小指侧朝前，掌心向下，右脚向前弹踢，脚面绷直，右拳收于腰间，拳心向上，目视左掌。(图 3-5-109)

Quickly grasp and clench the fist with the right palm, (Fig. 3-5-108) move the center of gravity forward to the left leg, push the left hand horizontally forward, with the little finger side forward, the palm center downward, the right foot forward to play and kick, the foot surface taut and straight, close the right fist to the waist, the fist center upward, and look at the left palm. (Fig. 3-5-109)

图Fig 3-5-108　　　　　图Fig 3-5-109

动作要点：抓握快速有力，抓握稍屈肘；弹踢力达脚尖，支撑腿稍屈膝。

Key points: grasp fast and forcefully, the kick force reaches to the toe, and standing leg slightly bend the knee.

41. 弓步推掌 Gongbutuizhang

右脚向后落于原位，仍成左弓步，右拳变掌向前推掌，掌指向上，左掌屈肘按于左膝上，掌心向下，目视右掌。(图 3-5-110)

The right foot goes back to the original position, still forming a left bow step. Change the right fist into palm and push forward. Bend the left elbow and press it on the left knee, the palm center is downward, and look at the right palm. (Fig. 3-5-110)

图Fig 3-5-110

动作要点：推掌快速有力，掌指与眉同高，两肩平齐下沉。

Key points: palms go quickly and powerfully, the fingers are as the same height as the eyebrows, and the shoulders are even and sinking.

42. 捋手十字脚 Lvshoushizijiao

右掌转腕使掌指从上向右绕环，拇指张开，右臂外旋，至下方时五指抓握成拳，肘稍屈，(图 3-5-111) 右拳屈肘收于腰间，拳心向上，重心前移左腿，左腿直立，右脚向前直腿摆踢，脚面绷平，左掌从下向后、向上、向前直臂立圆绕环后在胸前击拍右脚面，目视右脚。(图 3-5-112)

The right palm turns the wrist to make the palm finger circle from the top to the right, the thumb opens, the right arm turns outwards, and when it reaches the bottom, the five fingers grasp to form a fist, and the elbow slightly bends, (Fig. 3-5-111) the right fist bends the elbow to close at the waist, the fist heart is upward, the center of gravity moves forward to the left leg, the left leg is upright, the right foot is straight forward to swing the kick, the foot is flat, the left palm is straight from the bottom to the back, up, and forward to make a circle, and then hit the right foot in front of the chest, and look at the right foot. (Fig. 3-5-112)

图Fig 3-5-111　　　　　　图Fig 3-5-112

动作要点：收拳、踢腿、拍脚三动协调一致，快速完成，拍脚脆快、响亮。

Key points: fist drawing back, kicking and feet clapping should be done in coordinately and quickly.

43. 旋风脚 Whirlwind feet

右脚向前落步，两腿屈膝，右手向下、向后、向上直臂弧形绕环举起，(图 3-5-113) 上身左转，左脚提起，左掌放松直臂向下、向左、向后抡甩，(图 3-5-114) 右脚蹬地跳起，上身从左向上、向后翻转，右脚向左上里合腿踢摆，左掌迎击右脚底，目视右脚。(图 3-5-115)

Step forward with the right foot, bend the knees, lift the straight arm in an arc with the right hand downward, backward and upward, (Fig. 3-5-113) turn the upper body to the left, lift the left foot, release the left hand and swing the straight arm downward, left and backward, (Fig. 3-5-114) jump up with the right foot on the ground, turn the upper body upward and backward from the left, turn the right foot up to the left and close the leg, and hit the right foot bottom with the left palm, and look at the right foot. (Fig. 3-5-115)

图Fig 3-5-113　　　　　　图Fig 3-5-114　　　　　　图Fig 3-5-115

动作要点：同前旋风脚。

Key points: the same as that of Whirlwind feet in No.31

44. 提膝盘肘 Tixipanzhou

左脚落地，左掌举于左侧上方，右拳收于腰间，拳心向上，（图 3-5-116）右腿屈膝，脚面绷直；同时右拳向前内旋横贯打，拳心向下，贯打后平摆屈肘环抱，拳心向下，右臂端平，左掌屈腕向上横架掌，目视前方。（图 3-5-117）

Step the left foot on the ground, the left palm is raised above the left side, the right fist is closed at the waist, the fist heart is upward, (Fig. 3-5-116) the right leg is bent and raised, the foot is straight, the right fist is rotated forward and internally, the fist heart is downward, the fist heart is downward, the elbow is folded and encircled after the stroke, the fist heart is downward, the right arm is level, the left palm is bent and the wrist is upward to cross frame the palm, and look ahead. (Fig. 3-5-117)

图Fig 3-5-116　　　　图Fig 3-5-117

动作要点：落地站稳，左腿伸直，上身正直，右肘盘平，左肘稍向后张展。

Key points: stand firmly, straighten the left leg and upper body, level the right elbow, and slightly extend the left elbow backward.

45. 靠身掌 Kaoshenzhang

左腿屈膝略蹲，右脚向右斜前方落步，脚尖里扣，右腿伸直，上身左转，左掌落于右肩前，右拳变掌，臂外旋使掌心向上，屈肘伸向左侧，（图 3-5-118）右脚尖外转，右腿屈膝，上身右转 180°，左腿伸直成右弓步；同时，右掌向右上方直臂弧形平靠，掌心向上，左臂内旋掌心向下，向左直臂摆动，目视右掌。（图 3-5-119）

The left leg squats slightly with the knee bent, the right foot falls to the right obliquely in front, the toes buckle in, the right leg straightens, the upper body turns left, the left palm falls in front of the right shoulder, the right fist changes the palm, the arm turns outward to make the palm center upward, the elbow bends to the left, (Fig. 3-5-118) the right foot turns outward, the right leg bends the knee, the upper body turns right 180°, the left leg straightens into the right lunge; at the same time, the right palm straightens the upper right arm, the palm is upward, and the left arm is inward Rotate the palm center downward, swing the left straight arm, and look at the right palm. (Fig. 3-5-119)

图Fig 3-5-118　　　　图Fig 3-5-119

动作要点：靠身掌以右肩背向前挤靠，再以右肘臂向前靠，最后以右掌向前甩摆，动作连贯；上身挺胸、直背、塌腰，两胯下沉。

Key points: lean forward with the right shoulder and swing forward with the right palm are consistent; the upper body is straight and the two crotches sink.

46. 虚步栽拳 Xubuzaiquan

重心上提，身体左转180°，右脚跟外转，左脚回收半步以脚尖虚点地，右掌向上摆，掌尖向上，（图 3-5-120）右腿屈膝半蹲，左腿屈膝成左虚步；同时，右掌变拳内旋腕架拳，拳眼朝下，拳心向前，左臂内旋屈肘，左拳下栽附于左膝面，拳面向下，拳心向后，目视前方。（图 3-5-121-1、图 3-5-121-2）

Lift the gravity, turn the body 180° to the left, turn the right heel outward, take the left foot back half step to the ground with the toe attaching the ground, put the right palm upward and the palm tip upward, (Fig. 3-5-120) bend the right leg and squat half, bend the left leg and form the left empty step; turn the right palm to the fist, turn the fist inside, turn the fist eye downward, the fist heart forward, turn the left arm inside and bend the elbow, and the left fist is planted on the left knee, the fist face downward, the fist heart backward, and look ahead. (Fig. 3-5-121-1, Fig. 3-5-121-2)

图Fig 3-5-120　　　　　图Fig 3-5-121-1　　　　　图Fig 3-5-121-2

动作要点：右腿半蹲，两脚虚实分明，上身挺胸、拔背、塌腰，两肩下沉，两臂屈成半圆。

Key points: squat on the right leg straighten upper body, chest and back, loosen the waist and shoulders, and bend arms into a semicircle.

47. 收势 Ending up

图Fig 3-5-122　　　　　图Fig 3-5-123　　　　　图Fig 3-5-124

重心上提前移，身体左转 90°，右脚向前上一大步，右腿伸直站立，右拳下落至身体右侧，左拳随上步向身体左侧平摆，(图 3-5-122) 左脚向右脚并步，两腿靠拢，两拳收于腰间，拳心向上，目视左侧，(图 3-5-123) 两拳变掌向身体两侧自然下垂，掌指贴靠腿侧，成立正姿势。(图 3-5-124)

Move the weight forward, turn the body 90° to the left, take a big step forward with the right foot, stand straight with the right leg, drop the right fist to the right side of the body, swing the left fist to the left side of the body with the step up, (Fig. 3-5-122) move the left foot to the right foot, close the two legs, close the two fists at the waist, with the fist heart up, and look at the left side, (Fig. 3-5-123) change the palm of the two fists to the two sides of the body and naturally hang down, with the palm and finger close to the leg side, in an upright position.(Fig. 3-5-124)

动作要点：头端正，下颏内收，挺胸，直腰，沉肩，精神振作。

Key points: head straight, chin back, chest and waist straight, spirit up.

思考题：Questions for consideration

1. 红拳十三式技术特点？

1. What are the technical characteristics of Hongquan Shisanshi?

2. 红拳裙拦势动作的要点？

2. What are the key points of Quanlanshi in Hongquan?

3. 小红拳技术特点是什么？

3. What are the technical characteristics of Xiao Hongquan?

4. 翻子拳技术特点有哪些？

4. What are the technical characteristics of Fanzi Quan?

5. 华拳的运动节奏表现有哪些？

5. What are the movement rhythms of Hua Quan?

第四章 传统器械选编
Chapter 4 Selections of Traditional Instruments

第一节 盘龙棍
4.1 Dragon Club (Panlong Gun)

一、盘龙棍简介 Brief Introduction

盘龙棍是红拳古老而典型的棍法，相传其因宋太祖赵匡胤创始而得名。盘龙棍架式工整，技术动作直来直往，粗狂豪迈，练习者将整套棍法练完，留下的足印酷似一条凌空翱翔的巨龙：六个往返的足印巧妙地构成了龙身，折返点动作简繁差异留下的足印区分了龙首与龙尾，梢把并用手法配合的连环步组成了龙爪，整套动作的足迹摆出的龙栩栩如生，这也成为盘龙棍的一个传神来由。盘龙棍技法实用性强，被看做是红拳拳系器械技法的精要，透示着器械技艺的古典与珍贵。

Dragon Club is an ancient and typical club technique of Hongquan. It is said that the name was invented by Zhao Kuangyin, the first emperor of the Song Dynasty (960-1279). The moves in Dragon Club are neat and orderly with grand swing and beating. When the player finishes his practice of the club, the footprints left by the player are just like a giant dragon flying in the air: Six back and forth footprints cleverly form the dragon body, the simple or complex turning points of the movements can be used to distinguish the dragon head and tail, and the combination of the continuous steps forms the dragon claws. The dragon composed by the steps is so vivid that the club is named Dragon Club. It is very practical in real fighting and regarded as the classical instrument in Hongquan.

二、盘龙棍技法特点 Technical characteristics

盘龙棍顺势持棍，调把换势，梢把兼用，长短兼施，刚柔相济而著称，更有灵猛泼辣、密集如雨、气势恢弘的技法风格。盘龙棍序套一趟，正套六趟，分四门、四角，计五十六棍。盘龙棍讲究步形身法灵活自然，身棍协调，进退皆打，动作大劈、大开与小巧刁钻多变结合，劲整力齐，刚中带柔，柔中寓刚，动作各节紧凑，演练起来猛似蛟龙，快如飞凤，实而无华。盘龙棍的用法主要有劈、崩、抡、扫、缠、绕、绞、云、拦、点、拨、挑、撩、挂、戳等。

The playing of Dragon Club needs the combination of the player and the club and to embed the player's soul into the club. It's also known for its sharp, intense and magnificent moves. There is a sequence of six sets of Panlong Club, which are divided into "Simen" (four doors) and "Bajiao" (eight corners), altogether fifty-six acts. Panlong Club playing is flexible and natural in the form of steps, coordinated in the body and staff, playing in and out, combining big split and small drills, softness and hardness. The connected moves are like a flying dragon. The common moves used in Dragon Club are split, collapse, swing, sweep, wrap, twist, tilt, swirling, block, point, dial, pick, lift, hang, poke, etc.

盘龙棍技法讲究指东打西，点上扎下，大开大劈，稳扎稳打，快速换手；步法讲究闪、绽、腾、挪和偷步换势；势法则随势换法，灵活换把，每手换势，多含枪法。典型动作有躬身揽棍、日头照、寻营瞭哨、朝天一炷香、金鸡独立、转身贯耳、列枪势、三步三枪、偷步盖把、怀抱琵琶、进步贯扎、行步提撩、魁星点笔、白蛇吐信、撑补飞燕、凤点头、担山势、偷步偷枪等。

The technique of Dragon Club is very fexible and always confuses the enymy by beating the east while pointing the west. The club is used to prick, point, swing and sweep. The moves of the hands and feet change swiftly according to the club's direction. The names of the moves are closely related to the great nature, some animals' behavior or people's daily life and work such as "The Rooster standing on one leg", "the hissing snake" or "shouldering the hills".

盘龙棍歌（谱）诀

盘龙神棍莫可夸，招招实用好棍法，太祖跨杆世无双。
手提盘龙当头照，探营瞭哨把敌寻，休将盘龙当俗传。
三进步连环扎枪，一步一扎令人惊，枪枪中平势难挡。

偷步盖打身要急，拧身撩打龙抬头，太祖甩棒把道开。
指人头，扎脚面，指上打下人难防，千变万化妙计多。
前管后锁下平枪，迎面花子下拦腿，拨草寻蛇不用慌。
白蛇吐信先取心，雪花盖顶伤敌根，里慌外扎紧如风。
抡格横护龙伸爪，怀抱琵琶列枪势，挑拨转拧接连打。
棍中暗合拦拿扎，伤敌莫过棍头戳，盘龙兼枪最为良。
天下盘龙莫要问，行拳打棍要提防，太祖奇功江山定。

三、盘龙棍基本技法与组合图解 Illustrations of the Basic skills

（一）盘龙棍基本技法 Basic skills of the Dragon Club

1. 立举：右手握棍把，将棍竖直举于体前或体侧。

1.Vertical lift: hold the handle of the stick with the right hand, and lift the stick vertically in front of or on the side of the body.

2. 抱棍：两手开握、并握或两臂交叉握棍抱于体前或体侧。

2. Hold the club: hold the cudgel in front of or on the side of the body with two hands open, or with two arms crossed.

3. 肩上背棍：单手或双手握把端，将棍身平置于肩上。

3. Shoulder the club: hold the end of the stick with one hand or two hands, and put the stick body on the shoulder.

4. 背后背棍：单手屈臂握棍，将棍置于背后，棍身紧贴背部。

4. Back the club: hold the stick with one hand bent, put the stick on the back, and stick the body close to the back.

5. 劈棍：棍由上向下猛力劈出，力达棍前端。

5.Split: the stick is split from top to bottom with strong force, reaching the front end of the stick.

6. 夹棍：手握棍，将棍夹于腋下。

6.Press the club: hold the club in hand and put it under the armpit.

7. 撩棍：棍沿身体左侧或右侧立圆从下向前上快速抡出，力达棍前端。

7. Blow: the cudgel is quickly swung out from the bottom to the front along the left or right side of the body.

8. 扫棍：棍梢在腰以下平扫或以棍梢贴地、棍身倾斜迅猛扫出，力达棍前端。

8. Sweep: the top of the staff shall be flat below the waist or with the top of the staff close to the ground.

9. 平抡棍：棍梢在胸部以上向左或向右迅猛有力地做半周以上平抡，力达棍前端。

9. Swing the club horizontally: swing the top of the stick to the left or right above the chest for half circle.

10. 挂棍：用棍梢或棍把由前向侧后上方或侧后下方贴身拨摆，快速有力。

10. Hang the club: use the tip or handle of the stick to move from the front to the top or the bottom of the back, fast and powerful.

11. 云棍：棍在头前上方或上方向顺时针或逆时针平圆绕环一周。

11. Swirling: the stick circles clockwise or anticlockwise over the head.

12. 戳棍：双手握棍，使棍梢或棍把直线向前、向侧或向后戳击。

12. Stab: hold the stick with both hands, and make the stick tip or stick poke straight forward, sideways or backward.

13. 架棍：双手握棍由下向头上举起，棍身横平为平架棍，棍身斜平举为斜架棍。

13. Hold: hold the stick with both hands and lift it from the bottom to the top.

14. 挑棍：一手握棍把端，另一手握棍身中段，使棍的一端由下向前上方快速挑起，力达棍梢端。

14. Pick: hold the handle end of the stick in one hand and the middle part of the stick in the other hand, to make one end of the stick up quickly.

15. 压棍：棍横举后向下按压，力达棍身中段。

15. Press: press down after the stick is raised horizontally.

16. 点棍：棍梢向下方短促点击，力达棍梢。

16. Point: point with the top of the stick.

17. 崩棍：棍梢由下向上或向左右短促崩击，力达棍梢。

17. Shoot: shoot out the tip of the stick quickly.

18. 绞棍：棍身横置于身前，棍梢或棍把向内或向外绕立圆，力达棍梢或棍把。

18. Wring: the stick body is horizontally placed in front of the body, wring the stick inward or outward.

19. 舞花棍：棍在身体两侧立圆绕转，可原地和行进间连续进行。

19. Swing: swing the stick on both sides of the body in vertical round.

20. 提撩舞花：棍在身体两侧连续立圆撩棍转动。

20. Lift and swing: continuously rotating the stick on both sides of the body.

（二）盘龙棍组合动作图解 Illustrations of the combined actions

组合一： Combination 1

1. 预备姿势 Ready position

图Fig 4-1-1　　　　　图Fig 4-1-2　　　　　图Fig 4-1-3

（1）并步站立，右手握棍把竖直举于右侧，左手直臂垂于身体左侧，目视前方。(图 4-1-1)

(1) Standing on the parallel feet, hold the stick in the right hand and lift it vertically on the right side, with the straight arm of the left hand hanging on the left side of the body, and look ahead. (Fig. 4-1-1)

（2）左掌向左前方撩掌，掌心向上，与肩同高，目视左掌。(图 4-1-2)

(2) Lift the left palm to the left front, and look at the left palm. (Fig. 4-1-2)

（3）左掌收抱腰间，右手持棍向右前方推棍，目视右手。(图 4-1-3)

(3) The left palm is close to the waist, the right hand is holding the stick and pushing the stick to the right and front. Look at the right hand. (Fig. 4-1-3)

动作要点：撩掌、举棍手臂劲力饱满，目光锐利。

Key points: do with full strength and sharp eyes.

2. 躬身揽棍 Gongshenlangun

（1）右脚向右前方上步，右腿微屈，左手内旋腕握棍，与右手虎口相对，目视双手。

(图 4-1-4)

(1) Step up right front with right foot, slightly bend the right leg, turn the left wrist to hold the stick, and look at the both hands. (Fig. 4-1-4)

（2）重心前移右腿，双手拉开持棍，斜举棍贴于胸前，棍梢与膝同高，目视左侧。(图 4-1-5)

(2) Move the weight forward on the right leg, pull out the club with both hands, lift the it obliquely to the chest, keep the top of the it at the same height as the knee, and look at the left side. (Fig. 4-1-5)

（3）重心前移右腿，右腿直立，左腿屈膝上提，左脚背绷直；同时，双手持棍向左立推棍，上体左倾，目视左侧。(图 4-1-6)

(3) Move forward the weight of the right leg, keep the right leg upright, bend the left leg and lift it up, and straighten the back of the left foot; at the same time, hold the stick in both hands and push the stick to the left, lean the upper body to the left, and look at the left side. (Fig. 4-1-6)

图Fig 4-1-4　　　　　图Fig 4-1-5　　　　　图Fig 4-1-6

动作要点：推棍贴身前送，上体通肩伸臂，身体形成弧度，力达棍身。

Key points: pull the stick close to the body and send it forward.

3. 凤点头 Phoenix nodding

（1）左脚向左跨步，右脚再向左脚并步，右手持棍经上向右下劈点，左掌上架，目视右侧。(图 4-1-7)

(1) Step left with the left foot, and the right foot, hold the stick in the right hand and split up, right and down. the left palm up and look at the right side. (Fig. 4-1-7)

（2）身体左转 90°，左脚向前上步，左掌前穿掌，目视前方。(图 4-1-8)

(2) Turn your body 90° to the left, step forward with your left foot, put your palm in front of your left palm, and look ahead. (Fig. 4-1-8)

（3）身体左转，右脚向前上步，右手持棍随上步向前上撩棍，目视右手。(图 4-1-9)

(3) Turn your body to the left, step forward with your right foot, hold the stick with your right hand and lift the stick forward, and look at your right hand. (Fig. 4-1-9)

图Fig 4-1-7　　　　　　图Fig 4-1-8　　　　　　图Fig 4-1-9

（4）两脚开立，左手内旋腕握棍，目视左手。(图 4-1-10)

(4) Open your feet, turn your left wrist inward to hold the stick, and look at your left hand. (Fig. 4-1-10)

（5）身体左转 90°，双手持棍逆时针挂滚，棍把向上，目视左侧。(图 4-1-11)

(5) Turn the body 90° to the left, hold the stick in both hands and roll it anticlockwise, with the handle upward, and look to the left. (Fig. 4-1-11)

图Fig 4-1-10　　　　图Fig 4-1-11

（6）继续左转身体，左脚后撤步，双手持棍向左下挂棍，棍把向下，目视左侧。(图 4-1-12)

(6) Continue to turn left, step back with your left foot, hang the stick with both hands to

the left, hang the stick down with the handle, and look to the left. (Fig. 4-1-12)

（7）右脚向左脚并步，挂棍上举，右手持棍经上向右下劈点，左掌上架，目视棍梢。（图 4-1-13）

(7) Step the right foot to the left foot, hang the stick up, hold the stick in the right hand and split up, right and down. Look at the top of the stick. (Fig. 4-1-13)

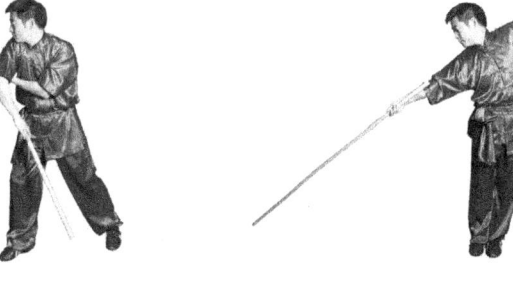

图Fig 4-1-12　　　　图Fig 4-1-13

动作要点：撩棍紧随上步，撩棍、挂棍贴近身体，劈点力达棍梢。

Key points: the stick close to the body, and the force reaches the top of the stick.

4. 寻营瞭哨 Watch out

（1）身体左转 90°，右手持棍拖地，两脚向前行进间跑三步，左脚先上步，左掌前穿掌，目视前方。（图 4-1-14、图 4-1-15、图 4-1-16）

(1) Turn your body 90° to the left, drag the stick in your right hand, run three steps, step on the left foot first, the left palm goes in front, and look ahead. (Fig. 4-1-14, Fig. 4-1-15, Fig. 4-1-16)

图Fig 4-1-14　　　　图Fig 4-1-15　　　　图Fig 4-1-16

（2）重心前移左脚，左腿直立，右腿向后撩腿，左掌向前上架掌，目视前方。（图 4-1-17）

(2) Move the weight forward on the left foot, keep the left leg upright, lift the right leg backward, and look ahead. (Fig. 4-1-17)

图Fig 4-1-17

动作要点：右手持棍拖地跟随，行进间三大步跑进，最后一步站稳脚步。

Key points:drag the stick on the ground, run in three steps, and stand firmly at the last step.

5. 日头照 Sunny shower

左脚贴地碾转，身体右后转180°左腿直腿站立，右腿屈膝上提，右脚背绷直；同时，右手外旋拖棍，左掌架掌，目视前方。(图 4-1-18)

The left foot turns the right back 180°, stand on the left leg, the right leg bend and lift, with the right foot back straight; rotate the stick with the right hand, and look ahead. (Fig. 4-1-18)

图Fig 4-1-18

动作要点：左脚碾转站稳，随转身外旋拖棍。

Action points: stand firm, and turn the stick with the body.

6. 朝天一炷香 A stick of incense in the sky

(1) 右脚尖外展向前上步，左手贴紧右手接握棍向右上抡棍，目视棍梢。(图 4-1-19)

(1) Step forward with the tip of the right foot outstretched, hold the stick tightly with the left hand, swing the stick to the right, and look at the top of the stick. (Fig. 4-1-19)

（2）两脚交叉不动，双手持棍继续向左抡棍，目视棍梢。(图 4-1-20)

(2) Keep your feet crossed, swing the stick to the left with both hands, and look at the top of the stick. (Fig. 4-1-20)

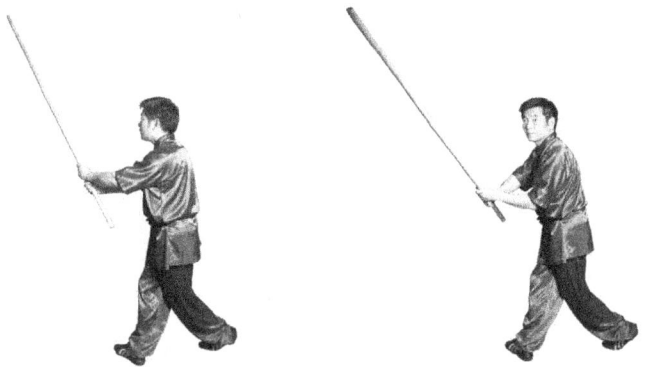

图Fig 4-1-19　　　　　图Fig 4-1-20

（3）身体右转 45°，左脚上步，两腿屈膝半蹲成马步，双手持棍立棍于体前，目视左侧。(图 4-1-21-1、图 4-1-21-2)

(3) Turn your body 45° to the right, step on your left foot, bend your knees and squat in a horse stance, and look at the left side. (Fig. 4-1-21-1, Fig. 4-1-21-2)

图Fig 4-1-21-1　　　　　图Fig 4-1-21-2

动作要点：持棍在体前立圆抡棍，力达棍身前端。

Key points: hold the stick in front of the body and swing the stick.

7. 丁步抱棍 T stance

（1）身体左转 90°，重心前移左腿成半弓步，右脚跟提起，双手向上滑把，棍把向前横打，力达棍把端，目视棍把。(图 4-1-22)

(1) Turn your body 90° to the left, move your weight forward and form a half bow step, lift your right heel, hit the handle forward and horizontally, and look at the handle. (Fig. 4-1-22)

（2）两脚不动，重心上提，双手持棍继续向左抡棍，右手向棍把端滑把，使棍竖立，目视棍把。（图 4-1-23)

(2) Keep your feet still, lift your weight up, swing the stick to the left with both hands holding the stick, make the stick stand upright, and look at the stick. (Fig. 4-1-23)

图Fig 4-1-22　　　　图Fig 4-1-23

（3）左手向右手滑把，双手持棍继续从头上方顺时针云棍，目视棍梢。（图 4-1-24)

(3) From the left hand to the right hand, swirl the stick clockwise from the top of the head, and look at the top of the stick. (Fig. 4-1-24)

（4）左脚向右脚靠拢，左脚尖点地，右腿全蹲成丁步；同时，双手持棍继续向左平云棍，左手向棍梢滑把，两手平抱棍于体前，目视左方。（图 4-1-25)

(4) The left foot toe on the ground, and the right leg is squatted into a T step; at the same time, keep holding the stick in both hands to swing left , slide the stick to the top of the stick in the left hand, hold the stick in front of the body with both hands, and look at the left side. (Fig. 4-1-25)

图Fig 4-1-24　　　　图Fig 4-1-25

动作要点：云棍平圆，左右手滑把迅速流畅，抱棍时棍贴身，左臂伸直。

Key points: Swirl the stick vertically, the left and right hand change quickly and smoothly, the stick is close to the body when holding the stick, and the left arm is extended straight.

组合二： Combination 2

8. 左右贯打 Right and Left Guanda

（1）左脚向前上步，重心前移左腿半蹲，右腿屈膝，右手向左手滑把，双手持棍向前右贯打，目视棍把。(图 4-1-26)

(1) Step forward with your left foot, move your gravity forward and squat on your left leg, bend your right leg, hold your stick in both hands and hit it forward and right, and watch the handle.(Fig. 4-1-26)

（2）右脚向前上步，重心前移右腿半蹲，左腿屈膝，双手依次向棍把滑把，双手持棍向前左贯打，目视棍梢。(图 4-1-27)

(2) Step forward with your right foot, move your weight forward, squat on your right leg, bend your left leg, slide your hands towards the handle of the stick in turn, hold the stick in your hands and hit it forward and left, and look at the top of the stick. (Fig. 4-1-27)

图Fig 4-1-26　　　　　图Fig 4-1-27

动作要点：左右手滑把迅速流畅，贯打与小腿同高。

Key points: the transfer of the club between left and right should be fast and smooth.

9. 舞花 Wuhua

（1）重心上提，两腿微屈，右手持棍上提，左手向棍中滑把，右手再向棍中滑把，双手持棍竖立右侧，目视左方。(图 4-1-28)

(1) Lift the gravity, slightly bend the legs, lift the stick with the right hand, slide the handle from the left hand to the middle of the stick, slide the handle from the right hand to the

middle of the stick, stand the right side with the stick in both hands, and look to the left side. (Fig. 4-1-28)

图Fig 4-1-28

（2）两脚不动，双手持棍在身体两侧立圆舞花棍，目视前方。(图4-1-29、图4-1-30、图4-1-31)

(2) Keep your feet still. Swing the stick in both hands on both sides in vertical round. Look ahead. (Fig. 4-1-29, Fig. 4-1-30, Fig. 4-1-31)

图Fig 4-1-29　　　　图Fig 4-1-30　　　　图Fig 4-1-31

动作要点：舞花棍立圆，贴近身体，身体配合舞花棍微左右转身。

Key points: swing the stick in a circle close to the body, and the body turns around slightly with the stick.

10. 进步压棍 Press the club

左脚向前上步，左腿屈膝半蹲成左弓步，左手滑把至棍把端，右手持握棍中，双手持棍向前下压棍，目视棍梢。(图4-1-32)

Step forward with your left foot, bend your left leg to form a left bow step, hand sliding to the end of the stick, hold the stick in your right hand, press the stick forward with both hands, and look at the top of the stick. (Fig. 4-1-32)

图Fig 4-1-32

动作要点：舞花压棍滑把换手要迅速，力达棍身。

Key points: the change of the hands on the club should be fast when swing the club.

11. 进步贯扎 Step forward and stab

（1）右脚向前上步，右腿直立，左腿屈膝上提，双手持棍向右后挂棍，目视棍梢。（图4-1-33）

(1) Step forward with your right foot, stand upright with your right leg, bend your left leg and lift it up, hold the stick in both hands and blow back to right, and look at the top of the stick. (Fig. 4-1-33)

（2）左脚向前落步成左弓步，双手持棍向前扣压棍，目视棍梢。（图4-1-34）

(2) Step your left foot forward into a left bow step, press the stick forward with both hands, and look at the tip of the stick. (Fig. 4-1-34)

（3）两脚不动，双手持棍向前扣压戳棍，目视棍梢。（图4-1-35）

(3) Keep your feet still, press the stick forward with both hands, and look at the top of the stick. (Fig. 4-1-35)

图Fig 4-1-33　　　　图Fig 4-1-34　　　　图Fig 4-1-35

动作要点：挂棍和压棍贴近身体，扣压戳棍右臂内旋。

Key points: hang the stick and press the stick close to the body, and press the right arm to rotate inside.

12. 中平枪 Zhongpingqiang

重心后移，两腿屈膝成马步；同时，双手迅速滑把换位，右手把握棍把端，目视棍梢。（图 4-1-36）

The gravity is shifted backward, and the legs are bent to form a horse stance; meanwhile, the hands quickly slide to change positions, the right hand holds the end of the handle, and look at the end of the handle. (Fig. 4-1-36)

图Fig 4-1-36

动作要点：两手倒手换把要牢稳快速，右手握棍把头。

Key points: change hands firmly and quickly, hold the head of the stick with the right hand.

13. 偷步盖把 Toubugaiba

（1）身体左转，重心前移左腿，右腿屈膝，左手滑把至棍梢，右手滑把至棍中，向前斜打棍把，目视棍把。（图 4-1-37）

(1) Turn your body to the left, move your weight forward to the left leg, bend your right leg, left hand slides to the top of the stick, right hand slides to the middle of the stick, and hit forward obliquely and look at the handle. (Fig. 4-1-37)

（2）身体左转，快速上右步，再向前插左步，两腿交叉；同时，右手滑把至棍把，左手滑把至棍中，双手持棍立圆从上向前盖打，目视棍梢。（图 4-1-38）

(2) Turn your body to the left, quickly step up to the right, then step left, legs crossed, slide your right hand to the handle of the stick, slide your left hand to the stick, blow up and down. (Fig. 4-1-38)

图Fig 4-1-37　　　　图Fig 4-1-38

动作要点：斜打棍把与盖打棍梢双手滑把要稳准快。

Key points: hands shift should be stable, accurate and fast.

14. 列枪势 Lieqiangshi

（1）身体左后转，左脚向右脚并步，两腿直立，双手持棍随转身立圆向前右撩棍，目视棍梢。(图 4-1-39)

(1) Turn your body back to the left, step your left foot to your right foot, stand upright with your legs, hold the stick with your hands, swing in a circle and blow forward and right, and look at the top of the stick. (Fig. 4-1-39)

（2）两脚不动，双手持棍向左后撩棍抡劈，目视棍梢。(图 4-1-40)

(2) Keep your feet still. Hold the stick in both hands and swing it to the left. Look at the end of the stick. (Fig. 4-1-40)

图Fig 4-1-39　　　　　　　　　图Fig 4-1-40

（3）两脚不动，上体微左转，左手向棍梢端滑把，双手拖棍于左侧，目视棍梢。(图 4-1-41)

(3) Keep your feet still, turn your upper body slightly to the left, slide your left hand to the end of the stick tip, drag the stick with both hands to the left, and look at the stick tip. (Fig. 4-1-41)

（4）右腿直立，左腿屈膝上提，双手持棍斜抱棍于体侧，目视前方。(图 4-1-42)

(4) The right leg is upright, the left leg is raised with the knees bent, the two hands hold the stick obliquely on the side of the body, and look ahead. (Fig. 4-1-42)

（5）右腿屈膝半蹲，左脚向前虚点脚尖成左虚步，双手持棍向前推棍，目视前方。(图 4-1-43)

(5) Bend your right leg and squat. Move your left foot forward to form a left virtual step. Push the stick forward with both hands and look ahead. (Fig. 4-1-43)

图Fig 4-1-41　　　　　图Fig 4-1-42　　　　　图Fig 4-1-43

动作要点：拖棍时左手以拇指扣握，左掌伸直拖棍。

Key points: hold the stick with the thumb button in the left hand and extend the stick with the left palm.

15. 日头照 Sunny shower

（1）左手握棍，右手滑把至把头，贴紧把头旋转成正握棍，右臂屈臂内旋伸直由脑后将棍从头上移至左肩，目视前方。(图 4-1-44)

(1) Hold the stick with the left hand, slide the handle with the right hand to the head, close to the head and rotate, bend the right arm and rotate, move the stick from the back of the head to the left shoulder, and look ahead. (Fig. 4-1-44)

（2）右手向前推送棍，左手滑把至棍把端，左手单手持棍点地，重心上提，右腿直立，左腿屈膝上提；右掌外旋上架，目视前方。(图 4-1-45)

(2) Push the stick forward with the right hand, slide the hand to the end of the stick, hold the stick, point on the land, lift the center of gravity upward, keep the right leg upright, and lift the left leg with the knee bent upward; and look ahead. (Fig. 4-1-45)

图Fig 4-1-44　　　　　图Fig 4-1-45

动作要点：右手不离棍，贴紧把头旋转，持棍裹脑，两臂和棍一条线。

Key points: keep your right hand holding the stick, rotate around the handle.

16. **收棍** End up

（1）左脚向左落步，身体右转90°，右手握棍把，左手向棍中滑把，目视棍梢。（图4-1-46）

(1) Step left with your left foot, turn right 90°, hold the handle with your right hand, slide the handle to your left hand, and look at the top of the stick. (Fig. 4-1-46)

（2）左脚向右脚并步，两腿直立，双手持棍收棍于身体右侧，目视右手。（图4-1-47）

(2) Step the left foot to the right foot, keep the legs upright, hold the stick in both hands to the right side of the body, and look at the right hand. (Fig. 4-1-47)

（3）并步站立，右手握棍把竖直举于体侧，左手直臂垂于左侧，目视前方。（图4-1-48）

(3) Stand in step, hold the stick in the right hand and lift it vertically on the side of the body, with the straight arm of the left hand hanging on the left side, and look ahead. (Fig. 4-1-48)

图Fig 4-1-46　　　　　图Fig 4-1-47　　　　　图Fig 4-1-48

动作要点：收棍笔直，精神饱满。

Key points: the club is straight and the player is energetic.

第二节　龙凤双刀
4.2 Dragon and Phoenix Double Blades

一、龙凤双刀简介 Introduction

龙凤双刀是红拳的双器械技法，命名取意龙凤呈祥，象征双器械的默契配合。龙凤双刀以精、气、神引领手、肘、肩、脚、膝、胯等势法运行，构成六合刀法技理思路。整套技术动作布局合理，衔接紧凑，刀法清晰，实用性强。刀法以劈、砍、撩、挂、扎、截、拦、缠头裹脑及舞花等基本技法构成，将红拳撑补、勾挂、缠粘、贴靠、巧击拳理表现得淋漓尽致。

Dragon and Phoenix Double Blades are the double instruments techniques of Hongquan. They are named after the meaning of dragon and Phoenix, symbolizing the tacit cooperation of the two instruments. The playing of Dragon and Phoenix Double Blades needs human's Qi to guid the moving and the actions of hands, legs and feet. The whole set of moves are close and tight composing the basic techniques of Liuhe blades. The basic skills include chopping, lifting, hanging, tying, cutting, blocking, wrapping and blades dancings, etc., which show the skill of supporting, hooking, sticking, leaning and skillfully hitting of Hongquan.

二、龙凤双刀技术特点 Technical characteristics

龙凤双刀多缠头裹脑与舞花技法，技法简单明快，攻防方法清晰，劲力饱满。双刀注重左右刀配合，左手刀防、右手刀攻或右手刀劈、左手刀斩随之，左右刀攻防为伍，主次分明、繁而不乱；双刀演练身法以侧身换膀、拧腰摆胯、腰带动双刀巧击刁打。双刀练习以拳术套路为基础，有了扎实的拳术基础才能体现出龙凤双刀技法圆转灵活、刀花较多、身步协调、刀如流水、步法如飞、气势磅礴、刚柔相济的技法风格特点。

The techniques are simple and bright, the attack and defense methods are clear, and the strength is full. The players should pay attention to the coordination of left and right sabers. The left and right sabers attack or split with the right and cut with the left. The left and right sabers attack and defense together. The body method of double sabers drill is to exchange arms with one side, twist waist and swing hips skillfully. The practice of double sabers is based on the Quan routine.

龙凤双刀歌（谱）诀

龙凤双刀法在走，起势先走风摆柳；
虚步亮刀显威风，双刀攻防紧相连；
龙游凤摆走连环，双双缠脖盖世间；
提劈撩砍虎翻身，双摆贯千护全身；
左格右砍龙形走，双刀变化显身手；
蝴蝶採花风火轮，飘柔绝技多惊人；
猫儿洗脸迎面转，果老骑驴向后看；

左格右砍缠腰刀，白蛇出洞水上飘；

马步藏刀身下势，滚刀妙法接连旋；

勤练技巧有诀窍，经典绝技留世上。

三、龙凤双刀基本技法与组合图解 Illustrations of the Basic skills and combination

（一）基本技法 Basic techniques

1. 抱刀礼：并步站立，左手抱刀，刀背贴于小臂上，刀刃向上，屈臂使刀斜横于胸前，右手拇指屈拢成斜侧立掌，以掌根附左腕内侧。（图 4-2-1）

1. Knife holding etiquette: stand in parallel, hold the knife in the left hand, stick the back of the knife to the small arm, with the blade upward, bend the arm to make the knife slant across the chest, bend the right thumb to form a slant side standing palm, and attach the palm root to the inside of the left wrist. (Fig. 4-2-1)

2. 推刀：持刀直臂前推，力达刀刃，分立推、平推、斜推。（图 4-2-2）

2.Push: hold the straight arm of the knife to push forward, reach the blade, and push separately, horizontally and obliquely. (Fig. 4-2-2)

3. 刺刀：刀尖向前直刺，臂与刀身成一直线，力达刀尖。（图 4-2-3）

3.Stab: the point of the knife is straight forward, the arm is in line with the blade, and the force reaches the point of the knife. (Fig. 4-2-3)

图Fig 4-2-1　　　　图Fig 4-2-2　　　　图Fig 4-2-3

4. 劈刀：刀由上向下挥动。手臂向上挥起时，臂与刀在同一垂面上，向下劈刀时，要松肩伸臂，臂、刀成一直线，力达刀刃。（图 4-2-4）

4.Cleave: the knife is swung from top to bottom. When the arm is swung upward, the arm and the knife are on the same vertical surface. When cutting downward, the shoulder should be loosened and the arm should be extended. The arm and the knife should be in a straight line, and the force should reach the blade. (Fig. 4-2-4)

5. 撩刀：刀刃领先，刀由下向前上运行。分右撩刀和左撩刀，右撩刀前臂外旋，手心朝上，身体向左拧转；左撩刀反之。（图 4-2-5）

5. Blow: the blade is in the lead, and the blade moves from bottom to top. It can be divided into right blade and left blade. The forearm of the right blade is turned outward, the palm of the hand is upward, and the body is turned to the left; the left blade is on the contrary. (Fig. 4-2-5)

6. 截刀：刀刃向斜上方或斜下方向迎击，上用于截腕，下用于截膝。（图 4-2-6）

6. Cut: the blade is used to cut the wrist and the knee. (Fig. 4-2-6)

图Fig 4-2-4　　　　　图Fig 4-2-5　　　　　图Fig 4-2-6

7. 点刀：刀尖随提腕动作猛力向下点击，力达刀尖。（图 4-2-7）

7.Point : with the wrist lifting action, click down sharply to reach the point. (Fig. 4-2-7)

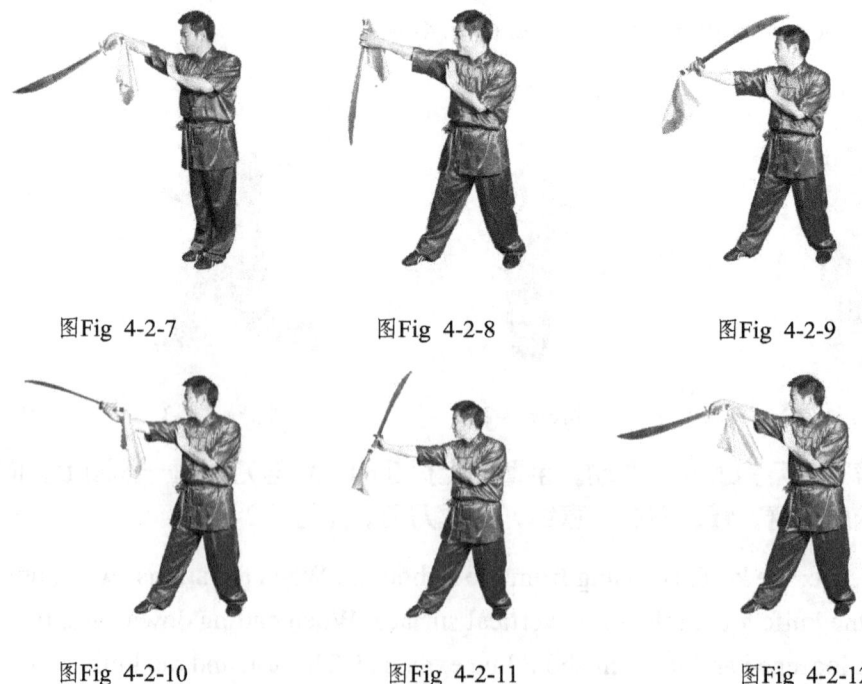

图Fig 4-2-7　　　　　图Fig 4-2-8　　　　　图Fig 4-2-9

图Fig 4-2-10　　　　　图Fig 4-2-11　　　　　图Fig 4-2-12

8. 剪腕花：以腕为轴，立刀在臂两侧向前下贴身立圆绕环，力达刀尖。（图 4-2-8、图 4-2-9、图 4-2-10、图 4-2-11、图 4-2-12）

8. Wrist twist: take the wrist as the axis, stand the knife on both sides of the arm and close to the body to form a circular ring, with the force reaching the tip of the knife. (Fig. 4-2-8, Fig. 4-2-9, Fig. 4-2-10, Fig. 4-2-11, Fig. 4-2-12)

9. 挂刀：刀尖由前向上、向后或向下、向后划弧，力达刀背前部。分为上挂刀：刀尖向上、向后贴身挂出；下挂刀：刀尖向下、向后贴身挂出；抡挂刀：刀贴身立圆抡一周。

9.Hang: the tip of the knife should arc from the front up, back or down, back to the front of the back. It can be divided into upper hanging knife: the tip of the knife goes up and back close to the body; lower hanging knife: the tip of the knife goes down and back close to the body; swing hanging knife: the blade is close to the body and stands for a circle.

10. 云刀：刀在头顶或头前上方做平圆绕转。

10. Swirling: make a circle around the top of the head or the front of the head.

11. 缠头刀：刀尖下垂，扣腕旋臂，刀背沿左肩紧贴背向右肩缠绕。左手持刀反之。

11.Wrap: the tip of the knife is down, the wrist is buckled and the arm is rotated, and the back of the knife is tightly attached to the left shoulder and twined to the right shoulder. Holding the knife with the left hand is the opposite.

12. 裹脑刀：刀尖下垂，刀背沿右肩紧贴背向左肩缠绕。左手持刀反之。

12. Rotate: the tip of the knife down, and the back of the knife clings to the right shoulder and twines to the left shoulder. Holding the knife with the left hand is the opposite.

（二）双刀技法组合 Double blades combination techniques

组合一： Combination 1

1. 预备姿势 Ready position

并步站立，双手各持刀，直臂垂于身体两侧，目视前方。（图 4-2-13）

Stand in step, each holding a knife, straight arms down on both sides of the body, and look ahead. (Fig. 4-2-13)

两腿不动，两手各持刀屈臂收至腰间，身体微左转，目视左方。(图 4-2-14)

Keep your legs still, bend your arms to your waist, turn left slightly, and look to the left. (Fig. 4-2-14)

图Fig 4-2-13　　　　　　图Fig 4-2-14

2. 捞月架刀 Moon fishing

(1) 两腿不动，俯身弯腰，两手各持刀向下伸直接近地面，刀刃均朝前，两刀交叉，目视双刀。(图 4-2-15)

(1) Keep your legs still, bend over, hold the knife in both hands and reach down straight to the ground. The blades are all facing forward. The two knives are crossed. Look at the two knives. (Fig. 4-2-15)

(2) 接上式起身，两臂伸直上抬至与肩同高，双臂微屈，两刀上架，左手刀在外，右手刀在内，交叉成"十"字状，转头，目视左方。(图 4-2-16)

(2) Follow the up moves and get up, straighten and lift both arms up to the same height as the shoulder, slightly bend both arms, hold up the two knives with the left outside and the right one inside, making a cross, turn your head and look to the left. (Fig. 4-2-16)

动作要点：十字架刀有力，双臂含圆，双臂旋腕有力。

Key points: powerful, the arms are round, and the arms rotate the wrist powerfully.

3. 腕花虚步分刀 Wrist twist

右脚向右后撤一步，两刀以手腕为轴各绕腕花一圈向下交叉，重心后移，右腿屈膝下蹲，左腿微屈脚尖虚点地成左虚步；双手向右带刀，左手刀在外，右手刀在内，交叉成"十"字状，目视左方。(图 4-2-17)

Step back with the right foot, cross the two knives around the wrist with the wrist as the axis, move the center of gravity backward, squat down with the right leg bent, slightly bend the toe of the left leg to form the left virtual step; take the knife with both hands to the right, with the left knife outside and the right knife inside, making a cross and look at the left side. (Fig. 4-2-17)

图Fig 4-2-15　　　　　图Fig 4-2-16　　　　　图Fig 4-2-17

动作要点：腕花与后撤步连贯协调。

Key points: wrist moves coordinately with the feet moving.

4. 弓步刺刀 Stab with bow step

（1）左脚向左侧跨一步成半马步，左手持刀成立刀，右手持刀屈臂向上带刀，两刀交叉，左刀刀刃向前，右刀刀尖向前，目视前方。(图 4-2-18)

(1) Step the left foot to the left to form a half horse step, hold the knife in the left hand to set up the knife, hold the knife in the right hand to bend the arm to bring the knife upward, cross the two knives, move the left knife edge forward, move the right knife tip forward, and look ahead. (Fig. 4-2-18)

（2）重心前移至左脚，右腿微屈，右脚跟提起，右手刀向前刺出，左手握刀随之收于腰间，目视刺刀方向。(图 4-2-19)

(2) Move the gravity forward to the left foot, slightly bend the right leg, lift the right heel, stab the right knife forward, hold the knife in the left hand and close it to the waist, and look at the knife. (Fig. 4-2-19)

（3）两腿不动，左手刀向前刺出，右手握刀随之收于腰间，目视刺刀方向。(图 4-2-20)

(3) Keep the legs still, stab forward with the left knife , draw back the knife in the right hand to the waist , and look at the knife. (Fig. 4-2-20)

图Fig 4-2-18　　　　　图Fig 4-2-19　　　　　图Fig 4-2-20

动作要点：刺刀伸臂顺肩，两刀刺刀快速协调，力达刀尖。

Key points: the knife stretches along the arms and shoulders, the knives go coordinately and rapidly.

5. **转身挂刺刀** Turn and stab

（1）两腿不动，右手刀向前刺刀后内旋腕左挂刀，左手刀藏刀于右腋下，目视前方。（图 4-2-21）

(1) Keep your legs still, turn your right knife forward, turn your wrist inward, hang it on the left, hide it under your right armpit, and look ahead. (Fig. 4-2-21)

（2）身体左转，重心前移至左脚，右腿屈膝，右脚背绷直，右手刀挂刀从上带至右侧，左手刀向左带刀，目视右刀。（图 4-2-22）

(2) Turn your body to the left, move your weight forward to the left foot, bend your right leg, straighten the back of your right foot, put the knife on your right knife from the top to the right, put the knife on your left knife to the left, and look at the right knife. (Fig. 4-2-22)

（3）身体左转，右脚向左脚外侧上步成右弓步，右手刀向前刺出，左手刀藏刀于右腋下，目视右手刀方向。（图 4-2-23）

(3) Turn your body to the left, step up the right foot to the outside of the left foot to form a right lunge, stab the right knife forward, hide the left knife under the right armpit, and look in the direction of the right knife. (Fig. 4-2-23)

图Fig 4-2-21　　　　图Fig 4-2-22　　　　图Fig 4-2-23

动作要点：挂刀立圆、贴身，刺刀随身体重心前移伸臂顺肩，力达刀尖。

Key points: The knife moves forward with the center of gravity of the body and stretches along arms and shoulders.

6. **缠头列刀** Chantouliedao

（1）身体左转，两腿微屈，右手持刀屈腕，双手持刀随转身向左带刀，目视左手刀。（图 4-2-24）

(1) Turn your body to the left, bend your legs slightly, hold the knife in your right hand and bend your wrists, hold the knife in both hands and turn to the left with the knife as you turn, and look at the left knife. (Fig. 4-2-24)

（2）两腿不动，左手提肘扣腕，使刀尖下垂、刀刃朝外向右绕至右肩外，右手握刀藏于左腋下，目视右侧。(图 4-2-25)

(2) Keep your legs still, lift your elbows and buckle your wrists with your left hand, so that the tip of the knife droops and the blade turns outwards and right to the outside of your right shoulder. Hold the knife with your right hand and hide it under your left armpit. Look to the right. (Fig. 4-2-25)

（3）两腿不动，左手刀贴背向左肩绕摆，右手握刀随之向右拉摆，目视右侧。(图 4-2-26)

(3) Two legs do not move, the left knife sticks to the back and swings around the left shoulder, the right hand holds the knife and then pulls it to the right, and looks at the right side. (Fig. 4-2-26)

（4）两腿不动，右手提肘扣腕，使刀尖下垂、刀刃朝外向右肩贴背裹脑，左手握刀藏于右腋下，目视右侧。(图 4-2-27)

(4) Keep your legs still, lift your elbows and clasp your wrists with your right hand, so that the point of the knife is drooping, the edge of the knife is facing outwards, the right shoulder is close to your back, the left hand holds the knife and hides it under your right armpit, and you can see the right side. (Fig. 4-2-27)

（5）两腿不动，身体微左转，右手刀裹脑绕背从左肩外下落胸前，左手握刀藏于右腋下，目视左侧。(图 4-2-28)

(5) Keep your legs still, turn your body slightly to the left, wrap your right knife around your back and fall to your chest from the outside of your left shoulder. Hold the knife in your left hand and hide it under your right armpit. Look at the left side. (Fig. 4-2-28)

（6）右脚向右前方上步，右腿屈膝半蹲成右弓步，右手提腕向上列刀，右刀尖向下，刀刃向前，左手持刀向左前屈腕平推，刀尖向右，目视左侧。(图 4-2-29)

(6) Step right forward with the right foot, bend the right leg and half squat to form a right lunge, lift the wrist with the right hand to form an upward row of knives, with the right tip downward and the blade forward, with the left hand holding the knife, bend the wrist to the left and push horizontally, with the tip right, and look at the left side. (Fig. 4-2-29)

图Fig 4-2-24　　　　　图Fig 4-2-25　　　　　图Fig 4-2-26

图Fig 4-2-27　　　　　图Fig 4-2-28　　　　　图Fig 4-2-29

动作要点：缠头裹脑时刀背贴身缠绕，藏刀刀背贴身，左右手刀协调。

Key points: when wrapping head, the back of the blade shall be wound close to the body, the back of it shall be close to the body, and the left and right hand shall be coordinated.

组合二：Combination 2

1. 虚步推刀 Xubutuidao

右脚后撤半步，重心移至右腿，右腿屈膝下蹲，左腿微屈脚尖虚点地成左虚步；同时，右手持刀屈臂向后带刀，刀尖向前，刀刃向下，左手持刀向前推刀，刀刃向前，刀尖向上，目视前方。(图 4-2-30)

The right foot retreats half a step, the center of gravity moves to the right leg, the right leg bends the knee and squats down, the left leg slightly bends the toe to form the left virtual step; at the same time, the right hand holds the knife and bends the arm to bring the knife backward, the knife point is forward, the knife edge is downward, the left hand holds the knife and pushes the knife forward, the knife edge is forward, the knife point is upward, and look ahead.(Fig. 4-2-30)

图Fig 4-2-30

动作要点：抬头挺胸，直臂推刀，刀身竖直。

Key points: raise your head, straighten your arms and push the knife. The blade is vertical.

2. 独立架刀 Dulijiadao

（1）左脚向左侧跨一步，重心前移至左脚，右腿微屈，右脚跟提起，右手刀向前刺出，左手握刀收于腰间，目视刺刀方向。(图 4-2-31)

(1) Step left to the left, move the center of gravity forward to the left foot, slightly bend the right leg, lift the right heel, stab the right knife forward, hold the knife in the left hand to the waist, and look in the direction of stabbing.(Fig. 4-2-31)

（2）重心后移至右腿直立，左腿屈膝上提，左脚背绷直；同时，右手刀后带刀，翻腕上架，刀尖向前，刀刃向上，左手带刀至右腋下藏刀，目视前方。(图 4-2-32)

(2) Move the weight back to the right leg and stand upright, bend the left leg and lift it up, and straighten the back of the left foot; at the same time, bring the knife behind the right knife, turn the wrist and go upward, with the tip of the knife forward, the blade upward, and take the knife with the left hand to the right armpit, and look ahead. (Fig. 4-2-32)

图Fig 4-2-31　　　　　　图Fig 4-2-32

动作要点：右手带刀贴身立圆，上架刀翻腕快速。

Key points: the right hand with the knife is close to the body, and the upper holding and wrist turning quickly.

3. 翻身抡劈刀 Fanshenlunpidao

（1）左脚外展向前落步，右手刀以刀尖为力点下抡左挂刀，目视刀前身。(图 4-2-33)

(1)Step forward with the left foot outstretched, swing the left knife with the right knife as the force point, and look at the front of the knife. (Fig. 4-2-33)

（2）右脚向前上步，右手刀向上绕至头上方，刀刃向上，刀尖向左。(图 4-2-34)

(2) Step forward with the right foot; turn the right knife upward to the top of the head, with the blade upward and the tip to the left. (Fig. 4-2-34)

（3）左脚向右脚后插步，右手刀向上绕至身体右侧平劈刀，左手刀随之下落，体前平置，两刀刃均朝下，刀尖向右，目视右刀。(图 4-2-35)

(3) Step backward from the left foot to the right foot, turn the right knife upward to the right side of the body, and then the left knife will fall, the front of the body is flat, both blades are facing down, the tip of the knife is right, and look at the right knife. (Fig. 4-2-35)

图Fig 4-2-33　　　　图Fig 4-2-34　　　　图Fig 4-2-35

（4）身体向左翻转成仰身，两脚贴地拧转成开立步；同时，两刀随身体翻转由下向上立圆绕转。(图 4-2-36)

(4) Turn the body to the left to turn it into a reclining body, and turn the feet to the ground to turn it into a opening step; at the same time, turn the two knives vertically and circularly from the bottom to the top with the body turning. (Fig. 4-2-36)

（5）上右步；同时，右手刀随上步转身绕至体右前方劈出，左手刀顺势收于体前横置，目视右手刀。(图 4-2-37)

(5) Step up and right; at the same time, the right knife turns around to the front of the body and splits out. The left knife is placed horizontally in front of the body and looks at the right knife. (Fig. 4-2-37)

（6）重心移至右腿直立，左腿屈膝上提，右手刀下劈，左手刀上提，目视右手刀。（图 4-2-38）

(6) Move the weight to the right leg and stand upright, bend the left leg and lift it up, split it down with the right knife, lift it up with the left knife, and look at the right knife. (Fig. 4-2-38)

图Fig 4-2-36　　　　图Fig 4-2-37　　　　图Fig 4-2-38

动作要点：右手劈刀随即上右步，左手劈刀插左步，翻腰上右步同时提左膝劈出右刀，动作要连贯流畅。

Key points: right hand cleaver immediately step up and right, left hand cleaver and step left, turn waist up and right step while raising left knee to cleave with right knife, the action should be coherent and fluent.

4. 左右撩花 Zuoyouliaohua

（1）身体右转，左脚向后落步，左脚跟提起，右手持刀外旋腕向前上右撩刀，左手持刀随之左撩刀，双手持刀合拢于胸前，目视前方。（图 4-2-39）

(1) Turn your body to the right, step backward with your left foot, lift the heel of your left foot, hold the knife in your right hand, turn your wrist outward, lift the knife forward and right, hold the knife in your left hand, then lift the knife in your left hand, hold the knife in your hands and close it to your chest, and look ahead. (Fig. 4-2-39)

（2）两腿不动，身体微左右转，双手持刀左右连环撩刀，目视前方。（图 4-2-40）

(2) Keep your legs still, turn your body slightly left and right, hold the knife in both hands and lift it left and right, and look ahead. (Fig. 4-2-40)

图Fig 4-2-39　　　　图Fig 4-2-40

动作要点：双手立圆撩刀，左右刀依次紧随，身体随撩刀微左右转身。

Key points: the left and right knives swing in turn, and turn slightly with the body.

5. 缠头裹脑 Chantouguonao

（1）左脚向前上步，身体右转，右手扣腕提肘使刀尖下垂、刀刃朝外从左肩贴背缠头刀，左手握刀藏于右腋下，目视左侧。(图 4-2-41)

(1) Step forward with the left foot, turn right, hold the elbow with the right hand to make the tip of the knife droop, the blade is outward from the left shoulder to the back, wrap the head, hold the knife with the left hand and hide it under the right armpit, and look at the left side. (Fig. 4-2-41)

（2）右手缠头刀收至左腋下，左手刀从右腋下向左横摆，扣腕提肘至左肩裹脑刀，目视左侧。(图 4-2-42)

(2) Turn the right hand wrapping knife to the left armpit, swing the left hand knife from the right armpit to the left, buckle the wrist and lift the elbow to the left shoulder wrapping the brain knife, and look at the left side. (Fig. 4-2-42)

图Fig 4-2-41　　　　　　　　图Fig 4-2-42

（3）两腿不动，身体微左转，左手裹脑刀向左平推刀，目视左侧。(图 4-2-43)

(3) Keep your legs still, turn your body slightly to the left, wrap the head with the left hand, push the knife to the left, and look at the left side. (Fig. 4-2-43)

（4）右脚向右前跨步，重心前移成右弓步；同时右手带刀上架，刀刃向上，刀尖向左，左手刀藏于右腋下，目视左侧。(图 4-2-44)

(4) Step right and forward with the right foot, and move the gravity forward into a right lunge. Put the right knife to block, with the blade upward and the tip to the left. Hide the left knife under your right armpit and look to the left. (Fig. 4-2-44)

图Fig 4-2-43　　　　　　　　图Fig 4-2-44

动作要点：缠头裹脑刀要刀背贴身，刀刃朝外、刀尖下垂。

Key points: wrap the head around to keep the back of the knife close to the body, with the blade facing outward and the tip drooping.

组合三 Combination 3

1. 弓步背刀 Gongbubeidao

右脚向右前跨步，重心前移成右弓步，右手带刀屈臂旋腕向体后背刀，左手持刀仰腕前推架刀，刀刃向上，刀尖向后，目视前方。(图 4-2-45)

Step right forward with your right foot, move your center of gravity forward into a right lunge, turn your back knife with your right arm bent with your knife, hold your knife with your left hand and lean your wrist forward to push the knife, with the blade upward, the tip backward, and look ahead. (Fig. 4-2-45)

图Fig 4-2-45

动作要点：背刀时随腕花向体后旋腕摆动，刀面贴近背部。

Key points: when carrying the knife, swing the wrist backward, and the knife is close to the back.

2. 蝴蝶采花 Butterfly picking flowers

（1）左脚向左前上步，身体左转，重心移至左腿成左弓步，右手持刀从背后随转

身腕花向前刺刀，左手持刀拉至体后，目视前方。(图 4-2-46)

(1) Step left and forward with left foot, turn left with body, move weight to left leg to form left bow step, hold knife with right hand from back and stab forward, pull knife with left hand back, and look ahead. (Fig. 4-2-46)

（2）重心后移至两腿之间，身体右转 90°，两腿微屈成开步站立，右手刀内旋臂，向右平拉至右侧屈臂翻腕撩刀，左手刀置于体前，目视右刀。(图 4-2-47)

(2) The center of gravity moves back between the two legs, the body turns 90° to the right, the legs are slightly bent to stand, the right knife rotates, the right arm is pulled horizontally, the wrist is turned and the knife is lifted, the left knife is placed in front of the body, and look at the right knife. (Fig. 4-2-47)

（3）右手刀向右后剪腕花，左手刀向右上撩腕花，目视右侧。(图 4-2-48)

(3) Swing the right knife with right hand, lift and swing the left knife with left hand, and look to the right side. (Fig. 4-2-48)

图Fig 4-2-46　　　　图Fig 4-2-47　　　　图Fig 4-2-48

（4）身体微左转，左手刀向左后剪腕花，右手刀向左上撩腕花，目视右手刀。(图 4-2-49)

(4) Turn your body slightly to the left, twist left knife, lift the and twist right knife to the left and look at the right knife. (Fig. 4-2-49)

（5）身体微右转，右手刀从左上立圆向右剪腕花下劈，左手刀向左剪腕花，目视右刀。(图 4-2-50)

(5) Turn your body slightly to the right. Cleave from upward with right knife by right hand, twist the left knife by left hand and look at the right knife. (Fig. 4-2-50)

（6）左手刀从左后经下向右上撩腕花，右手刀向右后剪腕花，目视左刀。(图 4-2-51)

(6) Lift and twist left knife with left hand from the back through the bottom to the right, twist right knife behind, and look at the left knife. (Fig. 4-2-51)

图Fig 4-2-49　　　　　图Fig 4-2-50　　　　　图Fig 4-2-51

（7）身体左转，左手刀从右上向左侧剪腕花下劈，右手刀向右后剪腕花，目视左刀。（图 4-2-52）

(7) Turn your body to the left, cleave and twist the left knife in left hand from upper right to lower left, twist right knife behind with the right hand toward right back, and look at the left knife. (Fig. 4-2-52)

（8）身体右转，右手刀从右后向上撩腕花，左手刀向左后剪腕花，目视右刀。（图 4-2-53）

(8) Turn your body slightly to the right. Cleave from upward with right knife by right hand, twist the left knife by left hand and look at the right knife. (Fig. 4-2-53)

（9）右脚踏实，左脚向右脚外侧上步，重心移至左腿，左腿直立，右小腿屈腿上摆；同时，右手刀翻腕上架刀，刀刃向上，刀尖向左，左手刀向左劈刀，目视左刀。（图 4-2-54）

(9) The right foot is firm, the left foot moves towards the outside of the right foot, the center of gravity moves to the left leg, the left leg is upright, and the right leg is bent up; at the same time, the right hand knife turns over the wrist, the blade is upward, the tip is left, the left knife cleaves to the left, and watch the left knife. (Fig. 4-2-54)

图Fig 4-2-52　　　　　图Fig 4-2-53　　　　　图Fig 4-2-54

动作要点：左右上方为撩腕花，左右下方剪腕花，背后背腕花，以腕关节为轴，刀花立圆，贴近身体。

Key points: the upper swing and lower swing are different.When swinging the knives, wrist joints should be the axis.

3. 弓步推刀 Gongbutuidao

（1）右脚向右前上步成右弓步，左手刀向前下压刀，与肩同高，刀刃向前，刀尖向右，右手刀收至腰间，目视左手刀。(图 4-2-55)

(1) The right foot moves forward to the right to form a right lunge, the left knife moves forward and downward to press the knife, which is the same height as the shoulder, the blade moves forward, the tip of the knife is right, the right knife retracts to the waist, and look at the left knife. (Fig. 4-2-55)

（2）两脚不动，上体微左转，右手刀向上刺刀，左手刀收回胸前随左转身向前平推刀，刀刃向前，刀尖向右，目视左刀。(图 4-2-56)

(2) Keep your feet still, turn the upper body slightly to the left, turn the right knife upward, take the left knife back to chest and push the knife forward with the left turning, move the blade forward, turn the tip to the right, and look at the left knife. (Fig. 4-2-56)

图Fig 4-2-55

图Fig 4-2-56

动作要点：推刀与转身协调一致。

Key points: push the knife and turn in harmony.

4. 弓步双劈 Gongbushuangpi

图Fig 4-2-57

图Fig 4-2-58

（1）重心移至右腿直立，左腿屈膝上提；同时，两手刀由前向右下截刀，目视刀身。(图 4-2-57)

(1) The center of gravity is moved to the right leg to stand upright, and the left leg is bent to lift; meanwhile, the two handed knives are cut from the front to the right, and look at the knife. (Fig. 4-2-57)

（2）左转身，左脚前落成左弓步；同时，双刀自右经头上向前下劈刀，目视左前方。（图 4-2-58）

(2) Turn left and make a left bow step. Split from overhead and look at the left front. (Fig. 4-2-58)

动作要点：双刀抡圆，平行一致。

Key points: the knives should swing round and parallel.

5. 连环推刀 Lianhuantuidao

（1）两脚不动，右手刀扣腕下压，左手刀收回再从右刀上向前推刀，刀刃朝前、刀尖向左，右手刀从左臂下收至左腋下，目视左手刀。（图 4-2-59）

(1) Keep your feet still, press down the wrist of the right knife buckle, recover the left knife and push the knife forward from the right knife, with the blade facing forward and the tip to the left, and take the right knife under the left arm to the left armpit, and look at the left knife. (Fig. 4-2-59)

（2）右手刀前推，左手刀回收，刀刃朝前、刀尖向左，目视右手刀。（图 4-2-60）

(2) Push the right-hand knife forward, retreat the left-hand knife, with the blade facing forward and the tip to the left. Look at the right-hand knife. (Fig. 4-2-60)

（3）左手刀前推，右手刀从左臂上收回至左肩内侧，刀刃朝前、刀尖向左，目视左手刀。（图 4-2-61）

(3) Push the left knife forward, retreat the right knife from the left arm to the inside of the left shoulder, with the blade facing forward and the tip to the left, and look at the left knife. (Fig. 4-2-61)

图Fig 4-2-59　　　　　　图Fig 4-2-60　　　　　　图Fig 4-2-61

动作要点：右手刀前推下压，左手刀顺势回收；左手刀迅速前推，右手刀顺势回收，两刀收推协调。

Key points: push the right knife forward and press it down, and the left knife will be recovered in accordance with the situation; push the left knife forward quickly, and the right knife will be recovered in accordance with the situation, and the two knives will be recovered and pushed in coordination.

6. 缠头双劈刀 Chantoushuangpidao

（1）身体右后转身，重心后移右脚，右脚外摆；同时，左手臂内旋，提肘使刀身垂直从右肩贴背缠头。(图 4-2-62)

(1) At the same time, rotate the left arm inward and lift the elbow to make the blade vertical from the right shoulder to the back. (Fig. 4-2-62)

（2）左脚向右脚前扣上步，身体随之右转；同时，右手刀从左向右上至右肩贴背裹脑，左手刀随绕至右腋下，目视前方。(图 4-2-63)

(2) The left foot buckles up to the right foot, and then the body turns right; at the same time, the right knife goes up from the left longitude to the right shoulder and wraps around the head, and the left knife goes around to the right armpit and look forward. (Fig. 4-2-63)

（3）两脚不动，继续右转身，两腿交叉拧转；同时，左、右手刀自身后经头上向右下劈刀，目视右下。(图 4-2-64)

(3) Keep your feet still, continue to turn right, and turn your legs crosswise; at the same time, cut the left and right knives to the right through the back of their own heads, and look at the right bottom. (Fig. 4-2-64)

图Fig 4-2-62

图Fig 4-2-63

图Fig 4-2-64

（4）左脚向左前上步，重心前移左腿成左弓步；同时，两手刀由右下向左前双劈刀，目视刀身。(图 4-2-65)

(4) Step left foot forward and step up, move left leg forward to form left bow step; cleave with knives in two hands from right bottom to left front, and look at the blade. (Fig. 4-2-65)

图Fig 4-2-65

动作要点：转身缠头裹脑紧凑贴身，双劈刀抡圆，平行一致。

Key points: turn around, wrap your head around with the hand, close to your body, swing your double cleavers round, parallel and consistent.

7. 收刀 End up

（1）身体右转，右腿屈膝成马步，两刀于体前合并收于左手，左手抱刀，刀背贴身，刀刃朝外，刀尖向上，右掌向右撩掌，目视右掌。(图 4-2-66)

(1) Turn your body to the right, bend your left leg to form a horse stance, merge the two sabres in front of your body and close to your left hand. Hold the sabre in your left hand, with the back close to your body, the blade facing out, the tip of the sabre facing up, and lift your right palm to the right, and look at your right palm. (Fig. 4-2-66)

（2）身体左转，左脚向右脚并步直立，右掌上提下按掌于腰间，目视左方。(图 4-2-67)

(2) Turn your body to the left, turn your left foot to your right foot and stand upright, lift your right palm up and down, press it on your waist, and look to the left. (Fig. 4-2-67)

图Fig 4-2-66 图Fig 4-2-67

动作要点：抱刀时手捧护手盘，手指不得触及刀刃，刀刃向前不得触身。

Key points: when holding the knife, hold the hand plate, fingers shall not touch the blade, and the blade shall not touch the body forward.

第三节 鞭杆
4.3 Biangan

一、鞭杆简介 Introduction

鞭杆属于武术短器械之一，鞭杆为木制短棍，长度约是使用者的一臂加一肘长，一头略粗，另一头略细，粗的一头称为"把"，细的一头称为"梢"。演练时，单手或双手握持，单双手互换使用，技法内容丰富，吸收和综合了传统武术长、短器械的多种运动方法，衍变出独特的运动风格。主要流行于甘肃、宁夏、山西、陕西等地，鞭杆技法独特，携带方便，有助于身体素质的全面提高，成为颇受喜爱的传统武术器械。鞭杆可以单练，也可以对练（鞭杆对打）。常见的鞭杆套路有八仙鞭、三十六鞭、十三鞭、三才鞭、陀螺鞭、子胥鞭杆、太师鞭杆、扭丝鞭杆、川龙鞭杆、五虎群羊鞭杆、黑虎鞭杆、缠海鞭杆等。

Biangan belongs to short instruments in Wushu. It is a short wooden stick, the length of which is about one arm plus one elbow of the user. One end is slightly thick, the other end is slightly thin, the thick end is called "Ba", and the thin end is called "Shao". During the drill, one hand or two hands hold each other and use them interchangeably. The technique is rich in content. It absorbs and synthesizes various sports methods of long and short instruments of Wushu and develops a unique sports style. It is mainly popular in Gansu, Ningxia, Shanxi, Shaanxi and other places. Its unique technique is convenient to learn and practice, which is conducive to the overall improvement of physical quality and becomes a popular Wushu instrument. It can be practiced individually or in pairs. The common sets are Baxianbian, 36 Bian, 13 Bian, Sancaibian, Tuoluo Bian, Zixu Biangan, Taishi Biangan, Niusi Biangan, Chuanlong Biangan, Five-tiger Biangan, Black-tiger Biangan, Chanhai Biangan, etc.

二、鞭杆技术特点 Technical characteristics

鞭杆基本技法有戳、劈、崩、击、搬、砸、扭、扣、挑、点、绞、挎、压、拦、截、拨、架、推、撩、舞花等。演练中要求手不离鞭，鞭不离身，走鞭换手，忽上忽下，忽左忽右，进退吞吐，起伏转折。技法运用讲求乘人之势，借人之力，出势伸展自如，劲力刚柔相济，动作声东击西，进退虚实随机。练习起来，梢把并用，调手换把，上撩下取，前劈后戳，左撩右拦，鞭法精妙，快速敏捷，一气呵成。

The basic techniques of Biangan are poke, split, collapse, strike, move, smash, twist, buckle, pick, point, hinge, hold, press, block, cut, dial, stand, push, lift, dance flower, etc. During the drill, it is required that the hand should not be separated from the stick, the stick should not be separated from the body, the stick should be used to change hands, up and down, left and right, forward and backward. The technique is to take advantage of the potential power of players with the strength of both hardness and softness, and move in and out randomly. In practice, the "Ba" and the "Shao" are shifted freely, the series moves are done continuously and finished in one breath.

缠海鞭杆歌（谱）诀

缠海势法先打手，提杆不怕枪扎喉；
裹身前进紧随身，倒手分鞭快似风；
左右横打如磨盘，右挂翻打左挡翻；
点扣缩肩立身齐，上打鼻梁下打膝；
左右里外神手变，上揭下打朝阳势；
鹞子扑鹌如流光，后打三棍彩蝶飞；
纵步飞腿藏揭打，退步埋伏把身藏；
倒打西歧回头望，闪绽左右晃鞭忙；
绞剪下防取胸膛，擒别刮挎在中央；
掠眉捧盘牛角抵，拧身挡架奔胸忙；
白蛇入洞似拨簧，拨草寻蛇里外去；
心熟手巧似猿猴，五星光辉扫八方。

三、基本技法组合图解 Illustrations of Basic techniques

组合一：Combination 1

预备式：自然直立，右手虎口朝下持握棍，右臂略屈，棍把贴小臂外侧，目视前方。（图 4-3-1）练习时，右手持棍向前点棍，目视棍梢。（图 4-3-2）

Ready pose: natural upright, holding the club with the thumb of the right hand downward, slightly bending the right arm, attach the head of the club to the outside of the forearm, and look ahead. (Fig. 4-3-1) During practice, hold the stick with your right hand and point it forward, and look at the top of the stick. (Fig. 4-3-2)

图Fig 4-3-1

图Fig 4-3-2

1. 虚步裹棍 Xubuguogun

图Fig 4-3-3

图Fig 4-3-4

图Fig 4-3-5

图Fig 4-3-6

(1) 右脚向右前方上步，右手持棍向左侧上挑，左手接握棍，两手虎口相对握棍。(图 4-3-3)

(1) Step up and right on the right foot, stick to the left with the right stick in the right hand, hold the stick with left hand, hold the stick with two hands opposite each other. (Fig. 4-3-3)

(2) 身体微左转，两手持棍向上、向身后带棍，目视棍梢。(图 4-3-4)

(2) Turn your body slightly to the left, hold the stick in both hands up and behind, and look at the top of the stick. (Fig. 4-3-4)

(3) 右腿直立，左腿屈膝上提，左脚背绷直，收于右腿内侧，两手持棍继续从后向下挑棍，目视左侧。(图 4-3-5)

(3) Stand upright on the right foot, bend the left knee and lift the left leg with left foot stretched straight and close to the inner side of the right leg. Pick from behind to the bottom

with the stick in both hands and look at the left side. (Fig. 4-3-5)

(4)右腿屈膝半蹲，左脚尖向前点地成左虚步，两手持棍向左前上方挑棍，目视棍梢。（图 4-3-6）

(4) The right leg is bent and half squatted, and the left toe points forward to form a left virtual step. Hold the stick in both hands, pick the stick to the left front and top, and look at the top of the stick. (Fig. 4-3-6)

动作要点：肩肘放松，两手握棍松紧适当；棍身贴紧身体，立圆向上挑棍，脆快有爆发力。

Key points: shoulders and elbows are relaxed, and the two hands hold the stick properly; the stick is close to the body, and the stick-picking is upright and upward, crisp and explosive.

2. 上步盖把 Shangbugaiba

左脚向左侧上步成半弓步，双手持棍向前盖打，(右手在前)，力达棍把段，目视前方。（图 4-3-7）

Step the left foot to the left to form a half bow step, hold the stick in both hands and beat forward (right hand in front), and look ahead. (Fig. 4-3-7)

图Fig 4-3-7

动作要点：左右手滑把协调快速，棍把立圆由上向前下盖打，握棍松紧适当。

Key points: the left and right hand sliding handles are coordinated quickly, the handle is vertical and round, and the grip is properly tightened.

3. 撩棍弹踢 Liaoguntanti

（1）身体左转，左脚尖外展，两手持棍向左后撩棍成竖立棍，棍把朝上，目视前方。（图 4-3-8）

(1) Turn to the left, extend the left foot tip, hold the stick in both hands and lift it to the left to form a vertical standing stick, with the handle facing up, and look ahead. (Fig. 4-3-8)

（2）左腿直立，右脚向前上弹踢，力达脚尖，目视前方。(图 4-3-9)

(2) The left leg is upright, the right foot is bouncing and kicking forward, reaching the toe, and look forward. (Fig. 4-3-9)

图Fig 4-3-8　　　　　　　图Fig 4-3-9

动作要点：撩棍靠腰转发力，弹踢快速，左腿挺直站稳。

Key points: stick swing by the waist force, play and kick quickly, stand straight on the left leg.

4. 提膝点棍 Tixidiangun

右脚向前落步，重心前移右脚，右腿直立，左腿屈膝上提，双手持棍左撩棍向前上举棍，(图4-3-10)双手持棍向前扣腕点棍，力达棍把端，同时右脚踏跳腾空，左膝上顶，左脚背绷直，目视棍端。(图 4-3-11)

Step forward with the right foot, shift the gravity to the right foot, keep the right leg upright, bend the left leg and lift, hold the left stick with both hands and lift the stick forward, (Fig. 4-3-10) hold the stick with both hands and bend the wrist to point stick forward, and step on the right foot, top the left knee, straighten the back of the left foot, and look at the end of the stick. (Fig. 4-3-11)

图Fig 4-3-10　　　　　图Fig 4-3-11

动作要点：撩棍贴身立圆，点棍、提膝踏跳协调一致，蹬腿快速，右腿挺直。

Key points: swing the stick close to the body in a vertical circle, stick point and knee lift and jump in harmony, fast kicking, right leg straight.

5. 双撩棍 Shuangliaogun

（1）左脚向前落步，左掌向身体后平伸，拇指侧朝上，右手单手握棍立圆贴身向上、向后再向前右撩棍，目视前方。(图 4-3-12)

(1) Step forward with your left foot, extend your left palm behind the body, thumb side up, hold the stick with the right hand, and close to the body, swing the stick forward and right again, and look ahead. (Fig. 4-3-12)

（2）两脚不动，右手单手握棍向上、向后经下向前左撩棍，右腕内旋反手持棍，目视棍把端。(图 4-3-13)

(2) Keep still, hold the stick in the right hand upward, backward, downward, forward and left, turn inside the right wrist to hold the stick, and look at the end of the stick. (Fig. 4-3-13)

图Fig 4-3-12　　　　　　图Fig 4-3-13

动作要点：撩棍贴身立圆，右撩正手，左撩反手。

Key points: stick attaches to the body and moves in a vertical circle, right swing with wrist outward, left swing with wrist inward.

6. 弓步立棍 Gongbuligun

身体右转，右脚向右后撤一大步，重心移至右脚成右弓步，右手持棍下落，左手接握棍，两手持棍随右转身横向右戳棍梢，继而向上戳，竖立棍，右手在上半握棍，目视左侧。（图 4-3-14）

Turn your body to the right, take a big step backward with your right foot, move your weight to your right foot to form a right lunge, drop the stick with your right hand, hold the stick with your left hand, turn your right hand to stab the tip of the stick horizontally with your right hand, then poke upward, erect the stick, hold the stick with your right hand in the upper half, and look at the left side. (Fig. 4-3-14)

图Fig 4-3-14

动作要点：双手横向戳棍与腰转协调一致、快速，幅度要远。

Key points: horizontal moves of the stick in both hands are consistent with the waist turning, fast and with wide covering.

7. 提膝横打 Tixihengda

重心上提，右腿直立，左腿屈膝上提；同时右手向下滑把，两手持棍回旋向左前横向击打，力达棍头，上体微向右前倾斜，目视棍把。(图 4-3-15)

Lift the gravity up, right leg upright, left leg knee bending up; slide the right hand down, swing the two hands with the stick to the left and strike horizontally, reaching the head of the stick, tilt the upper body slightly to the right and forward, and look at the stick handle. (Fig. 4-3-15)

图Fig 4-3-15

动作要点：横打倾身一致、快速，既有棍把横打又有棍把戳击。

Key points: the body is consistent with the horizontal beating, including horizontal strokes and stabbing with the stick.

8. 提膝横打 Tixihengda

左脚向左前落步，重心前移左脚，左腿直立，右腿屈膝上提；同时双手持棍在头上逆时针平圆一圈向右前横打，上体微向左前倾，目视前方。（图 4-3-16)

The left foot falls forward to the left, the center of gravity moves forward to the left foot, the left leg is upright, the right leg is knee bent and raised; at the same time, the two hands hold the stick on the head and make a circle to the right, the left hand hold the stick under the right arm, the upper body slightly leans forward to the left, and look ahead. (Fig. 4-3-16)

图Fig 4-3-16

动作要点：平圆横打与上步倾身一致、快速，既有棍身横打又有棍戳。

Key points of action: the horizontal and round strokes are consistent and fast with the leaning of the upper step. There are both strokes with the stick and stabs with the stick.

组合二： Combination 2

预备式：自然直立，右手虎口朝下持握棍，右手臂略屈，棍把贴小臂外侧，目视前方。

Preparatory pose: stand upright, holding the stick with the thumb of the right hand downward, slightly bending the right arm, stick the handle to the outside of the small forearm, and look ahead.

1. 起势 Start

(1) 右手持棍向左侧上挑，左手接握棍，两手正握棍。（图 4-3-17)

(1) The right hand holds the stick to pick from the left, the left hand holds the stick, and the two hands are holding the stick. (Fig. 4-3-17)

(2) 右手半握棍，上举于身体右侧，左手向棍梢滑把正握棍，目视左侧。（图 4-3-18)

(2) Hold the stick with half of the right hand , lift it up on the right side of the body, slide the left hand toward the end of the stick and hold the stick. Look at the left side. (Fig. 4-3-18)

图Fig 4-3-17　　　　　　图Fig 4-3-18

2. 弓步盖棍 Gongbugaigun

身体左转，左脚上步成左弓步；同时右手向下滑把，双手持棍向前盖打，目视前方。（图 4-3-19）

Turn your body to the left, step on your left foot to form a left bow step; at the same time, slide your right hand down, hold the stick in both hands and hit forward, and look ahead. (Fig. 4-3-19)

图Fig 4-3-19

动作要点：肩肘放松，两手滑把合顺，握棍松紧适当。

Key points: shoulders and elbows are relaxed, two hands' sliding handles are closed smoothly, and the stick is properly tightened.

3. 弓步扣打 Gongbukouda

（1）右脚向左脚内侧上步，重心移至右脚，左手握棍向左后直线拉回，右手滑把到棍把端，目视前方。（图 4-3-20）

(1) Step up the right foot to the inside of the left foot, move the center of gravity to the right foot, hold the stick in the left hand and pull it back to the left, slide the handle in the right hand to the end of the stick, and look ahead. (Fig. 4-3-20)

（2）左脚向前上步成左弓步，双手持棍向前横打棍梢，左手半握棍，目视前方。(图 4-3-21)

(2) Step forward with your left foot to form a left bow step. Hold the stick in both hands and hit with the top of the stick forward. Hold the stick in the left half and look ahead. (Fig. 4-3-21)

图Fig 4-3-20　　　　　　　图Fig 4-3-21

动作要点：滑把顺畅，横打棍梢与上步协调统一。

Key points: smooth handle-sliding, coordinated and unified cross stroke with the upper step.

4. 弓步截棍 Gongbujiegun

右脚上步成右弓步；同时，右手握棍向后拉，左手滑把到棍梢端，右手向左手滑把，双手持棍向前下斜打截击，右手半握棍，力达棍把端，目视前下方。(图 4-3-22)

Step on the right foot into a right lunge; at the same time, pull back with the right hand holding the stick, slide the left hand to the tip of the stick, slide the right hand to the left hand, and hit with both hands holding the stick forward and downward, hold the stick half with the right hand, and look ahead and down. (Fig. 4-3-22)

图Fig 4-3-22

动作要点：同上。

Key points : the same as above.

5. 偷崩棍 Toubenggun

左脚向左侧跨一大步，右脚跟进半步，左腿屈膝半蹲，右腿膝盖朝下成半弓步，重心前倾；同时，双手握棍向下向右在右臂下顺时针快速旋转一周向前崩棍，右手虎口半握棍，力达棍把端，目视前方。(图 4-3-23)

The left foot takes a big step to the left, the right foot follows a half step, the left leg bends and squats, the right leg knees fall into a half lunge, and the center of gravity leans forward; at the same time, hold the stick with both hands downward and to the right, turn it clockwise and quickly under the right arm to break the stick forward, hold the stick with the right tiger mouth half, reach the end of the stick, and look ahead. (Fig. 4-3-23)

图Fig 4-3-23

动作要点：双手握棍旋转要灵活，崩棍力点清晰、准确。

Key points of action: hold the stick with both hands and rotate it flexibly. The force point of breaking the stick is clear and accurate.

6. 马步扣压 Mabukouya

图Fig 4-3-24

右脚向后撤半步，身体微右转，重心后移两腿之间成半马步；同时，借势后撤双手向右外旋立圆挂棍一周向前扣压棍，右手滑把至棍身中间，目视前方。(图 4-3-24)

Take a half step backward with the right foot, turn slightly to the right, and move the gravity back between the legs to form a half horse stance. Take advantage of the situation, take back the hands and turn them to the right to hang a round stick and press it forward in a circle. Slide the right hand to the middle of the stick and look ahead. (Fig. 4-3-24)

动作要点：挂棍时双手旋转灵活，跟随棍的旋转路线双手把位调整，扣压立圆。

Key points: when hanging the stick, rotate your hands flexibly, adjust the position of your hands following the rotation route of the stick.

7. 苏秦刺剑 Suqin Cijian

身体稍右转成马步，左手持棍单手向前刺棍，右手变掌向后打开，目视棍把端。(图 4-3-25)

Turn the body slightly to the right into a horse stance, hold the stick in the left hand and stab forward with one hand holding the stick, the right palm goes backward, and look at the top of the stick. (Fig. 4-3-25)

图Fig 4-3-25

动作要点：刺棍以腰发力。

Key points: the force of stick-stabbing is generated from the waist.

8. 右撩棍 Right liaogun

（1）身体左转，左手持棍压腕使棍把向上、向后画弧，右手随之接握棍，目视前方。(图 4-3-26)

(1) Turn to the left, hold the stick in the left hand and press the wrist to make the handle upward and backward in an arc, then hold the stick in your right hand and look ahead. (Fig. 4-3-26)

（2）两脚不动，双手握棍继续立圆向左前撩棍，目视前方。(图 4-3-27)

(2) Keep your feet still, hold the stick with both hands, continue to stand up and lift the stick to the left, and look ahead. (Fig. 4-3-27)

图Fig 4-3-26　　　　　　　　图Fig 4-3-27

动作要点：撩棍走立圆，棍贴近身体，抡棍巧劲发力。

Key points : cudgeling in a circle, keep the stick close to the body, and swing the stick skillfully.

9. 蹬腿戳把 Dengtuichuoba

（1）双手握棍向左后撩棍，左腿直立，右腿勾脚向前蹬腿，目视前方。(图 4-3-28)

(1) Hold the stick with both hands and lift it to the left, keep the left leg upright, and lift the right leg forward, look ahead. (Fig. 4-3-28)

（2）右脚向前落步成右弓步，双手握棍滑把向前下戳棍梢，目视棍梢。(图 4-3-29)

(2) Step the right foot forward into a right lunge, hold the stick with both hands and poke forward and down, and look at the thin end of the stick. (Fig. 4-3-29)

图Fig 4-3-28　　　　　　　　图Fig 4-3-29

动作要点：蹬腿快速，左腿挺直站稳，蹬腿力达脚跟，棍贴身向前戳击。

Key points: fast kicking, left leg standing straight, kicking up with the heel, stick close to the body and poke forward.

10. 翻身盖压 Fanshengaiya

身体左转180°，两腿微屈，两脚碾转，左手滑把至棍把，双手握棍立圆盖压棍梢，目视棍梢端。(图 4-3-30)

Turn 180° to the left, bend the legs slightly, spin the feet, slide the handle of the left hand to the top of the stick, hold the stick with both hands, erect a round and press the handle, and look at the thin end of the stick. (Fig. 4-3-30)

图Fig 4-3-30

动作要点：转身与立圆盖压棍动作协调一致。

Key points: body turning and the stick swing in the vertical circle should be coordinated.

11. 左右贯打 Right and Left Guanda

（1）右脚向前上步，两腿微屈，双手握棍向右上回旋，目视前方。(图 4-3-31)

(1) Step forward with your right foot, slightly bend your legs, turn right and up with your hands holding the stick, and look ahead. (Fig. 4-3-31)

（2）重心前移右腿，右腿直立，左腿屈膝上提，上体微右倾；同时，双手握棍从右向前横贯打，目视棍梢端。(图 4-3-32)

(2) Move the gravity forward on the right leg, keep the right leg upright, bend the left leg and lift it up, lean the upper body slightly to the right; at the same time, hold the stick with both hands and hit from the right to the front, and look at the thin end of the stick. (Fig. 4-3-32)

（3）左脚向左前落地直立，右腿屈膝上提，上体微左倾；同时，双手握棍经头上逆时针一周向前横贯打，目视棍梢端。(图 4-3-33)

(3) The left foot is on the ground and upright, the right leg is bent and raised, and the upper body is slightly left leaning; at the same time, hold the stick with both hands and hit it forward one circle anticlockwise on the head to look at the thin end of the stick. (Fig. 4-3-33)

图Fig 4-3-31　　　　　　图Fig 4-3-32　　　　　　图Fig 4-3-33

动作要点：左右贯打配合身法，前倾上体，力达棍梢。

Key points: left and right penetrating beatings go along with body moves,body leans forward and the fore should reach the thin end.

12. 马步列杆 Mabuliegan

图Fig 4-3-34　　　　　　图Fig 4-3-35　　　　　　图Fig 4-3-36

（1）右脚向右落步，身体微左转，两腿微屈，右手握棍向右劈点棍，左掌向左横掌，目视棍梢端。(图 4-3-34)

(1) Turn your body slightly to the left, step your right foot to the right, bend your legs slightly, hold the stick with your right hand and split it to the right, turn your left palm to the left, and look at the thin end of the stick. (Fig. 4-3-34)

（2）两腿屈膝半蹲成半马步，右手握棍向上立挑棍，左掌屈臂下按，目视棍身。(图 4-3-35)

(2) Bend your knees and half squat into a half horse stance. Hold the stick in your right hand and stand up to pick it up. Bend your left palm and lower your arms and look at the body of the stick. (Fig. 4-3-35)

（3）身体左转180°，右手握棍向左斜架棍，左手下握棍梢，目视前方。(图 4-3-36)

(3) Turn your body 180° to the left, hold the stick in your right hand and tilt to the left, hold the handle in your left hand and look ahead. (Fig. 4-3-36)

动作要点：半马步转身，保持重心下沉。

Key points: turn in half horse-ride stance and keep your gravity down.

13. **缠头扫** Chantousao

（1）重心上提，两腿微屈，右手握棍右下截棍，左掌收于右腋下，目视前方。(图 4-3-37)

(1) Lift the gravity of the body, bend the legs slightly, hold the right stick in the right hand and cut down, then close the left palm to the right armpit and look ahead. (Fig. 4-3-37)

（2）右手握棍扣腕上提，棍身贴于左肩，左掌收于右腋下，目视前方。(图 4-3-38)

(2) Hold the stick in your right hand, buckle the wrist and lift the stick up. Close the stick to your left shoulder, and close your left palm to your right armpit. Look ahead.(Fig.4-3-38)

图Fig 4-3-37　　　　　　　　图Fig 4-3-38

（3）重心半蹲，右手握棍从左肩上向后贴背缠绕头至右下，左掌向左挂掌，目视前方。(图 4-3-39)

(3) Half squat with the gravity, hold the stick with the right hand from the left shoulder to the back, swing around the head to the right bottom, hang the left palm to the left, and look ahead. (Fig.4-3-39)

（4）重心前移左腿，右腿屈膝，右脚跟提起，上体微前倾，右手握棍向前横扫棍，左掌向后挂掌，目视前方。(图 4-3-40)

(4) Move the gravity forward on the left leg, bend the knee on the right leg, lift the right heel, lean forward slightly on the upper body, sweep the stick forward with the right hand, hang the palm backward on the left palm, and look ahead. (Fig. 4-3-40)

图Fig 4-3-39　　　　　　　　图Fig 4-3-40

动作要点：右手握棍贴背缠绕，横打力贯棍身，棍和右臂顺直。

Key points: hold the stick with the right hand and wrap it around the back. The horizontal beating should be full of strength. The stick and the right arm are parallel.

14. 撑补飞燕 Chengbufeiyan

身体右转 180°，两腿屈膝半蹲成半马步，右手握棍屈臂扣腕横架棍，棍平放于右臂上，左掌置于右腕处，目视前方。(图 4-3-41)

Turn your body 180° to the right, bend your knees and squat into a half horse stance, hold the stick in your right hand, bend your arms and buckle your wrists. Place the stick on your right arm, place your left palm on your right wrist, and look ahead. (Fig. 4-3-41)

图Fig 4-3-41

动作要点：马步和棍方向一致，平肘架棍，抬头挺胸。

Key points: the directions of the step and the stick are the same, the elbow is flat when support the stick, the chest is up.

15. 提膝列棍 Tixiliegun

左手从右臂上握棍，右手向棍把滑把，重心前移右脚，右腿直立，左腿屈膝上提，上体微左转，双手握棍向左斜列棍，棍梢斜向下，目视左侧。(图 4-3-42)

The left hand holds the stick from the right arm, the right hand slides towards the handle, the center of gravity moves forward to the right foot, the right leg is upright, the left leg is bent and lifted, the upper body turns slightly to the left, the two hands hold the stick to the left, the tip of the stick is inclined downward, and watch the left side. (Fig. 4-3-42)

图Fig 4-3-42

动作要点：列棍贴紧身体，站立稳定。

Key points: attach the club to the body tightly and stand stably.

16. 收棍 Ending up

图Fig 4-3-43　　　　图Fig 4-3-44　　　　图Fig 4-3-45

（1）左脚落地，两腿微屈，右手单手握棍向右劈点地，左掌收至腰间，掌心向上，目视棍梢。(图 4-3-43)

(1) The left foot is on the ground, the legs are slightly bent, the right hand holds the stick and splits to the right, the left palm is closed to the waist, the palm is upward, and watch the thin end. (Fig. 4-3-43)

（2）重心上提，左脚向右脚并步，两腿直立，右手握棍向左前撩棍，目视棍梢端。(图 4-3-44)

(2) Lift the gravity, step left foot to right foot, keep legs upright, hold the stick with right

hand and lift it forward to the left, and look at the tip of the stick. (Fig. 4-3-44)

（3）两脚不动，右手握棍右腕花一周向右脚前点立棍，目视左侧。（图 4-3-45）

(3) Keep your feet still, hold the right wrist of the stick with your right hand, spin around in a circle to stand the stick in front of your right foot, and look at the left side. (Fig. 4-3-45)

动作要点：收棍时撩棍和右腕花立棍沉稳。

Key points: at the end, lift the stick steadily and erect the right wrist to twist the club steadily.

第四节　三节棍
4.4 Three-Section Club

一、三节棍简介 Introduction

三节棍，软器械之一。它由三条长度相近的短棍中间以铁环连接而成，又称"三节鞭"，又有长三节棍和短三节棍之分，长三节棍总长相当于人体直立直臂上举到手指尖的高度。三节棍使用轻巧方便，可近可远，可方可圆，可长可短，可伸可缩，放开如同长器械一般，可作远距离击打，折叠则是短棍，约同臂长，可作自卫防身的随身物。三节棍握法丰富，双手分握两个梢节或一手握梢节、另一手握中节，或单手握棍，方法灵活多样。

Three-Section Club, one of the soft instruments. It is made of three short sticks of similar length connected by iron rings, also known as "Three-Section Whip". There are also long Three-Section Club and short Three-Section Club. The length of the long Three-Section Club is equal to the height of the upright arm of the human body raised to the tip of the finger. The Three-Section Club is light and convenient to use, can be used near or far, can be square to round, long or short, be extended or retracted, and can be used as a long-distance strike when it is released. Folded, it is a short stick, about the same arm length, which can be used as a self-defense weapon. There are many ways to hold the Three-Section Club, such as holding two tips with two hands, holding the tip with one hand, holding the middle section with the other hand, or holding the stick with one hand.

二、三节棍技术特点 Technical characteristics

三节棍是三节短棍相连，节节能用，三节互换，攻守兼备，基本棍法有劈、砸、抡、扫、架、戳、格、缠、撩、挂、挑、截、封、压、绞以及各种舞花等，套路练习时还有背棍、抛棍等动作，对练套路有三节棍对枪、三节棍进盾牌刀等。三节棍技法特点是招招有势、势势有法、长短兼用、势法齐整、变化多端、软硬兼施、气势逼人。

The Three-Section Club is connected by three sections of short sticks which can be used separately or swapped. It can be used as an attacking and defending weapon. The basic practicing techniques are split, smash, swing, sweep, frame, poke, grid, entwine, lift, hang, pick, cut, seal, press, twist, etc. In the routine practice, there are also club club backing, club throwing and other actions. In the practice of pair work, there are Three-Section Club vs. Spear, Three-Section Club vs. Shield and so on. The characteristics of the skills of the Three-Section Club are the combination of hardness and softness, flexibility and various changes in the moves.

三节棍歌（谱）诀

三节短棍软有硬，呼呼生风人难防；
舞花翻身立圆劈，单手背花巧换技；
乌龙摆身顾首尾，左格右打遵变数；
力劈华山雪盖顶，招法奇快一条鞭；
就地滚翻讲艺法，扫转攻防有规程；
面花缠腰回身转，绕颈护身谁敢来；
灵便伸缩如破竹，能软能硬方泼辣；
劈撩抡打势威武，全凭德艺双修悟。

三、三节棍基本技法组合图解 Illustrations of basic skills

（一）三节棍基本持握法 Basic holding methods

1.持棍：并步直立，棍折叠持握于右手，右臂平举，左手贴身，目视前方。（图4-4-1）

1. Chigun: stand upright in parallel steps, fold the stick and hold in the right hand, raise the right arm horizontally, keep the left hand close to the body, and look ahead. (Fig. 4-4-1)

2. 握棍：双手把握中节，（图 4-4-2）单手把握一端，（图 4-4-3）双手分握相连的两节或把握两端棍节。（图 4-4-4、图 4-4-5）

2. Wogun: hold the middle section with both hands, (Fig. 4-4-2) hold one end with one hand, (Fig. 4-4-3) hold the two ends of the middle section with two hands or hold the sections separately. (Fig. 4-4-4, Fig. 4-4-5)

图Fig 4-4-1　　　　　　　　图Fig 4-4-2

图Fig 4-4-3　　　　图Fig 4-4-4　　　　图Fig 4-4-5

（二）三节棍技法组合 Skills of the combinations

1. 预备姿势 Ready

并步站立，右臂平举，右手持握折叠三节棍，左手贴身，目视前方。（图 4-4-6）

Stand on the parallel legs, raise your right arm horizontally, hold the folding three section stick in your right hand, keep your left hand close to your body, and look ahead. (Fig. 4-4-6)

图Fig 4-4-6

动作要点：持握棍时注意三节折叠次序，便以左手接握。

Key points: when holding the stick, pay attention to the folding order of the three sections, so as to pass to the left hand.

2. 马步列棍 Mabuliegun

（1）身体微右转，左手持握棍，两手分握两端棍节根部，目视左手。(图 4-4-7)

(1) Turn slightly to the right, hold the stick in your left hand, hold the ends of the 1st and the 3rd sections with two hands, and look at your left hand. (Fig. 4-4-7)

（2）右脚向右跨步，两脚分立，双手持棍向左列棍，左手棍前推，两端棍节交叉，目视左前方。(图 4-4-8)

(2) Step right with the right foot, separate the two feet, hold the stick in both hands, push the stick forward with the left hand, cross the 1st and the 3rd sections , and look at the left front. (Fig. 4-4-8)

（3）身体右转，两手持棍向右刺棍，力达右手棍前端，目视右手。(图 4-4-9)

(3) Turn to the right, hold the stick in both hands and stab to the right, force reaching the front of the right stick, and look at your right hand. (Fig. 4-4-9)

（4）身体左转，两腿屈膝半蹲成半马步，重心偏于右腿，左脚外展，两手持棍随转身向左前平推棍，力达左手棍前端，右手棍竖立，目视前方。(图 4-4-10)

(4) Turn your body to the left, bend your legs and half squat into a half horse stance, with the center of gravity on the right leg, extend your left foot, push the stick to the left with both hands holding the stick as you turn to the left, with the force reaching the front of the left stick, stand the right stick upright, and look ahead. (Fig. 4-4-10)

图Fig 4-4-7　　　　图Fig 4-4-8

图Fig 4-4-9　　　　图Fig 4-4-10

动作要点：动作贴身立圆划弧，推棍臂直。

Key points: the stick moves in a vertical circle close to the body, the pushing with arm straight.

3. 点劈棍 Dianpigun

（1）身体左转，重心上提前移成半弓步，右脚跟提起，左手持棍向左后带棍，右手向前抛刺棍，右手回握中节棍，目视前方。（图 4-4-11）

(1) Turn your body to the left, lift up the gravity and step forward in half lunge, lift the right heel, hold the stick in your left hand and bring it back to the left, throw the stick forward in your right hand, hold the middle stick back in your right hand, and look ahead. (Fig. 4-4-11)

（2）右脚向前上步，两腿微屈，双手持棍向右后带棍下抢，目视棍梢。（图 4-4-12）

(2) Step forward with your right foot, bend your legs slightly, swing the stick with your hands to the right and back, and look at the top of the stick. (Fig. 4-4-12)

（3）两脚不动，双手持棍从右向上向前下抢，目视棍梢。（图 4-4-13）

(3) Keep your feet still, swing the stick from right to up and down with both hands, and look at the top of the stick. (Fig. 4-4-13)

（4）两脚不动，重心下沉前倾，双手持棍向前劈棍，目视棍梢。（图 4-4-14）

(4) Keep your feet still and lean forward with your weight down. Split forward with your hands and look at the tip of the stick. (Fig. 4-4-14)

（5）身体左转，左脚经右脚后向前插步；同时，双手持棍从左侧反手向前抢劈，目视棍梢。（图 4-4-15）

(5) Turn your body to the left and cross your left foot behind your right foot. At the same time, swing forward with the stick in both hands and look at the top of the stick. (Fig. 4-4-15)

图Fig 4-4-11

图Fig 4-4-12

图Fig 4-4-13

图Fig 4-4-14　　　　　　　　　图Fig 4-4-15

动作要点：左右抡劈立圆贴身，抡棍笔直，劈点清晰，左手跟随右手。

Key points: swing right and left close to your body, the force should be straight and sharp, follow your right hand with your left hand.

4. 舞花棍 Wuhuagun

（1）身体左后转身，双手持棍随转身立圆向右侧立圆抡劈，目视棍梢。（图 4-4-16）

(1) Turn your body to the right, step backward with your left foot, hold the stick with your hands and swing it from the left side to the right side, and look at the top of the stick. (Fig. 4-4-16)

（2）双手持棍向左带棍，调整双手把位，目视前方。（图 4-4-17）

(2) Carry the stick with both hands to the left, adjust the handle position of both hands, and look ahead. (Fig. 4-4-17)

图Fig 4-4-16　　　　　　图Fig 4-4-17　　　　　　图Fig 4-4-18

（3）两脚不动，身体微左右转，双手持棍左右立圆舞花，目视前方。（图 4-4-18、图 4-4-19、图 4-4-20、图 4-4-21）

(3) Keep your feet still, turn slightly to the left and right, hold the middle part in both

hands and swing in vertical round, and look ahead. (Fig. 4-4-18, Fig. 4-4-19, Fig. 4-4-20, Fig. 4-4-21)

图Fig 4-4-19　　　　　　　图Fig 4-4-20　　　　　　　图Fig 4-4-21

动作要点：棍在身体两侧立圆绕行，贴近身体，两手旋腕灵活，棍笔直。

Key points: rotate the stick in vertical circle on both sides of the body, two wrists rotate flexibly, keep the stick straight.

5. 虎尾鞭 Huweibian

左脚向前上步，身体右转，舞花棍至身体右侧斜背棍，右臂屈肘扣腕将棍的一节送至左肩上，右脚经左脚后插步，身体迅速右转360°，重心半蹲成右弓步，右手从左肩把握一端棍节立圆抡劈，左掌向后挑掌，目视前方。（图4-4-22）

Step forward with the left foot, turn right, twist the stick to the right side of the body, bend the elbow and buckle the wrist sending one section of the stick to the left shoulder, cross step with the right foot behind the left foot, turn right 360° quickly, squat into the right lunge, hold one end of the section with the right hand from the left shoulder, and swing, lift the left hand backward and look ahead. (Fig. 4-4-22)

图Fig 4-4-22

动作要点：右臂扣腕屈臂背棍贴紧背部，借转身松开右手，靠背部维持棍稳定，单手把握棍端节立圆抡劈。

Key points: the right wrist buckles inner ward, make the stick close to the back, release the right hand when turn around, maintain the stability of the stick on the back, hold the end of the stick with one hand, and swing vertically.

6. 仙人收宝 Xianrenshoubao

图Fig 4-4-23

两脚不动，身体左转180°，两脚碾转重心移至左脚成左弓步，右手单手随转身向左前上撩棍，抖腕使棍节回弹折叠收于右手，左掌向后挑掌，目视右手。(图 4-4-23)

Keep your feet still, turn your body 180° to the left, turn the weight of your feet and move to the left foot to form a left bow step, turn your right hand to the left and lift up the stick, shake your wrist to make the sections spring back and fold in your right hand, turn your left palm backward and look at your right hand. (Fig. 4-4-23)

动作要点：单手撩棍注意控制节奏和高度，棍向内折叠，回弹收棍要抓握稳固。

Key points: control the rhythm and height when swing the stick single handed , fold the stick inward, and grasp firmly.

7. 云棍拍脚 Yungunpaijiao

（1）右手持棍上举逆时针云棍一周，左手上举接握棍，两脚碾转，身体右转180°，右掌下落，目视左手。(图 4-4-24)

(1) Hold the stick in the right hand and lift the stick and swing anticlockwise in a circle. Hold the stick in the left hand and spin on both feet. Turn the body 180° to the right. Drop the right palm and look at the left hand. (Fig. 4-4-24)

（2）左脚向前上步，右掌上举，掌尖向上，左手持棍收至腰间，目视前方。(图 4-4-25)

(2) Step forward with the left foot, raise the right palm, with the tip of the palm upward, hold the stick in the left hand to the waist, and look ahead. (Fig. 4-4-25)

（3）左脚不动，右腿直腿向上摆踢，脚背绷直，右手迎击右脚背，目视右手。（图 4-4-26）

(3) The left foot doesn't move, the right leg is straight and kicks upward, the instep is taut and straight, the right hand hits the right instep and look at the right hand. (Fig. 4-4-26)

图Fig 4-4-24　　　　图Fig 4-4-25　　　　图Fig 4-4-26

动作要点：转身以脚前掌碾转，拍脚清脆。

Key points: turn around on the forefoot, pat the foot clear and crisp.

8. **虚步架棍** Xubujiagun

（1）右脚向前落步，身体左转 45°，左脚向右脚后插步，左前脚掌点地，两臂前后斜分掌，目视右手。（图 4-4-27）

(1) Step forward with the right foot, turn left 45°, cross step with the left foot to the back of the right foot, point to the ground with the left front foot, split the two arms back and forth obliquely, and look at the right hand. (Fig. 4-4-27)

（2）身体左转 45°，左脚向左前虚点地，重心后移，右腿屈膝下蹲成左虚步；同时，左手持棍向右侧斜架，右掌驾于左腕上，目视左前方。（图 4-4-28）

(2) Turn the body 45° to the left, move the left foot forward to the left, move the center of gravity backward, and squat down with the right leg bent to form a left virtual step; at the same time, hold the stick in the left hand and lean to the right, drive the right palm on the left wrist, and look at the left front. (Fig. 4-4-28)

图Fig 4-4-27　　　　图Fig 4-4-28

动作要点：两臂前后斜分呈一条线，动作起伏沉降节奏鲜明，虚步静定，抬头挺胸，架棍右推有力。

Key points: the two arms are inclined to form a line in front and back, the rhythm of movement ups and downs is distinct, the virtual step is static, the head is straight, the stick is pushed right forcefully.

9. 并步收势 Ending up

（1）右脚后撤半步，身体右后转，左手持棍随转身立圆下压横棍，右手握拳抱腰，目视左手。（图 4-4-29）

(1) Step back with your right foot, turn right back, hold the stick in your left hand and press it down, hold your waist with your right hand, and look at your left hand. (Fig. 4-4-29)

（2）身体左转，左脚向右脚并步，左手持棍斜收于腰，右拳向右内旋臂横架拳，拳眼向下，拳心朝外，目视左前方。（图 4-4-30）

(2) Turn your body to the left, move your left foot to the right foot, hold the stick in your left hand and close to your waist, turn your right fist to the right, turn your arm right and uphold, with fist eye down and fist heart outward, and look at the front left. (Fig. 4-4-30)

图Fig 4-4-29

图Fig 4-4-30

动作要点：左右手交接棍稳定准确，调整呼吸。

Key points: when transfering the stick between the left and right hand, the action should be stable and accurate, and the breathing is balanced.

第五节 朴 刀
4.5 Long-Hilt Broadsword (Pudao)

一、朴刀简介 Brief introduction

朴刀，又称双手带，大刀的一种，是一根木柄上安有长而宽刀刃的武术古兵器。使用时双手持刀，像使用大刀那样，利用刀刃和刀身重量来劈杀。朴刀长度一般不低于本人身高，柄长以双手分开握持运用自如为度。柄尾部亦称刀根，有铁环，刀身呈浅弧形，前部为刀头，一侧为刃，一侧为背。朴刀有别于刀柄较长的大刀，兼有短兵器之利，也有别于柄短的单刀，兼有长击。

Long-Hilt Broadsword (Pudao), also known as Shuangshoudai, is a kind of big broadsword. It is an ancient Wushu weapon with a long and wide blade on a wooden handle. When using it, hold the knife with both hands, and use the sharp blade and the weight of the knife to cut and kill like using a broadsword. Generally, the length of the knife is not less than the height of a person, and the handle length is measured by the degree that the two hands can hold and operate freely separately. The tail of the handle is also called the root of the knife. It has an iron ring. The blade is in a shallow arc. The front part is the head of the knife, one side is the blade, and the other side is the back. The knife is different from the big knife with a long handle, and it has the advantages of short weapons, and also different from the single knife with a short handle, and it has a long strike.

二、朴刀技法特点 The Technical characteristics

朴刀兼有大刀和单刀技法，主要刀法有劈、撩、斩、扇、抹、挂、剁、托、扫、云、舞花等。朴刀动作方法清楚，以劈为主，灵活多变，长短兼用。朴刀技法特点为：刀快法诈、勇猛刚劲、泼辣彪悍、气势雄伟、动作紧凑、姿势舒展、动速静定、节奏鲜明、劲力顺达。

Pudao has both Dadao and Dandao techniques. The main techniques are splitting, pulling, chopping, chopping, supporting, sweeping, twisting, etc. The actions are mainly splitting with flexible changes of the routes.The characteristics of Pudao's practices are as follows: quick and deceitful moves, bravery and forcefulness, shrewdness and ferocity, majestic and compact momentum, stretching posture, steady moving speed, distinct rhythm and smooth strength.

朴刀歌（谱）诀

朴刀刚猛在顶手，手抵刀盘法在理；

手眼身法多灵活，迎敌制胜来变化；

刀法前削和劈挂，闪展腾挪心法静；

朴刀缠身巧变换，上挑翠云雪花顶；

下砍坐盘立威风，以静制动胜法定；

迎面花子绕身转，刀劈三关接连劈；

玉尺量天双手换，背刀弓步多威严；

朴刀练出精气神，中华瑰宝传下来。

三、朴刀基本技法与组合图解 Illustrations of the Basic Combination Skills

（一）朴刀基本技法 Basic skills of Pudao

1. 持刀：右手虎口向上贴近护手盘抓握刀柄上部。刀身竖直，刀尖朝上，刀刃向前。

1.Holding: hold the upper part of the handle with the right thumb up close to the hand guard plate. The blade is vertical, the tip is up, and the blade is forward.

2. 劈刀：双手握刀柄，使刀由上向前、向下劈砍。劈刀有正劈与斜劈；正劈为刀由头上向正前方劈落，斜为由斜上向前、向异侧斜下劈落。要求转腰带刀，身械一体，力达刀刃。

2. Cleaving: hold the handle of the knife with both hands to cleave from top to front and down. There are two kinds of cleaving: straight and oblique. Straight means the blade falls from the head to the front, and oblique cleaving from the top to the front and from the opposite side. It is required the blade go along with the waist turning.

3. 斩刀：双手握刀柄，刀身平，高与胸齐，由身体一则经前向另一侧平摆击出。要求动作短促有力，力达刀刃，两手同时向一侧用力；推斩则两手反相用力。

3.Chopping: hold the handle with both hands, the blade is flat, high to the chest level, and swing from one side of the body to the other side horizontally. The action is required to be short and powerful, force reaching the blade, and both hands are forced to one side at the same time; pushing and chopping is the opposite force of both hands.

4. 抹刀：双手握刀，刀身呈水平，高与胸齐，由体侧经前向异侧平行挥摆后稍回带。

4.Smearing: hold the knife with both hands, the blade is horizontal, high to chest level, and swing from the body side to the opposite side in parallel, then bring it back slightly.

5. 挂刀：双手握刀柄，用刀背由前向下沿体侧向后弧形挂转，力达刀背。挂刀有左、右之分，由握刀开始右臂内旋使刀背沿身体左侧向后挂起为左挂刀；反之右挂刀，其用法为挂格对方攻击的动作。

5.Hanging: hold the handle with both hands, and use the back of the knife to rotate from the front down along the body side to the back in an arc, with the force reaching the back of the knife. The hanging knife can be divided into left and right. It is left hanging knife when the back of the knife is hung backward along the left side of the body from the beginning of holding the knife and turning the right arm inside. On the contrary, it is used to hang the knife on the right side, which is the action of attacking the opponent.

6. 扫刀：双手握刀，置刀于体右侧，刀身呈水平，向左转体；同时右手滑握至左手处，使刀刃领先由右经前向左侧平扫，力达刀刃。

6.Sweeping: hold the knife with both hands, place the knife on the right side of the body, and the blade is horizontal. Turn to the left, and slide the right hand to the left hand, so that the blade is ahead of the others and sweep from the right to the left.

7. 架刀：双手握刀（右手握刀柄上部，左手握下部）由体前上举至头上方，刀刃向上，刀尖向右，以刀柄中部着力。

7. Supporting: hold the knife with both hands (hold the upper part of the handle with the right hand, and hold the lower part with the left hand) from the front of the body to the top of the head, with the blade upward and the tip to the right, with the force in the middle of the handle.

8. 云刀：双手握刀，使刀尖向左经上向右在头上云转一周。

8. Swirling: hold the knife with both hands, make the point of the knife turn left, up, right and around the head.

9. 背刀：右手握持刀柄上部，将刀置于身体右后方，刀尖向下，刀刃向后，刀柄紧贴于后背。

9. Carrying: hold the upper part of the handle with the right hand, place the knife at the right rear of the body, with the tip downward, the blade backward, and the handle close to the back.

10. 舞花刀：两手握刀柄，使刀在身体两侧连续做立圆舞动。

10. Twisting : hold the handle of the knife with both hands, so that the knife can make a continuous vertical and circular ring on both sides of the body.

（二）朴刀技法组合 Skill combinations

组合一：Combination 1

1. **预备姿势** Ready

两脚并步直立，左手自然垂于身体左侧，右臂屈臂平肘，右手正握扑刀把立于身体右侧，刀刃向前，目视前方。(图 4-5-1)

Stand upright with both feet together, the left hand naturally hangs on the left side of the body, the right arm bends the elbow, the right hand holding the handle of knife on the right side of the body, the blade is forward, and look ahead. (Fig. 4-5-1)

图Fig 4-5-1

动作要点：身体保持正直，挺胸、塌腰、沉肩。

Key points: keep your body straight, chest up, waist down, shoulder down.

2. **撩掌推刀** Liaozhangtuidao

图Fig 4-5-2　　　　　图Fig 4-5-3　　　　　图Fig 4-5-4

（1）正身站立，两脚并步，左臂屈臂，左掌收至腰间，掌心向上，悬头竖项，自然呼吸，目视左方。（图 4-5-2）

(1) Stand upright, walk with both feet together, bend your left arm, put your left palm to your waist, palm up, breathe naturally, and look to the left. (Fig. 4-5-2)

（2）左掌向下向左前方撩掌，掌心向上，掌尖朝前，与肩同高，目视左掌方向。(图 4-5-3)

(2) Lift the left palm down to the left front, palm center up, palm tip forward, shoulder height, and look in the direction of the left palm. (Fig. 4-5-3)

（3）两脚并步直立，左掌收至腰间，掌心向上，右手持刀向右前方推刀，刀刃向前，目视刀背。(图 4-5-4)

(3) Stand upright with both feet together, with the left palm closed to the waist, the palm center upward, the right hand holding the knife, push the knife to the right front, the blade forward, and look at the back of the knife. (Fig. 4-5-4)

动作要点：提掌转头迅速，推刀与收掌转头协调一致。

Key points: raise the palm and turn the head quickly. Push the knife and turn the head in coordination.

3. 弓步截刀 Gongbujiedao

（1）左腿直立，右脚提起用脚内侧向左踢扑刀底部，目视下方。（图 4-5-5)

(1) The left leg is upright, the right foot is lifted and the inside of the foot is used to kick the bottom of the knife to the left, and look down. (Fig. 4-5-5)

（2）右脚经左脚向左侧落步，左手握刀柄，左脚再向前上一大步，重心前移下蹲成左弓步；同时，双手持刀经头上方顺时针云刀向前平截刀，与头同高，刀刃朝左，刀尖向前，目视前方。(图 4-5-6)

(2) Step to the left with the right foot through the left foot, hold the handle with the left hand, take a big step forward with the left foot, move the center of gravity forward and squat into the left bow step; at the same time, hold the knife in both hands and move forward with the knife clockwise above the head, with the same height as the head, the blade to the left, the tip to the front, and look ahead. (Fig. 4-5-6)

图Fig 4-5-5   图Fig 4-5-6

动作要点：双手云刀配合上步节奏，云刀以刀背带动刀刃平圆一圈，截刀与身体重心一致，力达刀刃前部。

Key points: the two hands rotate the knife swiftly matched with the rhythm of stepping up. The knife moves in a circle with the back part leading the blade. The center of gravity of the knife is the same as that of the body, the force reaches the front of the blade.

4. 云刀摆莲 Yundaobailian

（1）重心上提，两腿直立，双手持刀逆时针上平举，刀尖向右，抬头目视右手。(图 4-5-7)

(1) Lift up the gravity, keep legs upright, hold the knife in both hands and lift it horizontally anticlockwise, with the tip of the knife to the right, look up to see your right hand. (Fig. 4-5-7)

图Fig 4-5-7   图Fig 4-5-8

图Fig 4-5-9　　　　　　　　图Fig 4-5-10

（2）身体右转，双手持刀继续逆时针平云刀至右下方，右手单手背刀，（图 4-5-8）上左脚，重心前移至左脚，右腿向左上方外摆踢腿，左掌迎击右脚背，目视左掌。（图 4-5-9）

(2) Turn your body to the right, hold the knife with both hands and continue to rotate the knife anticlockwise to the lower right, support the knife with the right hand, (Fig. 4-5-8) to move the left foot, move the gravity forward to the left foot, the right leg swings the upper left and outward, hit the right foot back with the left palm, and look at the left palm. (Fig. 4-5-9)

（3）右脚向右前落步成右弓步，左手从右腋下握刀把，双手持刀经身体右侧立圆向前撩刀，刀刃向上，右手与额头同高，目视刀刃。(图 4-5-10)

(3) The right foot falls forward to form a right lunge, the left hand holds the knife handle from the right armpit, the two hands hold the knife and lift the knife forward through the vertical circle on the right side of the body, the blade is upward, the right hand is the same height as the forehead, and look at the blade. (Fig. 4-5-10)

动作要点：云刀平圆旋转，外摆击响声音清脆，撩刀立圆。

Key points: the knife rotates in a flat circle, the sound of external swing is clear, and the knife is lifted to swing in a vertical circle.

5. 叉步反刺刀 Chabufancidao

左脚经右腿后向前插步，上体向右腿方向前倾，双手持刀随转体回带刀，右手内旋，双手持刀向前上反手刺刀，刀刃向上，目视刀身。(图 4-5-11)

After the left foot passes through the right leg and step forward, the upper body leans forward towards the right leg, the two hands hold the knife to bring back the knife along with the body's rotation, the right hand rotates inward, the two hands hold the knife to move forward and stab, the blade is upward, and look at the blade. (Fig. 4-5-11)

图Fig 4-5-11

动作要点：回带刀贴近身体，右旋臂刺刀臂直。

Key points: rotate back with the knife close to the body, right arm straight.

6. 马步挂刀 Mabuguadao

（1）重心上提，两腿直立，双手持刀向右腿方向立圆撩刀，刀柄收落于右臂外侧，刀身竖直，刀尖向上，左掌收至右肩前。(图 4-5-12)

(1) The gravity is lifted, the legs are upright, the two hands hold the knife to the right leg, the handle is closed to the outside of the right arm, the blade is vertical, the tip is up, and the left palm is closed to the front of the right shoulder. (Fig. 4-5-12)

（2）右手单手持刀不动，刀刃朝左，身体左转，重心移至左脚，右腿屈膝上提，脚背绷直，目视左侧。(图 4-5-13)

(2) Hold the knife with the right hand, turn the body to the left with the blade to the left, move the weight to the left foot, bend the right leg and lift up, straighten the instep, and look at the left side. (Fig. 4-5-13)

（3）右手单手持刀不动，刀刃朝左，右脚向左脚外侧震脚落步，左脚向前跨步，两腿屈膝下蹲成马步，左掌向前推掌，掌尖向上，目视左掌。（图 4-5-14）

(3) Hold the knife with the right hand, the blade is to the left, the right foot steps down outside of the left foot. The left foot steps forward, the two legs are bent to squat into a horse step, the left palm pushes forward with fingers up, and watch the left palm. (Fig. 4-5-14)

图Fig 4-5-12　　　　图Fig 4-5-13　　　　图Fig 4-5-14

动作要点：撩刀要立圆，收刀竖立稳定，右臂外旋翻肘。

Key points: blade swinging in a vertical circle, make the knife stand stably, turn the right arm outside.

7. 云手舞花 Yunshouwuhua

（1）身体立起左转，重心移至左脚，右脚向前跟半步，右脚跟提起，右手向前下落，左手从右肩接握刀柄，目视前方。(图 4-5-15)

(1) Stand up and turn left, move the weight to the left foot, the right foot half a step forward, lift the right heel, drop the right hand forward, hold the hilt with the left hand from the right shoulder, and look ahead. (Fig. 4-5-15)

（2）两脚不动，双手持刀向右下挂刀，刀尖向下，目视前方。(图 4-5-16)

(2) Hold the knife in both hands and hang the knife to the right with the tip down. Look ahead. (Fig. 4-5-16)

图Fig 4-5-15　　　　　图Fig 4-5-16　　　　　图Fig 4-5-17

（3）右脚向前上步，双手持刀向左挂刀，紧接着左右立圆舞花，目视前方。(图 4-5-17、图 4-5-18、图 4-5-19、图 4-5-20)

(3) Hold the knife with both hands to the left and hang it to the top left. Turn your body slightly to the right. Hold the knife with both hands to hang it to the right. Rotate knife in vertical circle on the left and right sides of the body and look ahead. (Fig. 4-5-17, Fig. 4-5-18, Fig. 4-5-19, Fig. 4-5-20)

图Fig 4-5-18　　　　　图Fig 4-5-19　　　　　图Fig 4-5-20

（4）双手持刀舞花至身体左侧，刀尖向下，目视前方。(图 4-5-21)

(4) Hold the knife and rotate in in vertical circle to the left side of the body, with the tip down and look ahead. (Fig. 4-5-21)

图Fig 4-5-21

动作要点：舞花刀要快，立圆贴身，重心前后调整，身体左右微转动。

Key points of action: the twists should be fast in vertical circle with the shift of the gravity, the body should slightly adjust between the left and the right.

8. 绕脖刀 Raobodao

（1）身体左转，重心微下沉，左脚向前插步，左脚跟提起，双手持刀舞花至平举，刀尖向右，目视前方。(图 4-5-22)

(1) Turn your body to the left, slightly sink your center of gravity, cross step your left foot forward, lift your left heel, hold the knife with both hands and rotate in a circle, knife tip to the right, and look ahead. (Fig. 4-5-22)

（2）身体继续左转，双手持刀随身体左转向下向前立圆上撩刀，刀平放于右肩，左掌收于右肩前，目视前方。(图 4-5-23)

(2) The body continues to turn to the left, holding the knife with both hands swing down and forward with the body turning to the left, put the knife flat on the right shoulder, closing the left palm in front of the right shoulder, and look ahead. (Fig. 4-5-23)

（3）继续左转身180°，右手单手持刀从右肩贴背部裹脑，刀柄绕脖至左肩，左手收于右肩，刀尖向上，目视前方。(图 4-5-24)

(3) Continue turning 180° to the left, with the right hand holding knife to swing close the back and wrap the head from the right shoulder, the handle of the knife around the neck to the left shoulder, the left hand closing to the right shoulder, the tip of the knife upward, and look ahead. (Fig. 4-5-24)

（4）右手单手持刀从左肩下落，左手接握刀柄，目视前方。(图 4-5-25)

(4) The right hand with knife falls from the left shoulder, the left hand receives the handle of the knife and look forward. (Fig. 4-5-25)

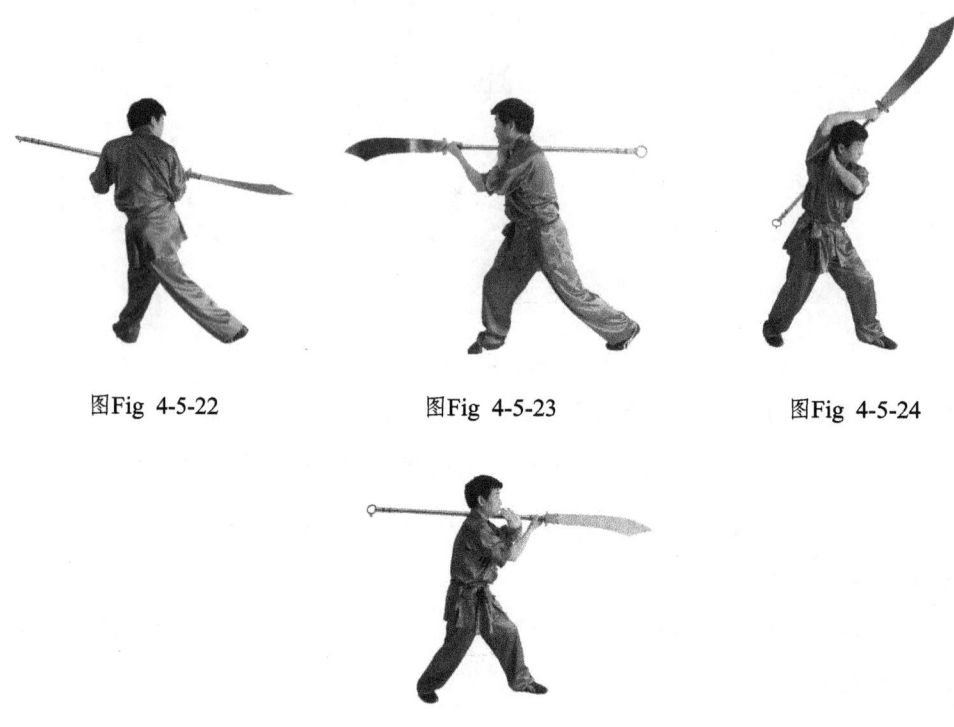

图Fig 4-5-22　　　　　图Fig 4-5-23　　　　　图Fig 4-5-24

图Fig 4-5-25

动作要点：绕脖时刀柄竖立贴背，左手接握要快。

Key points: when winding around the neck, the hilt should be upright and stick to the back, and the left hand should be grasped quickly.

9. 挂劈刀 Guapidao

（1）两脚不动，双手持刀向右下挂刀，刀尖向下，目视前方。(图 4-5-26)

(1) Hold the knife in both hands and hang the knife to the right with the tip down. Look ahead. (Fig. 4-5-26)

（2）上右步，双手持刀向左下挂刀，刀尖向下，目视前方。(图 4-5-27)

(2) Keep your feet still, hold the knife with both hands and hang it to the left, the tip of the knife is down, and look ahead. (Fig. 4-5-27)

（3）重心移至左腿，右腿屈膝上提，脚背绷直，双手挂刀立圆上举，刀尖向上，目视前下方。(图 4-5-28)

(3) Move the weight to the left leg, bend the right leg and lift it up, straighten the instep,

hang the knife with both hands and lift it up in a circle, with the tip of the knife upward and look at the front and bottom. (Fig. 4-5-28)

（4）右脚向前落步，身体左转，两腿屈膝半蹲成马步；同时，双手持刀由上向下劈刀，刀与肩同高，刀刃向下，目视前下方。(图 4-5-29)

(4) Step forward with your right foot, turn left, bend your knees and squat into a horse stance; at the same time, hold the knife with both hands, Cleave from top to bottom, the blade is the same height as the shoulder, the blade is downward, look at the front and bottom. (Fig. 4-5-29)

图Fig 4-5-26　　　　　　　图Fig 4-5-27

图Fig 4-5-28　　　　　　　图Fig 4-5-29

动作要点：左右挂刀立圆贴身，以刀背领先，劈刀力达刀刃，右手抵握刀盘。

Key points: hang the knife on the left and right to stand round and close to the body, back of the knife forward, and hold the handle with the right hand.

10. 独立扎刀 Dulizhadao

重心移至右腿，左腿屈膝上提，脚背绷直，双手持刀向下扎刀，刀尖向下，目视前下方。(图 4-5-30)

Move the gravity to the right leg, bend the left leg and lift up, straighten the foot back, hold the knife in both hands and pierce downward, with the tip of the knife downward, and look forward and downward. (Fig. 4-5-30)

图Fig 4-5-30

动作要点：身体微前倾，与下扎刀配合协调。

Key points: lean forward slightly and coordinate with the lower stabbing.

11. 云背刀 Yunbeidao

（1）左脚落地，两脚开立，身体右转180°，两脚碾转，两腿交叉，重心移至右脚，左脚跟提起，双手持刀上举逆时针云刀一周下落至右臂后背刀，左掌收至右肩，目视刀刃。（图 4-5-31）

(1) The left foot lands on the ground, the two feet open, the body turns 180° to the right, the two feet crossed, the gravity on the right foot, the left foot heel lifts, the two hands hold the knife and lift up anticlockwise, the knife falls down to the back of the right arm, the left palm is folded to the right shoulder, and watch the blade. (Fig. 4-5-31)

（2）左脚向前上一大步，左腿屈膝半蹲成左弓步，右手背刀不动，左掌向前推掌，掌尖向上，目视前方。（图 4-5-32）

(2) Take a big step forward with your left foot, bend your left leg and half squat into a left bow step, keep the knife still, push your left palm forward, with the tip of your palm up, and look ahead. (Fig. 4-5-32)

图Fig 4-5-31　　　　　　图Fig 4-5-32

动作要点：云刀要平圆，下落右背刀时刀柄要贴背。

Key points: the cloud knife should be flat and round, and the handle should stick to the back when the knife is falling.

组合二：Combination 2

1. 弓步持刀 Gongbuchidao

右脚向右前方上一大步，重心右移，左腿蹬直，右腿屈膝成右弓步；同时，双手持刀贴身从左向右、向上撩刀，抱刀竖于身体右侧，刀刃向前，目视左侧。(图 4-5-33)

Take a big step forward to the right, shift the weight to the right, straighten the left leg, bend the right leg to form a right lunge; at the same time, lift the knife from left to right and upward with both hands holding the knife close to the body, hold the knife upright on the right side of the body, the blade forward, and look at the left side. (Fig. 4-5-33)

图Fig 4-5-33

动作要点：刀撩起后右手迅速外旋竖立刀柄。

Key points: the knife is lifted and rotated quickly with the handle upright.

2. 提膝扎刀 Tixizhadao

图Fig 4-5-34　　　　　　图Fig 4-5-35

图Fig 4-5-36　　　　　　　图Fig 4-5-37

（1）重心上提，身体立起，左脚向右脚前挪步，两脚开立，双手持刀直臂上举于头上部，刀刃向右，目视刀柄。(图 4-5-34)

(1) Lift the gravity, stand up, move the left foot forward to the right foot, open the two feet, hold the knife with both hands and lift it on the top of the head with straight arms, the blade to the right, and look at the handle. (Fig. 4-5-34)

（2）双手握刀向右上方举刀，左臂屈肘收于右胸前，刀刃朝右，(图 4-5-35) 双手持刀由上至下劈刀，刀刃向下，目视右下方。(图 4-5-36)

(2) Hold the knife in both hands and lift it up to the right. Bend your elbow to the right chest with the blade facing right, (Fig. 4-5-35) hold the knife in both hands and split from top to bottom. The blade is downward. Look at the right down. (Fig. 4-5-36)

（3）重心移至左腿，左腿直立，右腿提膝；同时，双手持刀回收于胸前再向前扎出，刀刃向下，目视前方。(图 4-5-37)

(3) The gravity is moved to the left leg, the left leg is upright, and the right knee raise up; at the same time, the two hands hold the knife back in front of the chest and then pierce forward, the blade is downward, and look ahead. (Fig. 4-5-37)

动作要点：双手持刀由上至下成立圆劈刀；扎刀与提膝同时完成。

Key points: cleave in vertical round with both hands holding the knife from top to bottom; finish the stabbing and knee lifting at the same time.

3. **歇步抱刀** Xiebubaodao

右腿后撤落步，两腿屈膝全蹲成左歇步；同时，双手持刀回抱旋腕于胸前，刀刃向上，目视刀刃。(图 4-5-38)

The right leg retreats and falls, the two legs bend to form a left cross-legged crouch stance; at the same time, hold the knife back with both hands and rotate the wrist in front of the chest, with the blade upward, and look at the blade. (Fig. 4-5-38)

图Fig 4-5-38

动作要点：歇步与旋腕抱刀同时完成。

Key points: the cross-legged crouch stance and the wrist rotating should be done simultaneously.

4. 上步撩刀 Shangbuliaodao

（1）身体立起并右转身，左手持刀柄至头左上方，使刀下带于右腿外侧，刀刃向下，目视前下方。(图 4-5-39)

(1) Stand up and turn right. Hold the handle of the knife to the top left of the head with your left hand, so that the lower part of the knife is on the outside of the right leg, the blade is downward, and look at the front and lower part. (Fig. 4-5-39)

（2）身体继续右转，两脚随身体右转跟着碾转，使刀由下向上划弧带于右上方，重心移至右腿，左脚上步，脚尖外展，上体略前俯；同时，双手持刀由上向后、向下撩刀，左、右手臂成交叉握刀，刀刃向下，目视左下方。(图 4-5-40)

(2) Continue to turn your body to the right, turn your feet to the right and follow the rolling, make the knife swing from the bottom to the upper right, move the center of gravity to the right leg, step up the left foot, and slightly lean the upper body forward; at the same time, lift the knife with both hands from the top to the back and down, and hold the knife with the left and right arms crossed, the blade downward, and look at the lower left. (Fig. 4-5-40)

（3）两腿直立，右脚跟抬起，身体右转，双手持刀由下至前撩刀，刀刃向上，目视刀身。(图 4-5-41)

(3) Keep your legs upright, raise your right heel, turn your body to the right, hold the knife in both hands and lift it from the bottom to the front, with the blade upward, and look at the blade. (Fig. 4-5-41)

图Fig 4-5-39　　　　　　图Fig 4-5-40　　　　　　图Fig 4-5-41

动作要点：撩刀随身体的转动在两侧成立圆走转，刀贴身。

Action points: lift the knife with the rotation of the body to form a circle on both sides, the knife is close to the body.

5. 提膝举刀 Tixijudao

（1）身体右转180°，右脚经左腿随转体撤步成交叉步，右脚尖外展，双手持刀由上至下劈刀，刀刃向下，目视刀身。（图4-5-42）

(1) Turn your body 180° to the right, turn your right foot through the left leg and take a step with the turning body to form a cross step, extend the right foot tip, split the knife from top to bottom with both hands holding the knife, and look at the blade. (Fig. 4-5-42)

（2）身体右转90°，两腿直立，双手持刀右臂外旋，持刀由前向后、向右带刀，刀刃朝前下，目视右下方。（图4-5-43）

(2) Turn your body 90° to the right, keep your legs upright, turn your right arm with the knife in both hands, bring the knife downward, bring the knife from front to back and to the right, with the blade facing forward and downward, and look down. (Fig. 4-5-43)

（3）身体左转90°，左脚尖外展，右脚跟抬起，双手持刀继续向上带刀于头上，刀刃向前，目视刀身。（图4-5-44）

(3) Turn your body 90° to the left, extend the tip of your left foot, raise your right heel, hold the knife in both hands and continue to bring the knife on your head, move the knife forward, and look at the knife body. (Fig. 4-5-44)

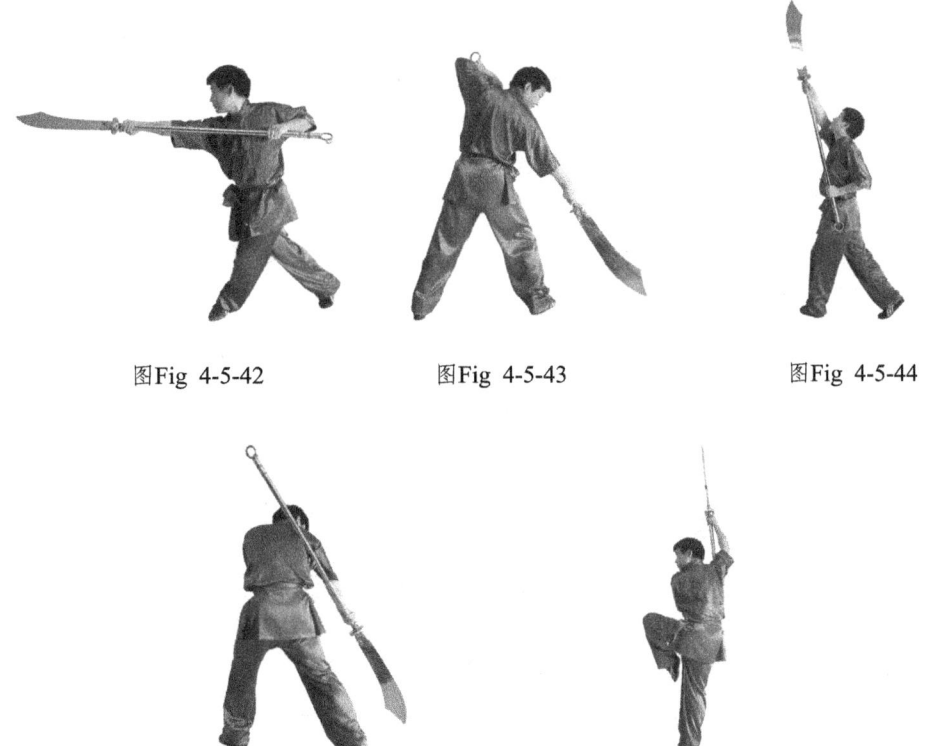

图Fig 4-5-42　　　　图Fig 4-5-43　　　　图Fig 4-5-44

图Fig 4-5-45　　　　图Fig 4-5-46

（4）身体右转，左脚内扣，重心右移，双手持刀向下、向右带刀于右下方，刀尖向下，刀刃朝后，目视右下方。（图4-5-45）

(4) Turn the body to the right, turn inside the left foot, gravity on the right, hold the knife with both hands downward and right, with the tip downward and the blade backward, and look at the lower right. (Fig. 4-5-45)

（5）重心移至右腿，右腿直立，左腿屈膝提起，上体略左转，双手持刀举于右胸前，刀刃向右，目视左前方。（图4-5-46）

(5) Move the gravity to the right leg, keep the right leg upright, lift the left leg with the knees bent, turn the upper body slightly to the left, hold the knife with both hands in front of the right chest, turn the blade to the right, and look at the left front. (Fig. 4-5-46)

动作要点：臂外旋、摆头、提膝同时完成，以示动作完整性。

Key points: rotate the arm outward, head swing the and knee lift should be done simultaneously to show the integrity of the action.

6. 弓步斩刀 Gongbuzhandao

身体左转，左脚向前上步，左腿屈膝成左弓步；同时，双手持刀随身体左转向前平斩刀，刀刃向左，目视刀身。(图 4-5-47)

Turn your body to the left, step forward with your left foot, and bend your left leg to form a left bow step. At the same time, hold the knife with both hands and turn left with your body, and then cleave horizontally. Look at the blade to the left. (Fig. 4-5-47)

图Fig 4-5-47

动作要点：从竖抱刀至斩刀要平圆前推。

Key points: from holding the knife vertically to knife cutting, the knife is pushed in a horizontal circle.

7. 弹腿抱刀 Tantuibaodao

（1）重心前移左脚，左腿直立，右腿由后向前弹踢；同时，双手持刀向右下截刀，目视刀身。(图 4-5-48)

（1）The gravity moves the left foot forward, the left leg stands upright, and the right leg bounces and kicks from the back to the front; at the same time, both hands hold the knife to cut the knife to the right and lower the knife, and look at the body of the knife. (Fig. 4-5-48)

（2）右腿向后落步成左弓步，上体右转，同时，双手持刀旋腕上抱于胸前，左臂伸直，右臂屈肘收于胸前，刀背贴于右大臂，刀刃向上，目视刀身。(图 4-5-49-1、图 4-5-49-2)

(2) The right leg falls backward to form a left bow step, the upper body turns right, at the same time, hold the knife with both hands, rotate the wrist and hold it in front of the chest, extend the left arm, bend the elbow of the right arm to close to the chest, stick the back of the knife to the right arm, with the blade upward, and look at the body of the knife. (Fig. 4-5-49-1, Fig. 4-5-49-2)

图Fig 4-5-48　　　　　图Fig 4-5-49-1　　　　　图Fig 4-5-49-2

动作要点：向前弹腿与后落步旋腕抱刀同时完成，节奏一致。

Key points: the forward spring leg and the backward step are completed at the same time, with the same rhythm.

8. 丁步下扎刀 Dingbuxiazhadao

重心移至右腿，左脚收于右脚内侧，脚尖点地，两腿屈膝成左丁步；同时，右手内旋持刀向右下方扎刀，刀与膝同高，刀刃向下，目视右下方。(图 4-5-50)

Move the center of gravity to the right leg, close the left foot to the inner side of the right foot, tiptoe down, bend the knees to form a left T step; at the same time, hold the knife in the right hand to stab lower right. The knife is the same height as the knee, the blade is downward, and look at the lower right. (Fig. 4-5-50)

图Fig 4-5-50

动作要点：身体重心压于右腿，左脚尖虚点地面，身体随扎刀微向前探。

Key points: press the gravity on the right leg, the left tiptoe down on the ground, the body slightly lean forward with the stab.

组合三 Combination 3

1. 弓步架刀 Gongbujiadao

（1）重心上提直立，身体左转180°，左脚向后撤步，重心移至左脚，左腿支撑直立，右腿提膝；同时，双手持刀随转身由右下向前上屈臂旋腕撩刀，刀刃向上，目视前方。（图 4-5-51）

(1) Lift the gravity vertically, turn the body 180° to the left, step backward with the left foot, move the center of gravity to the left foot, support the left leg upright, lift the right knee; at the same time, hold the knife with both hands and turn from the right bottom to the front, bend the arms and rotate the wrist to lift the knife, with the blade upward, and look forward. (Fig. 4-5-51)

（2）右腿向前落步成右弓步，双手持刀由胸前向上架刀，刀刃向上，目视前方。（图 4-5-52）

(2) Step forward with your right leg into a right lunge, hold the knife in both hands and hold it from the chest to make an upper frame, with the blade upward, and look ahead. (Fig. 4-5-52)

图Fig 4-5-51　　　　　　　图Fig 4-5-52

动作要点：①双手持刀贴身旋腕上挑撩刀，右手旋腕与左手下压刀柄要有爆发力。②落步成弓步与架刀摆头要完整，一气呵成。

Key points: ① hold the knife in both hands, close to the body, rotate the wrist. The wrist in the right hand rotating and pressing down with the left hand should be fast. ② Bow step forming and head swing go together.

2. 提步撩刀 Tibuliaodao

（1）重心移至左脚成左弓步，双手持刀向下带刀于身体右侧，刀刃向下，目视刀身。

(图 4-5-53)

(1) Move the center of gravity to the left foot to form a left bow step, hold the knife with both hands down to the right side of the body, with the blade down, and look at the blade. (Fig. 4-5-53)

（2）身体左转，重心移至左腿，左腿直立，右腿提膝；同时，双手持刀由后向前贴身撩出，双臂屈臂持刀收于胸前，刀尖与右脚尖同高，刀刃向上，目视刀身。(图 4-5-54)

(2) Turn your body to the left, move your weight to your left leg, keep your left leg upright, and lift your right leg to your knees. At the same time, blow the knife with both hands from the back to the front, bend your arms and hold the knife in front of your chest. The tip of the knife is the same height as the tip of your right foot, with the blade upward, and look at the blade. (Fig. 4-5-54)

（3）右腿向前落步，左腿蹬直，右腿屈膝成右弓步；同时，双手持刀由下向上撩刀，刀刃向上，目视前方。(图 4-5-55)

(3) Step forward with the right leg, step straight with the left leg, bend the right leg to form a right lunge; at the same time, hold the knife with both hands and lift the knife from the bottom to the top, with the blade upward, and look ahead. (Fig. 4-5-55)

图Fig 4-5-53　　　　图Fig 4-5-54　　　　图Fig 4-5-55

动作要点：弓步与撩刀同时进行，力达刀刃。

Key points: the feet moves and the hand moves are carried out at the same time, the force should reach the blade.

3. 提膝撩刀 Tixiliaodao

（1）重心上提，两腿微屈，双手持刀上撩至右上方，刀刃向上，目视刀身。(图4-5-56)

(1) Lift the gravity, bend the legs slightly, hold the knife with both hands and lift it to the upper right, with the blade upward, and look at the blade. (Fig. 4-5-56)

（2）右腿微屈，左腿伸直，双手持刀由右上方向左带刀至左下方，刀刃向下，目视刀身。（图 4-5-57）

(2) Slightly bend the right leg, straighten the left leg, carry the knife with both hands from the top right to the bottom left, with the blade downward, and look at the blade. (Fig. 4-5-57)

（3）身体右转 90°，左脚尖外展向前上步，右脚跟抬起；同时，双手持刀由身体左下侧向前方反撩，刀刃向上，目视刀身。（图 4-5-58）

(3) Turn your body 90° to the right, step forward with the tip of your left foot outstretched and the heel of your right foot raised; at the same time, hold the knife with both hands and lift it from the bottom left to the front, with the knife upward and look at the body. (Fig. 4-5-58)

图Fig 4-5-56　　　　　图Fig 4-5-57　　　　　图Fig 4-5-58

（4）身体继续右转，双手持刀继续上撩至右上方立刀，刀刃向前，目视前方。（图 4-5-59）

(4) Continue to turn your body to the right, hold the knife with both hands and continue to lift it up to the top right to stand the knife, with the blade forward and look ahead. (Fig. 4-5-59)

（5）重心移至右脚，右腿直立，左腿提膝；同时，双手持刀由头上向下再向前成立圆撩出，刀刃与肩同高，刀刃向上，目视前方。（图 4-5-60）

(5) The center of gravity is shifted to the right foot, the right leg is upright, and the left leg raises the knee; at the same time, the two hands hold the knife from the head down to the front to form a circle, the blade is the same height as the shoulder, the blade is upward, and look ahead. (Fig. 4-5-60)

图Fig 4-5-59   图Fig 4-5-60

动作要点：撩刀在身体两侧成立圆，提膝撩刀力达刀刃。

Key points: set up a circle on both sides of the body and lift the knee with the blade.

4. 上步左右抹刀 Shangbuzuoyoumodao

左腿向前落步，双手持刀由前向上撩至头上，继续上右步，左小腿屈膝抬起，双手持刀臂内旋向左平抹刀，与肩同高，刀刃向左，目视刀身。(图 4-5-61)

Step forward with the left leg, lift the knife with both hands from the front to the head, continue to step up and right, lift the left leg with knees bent, turn the knife with both hands inward to the left, the same height as the shoulder, the blade to the left, and look at the blade. (Fig. 4-5-61)

图Fig 4-5-61

动作要点：上步与抹刀要同时进行。

Key points: step up and knife smearing should be carried out at the same time.

5. 马步劈刀 Mabupidao

（1）左腿向前震脚落步，同时右膝提膝，双手持刀由前外旋向上举至肩上部，刀刃向下，目视前方。(图 4-5-62)

(1) The left leg steps down forward, while the right knee raised, both hands hold the

knife and swing from the front to the upper part of the shoulder, the blade is down, and look ahead. (Fig. 4-5-62)

（2）右脚向前落步，身体左转，两腿屈膝半蹲成马步；同时，双手持刀由上向下劈刀，刀刃向下，目视前下方。(图 4-5-63)

(2) Step forward with your right foot, turn your body to the left, bend your legs and squat to form a horse stance; at the same time, split with both hands from the top to the bottom, with the blade downward, and look down ahead. (Fig. 4-5-63)

图Fig 4-5-62　　　　　图Fig 4-5-63

动作要点：马步劈刀前，左脚落步震脚与右腿提膝节奏统一，劈刀力达刀刃。

Key points: before cleaving with horse-ride step, the left foot falls to the ground and the right leg raises rhythmically.

6. 换手刀 Huanshoudao

（1）两脚不动，身体重心上提右转，重心前移右脚；同时，刀向前上方送出，右手滑握刀柄中部，左手仍握刀柄尾部，刀刃向下，目视前方。(图 4-5-64)

(1) Keep your feet still, turn your body to the right, and move your weight forward to your right foot. At the same time, send the knife forward and upward,Slide the right hand to the middle of the handle, the left hand to the end of the handle, the blade down, and look ahead. (Fig. 4-5-64)

（2）重心前移，右脚尖外展，左脚跟提起，右手继续下滑握于左手上方，刀刃向下，目视前方。(图 4-5-65)

(2) Move the gravity forward, extend the right toe, lift the left heel, continue to slide the right hand and hold it on the top of the left hand, with the blade downward and look ahead. (Fig. 4-5-65)

第四章 传统器械选编 317

图Fig 4-5-64　　　　　　　　图Fig 4-5-65

（3）两脚不动，上体微右转，左手松开握刀，上举于头上方，目视刀身。(图 4-5-66)

(3) Keep your feet still, turn your upper body slightly to the right, release your left hand to hold the knife, lift it up above your head, and look at the blade. (Fig. 4-5-66)

（4）左腿上步，上体右转；同时，左手换握于刀盘处，右手握于刀柄把端，双手持刀由上至下成马步劈刀，刀与膝同高，刀刃向下，目视左前下方。(图 4-5-67)

(4) Step up on the left leg, turn the upper body to the right; at the same time, change the left hand to the cutter head, hold the right hand to the handle end of the knife, hold the knife in both hands from top to bottom to form a cleaving with horse-ride step , the knife is the same height as the knee, the blade is downward, and look at the front left and the bottom. (Fig. 4-5-67)

图Fig 4-5-66　　　　　　　　图Fig 4-5-67

动作要点：左、右手换刀要快，滑把顺畅，与上步协调进行。

Key points: shift the knife quickly between the left and right hand, and coordinate with the previous step.

7. 提膝绞截刀 Tixijiaojiedao

（1）两脚不动，身体迅速右转，右腿屈膝，左腿伸直，双手持刀下带刀，刀刃向下，目视刀身。(图 4-5-68)

(1) Keep your feet still, turn your body to the right quickly, bend your right leg to the knees, straighten your left leg, hold the knife with both hands, keep the blade down, and look at the blade. (Fig. 4-5-68)

（2）重心移至右腿，身体左转，左腿屈膝上提；同时，双手持刀臂内旋向上绞截刀，刀与头同高，刀刃向上，目视刀身。（图4-5-69）

(2) Move the gravity to the right leg, turn the body to the left, bend the left leg and lift up; hold the knife in both hands and twist the blade, the knife is the same height as the head, the blade is upward, and look at the blade. (Fig. 4-5-69)

图Fig 4-5-68

图Fig 4-5-69

动作要点：双手持刀内、外旋转臂与提膝协调统一，上提微前倾，力达刀刃。

Key points: the inside and outside rotating are coordinated with the knee lifting, and the body slightly leans forward to reach the blade.

8. 换手刀 Huanshoudao

（1）左脚向前落步，重心前移；同时，刀向前上方送出，左手下滑握刀柄中部，右手仍握刀柄尾部，刀刃向下，目视前方。（图4-5-70）

(1) Step forward with the left foot, and move the center of gravity forward; at the same time, send out the knife forward and upward, slide the left hand down and hold the middle of the handle, and still hold the tail of the handle with the right hand, with the blade downward, and look ahead. (Fig. 4-5-70)

（2）重心前移，右腿上步，左脚跟提起，右手换握于刀盘处，左手下滑握于刀柄，刀刃向下，目视刀身。（图4-5-71）

(2) Move the center of gravity forward, step up on the right leg, lift the left heel, change the right hand to the cutter head, slide the left hand to the handle, and hold the blade downward. Look at the blade. (Fig. 4-5-71)

（3）两脚不动，两腿屈膝成马步，双手持刀由上至下成马步劈刀，刀刃向下，目视刀刃。（图4-5-72）

(3) Keep your feet still, bend your legs to form a horse stance, hold the knife in both hands to form a horse stance cleaver from top to bottom, the blade is downward, and look at the blade. (Fig. 4-5-72)

图Fig 4-5-70　　　　　图Fig 4-5-71　　　　　图Fig 4-5-72

动作要点：左、右手换刀要快、稳准，换手与上步协调进行。

Key points: shifting the knife between left and right hands should be fast and stable, and the moves should be coordinated with the previous step.

9. 叉步刺刀 Chabucidao

（1）重心移至右腿，身体左转 90°，右腿直立，左腿屈膝向左弹踢；同时，双手持刀向左平顶刀把，刀刃向上，目视左侧。（图 4-5-73）

(1) Move the gravity to the right leg, turn the body 90° to the left, keep the right leg upright, bend the knee of the left leg and kick to the left; at the same time, hold the knife with both hands to the left flat, with the blade upward, and look at the left side. (Fig. 4-5-73)

（2）左腿经右腿后向右插步，右腿屈膝，脚尖外展，左腿伸直，脚跟抬起；同时，双手持刀内旋臂向右平刺刀，刀刃下下，目视刀身。（图 4-5-74）

(2) Step the left leg to the right through the right leg, bend the right knee, extend the toe, straighten the left leg and lift the heel; hold the knife with both hands swing inside and stab to the right, and look at the blade. (Fig. 4-5-74)

图Fig 4-5-73　　　　　图Fig 4-5-74

动作要点：弹踢屈膝快速，力至脚尖，叉步要远，刺刀伸直右臂。

Key points: fast knee bending, force reaches to the toe, the cross step should be wide, straight right when stabing.

10. 绕脖舞花刀 Raobowuhuadao

图Fig 4-5-75　　　　　　图Fig 4-5-76　　　　　　图Fig 4-5-77

（1）身体立起，身体左转，双手持刀随身体左转向下向前立圆撩刀，刀柄放于右臂外侧，左掌收于右肩前，目视前方。(图 4-5-75)

(1) Stand up and turn left. Hold the knife with both hands and move it forward with the body turning left. Place the handle on the outside of the right arm. Place the left palm in front of the right shoulder and look ahead. (Fig. 4-5-75)

（2）继续左后转身，右手单手持刀从右臂外贴背部绕脖至左肩，(图 4-5-76) 左手接握刀，双手持刀向右下挂刀，刀尖向下，目视前方。(图 4-5-77)

(2) Continue to turn left, with the right hand holding the knife, blow along the back and through the neck to the left shoulder, (Fig. 4-5-76) shift the knife to the left hand, hang the knife to the right with both hands, the tip of the knife downward, and look ahead. (Fig. 4-5-77)

（3）双手持刀左右舞花刀，目视前方。(图同前云手舞花)

(3) Hold the knife in both hands and twist the knife left and right. Look ahead. (The picture is the same as the previous Yunshouwuhua)

动作要点：转身绕脖与舞花刀成立圆，舞花刀与上步配合协调。

Key points: the twist of the knife around the neck should be in a vertical circle. The knife twist coordinates with the feet step.

11. 背刀拍脚 Beidaopaijiao

（1）双手舞花刀至右侧时立圆挂刀右下侧，右后背刀，刀刃向后，右脚上步，右

腿直立，左脚跟提起，左掌收于右肩前，目视前方。(图 4-5-78)

(1) When the knife twisting with two hands reaches the right side, hang the knife lower right side. The blade backward, the right foot stepped up, the right leg upright, the left heel lifted, the left palm closed in front of the right shoulder, and look ahead. (Fig. 4-5-78)

（2）左脚向前上步，右手背刀不动，左手上举，目视前方。(图 4-5-79)

(2) Step forward with the left foot, hold the knife on the back of the right hand, raise the left hand, and look ahead. (Fig. 4-5-79)

（3）重心前移左脚，右腿向上直摆踢腿，脚背绷直，左手拍击右脚面，目视左掌。(图 4-5-80)

(3) Move the weight forward on the left foot, swing the right leg straight up, straighten the instep, tap the right foot with the left hand, and look at the left palm. (Fig. 4-5-80)

图Fig 4-5-78　　　图Fig 4-5-79　　　图Fig 4-5-80

动作要点：挂刀立圆，上步协调一致，拍脚击响清脆有力。

Key points: swing the knife and in a vertical circle, and tap the foot with clear and powerful sound.

12. 震脚弓步推掌 Zhenjiaogongbutuizhang

（1）右腿向前震脚落步直立，左腿屈膝提起，左掌收于右肩前，目视前方。(图 4-5-81)

(1) Stamp forward with the right leg and stand upright. Lift the left leg with the knees bent. Close the left palm in front of the right shoulder and look ahead. (Fig. 4-5-81)

（2）左脚向前落地成左弓步，左手向前推掌，与肩同高，右手背刀，刀刃向上，目视前方。(图 4-5-82)

(2) The left foot falls forward into a left bow step, the left palm pushes forward to the same height as the shoulder, the right hand holding the knife, the blade upward, and watch the front. (Fig. 4-5-82)

图Fig 4-5-81　　　　　　图Fig 4-5-82

动作要点：右震脚与左提膝同时完成。

Key points: right foot stamping and left knee lifting are completed at the same time.

13. **虚步斩刀** Xubuzhandao

（1）身体略上起，左手回握于刀把，双手持刀向左上云刀至刀刃向右，目视右后方。（图4-5-83）

(1) Slightly up the body, hold the knife handle with the left hand, hold the knife with both hands swing the knife up and right, and look at the right rear. (Fig. 4-5-83)

（2）重心右移，左脚向右脚后插步；同时，双手持刀向右后下方截刀，目视刀刃。（图4-5-84）

(2) Move the gravity to the right, and cross step from left foot to right foot; at the same time, hold the knife with both hands and blow to the right and back to the bottom, and watch the blade. (Fig. 4-5-84)

（3）重心移至右脚，左脚向左前上半步，脚尖点地，右腿屈膝成左虚步；同时，双手持刀向左前斩刀，刀刃向左，目视刀刃。（图4-5-85）

(3) Move the gravity to the right foot, move the left foot forward half a step to the left, tiptoe the ground, and bend the right leg to form a left empty step; at the same time, hold the knife in both hands and blow forward to the left, the blade to the left, and look at the blade. (Fig. 4-5-85)

图Fig 4-5-83　　　　图Fig 4-5-84　　　　图Fig 4-5-85

动作要点：向后斩刀与左脚插步统一，撩刀、虚步、摆头要同时完成。

Key points: the back cutting and left foot step are unified, and the lifting knife, empty step and head swinging should be completed at the same time.

14. 并步持刀推掌 Bingbuchidaotuizhang

图Fig 4-5-86　　　　　图Fig 4-5-87

（1）重心上起，身体右转，右脚后撤半步，双手持刀随身体右转，由前向后垂放于身体右侧，目视刀身。(图 4-5-86)

(1) Lift the gravity, turn your body to the right, step backward with your right foot, turn right with your hands holding the knife, hang it on the right side of your body from the front to the back, and look at the knife. (Fig. 4-5-86)

（2）左脚向右腿并步直立，同时，左掌向身体左侧推出，与肩同高，右手持刀立于身体右侧，刀刃向前，目视左掌。(图 4-5-87)

(2) The left foot is straight to the right leg, at the same time, the left palm is pushed out to the left side of the body, which is the same height as the shoulder. The right hand holds the knife on the right side of the body, and the blade is forward. Look at the left palm. (Fig. 4-5-87)

动作要点：并步直立与推掌、摆头协调完成。

Key points: step upright is coordinate with palm pushing and head turning.

15. 收势 Ending up

两腿并步直立，左手收于体侧，自然下垂，右手持刀立于身体右侧，刀刃向前，目视前方。(图 4-5-88)

Stand upright with both legs together, with the left hand at the side of the body, hanging down naturally. Stand on the right side of the body with the knife in the right hand, with the blade forward, and look ahead. (Fig. 4-5-88)

图Fig 4-5-88

动作要点：身体姿势要求挺胸、沉肩，精神饱满。

Key points: the body posture requires chest up, shoulders down and full of energy.

第六节　小连枷
4.6 Xiao Lianjia

一、小连枷简介 Brief Introduction

小连枷又称小梢子棍，古时称连挺、连筵、铁链夹棒等，因其源于农家打麦脱粒用的连枷，故俗称连枷棍。连枷棍是一种很古老的武术兵器，据《墨子·备城门》记载："二步置连挺、长斧、长椎各一物，枪二十枚。"另有"当敌人附借云梯、密集如蚁，缘城墙而上时，用火烧之，用连筵击之。"由此可见，连枷棍在春秋战国时代就已经是守城御敌的重要兵器了。唐代杜佑在《通典》中记载："连挺，如打禾连枷状，打女墙外上城敌人。"意思是说当攻城的敌人沿梯攀登到接近城蝶时，守军居高临下，用连枷击打敌人。宋代时，连枷不但仍用于守城御敌，而且成为一种非常重要的马上兵器。据《武经总要》记载："铁链夹棒，本出西戎，马上用之，以敌汉之步兵，其状如农家打麦之连枷，以铁饰之，利用自上击下，故汉兵善用者巧于戎人。"

Xiao Lianjia is also called Xiao Shaozigun. It was called Lianting, Lianyan and Iron-chain-stick in ancient times, because it originated from the instrument used by farmers to thresh wheat, commonly known as flail stick. It is a very old weapon of Wushu. According to *Mozi·City Gate*, "there are two steps to set up Lianting, long axe and long vertebra. These things can be used to fight against the enemies who climb up the city defending wall by high ladders." It can be seen that the Xiao Lianjia has been an important weapon to defend the city and resist the enemy since the Spring and Autumn period and the Warring States period. In other historical books in the Tang dynasty and the Ming Dynasty, this practical staff can be found to be used to collect and clean the wheat, then to defend the city and resist the enemy, and became a very important weapon. According to the book of Wushu, it is recorded that 'iron chains and sticks originally came out of western minority and were used immediately by the Han soldiers. Therefore, the Han soldiers were skilled at using them."

连枷棍分为大连枷和小连枷。大连枷也称大梢子棍，由一根长棍和一根短棍以铁环连接而成，短棍约长40-50厘米，称"梢子"，长棍约长140-155厘米，称为"棍身"，属于长软器械，一般双手执用。小连枷也称小梢子棍，梢子约长15-20厘米，棍身长约40-60厘米，一般双手各执一棍，属于短兵中的双软器械。

Lianjia club can be divided into big one (Da Lianjia) and small one (Xiao Lianjia). Da Lianjia is known as Da Shaozigun, which is made of a long stick and a short stick connected by an iron ring. The short stick is about 40-50cm long, which is called "Shaozi". The long stick is about 140-155cm long, which is called "stick body". It belongs to long soft instrument, which is usually held by both hands. Xiao Lianjia is also called Xiao Shaozigun. The Shaozi is about 15-20cm long and the main body is about 40-60cm long. Generally, each hand holds a stick, which belongs to the double soft instrument.

二、小连枷技法特点 The Technical characteristics

小连枷形制特别，携带方便，灵活实用，兼长、短、软、硬、双器械的诸多特点，基本技法有抡、劈、戳、甩、撩、砸、扫、云以及舞花、撩弹、盖扑、抽斩、摇挂、圈缠、拨拦等方法。技术套路短小精悍，演练时勇猛泼辣，左右连环，软中带硬，边走边舞，棍势急厉，气势磅礴，威力强大，挥舞起来叮当作响，威猛彪悍，将棍技法发挥得淋漓尽致。

Xiao Lianjia is special in shape and easy to carry. It is flexible and practical, and has many characteristics of long, short, soft, hard and double instruments. The basic techniques include swing, split, poke, swing, lift, smash, sweep, twist, hit, lift, cover, chop and block. The technical routine is short and pithy. One can play it while walking. The staff's momentum is sharp and powerful. It's jingling when waving. It represents the essence technique of Gun Shu.

小连枷主要动作有捞月架、坐马势、雪花盖顶、古树盘根、金鸡过岭、背后插花、野马分鬃、朝天开花、就地十八滚、乌龙摆尾、狮子大张口、怪蟒翻身、偷步走门子、鹞子翻身、拧手三花、面背三花等。主要步法有跃步、跟步、弧行步等；步型主要有马步、半马步、虚步、仆步、跪步、丁步、弓步等；腿法有侧踢、弹腿、撩阴腿等。

The main actions of Xiao Lianjia are moon-fishing, horse-riding, snow covering the mountain top, the twisted roots of old trees, the golden rooster crossing the hills, inserting flowers from the back, dividing the mane of wild horses, blooming towards the sky, rolling on the spot, black dragon swinging the tail, the lion opening the big mouth, strange snake turning over the body and so on. The main footsteps include leaping, following and arc walking; the step mainly includes horse-riding step, half horse-riding step, empty step, kneeling step, T step, bow step, etc.; the leg skills include side kick, leg spring, leg swing, etc.

小连枷歌（谱）诀

小小连枷成双对，本自农具出兵刃；
左扑右斩弹劈撩，左右连环不及防，
滚身花子连三劈；雪花盖顶下扫腿，
偷步转身走门子，拧手舞花翻身打；
顺地抡扫抡上弹，退步提撩坐马势，
蝴蝶采花护尽全；圈缠拨拦有妙法，
棍急法厉势奔放；无影无形显神威。

三、小连枷基本技法与组合图解 Illustrations of basic techniques and combinations

（一）小连枷基本技法 Basic skills

1. 小连枷握把法：一般双手各执长棍把端。（图 4-6-1）

1.Carrying: each hand holds the two ends of the longer section of Xiao Lianjia. (Fig. 4-6-1)

2. 架法：双手各执折叠连枷长短棍，体前交叉平推。（图 4-6-2）

2.Propping: hold the folding two parts with both hands, and push horizontally in front of the body. (Fig. 4-6-2)

3.刺法：手握折叠连枷长短棍向前直戳，臂与连枷成一直线，力达棍头。(图4-6-3)

3.Stabbing: hold the folding club and poke it straight forward. The arm is in line with the flail body and reaches the head of the staff. (Fig. 4-6-3)

图Fig 4-6-1　　　　　　图Fig 4-6-2　　　　　　图Fig 4-6-3

4. 劈法：手握连枷长棍把端由上向下挥动。

4.Splitting: hold the end of the long part and wave from top to bottom.

5. 撩法：手握连枷长棍把端由下向前、向上挥击。

5.Lifting : hold the end of the long part and swing down to forward and upward.

6. 云法：手握连枷长棍把端在头顶或头前上方做平圆绕环。

6.Swinging: hold the end of the long part and make a flat circle over the head or before the head.

7. 缠头法：手握连枷长棍把端扣腕旋臂，贴背绕肩，与双刀缠头相同。

7.Chantou: hold the end of the long part, buckle the wrist and rotate the arm, close the back and wrap the shoulder, which is the same as the moves of Shuangdaochantou.

8. 裹脑法：手握连枷长棍把端扣腕旋臂，贴背绕头，与双刀裹脑相同。

8.Guonao: hold the end of the long part, wrist and rotate inward, the arm rotates back, which is the same as the moves in Shuangdaoguonao.

（二）小连枷技法组合图解 Illustrations of techniques combinations

组合一：Combination 1

1. 预备姿势 Ready pose

图Fig 4-6-4　　　　　　图Fig 4-6-5

（1）并步站立，折叠连枷长短棍，双手各执一棍，直臂垂于身体两侧，目视前方。（图 4-6-4）

(1) Stand with feet paralleled, fold the long and short parts of each Xiaolianjia, hold one in each hand, hang your arms on both sides of your body, and look ahead. (Fig. 4-6-4)

（2）两腿不动，双手各执棍屈臂收至腰间，身体微左转，目视左方。（图 4-6-5）

(2) Keep your legs still, bend your arms to your waist with the set in each hand, turn your body slightly to the left, and look to the left. (Fig. 4-6-5)

2. 捞月架 Moon-fishing posture

(1) 两腿不动，俯身弯腰，双手各执棍向下伸直接近地面，棍环朝前，目视棍环。（图 4-6-6-1、图 4-6-6-2）

(1) Keep your legs still, bend over, hold one set in each hand and with one part close down to the ground, with the stick ring facing forward, and look at the stick ring. (Fig. 4-6-6-1, Fig. 4-6-6-2)

图Fig 4-6-6-1　　　　　　图Fig 4-6-6-2

图Fig 4-6-7　　　　　　图Fig 4-6-8　　　　　　图Fig 4-6-9

(2) 上体直立，两臂伸直上抬至与肩同高，双臂微曲，两棍交叉成"十"字上架，左手棍在外，目视两棍。(图 4-6-7)

(2) Stand upright, the two arms are straight and raised to the same height as the shoulder, the arms slightly bent, the two sets crossed, the left set outside, and look at the two sets. (Fig. 4-6-7)

(3) 两腿不动，两臂伸直向两侧横棍，目视左方。(图 4-6-8)

(3) Keep your legs still, extend your arms to both sides, and look left. (Fig. 4-6-8)

(4) 两腿不动，双手执棍屈臂收至腰间，目视前方。(图 4-6-9)

(4) Keep your legs still, bend your arms to your waist, and look ahead. (Fig. 4-6-9)

动作要点：十字架棍有力，双臂旋腕有力。

Key points: to cross the sets powerfully, and the arms are strong.

3. 坐马势 Horse sitting posture

图Fig 4-6-10　　　　　　图Fig 4-6-11

图Fig 4-6-12　　　　　图Fig 4-6-13　　　　　图Fig 4-6-14

（1）两腿不动，右手执棍向右下穿棍，目视右手。（图 4-6-10）

(1) Keep your legs still, hold the stick with your right hand and go down to the right, and look at your right hand. (Fig. 4-6-10)

（2）两腿不动，右手执棍由右下向右上穿棍，目视右手。（图 4-6-11）

(2) Two legs do not move, the right hand holding stick goes from right down to right up, look at the right hand. (Fig. 4-6-11)

（3）右手执棍由右上旋臂向左上横拦棍，目视右手。（图 4-6-12）

(3) Hold the stick in the right hand, turn the right upper arm to the left to block the stick, and look at the right hand. (Fig. 4-6-12)

（4）左手执棍由右臂内向上穿棍，右手执棍收至右下方，目视左手。（图 4-6-13）

(4) The left hand holding stick goes from the right inward arm, the right hand holding stick retreats to the lower right, and look at the left hand. (Fig. 4-6-13)

（5）左脚向左侧跨步，两腿屈膝半蹲成半马步，左手执棍旋臂向下横棍扣压，右手执棍外旋上架棍，目视前方。（图 4-6-14）

(5) Step to the left with your left foot, bend your knees and half squat into a half horse-riding stance, press down horizontally with your left hand holding the stick, and turn the stick with your right hand outward, and look ahead. (Fig. 4-6-14)

动作要点：穿棍时棍与手臂贴紧成一直线，扣、压、架棍和横棍有力。

Key points: when the stick goes, the stick and the arm are close in a straight line, and the moves of the stick are powerful.

4. 弓步连戳 Gongbulianchuo

（1）重心前移至左腿成左弓步，右手执棍向前戳棍，左手执棍收至腰间，左手执棍向前戳棍，右手执棍收至腰间，目视左手。（图 4-6-15）

(1) Move the gravity forward to the left leg to form a left bow step, the right set stabs forward the left closet to the waist; the left set stabs forward with the right set back to the waist, and look at the left hand.(Fig. 4-6-15)

（2）重心前移，右脚跟提起，上体前倾，右手执棍再向前戳棍，左手执棍收至右腋下，目视右手。（图 4-6-16）

(2) Move the gravity forward, lift the right heel forward, lean the upper body forward, poke forward the right set, hold the left set under the right armpit, and look at the right hand. (Fig. 4-6-16)

图Fig 4-6-15　　　　　　图Fig 4-6-16

动作要点：快速连环戳棍，棍身贴紧前臂，力达棍环。

Key points: the connected poking is quickly; the stick goes close to the forearm, and the force reaches the stick ring.

5. 双开花 Double blooming

（1）身体左转90°，右脚扣于左膝后，右手执棍内旋臂，左手执棍收至右腋下，目视右手。（图 4-6-17）

(1) Turn your body 90° to the left, the right foot behind the left knee, swirl inside the right set, hold the left set under the right armpit, and look at the right hand. (Fig. 4-6-17)

（2）身体左转90°，右脚随转身上步成右弓步，左手执棍向前戳棍，右手执棍立圆挂棍一圈，目视左手。（图 4-6-18）

(2) Turn your body 90° to the left, turn your right foot and step up to form a right lunge, stick forward with the left set swing right in a vertical circle, and look at the left hand. (Fig. 4-6-18)

（3）两腿不动，右手执棍向前戳棍，左手执棍收至腰间，目视右手。（图 4-6-19）

(3) Keep your legs still, poke forward with the right set, put the left set to the waist, and look at the right hand. (Fig. 4-6-19)

图Fig 4-6-17　　　　　　图Fig 4-6-18　　　　　　图Fig 4-6-19

（4）身体左转180°成左弓步，左手执棍向前戳棍，目视左手。（图 4-6-20）

(4) Turn your body 180° to the left to form a left lunge. Hold the stick in your left hand and poke it forward. Look at your left hand. (Fig. 4-6-20)

（5）两腿不动，右手执棍向前戳棍，与左手平行，目视前方。(图 4-6-21)

(5) Keep your legs still, stick forward with the right set, parallel to the left hand, and look ahead. (Fig. 4-6-21)

（6）两腿不动，双手执棍向前抛送，双手贴棍滑把紧握棍把端，目视前方。(图 4-6-22)

(6) Keep your legs still, throw the sets forward with both hands, hold the end of the sets tightly after sliding down the handle, and look ahead. (Fig. 4-6-22)

图Fig 4-6-20　　　　　图Fig 4-6-21　　　　　图Fig 4-6-22

动作要点：戳棍手臂伸直，挂棍与左手戳棍协调配合，扣腿翻身迅速。

Key points: stick poking needs the arm to be straight; the moves of the two hands should be coordinated.

6. 拧手舞花 Ningshouwuhua

图Fig 4-6-23　　　　　图Fig 4-6-24

图Fig 4-6-25　　　　　图Fig 4-6-26

（1）右脚向前上步，双腿微屈，右手执棍向右下抡棍，目视前方。(图 4-6-23)

(1) Step forward with your right foot, slightly bend your legs, swing the stick with your right hand to the down right, and look ahead. (Fig. 4-6-23)

（2）两脚不动，双手执棍向前立圆左右舞花棍，目视前方。(图 4-6-24、图 4-6-25、图 4-6-26)

(2) Two feet do not move, holding the sets in both hands, standing forward to swirl the sets in vertical round, and watch ahead. (Fig. 4-6-24, Fig. 4-6-25, Fig. 4-6-26)

动作要点：舞花棍时棍在身体两侧立圆贴身绕行。

Key points:when twist the sets, make sure that the sets move in vertical circle on both sides of the body.

7. 鹞子翻身 Yaozi fanshen

（1）身体右转，左脚向前上步，左手执棍向前劈棍，右手执棍上举，目视左手。(图 4-6-27)

(1) Turn your body to the right, step forward with your left foot, split forward with the left set, hold up the right set, and look at the left hand. (Fig. 4-6-27)

（2）身体左转180°，右脚向前上步成马步，右手执棍向前劈棍，左手执棍向左带棍，目视右手。(图 4-6-28-1、图 4-6-28-2)

(2) Turn your body 180° to the left, step forward with your right foot into a horse-riding stance, split forward with the right set, bring the left set to the left, and look at the right hand. (Fig. 4-6-28-1, Fig. 4-6-28-2)

图Fig 4-6-27　　　　　　图Fig 4-6-28-1　　　　　　图Fig 4-6-28-2

（3）左腿屈膝上提，右脚踏跳，上体左后转，目视右手。(图 4-6-29)

(3) Bend the left leg and lift, step on the right foot, turn the upper body to the left and look at the right hand. (Fig. 4-6-29)

（4）右脚踏跳，身体腾空左后转360°，右手执棍上举，目视前方。（图4-6-30）

(4) Step on your right foot, turn your body 360° to the left, hold up the right set, and look ahead. (Fig. 4-6-30)

（5）左脚先落地，右脚继而向前落地，重心下蹲成马步，双手执棍同时向前劈棍，目视右棍。（图4-6-31）

(5) The left foot lands first , then the right foot, squat into a horse stance, hold the sticks with both hands and split forward at the same time, and look at the right set. (Fig. 4-6-31)

图Fig 4-6-29　　　　　图Fig 4-6-30　　　　　图Fig 4-6-31

动作要点：劈棍立圆，力达短棍棍梢；翻身踏跳迅猛，落地下蹲，劈棍前伸手臂。

Key points: stick going in vertical circle, the force should reaches to the tip of the short part; all the moves should be fast, the arms should stretch forward before the chopping.

8. 叉步反劈 Chabufanpi

左脚经右脚后插步，两腿交叉下蹲，双手执棍同时向前抡劈棍，目视右棍。（图4-6-32-1、图4-6-32-2)

The left foot crosses the right foot and squats down with two legs crossed. Hold the sticks with both hands and swing them forward at the same time. Look at the right stick. (Fig. 4-6-32-1, Fig. 4-6-32-2)

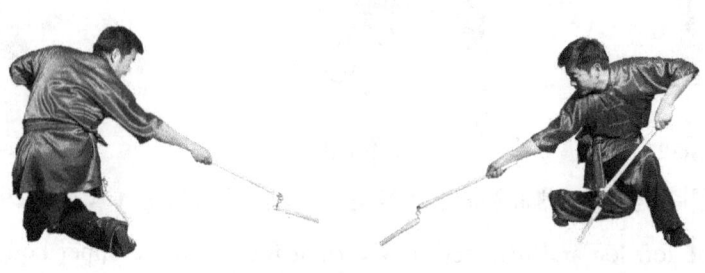

图Fig 4-6-32-1　　　　　图Fig 4-6-32-2

动作要点：双手执棍随叉步立圆抡劈，力达短棍棍梢。

Action points: holding the stick with both hands, standing with fork steps, swinging and chopping,the force reaches the end of the short stick.

9. 左走门子 Left Zoumenzi

（1）身体重心上提左转，左脚上步成左弓步，右手执棍向左上平抡棍，左手执棍带至右腋下，目视前方。(图 4-6-33)

(1) Turn left when lift the gravity of the body, form a left bow step, swing the right set, bring the left set to the right armpit in the left hand, and look ahead. (Fig. 4-6-33)

（2）两腿不动，右手执棍从头上顺时针平云棍一周向前横扫棍，左手执棍从右腋下向上顺时针云棍，目视右手。(图 4-6-34)

(2) Keep your legs still. Swing the right set over head clockwise. Swing the left set upward clockwise. Look at the right hand. (Fig. 4-6-34)

（3）左手执棍从头上顺时针云棍向左前横打，右手执棍收至左腋下，目视前方。(图 4-6-35)

(3) Swing the left set clockwise over the head, and pull the right set to the left armpit, and look forward. (Fig. 4-6-35)

图Fig 4-6-33　　　　图Fig 4-6-34　　　　图Fig 4-6-35

动作要点：两手执棍云棍平圆。

Key points: swing the sets in horizontal circle.

10. 右走门子 Right Zoumenzi

（1）右脚向右前方上步成右弓步，右手执棍向右前方上平抡棍，目视前方。(图4-6-36)

(1) Step right forward with your right foot to form a right lunge, hold the stick with your right hand and swing the stick to the right front, and look ahead. (Fig. 4-6-36)

（2）两腿不动，右手执棍上提屈腕，使棍从头右上贴背裹脑，左手执棍带至右腋下，

目视前方。（图 4-6-37）

(2) Keep your legs still. Swing the right set with the wrist bend, around the head from the top to the right. Hold the left set under the right armpit and look ahead. (Fig. 4-6-37)

（3）右手执棍从右上裹脑至左肩向右前横打，左手执棍收至右腋下，目视前方。(图 4-6-38)

(3) Swing the right set around the head to the left shoulder and forward, pull the left set under the right armpit, and look forward. (Fig. 4-6-38)

图Fig 4-6-36　　　　　图Fig 4-6-37　　　　　图Fig 4-6-38

动作要点：两手执棍云棍平圆，向右横打配合身体转向。

Key points: swing the sets in horizontal circle, then blow to the right with the body turning.

组合二： Combination 2

1. 狮子大张口 Roaring Lion

图Fig 4-6-39

左脚向前上步，两腿屈膝半蹲成半马步，右手执棍上举，左手执棍从右腋下向前平推棍，目视前方。（图 4-6-39）

Step forward with your left foot, bend your knees and squat in a half horse-riding stance, hold the stick in your left hand, and push the stick forward from your right armpit, and look ahead. (Fig. 4-6-39)

动作要点：半马步身体重心偏于右腿，推棍横置体前，右手执棍竖立。

Key points: the gravity of half horse-riding stance is inclined to the right leg, push the stick horizontally in front of the body, and hold the stick upright in the right hand.

2. **左右撩花 Right and Left Liaohua**

（1）重心上提，右脚向前上步，两腿微屈，右手执棍从上向前撩棍，左手执棍从下向前撩棍，目视前方。（图 4-6-40)

(1) Lift the gravity up, step forward with your right foot, slightly bend your legs, hold the stick in your right hand and swing to the front, hold the left stick and swing from bottom to the front, and look ahead. (Fig. 4-6-40)

（2）两腿不动，两手执棍在身体两侧向前依次立圆撩花，目视前方。（图 4-6-41、图 4-6-42)

(2) Keep your legs still, swing the sticks forward beside the body, and look ahead. (Fig. 4-6-41, Fig. 4-6-42)

图Fig 4-6-40　　　　图Fig 4-6-41　　　　图Fig 4-6-42

动作要点：撩花贴近身体，两手腕旋腕协调，棍立圆走转。

Action points: keep the sticks close to the body, the left and right swings should be coordinated, and the stick goes in vertical circle.

3. **朝天蹬 Chaotiandeng**

（1）左脚向前上步直立，右脚跟提起，左手执棍撩棍上举，右手执棍收于左腋下，目视前方。（图 4-6-43)

(1) Step forward and stand upright with left foot, lift the right heel, blow and swing the left stick, hold the right stick close under the left armpit, and look ahead. (Fig. 4-6-43)

（2）重心前移左脚直立，右腿向上蹬踢，力达脚跟，目视前方。（图 4-6-44）

(2) Move the weight forward, kick upright, and the force reaching to the heel, and look ahead. (Fig. 4-6-44)

图Fig 4-6-43　　　　图Fig 4-6-44

动作要点：蹬腿勾脚尖，左腿独立站稳，上体中正。

Key points: kick with the toe hook, stand on the left leg independently, and keep the upper body straight.

4. 弓步横打 Gongbuhengda

右脚向前落步，右腿屈膝成右弓步，右手执棍向前横打，左手执棍收于腰间，目视前方。(图 4-6-45)

Step forward with your right foot, bend your right leg to form a right bow, hold the stick in your right hand to fight forward, hold the stick in your left hand to your waist, and look ahead. (Fig. 4-6-45)

图Fig 4-6-45

动作要点：横打前臂发力，带动短棍向前抽打。

KKey points: use forearm to generate force, use the long parts to drive short parts forward.

5. 丁步群拦 T-step Qunlan

右脚内扣，重心移至右脚，左脚收至右脚内侧，左脚尖点地，左手执棍向左侧拉开，身体左转90°，右腿屈膝半蹲成丁步，两手执棍向两侧斜举棍，目视左前方。(图4-6-46)

The right foot lean inner ward, move the gravity to the right foot, put the left foot to the inside of the right foot, point the left foot to the ground, pull the left stick to the left, turn the body 90° to the left, bend the right leg knee and squat into a T step, hold the sticks in both hands obliquely to both sides, and look at the left front. (Fig. 4-6-46)

图Fig 4-6-46

动作要点：丁步时两腿贴紧，身体徐徐左转站稳，两臂向两侧撑架。

Key points: keep your legs close to each other in T step, turn your body slowly to the left and stand steadily, and stretch your arms to both sides.

6. 双撩 Shuangliao

重心上提，左脚向左前方上步成左弓步，两手执棍向左前撩棍，目视前方。(图4-6-47)

Lift the gravity up, step left foot forward to form a left bow step, swing the sticks left forward, and look ahead. (Fig. 4-6-47)

图Fig 4-6-47

动作要点：双撩时，两臂外旋腕合拢，撩棍平行一致。

Key points: swing with both wrists turning outside, together, and the sticks are parallel.

7. 收棍 Ending up

（1）两腿不动，两棍折叠交于左手，右掌收至腰间，目视左手。(图 4-6-48)

(1) Keep your legs still, fold the two sticks to your left hand, put your right palm to your waist, and look at your left hand. (Fig. 4-6-48)

（2）身体右转180°，重心移至右腿成右弓步，左手握棍收于腰间，右掌向右前撩掌，掌心向上，与肩同高，目视右掌。(图 4-6-49)

(2) Turn 180° to the right, move your weight to your right leg to form a right lunge, hold the sticks in your left hand and close them to your waist, lift your right palm to the right and forward, palm up, shoulder high, and look at your right palm. (Fig. 4-6-49)

图Fig 4-6-48　　　　　图Fig 4-6-49

图Fig 4-6-50　　　　　图Fig 4-6-51

（3）左脚向右脚并步直立，右掌下按掌于腰间，目视左侧。(图 4-6-50)

(3) The left foot is straight to the right foot. Press the right palm to the waist, and look at the left side. (Fig. 4-6-50)

（4）并步站立，两臂垂于身体两侧，目视前方。(图 4-6-51)

(4) Stand in parallel, with your arms down on both sides of your body, and look ahead. (Fig. 4-6-51)

动作要点：收棍时右手先收两棍把，借助挑弹折叠后左手收棍，注意收紧链环，两棍收齐。

Key points: At the end of the performance, the right hand should catch the ends of the sticks and then the left hand catch the other parts with the help of inertia after folding. Tighten the chain link and keep the two sticks alignment.

思考题：Questions for consideration

1. 盘龙棍的用法主要有哪些?
1. What are the main usages of Panlonggun?

2. 双刀技术特点有哪些?
2. What are the characteristics of double knife technique?

3. 缠头刀动作过程?
3. What's the action process of Chantoudao?

4. 鞭杆技法运用讲求有哪些?
4. What are the requirements for the use of Biangan techniques?

5. 朴刀技法特点是什么?
5. What are the characteristics of Pudao techniques?

6. 小连枷技法特点有哪些?
6. What are the characteristics of Xiao Lianjia techniques?

第五章　武术桩功选编
Chapter 5 Selections of Wushu Zhuang Gong

第一节　武术桩功简介
5.1 Brief Introduction to Wushu Zhuang Gong

桩功是传统武术内功功法之一，在传统武术流派中都有各自不同的站桩、坐桩、打坐功法，这些功法保持一定的拳式姿势以站式、盘坐静功或动功来提升练功效果，追求内在的调息理气和外部的壮力固本。站桩是比较简单易行的操作功法，站桩功练习时要求姿势准确，精力集中，形、意、气、力四者有机配合，相互作用，浑然一体。通过站桩锻炼身体体型和精神气，无论男女老少都可以学习基础的站桩，只要持之以恒，注意全身各处动作的正确练习要求，对人的健康非常有好处。近年来，站桩功单独作为一种简单易行的强身保健功法得到推广。

Zhuang Gong(stake work) is one of the Nei Gong skills of traditional Wushu. In the traditional Wushu schools, there are stake standing, stake sitting and other skills. These skills help people to keep or improve the inner Qi or the physical health by keeping a certain posture, such as standing, sitting, static or moving on the stake. Such practices require accurate posture, concentration and the perfect coordination of shape, tension, Qi and strength. They also can optimize body shape and spiritual state for men, women, the old and the young. As an effective and simple way to keep mental and physical health, Zhuang Gong is attracting more and more people's attention.

桩功是在"清虚其心、轻松其体"的原则下，通过多种静止的姿势或柔缓的动作，使人心理安静、意念集中，借以调节人体中枢神经的兴奋和抑制过程，清除大脑皮层的紊乱和疲劳，同时随着中枢神经发出多种良性刺激信号和一系列的功法操练，活跃人体各系统的生理机能，增强和改善内脏器官的功用，从而起到内壮外强、养生保健的功效。

Under the principle of "soothing the heart and relaxing the body", Zhuang Gong can make man calm and concentrate their mind through various static postures or gentle movements, so as to regulate the excitation and inhibition process of the central nervous system of the body and clear the disorder and fatigue of the cerebral cortex. At the same time, the central nervous system sends out a variety of benign stimulation signals and a series of exercises to activate the physiological functions of various systems of the human body, strengthen and improve the functions of internal organs, so as to play the role of internal strengthening and external strengthening, and health care.

练习桩功要虚、松、顺、沉。在具体姿势上，还对应各个部位有具体要求。

The practice of stake skill should be empty, loose, smooth and low-gravity. In the specific posture, there should be specific requirements for each part.

虚，主要是指练功时心里要安静，要做到意念专一，心平气和，避免杂念。

Emptiness mainly refers to the quietness of mind, the concentration of mind, the calmness of mind and the avoidance of distractions.

松，练功要保持自然舒松的身体状态。在意识中要做到"体静神舒，心畅神怡，情绪饱满"，在姿势上要做到舒展大方，保持圆润自然。

Looseness. Keep your body in a natural and relaxed state in practicing. In consciousness, it is necessary to achieve "the body is still, the mind is smooth, and the mood is full". In the posture, it is necessary to be relaxed and natural.

顺，包括"调息"和"调体"两个方面。调息要在自然下使气息深长、匀细，呼吸平缓；调体主要调配好全身上下，左右各部位浮沉、虚实、动静，使全身肌肉、关节、部位上下合顺，均衡自然，保持姿势舒松圆活、轻灵稳健。

Smoothness, including "regulating breath" and "regulating body". The breath should be deep, even and gentle; the body should be adjusted to up and down, the left and right parts floating, empty and solid, moving and static, so that the whole muscles, joints, parts up and other organs are smooth, balanced and natural, and the posture should be relaxed, flexible and stable.

沉，指"气沉丹田"，意念引导，通过肌肉、关节的放松、舒展来实现，不可努气使力。

Low-gravity refers to "Qi sinks into the Dantian (the part under your belly button)".

Mind guidance is realized through the relaxation and stretching of muscles and joints. Do not use Qi to exert force.

掌握了心静体松、内外合顺的要领，就会觉得上体越站越轻松，下肢越站越稳固，呼吸深长、匀细，心神舒畅安怡，身体各部关节肌肉都有舒松自然，向下沉实的感觉，全身也觉得融和通畅。

After mastering the key points of calming the mind and relaxing the body, the more relaxed the upper body is, the more stable the lower limbs are, the longer the breath is, the finer the body is, the more relaxed the mind is, the more comfortable the body is. All the joints and muscles of the body are relaxed and natural, and the body feels calm and smooth.

第二节　四段功
5.2 Siduan Gong

一、四段功简介 Brief introduction

四段功是流传有序的传统武术养生功法，其功法与八段锦相仿，少林武术就将四段功作为七十二艺软硬功夫的练习基础。中国中医学养生将人体内脏各器官划分为三焦，横膈以上的心肺称为上焦，横膈以下至脐以上的脾与胃称为中焦，脐以下的肾、大肠、小肠、膀胱等称为下焦，认为三焦是人体通行元气和运化水谷的主要部位，保持三焦功能的正常和强壮，也就能够保持人体的强实与健康。四段功就是通过肢体的动作以及躯干的屈伸配合呼吸来达到增强内脏功能，调理三焦的目的。

Siduan Gong is a well-organizend traditional health care practice, which is similar to Baduan Jin and the basis of 72 types soft and hard Gongfu of Shaolin Gongfu. According to traditional Chinese health care medicine, the organs of the body are divided into three categories (Jiao), the heart and lung above the diaphragm are called the upper Jiao, the spleen and stomach below the diaphragm and above the umbilicus are called the middle Jiao, and the kidney, large intestine, small intestine, bladder below the umbilicus are called the lower Jiao. It is believed that Sanjiao are the main parts of the human body to pass the vital energy and transport the water, so as to maintain the normal and strong function of Sanjiao, so as to maintain the strong and solid health body. Siduan Gong is to enhance the internal organs function and regulate the Sanjiao by the movement of limbs, the flexion and extension of trunk and the cooperation of breath.

四段功动作技术简单，易于操作，不受场地限制，随着练习兴趣愈增，功效也更为显著。练习时要求精神专注，以意念引领呼吸运行，做到静气、呼吸自然，动作柔和缓慢。适合不同人群习练，早、中、晚皆可练习。四段功由四组招式动作构成，分别是第一式：托天提地理三焦；第二式：五痨七伤往后瞧；第三式：推窗望月去心火；第四式：抓空打空力不瘠。坚持练习，可以强壮体魄，而且为习拳练功打好坚实素质基础。

The moves technique of Siduan Gong is simple, easy to operate and not limited by the field. With the increasing interest in practice, the effect is more significant. During the practice, it is required to focus on the spirit, breathing operation with the mind, and keep the breath naturally, and slowly. It is suitable for different groups of people at different ages. It is composed of four parts: part one is to hold the heaven and lift the ground to sooth SanJiao; the second one is to look back to stretch the neck; the third one is to push the window and watch the moon; the fourth one is to beat the air. Persisting in such practice can make you have a good health.

二、四段功动作分解 Illustrations of Siduan Gong

1. 第一式：托天提地理三焦 Part one: hold the heaven and lift the ground

（1）两腿并拢站立，两臂自然垂放体侧，目视前方。（图 5-2-1）

(1) Stand with your legs together, your arms hanging down naturally, and look ahead. (Fig. 5-2-1)

（2）两脚尖分开成八字，两掌从身体两侧慢慢向腹前抬起，五指自然分开，两手指十字交叉，继续向上，至胸前内旋外翻，掌心向上，继续向上推出，举于头上方，两足跟靠拢提起，以两前脚掌支撑身体，抬头目视双掌背，保持姿态，以 36 个意念呼吸为一组。（图 5-2-2-1、图 5-2-2-2）

(2) The tips of the two feet rotate outward a little. The two palms are slowly raised from both sides of the body to the front of the abdomen, the five fingers are naturally separated, the fingers of the two hands cross each other, continue to upward, turn outward in front of the chest, the palms are upward, continue to push upward, above the head, the two heels are close and lift up, support the body with the two front feet, look up at the back of the

palms, maintain the posture, and breathe 36 times. (Fig. 5-2-2-1, Fig. 5-2-2-2)

图Fig 5-2-1

图Fig 5-2-2-1

图Fig 5-2-2-2

（3）结束时双掌从头顶向两侧自然下落，做三次大呼吸。两脚自然开立，两掌从两侧向小腹前自然穿掌，（图 5-2-3）手臂交叉上翻，（图 5-2-4）抬头扩胸，两掌向上从两侧自然下落，两掌穿掌向上时吸气，从上向两侧下落时呼气。（图 5-2-5）

(3) At the end, the palms fall from the top to both sides, and take three big breaths. Open your feet naturally, put your palms in front of your abdomen from both sides, (Fig. 5-2-3) turn your arms up and cross, (Fig. 5-2-4) raise your head and expand your chest, let your palms fall down naturally from both sides, inhale when you put your palms crossed upward, and exhale when you fall from both sides. (Fig. 5-2-5)

图Fig 5-2-3

图Fig 5-2-4

图Fig 5-2-5

（4）还原站立姿势。

(4) Return to standing position.

2. 第二式：五痨七伤往后瞧 Part two: look back and get rid of all the diseases

（1）两腿并拢站立，两臂自然垂放体侧，目视前方。

(1) Stand with your legs together, your arms hanging down naturally, and look ahead.

（2）身体保持不动，身体正立，头向右后转，身不动，肩不斜，目光尽力注视正后方，

保持姿态，以 36 个意念呼吸为一组。(图 5-2-6)

(2) Keep your body still, stand upright, turn your head to the right and back, keep your shoulders still, try your best to look at the back, keep your posture, and breathe 36 times. (Fig. 5-2-6)

（3）右侧结束换左侧，动作相同，方向相反。(图 5-2-7)

(3) The left action is the same, the direction is opposite. (Fig. 5-2-7)

图Fig 5-2-6　　　　　图Fig 5-2-7

（4）结束时做三次大呼吸成还原站立姿势。

(4) At the end, take three long breaths to be back to the standing position.

3. 第三式：推窗望月去心火 Part three: open the window to watch the moon

（1）两腿并拢，两臂自然垂放体侧，目视前方。

(1) The two legs are close together, the two arms are naturally placed on the side of the body, and look ahead.

（2）左式：左脚向左侧跨一大步，重心半蹲成左弓步，左掌向左侧前伸，与肩同高，掌心向上，右臂内旋反手直臂向上与肩同高，右手成勾手，勾尖向上，头向左侧倾斜并右转头，目视天空，以 36 个意念呼吸为一组。(图 5-2-8)

(2) Left style: take a big step to the left, half squat into a bow step, extend the left palm to the left, with the shoulder at the same height, palm is up, turn the right arm inside and push upward to the shoulder, form a hook with the right hand, hook tip up, tilt the head to the left and turn the head to the right, look at the sky, breathe 36 times. (Fig. 5-2-8)

（3）右式：右脚向右侧跨一大步，重心半蹲成右弓步，右掌向右侧前伸，与肩同高，掌心向上，左臂内旋反手直臂向上与肩同高，左手成勾手，勾尖向上，头向右侧倾斜并左转头，目视天空，以 36 个意念呼吸为一组。(图 5-2-9)

(3) Right style: take a big step from the right foot to the right, squat half into the right lunge, extend the right palm to the right, high as the shoulder, rotate inside the left arm upward

to the shoulder, form a hook with the left hand, hook tip up, tilt the head to the right and turn the head left, look at the sky, and breathe 36 times. (Fig. 5-2-9)

图Fig 5-2-8　　　　　　　图Fig 5-2-9

（4）结束时做三次大呼吸成还原站立姿势。

(4) At the end, take three long breaths to be back to the standing position.

4. 第四式：抓空打空力不劳 Part four: beat in the air without vain

（1）两腿并拢，两臂自然垂放体侧，目视前方。

(1) The two legs are close together, the two arms are naturally placed on the side of the body, and look ahead.

（2）两脚左右分开，重心下蹲成半马步，两手握拳，屈肘抱拳于两肋，右拳向前直臂冲拳，冲出后内旋前臂成平拳，拳心向下，左拳仍抱于腰间不动，（图 5-2-10）右拳变掌，五指张开，（图 5-2-11）右手空抓紧握拳快速向后收，屈肘于肋下；左拳向前直臂冲拳，与右拳动作相同。（图 5-2-12、图 5-2-13）回抓时吸气，冲拳呼气，冲拳回抓配合呼吸，36 个呼吸为一组，目视前方。

(2) The left and right feet are separated, the gravity is down on the half-horse-riding-stance, the two hands are clenched, the right fist punches forward and rotates inside, the heart of the fist down, the left fist beside the waist, (Fig. 5-2-10) the right fist changes into the palm. (Fig. 5-2-11) The right hand clenches tightly and quickly retracts, the elbow is bent beside the ribs; the left fist punches forward, the same as the right fist. (Fig. 5-2-12, Fig. 5-2-13) Inhale with pulling back, exhale with punching forward. Breathe 36 times and look forward.

图Fig 5-2-10　　　　　　　图Fig 5-2-11

图Fig 5-2-12　　　　　　　图Fig 5-2-13

（3）结束时做三次大呼吸成还原站立姿势。

(3) At the end, take three long breaths to be back to the standing position.

第三节　十三太保功
5.3 Shisantaibao Gong

一、十三太保功简介 Introduction

十三太保功是古代导引术、气功和武术相结合的一种锻炼功法，是以不同身体姿势配合呼吸的站桩功法。练功要求心静用意，内外相合，呼吸吐纳引导内心安宁与肢体有度拉伸，将调身、调心和调息有机结合，使人身心安舒，通经活络、通畅气血，以求内部脏腑运化功能和外部肢体肌肉筋脉的强实。

Shisantaibao Gong is an ancient exercise combining ancient Daoyin(transition and guiding), Qigong and Wushu. This exercise is based on the method of Zhuang Gong. focusing on body posture and breathing tune on the stake. Practicing requires calm mind and the consistency of internal and external world. Practicing this Gong can make you healthy mentally and physically.

十三太保功是由七个相对固定的动作势法组成。功法内容有：韩湘子卧床、夜叉探海、魁星提斗、摘星换斗、观音纺线、犀牛望月和招空打空，前六个动作分左右练习，共构成十三个姿势桩功，坚持练习，可以提升身体机能和气息的运化，增强体质，为修持武术功力夯实身体基础。

Shisantaibao Gong is composed of seven main postures. The content includes: Han

Xiangzi in rest, the monster cruising, Kuixing lifting, Stars picking, Guanyin spinning, Rhinoceros watching the moon and Zhaokong Dakong.The first six movements are divided left and right style. Altogether there 13 moves. Persisting in this exercises can improve the organs function and strengthen the physique, and cultivate the internal Qi.

二、十三太保功动作分解 The Illustrations of the movements

1. 韩湘子卧床 Han Xiangzi in rest

图Fig 5-3-1　　　　　　　　　图Fig 5-3-2

（1）两腿并拢，两臂自然垂放体侧，目视前方。(图 5-3-1)

(1) The two legs are close together, the two arms are naturally placed on the side of the body, and look ahead. (Fig. 5-3-1)

（2）右式：右脚站稳支撑身体，上体向右倾倒，左腿随上体自然伸直，身体与地面平行，右臂屈肘，右手握拳支撑头部（太阳穴位），左臂屈肘，左掌贴于左腰，仿佛侧卧床榻，幽静自然，以36个意念呼吸为一组。(图 5-3-2)

(2) Right style: stand on your right foot, with the upper body toppling to the right, with the left leg naturally straightened, the body is parallel to the ground, bend the right arm, support your head with the right fist, bend the left and attach the left fist to the left waist, as if lying on on one's side, quiet and natural, breathe 36 times. (Fig. 5-3-2)

（3）左式：动作与右式相同，左右相反。

(3) Left style: the movement is the same as the right movement, right is replaced by left.

（4）结束时还原站立，做三次大呼吸。

(4) Back to standing state at the end and take three long breaths.

2. 夜叉探海 Monster cruising

（1）两腿并拢，两臂自然垂放体侧，目视前方。

(1) The legs are close together, the arms are naturally placed on the sides of the body, and look ahead.

（2）右式：右腿单腿站立，上体前俯，左腿直腿后伸，脚面崩平，两掌掌尖相对，前推，掌心均朝前下方，两臂伸直，抬头目视掌背，以36个意念呼吸为一组。(图 5-3-3)

(2) Right style: stand on the right leg, lean the upper body forward, extend the left leg backward, flatten the foot, push the palms forward with the fingers facing forward and push forward, straighten the arms, look up at the back of the palms, and breathe 36 times. (Fig. 5-3-3)

图Fig 5-3-3

（3）左式：动作与右式相同，左右相反。

(3) Left style: the movement is the same as the right movement, right is replaced by left.

（4）结束时还原站立，做三次大呼吸。

(4) Back to standing state at the end and take three long breaths.

3. 魁星提斗 Kuixing lifting

（1）两腿并拢，两臂自然垂放体侧，目视前方。

(1) The legs are close together, the arms are naturally placed on the sides of the body, and look ahead.

（2）右式：右腿屈膝提起，左腿直立支撑，右臂微屈，右拳拳心向下放于右大腿上方，左臂内旋，左拳心朝上，架于头上方，抬头，目视左拳，以36个意念呼吸为一组。(图 5-3-4)

(2) Right style: lift the right leg with knee bending the, standing on the left leg, slightly

bent the right arm, put the right fist on the upper part of the right thigh, rotate inward the left arm, the heart of the left fist facing up, put the right fist over the head, and look at the left fist and breathe 36 times. (Fig. 5-3-4)

（3）左式：动作与右式相同，左右相反。(图 5-3-5)

(3) Left style: the movement is the same as the right movement, right is replaced by left. (Fig. 5-3-5)

图Fig 5-3-4　　　　　图Fig 5-3-5

（4）结束时还原站立，做三次大呼吸。

(4) Back to standing state at the end and take three long breaths.

4. **摘星换斗** Stars Picking

（1）两腿并拢，两臂自然垂放体侧，目视前方。

(1) The legs are close together, the arms are naturally placed on the sides of the body, and look ahead.

（2）右式：两脚左右开立，左腿屈膝全蹲，右腿挺直成右仆步，左拳向右脚背平伸，拳心朝上，右拳内旋，向正上方直臂上举，头向右拳方向拧转，目视右拳，以 36 个意念呼吸为一组。(图 5-3-6)

(2) Right style: separate the left and right foot, bend the left leg and squat completely, straighten the right leg into a right footstep, extend the left fist horizontally to the right foot, with the heart of the fist upward, turn the right fist inward, lift the right arm straight upward, turn the head toward the right fist, and look at the right fist. Breathe 36 times. (Fig. 5-3-6)

（3）左式：动作与右式相同，左右相反。(图 5-3-7)

(3) Left style: the movement is the same as the right movement, right is replaced by left. (Fig. 5-3-7)

图Fig 5-3-6 　　　　图Fig 5-3-7

（4）结束时还原站立，做三次大呼吸。

(4) Back to standing state at the end and take three long breaths.

5. 观音纺线 Guanyin spinning

（1）两腿并拢，两臂自然垂放体侧，目视前方。

(1) The legs are close together, the arms are naturally placed on the side of the body, and look ahead.

（2）右式：两脚左右开立，比肩略宽，双手五指自然分开，两手指十字交叉，两大拇指指尖相对，掌心涵空，身体右后转180°，重心半蹲，两脚随上体转身拧转站稳成歇步，目视双手掌心，以36个意念呼吸为一组。(图 5-3-8)

(2) Right style: the two feet are separated, slightly wider than the shoulder. Fingers are naturally separated, and cross each other, the tips of the two thumbs are opposite, the palm is hollow, the body turns 180° to the right, half squatted, the two feet turn with the upper body and stand firmly in a rest step, and look at the palm center, breathe 36 times. (Fig. 5-3-8)

（3）左式：动作与右式相同，左右相反。(图 5-3-9)

(3) Left style: the movement is the same as the right movement, right is replaced by left. (Fig. 5-3-9)

图Fig 5-3-8 　　　　图Fig 5-3-9

（4）结束时还原站立，做三次大呼吸。

(4) Back to standing state at the end and take three long breaths.

6. 犀牛望月 Rhinoceros watching the moon

（1）两腿并拢，两臂自然垂放体侧，目视前方。

(1) The legs are close together, the arms are naturally placed on the side of the body, and look ahead.

图Fig 5-3-10　　　　　图Fig 5-3-11

（2）右式：两脚左右开立，左脚向右脚后插步半蹲，左臂伸直，左掌屈腕向前上架掌，右臂内旋反手于体后成勾手，勾尖向上，身体右转，目视右侧方向，以36个意念呼吸为一组。(图 5-3-10)

(2) Right style: separate the left and right feet, cross the left foot to the back of the right foot to half squat, extend the left arm, bend the left wrist to push forward, turn the right arm inward to form a hook behind the body, hook tip up, turn the body to the right, and look at the right direction, breathe 36 times. (Fig. 5-3-10)

（3）左式：动作与右式相同，左右相反。(图 5-3-11)

(3) Left style: the movement is the same as the right movement, right is replaced by left. (Fig. 5-3-11)

（4）结束时还原站立，做三次大呼吸。

(4) Back to standing state at the end and take three long breaths.

7. 招空打空 Zhaokongdakong

（1）两腿并拢，两臂自然垂放体侧，目视前方。

(1) The legs are close together, the arms are naturally placed on the sides of the body, and look ahead.

（2）两脚左右分开，重心下蹲成半马步，两手握拳，屈肘抱拳于腰间，右拳向前直臂冲拳，冲出后内旋前臂成平拳，拳心向下，(图5-3-12)右拳回收时快速冲左拳，(图5-3-13)再快速冲右拳，右左右三拳为一个呼吸，收右拳时吸气，连冲三拳时呼气，36个呼吸为一组，目视前方。

(2) Separate the left and right foot, squat into a half horse stance, bend the elbows beside the waist, punch forward the right fist and rotate inside, the heart of the fist down, (Fig. 5-3-12) with the right fist pulling backward, punch the left fist quickly, then the right fist.(Fig. 5-3-13) The right-left-right punches are in one breath. Inhale with the right fist back, and exhale with three punches, and breathe 36 times. Watch ahead.

图Fig 5-3-12　　　　图Fig 5-3-13

（3）结束时还原站立，做三次大呼吸。

(3) Back to standing state at the end and take three long breaths.

第四节　开合功
5.4 Kaihe Gong

一、开合功简介 Brief introduction

开合功是强调呼吸锻炼为主的养生练功方法，也是炼气、行气、调气的吐纳基础功，通过身体开合调身、调息来培植人体内气的运行和滋养身心活动。

Kaihe Gong is a kind of Gong, which focuses on the health exhaling and inhaling. It is also the basic work of adjusting and practicing breath to improve the movement of one's Qi and the physical and mental health.

二、开合功动作分解 The Illustrations of the movements

1. 开合功 Kaihe Gong

（1）两腿并拢，两臂自然垂放体侧，目视前方。

(1) The two legs are close together, the two arms are naturally placed on the side of the body, and look ahead.

图Fig 5-4-1　　　　　　　图Fig 5-4-2

（2）左脚向左侧开步，两脚比肩略宽，两腿微屈，身体放松，两臂屈臂抬肘置于体前，两掌尖向上，掌心相对，与脸同宽，（图5-4-1）慢速扩胸，两臂两掌向两侧拉开至比肩略宽时停止，（图5-4-2）再慢慢向中间合推，至两掌与脸同宽为止，拉开时吸气，合推时呼气，30个呼吸为一组，目视前方。

(2) Move the left foot to the left side, wider than the shoulder, the legs slightly bent, the body relaxed, the bent arms in front of the body, the fingers upward, the palms face to face. (Fig. 5-4-1) Slowly expand the chest, pull the arms to both sides until they are slightly wider than the shoulders, (Fig. 5-4-2) push them to the middle slowly, until the palms are the same width as the face, inhale when pulling, and exhale when pushing, breathe 36 times and look ahead.

（3）结束时，双掌从下向上抬起，（图5-4-3）至胸部内旋翻腕轻轻下按至腹前，（图5-4-4）双掌上升时吸气，下按时呼气，做3次。

(3) At the end, lift the palms from the bottom to the chest, (Fig. 5-4-3) and turn the wrists gently down to the front of the abdomen, (Fig. 5-4-4) inhale when the palms rise, and exhale when the palms press down, do three times.

图Fig 5-4-3　　　　　　　　　图Fig 5-4-4

2. 内合功 Neihe Gong

（1）两腿并拢，两臂自然垂放体侧，目视前方。

(1) The two legs are close together, the two arms are naturally placed on the sides of the body, and look ahead.

（2）左脚向左侧开步，两脚比肩略宽，两腿微屈，身体放松，两臂伸直，掌心向上，慢慢屈腕，掌心朝内，（图 5-4-5）两小臂带动两掌向回收，（图 5-4-6）两掌收至胸前内旋至掌心向前，徐徐向前推，（图 5-4-7）推至两臂伸直为止，两掌回收时吸气，前推时呼气，30 个呼吸为一组，目视前方。

(2) The left foot moves to the left, the distance between the feet is slightly wider than the shoulders. The legs are slightly bent, the body is relaxed, the arms are straight, the palms are upward, the wrists are slowly bent with the palms center inward. (Fig. 5-4-5) The two forearms drive the two palms back, (Fig. 5-4-6) the two palms are retracted to the chest, rotate inward and slowly push forward, (Fig. 5-4-7) till the two arms are extended straight. Inhale when pull back, and exhale when push forward. Breathe 30 times in one round and look ahead.

图Fig 5-4-5　　　　　　图Fig 5-4-6　　　　　　图Fig 5-4-7

（3）结束时，（同开合式结束收纳吐气）

(3) The end is as above.

3. 元神功 Yuanshen Gong

（1）两腿并拢，两臂自然垂放体侧，目视前方。

(1) The two legs are close together; the two arms are naturally placed on the sides of the body, and look ahead.

（2）右式：右脚向右前上步成右弓步，两臂屈臂对握拳，右臂在上，右拳拳心向下，与左拳拳心相对，30个呼吸为一组，目视左侧，（图5-4-8）

(2) Right style: Move the right foot forward to the right to form a right lunge, bent the two arms and clench the fists, the right arm on the top, the right fist center down, opposite to the left fist center, take 30 breaths, and look at the left side.(Fig. 5-4-8)

（3）左式：动作与右式相同，左右相反。30个呼吸为一组，目视右侧，（图5-4-9）

(3) Left style: the same as the right style.Left and right are opposite. 30 breaths in one round, look at the right side, (Fig. 5-4-9)

（4）两腿开立比肩略宽，身体放松，两腿微屈，两臂体前微屈平举，两手握拳，拳心向内，30个呼吸为一组，目视前方。（图5-4-10）

(4) Stand with two feet separated, wider than the shoulders, relaxed, bend the legs slightly, the arms are slightly bent in front of the body, fists clenched, the hearts of the fists are inward. Take 30 breaths in a round, and look ahead. (Fig.5-4-10)

图Fig 5-4-8　　　　　图Fig 5-4-9　　　　　图Fig 5-4-10

（5）结束时，（同开合式结束收纳吐气）

(5) The end is the same as the above.

思考题：Questions for consideration

1. 桩功的健身机理是什么？

1. What is the mechanism of Zhuang Gong?

2. 练习桩功有哪些具体要求？

2. What are the specific requirements for Zhuang Gong practicing?

3. 四段功动作谱诀是哪些？

3. What is the guide of the Siduan Gong?

4. 十三太保功动作名称有哪些？

4. What are the names of the movements of Shisantaibao Gong?

5. 开合功的健身机理是什么？

5. What is the mechanism of Kaihe Gong?

6. 练习桩功如何做到虚、松、顺、沉？

6. How to practice stake skill to be empty, loose, smooth and deep?

第六章　擒拿与解脱术
Chapter 6 Capture and Escape (Qinnashu)

第一节　擒拿术简介
6.1 Brief Introduction to Qinnashu

擒拿术是我国的一门独特技击术。明代嘉靖年间，擒拿已风靡一时，戚继光在《纪效新书·拳经》中对"鹰爪王的拿"便有赞誉。擒拿术是使用刁、拿、锁、扣、扳、点、缠等招法进行擒伏与解脱、控制与反控制的中国武术专门技术。擒拿术是武术技击"踢、打、摔、拿"四大技法之一，凡习武之人都以此四法为基本学习的目标，而拿法牵一发而制全身，往往能达到出奇制胜的效果。武术各流派均有擒拿术，被看作武术技艺的一个至高点。

Qinnashu (Capture Technique) is an important part in Chinese Wushu. In the Jiajing period of the Ming Dynasty (1522 - 1566), capture was very popular. Qi Jiguang praised the "Eagle King's Capture" in *Ji Xiao Xin Shu•Quan Jing*. Qinnashu is a special technique which uses the movements such as pick, catch, lock, buckle, pull, point and twine to capture or escape. It is one of the four techniques of Wushu. All schools of Wushu regard Qinnashu as the highest level of Gongfu techniques.

擒拿术以控制关节为主，劲力内含，以柔制刚，虽然动作不大杀伤力却很强，多制人于无形之中，从民间流传的多种擒拿方法中可以看到突出的技击本质，实用效果非常显著，有变化莫测之妙，充分体现了中华武术"巧打拙、柔克刚"的特点。这些绝招妙技所蕴含的深奥法理，不仅毫不神秘，而且完全符合现代生理学和运动力学原理。

Qinnashu is to make full use of the joints of the opponent to put him under control. This technique is not the severe beating or attacking but to use some skillful anti- joints movements to freeze the opponent. It is usually unpredictable but practical, which fully embodies the characteristics of Chinese Wushu. The unique skills in Qinnashu are not mysterious, and thay are also fully in line with the principles of modern physiology and sports mechanics.

擒拿术技法包括擒拿的基本手法、擒拿基本技术和徒手对凶器擒拿。擒拿基本技术有死手擒拿和活手擒拿，死手擒拿以死把位被动擒拿解脱为主，活手是快速踢打对战变化中的擒拿技术。擒拿术内容丰富，主动擒拿对方的技法受制于力量、技巧、人体关节的精准把握和瞬息变化的格斗态势，而死把位被动擒拿解脱相对容易，在技巧、力量和急速反应中往往能从被擒中获得解救或者占有主动权。

The techniques of Qinnashu include the basic techniques of hands, the basic techniques of capture and the unarmed capture of the armed. There active capture and passive capture. Generally, the active capture is subject to the grasp of the strength, joints and the rapidly changing fighting situation. The passive capture is relatively easy since it is used to escape from the capture. It needs skills and fast-reaction. It also can turn the captured into the catcher.

一、擒拿技法原理与特点 Principles and Characteristics of Qinnashu

擒拿术技法巧妙利用力学的杠杆、力偶、惯性、合力、旋转原理等使对方身体旋转后受控或摔倒，产生四两拨千斤的效果。力功、技巧和快速是掌握擒拿术的基础要素。

Qinnashu skillfully uses the mechanical lever, couple, inertia, resultant force, rotation principle, etc. to make the opponent's body be controlled or fall after rotation, resulting in the effect of "pulling one ton with tiny gram". Strength, skill and quickness are the basic elements of Qinna.

力量是擒拿术运用的必备条件，"百巧百能，无力不实"，力与功淳厚的人能最快掌握擒拿技法和战略、战术，临阵应敌自如，能巧妙地使用避实击虚和刚柔相济的方法。擒拿只具功力是不够的，还要善于用巧劲、施妙招伺机而动，完成动作时要避实就虚随机应势，顺势应招，轻取关节，巧施裹缠，使之受控。擒拿以巧取胜、以技制人为根本。技巧包含对擒拿技术方法和人体关节的高度精准化运用，其动有方，其用有法，使法必准，针对人体关节特性和弱点精准拿制，迫使对方的关节反折或受挫丧失反抗能力束手就擒，充分体现"手到擒拿"的功用。快速是能主动灵活、一快制百慢，能在快速中赢得致胜的时间。

Strength is a necessary condition for the use of Qinnashu. People who are rich in strength and Gong can master the skills of Qinna. They can skillfully use the methods of avoiding the strong and fighting the weak and combining the hard with the soft. It's not enough to capture only with skill, but also to be good at using skillful force and clever moves to wait for the opportunity to capture the opponent. The skills include highly precise application of capture technology and human joints, with proper movement and application, which will make the method accurate. For the characteristics and weaknesses of human joints, accurate capture will force the joints of the other side to fold or be frustrated, and lose the resistance ability to capture without hesitation.

擒拿以力学为理、巧妙施用，突出了其以巧取胜、以技制人、抓筋拿脉、拿中有解、解中有拿和一招制敌的技法特点，其动作技法可归纳为：巧、快、稳、准、狠、活。

Taking mechanics as the principle and ingenious application of capture, it highlights its technical characteristics of skillfully winning, using techniques to control the opponent, grasping tendons and vessels, taking one move to control the enemy. Its action techniques can be summarized as follows: craft, fast, stable, accurate, hard and flexible.

二、擒拿术手法 Hand Moves

擒拿术手法主要以拿、缠、锁、扣、刁、顺、抱、卷、背、踩、转、拧、点、击、扳、托等方法进行擒拿与解脱。

The hand moves of Qinnashu are mainly grasp, wrap, lock, buckle, peck, hold, roll, back, step, turn, twist, point, hit, pull and hold.

（1）拿：手指掐握对方要害部位及肢体关节，并使其内旋或外旋至疼痛异常。

(1) Na: grasp the key parts and limb joints of the other side with fingers, and make them rotate inward or outward until the pain is abnormal.

（2）缠：手、腕和上、下肢的内外旋转围绕对方身体某部位，使对方受控失去反抗能力或重心。

(2) Chan: the internal and external rotation of the hands, wrists, upper and lower limbs revolves around a certain part of the body of the other party, making the other party lose the resistance ability or center of gravity under control.

（3）锁：手脚控制对方的手和脚及肩胛咽喉等部位，施加压力锁固，使其不能移动、逃脱和活动受阻。

(3) Suo: lock up the hands, feet, scapula, throat and other parts of the opponent, and

apply pressure so that one can not move nor escape.

（4）扣：用手扣按压对方指、腕、肩、肘、膝等部位，使肢体关节过伸受制。

(4) Kou: press the fingers, wrists, shoulders, elbows, knees and other parts of the other side with the hand buckle, so that the limb joints are subject to over extension.

（5）刁：刁抓对方要害部位或对衣袖进行提拉。

(5) Diao: grab the key parts of the other side or lift the sleeves.

（6）顺：借势或劲力反击要害，借力打力。

(6) Shun: take advantage of momentum or strength to fight back.

（7）抱：双手环形搂抱对方头、腰、肩、腿、臂等部位，配合周身动作向某一个方向转动，摔倒对方或控制其肢体。

(7) Bao: hold the head, waist, shoulder, leg, arm and other parts in a circular way with both hands, rotate in a certain direction with the whole body action, fall the other side or control its limbs.

（8）卷：使关节过度屈曲，如卷肘、卷腕、卷指。

(8) Juan: to cause excessive curly of joints, such as elbows, wrists, and fingers.

（9）背：将对方肢体反关节背负肩背上，使其过度伸展，如背肩、肘、腰。

(9) Bei: carry the opposite body on the back anti-jointed.

（10）踩：蹬踩对方腿部，使关节过度内翻或反张。

(10) Cai: step on the leg of the other side to make the joint turn inward or reverse.

（11）转：扭转对方肢体关节或躯干，如挫颈、转臂、挫肩等。

(11) Zhuan: twist the other side's joints or trunk, such as neck, arm, shoulder, etc.

（12）拧：抓住对方某一部位向相反方向用力拧扯。

(12) Ning: grasp one part of the other side and pull it in the opposite direction.

（13）点：力量集中在一点来触击对方要害与穴位。

(13) Dian: focus on one point to touch the other's key points and acupoints.

（14）击：以手、脚、肘、膝攻击对方要害。

(14) Ji: attack the opponent's vital points with hands, feet, elbows and knees.

（15）扳：借助杠杆力使关节过度展转，如扳头、扳腿等。

(15) Ban: to make the joint rotate excessively with the help of lever force.

（16）托：紧握肢体一端，反关节用力向上托，如托肘等。

(16) Tuo: hold one end of the limb tightly, and use the anti joint force to hold up, such as

the elbow.

（17）别：用自己上肢或者下肢控制和固定住对方肢体末节，用自己另一肢或者身体其他部位对受控关节施加外力。

(17) Bie: use your own upper or lower limbs to control and fix the other end of the limb, and use your own other limb or other parts of the body to exert external force on the controlled joint.

（18）掐：用单手或者双手掐拿对方手、肘、颈、咽、裆等部位及一些要害穴位筋脉，致使其疼痛、麻木、丧失反抗能力。

(18) Qia: use one or both hands to pinch the other's hands, elbows, neck, pharynx, crotch and other parts and some vital acupoints, causing pain, numbness and loss of resistance.

另外，还有压、分、推、挫、绞、扭、牵、切、封、砸等技法，使对方反关节、分筋、分指、挫骨、推颈、点穴等，迫使对方违反人体关节的活动范围和生理机制的特点，达到制服对手的目的。

In addition, there are pressing, splitting, pushing, faltering, twisting, pulling, cutting, sealing, smashing and other techniques to force the opponent to violate the range of motion and physiological mechanism of human joints, so as to subdue the opponent.

三、擒拿技法应用原则 The Application Principle of Qinnashu

（一）手法纯熟，巧施妙招 Skillful technique and unexpected tricks

擒拿技法应用要"内外合一，形神一致"。意、气、劲、技运用纯熟，利用人体运动链结构和相邻关节锁定效应，预判对方多种可能性，感知对方劲力趋势，听劲、懂劲、化劲和巧施妙招，达到拿一点而控全身，运用以"巧"为先的原则。针对每一环节，每一关节有一整套擒拿技法系统，要有相应技法随机策变能力。同时，对指、腕、臂、腰背和下肢力训练来增强功力效果，在循序渐渐喂招对抗练习中掌握各种实用擒拿技术。

The application of capture techniques should be "unity of internal and external, as well as form and spirit". The spirit, Qi, strength and technique are used to predict the other side's multiple possibilities, perceiving the trend of the other side's strength by listening, understanding, transforming and skillfully applying some tricks, so as to control the whole body with a little bit. For each joint, there is a set of capture technique system, and the corresponding strategy. The strength training of fingers, wrists, arms, waist and back and lower limbs can enhance the affections.

（二）上下相随、身手一致 Coherence of body and limbs

擒拿技法应用依赖步法与身法密切配合。锁拿对方上肢关节或反擒拿解脱，就要迅速上步进身，绊锁其下肢或通过力的传递使其随我意图移动而无法应势变化，以满足自身重心、技法实施需要。身法与步法是运劲、发劲的关键，在技击实战中，身与步占有特殊重要的位置。

The application of Qinnashu depends on the coherence of step and body movements. In order to lock the upper limb joints of the opponent or release from reverse capture, we should step up quickly, trip his lower limbs, or make him unable to change with my intention through the transfer of force, so as to meet the needs of his own center of gravity and technique implementation. Step and body movements are the key of driving force.

（三）拿脱为主，打摔兼用 Capture and escape

擒拿技法必须和踢、打、摔综合运用，只拿不打或只拿不摔都是不可取的，要综合武术各技之长灵活运用，做到"控敌为主，打摔兼施"。学会打、摔、拿配合运用，宜拿则拿，宜打则打，可摔则摔，随机就势，拿中含打，打中带拿，方法多变。

Qinnashu must be used in combination with kicking, hitting and wrestling. It is not advisable to only take and not hit or just take and not wrestle. It is necessary to integrate the advantages of various techniques of Wushu and use them flexibly, so as to "control the enemy at first time". One should learn how to cooperate the hitting, plunging and catching. You can make good advantages of these various methods.

（四）随机应势，审势而变 Change flexibly

擒拿依据对方身高体重、力量大小、技术动作、劲力虚实以及地理位置等审势而行，不顶不抗，顺其势，顺其劲，随机变化、策变招法，充分利用双方肢体接触后所形成的运动态势，运用支点和借用"杠杆""反向合力"集中于所擒的骨关节上实施拿筋挫骨。

Qinna should be based on the height, weight, strength, technical action, strength and geographical position of the other party. To follow the trend and the strength, and then make changes can make full use of the movement situation formed by the contact between the two sides. Use the fulcrum, leverage and reverse force to focus on the captured bone joints to carry out tendon and bone contusion.

（五）合力避险，远离反攻 Ready to attack

以双手合力控制对方关节，使用旋拧的混合劲向对方外侧螺旋用力，让其可能反攻的一侧远离自己，在力的使用上将缠裹钻劲和冷脆快相结合，保证技法应用有效。

Control the opponent's joint with your own hands, use the mixed strength of screwing to spiral to the outside of the opponent's side, and keep the side of the possible counter attack away from yourself. In the use of force, the combination of wrapping drilling force and cold crisp fast ensures the effective application of techniques.

擒拿技法千变万化，手法技术内容广泛，招数不可尽数，名称道理繁复无穷，只要掌握了各部分擒拿术的基本形态和规律，长时间刻苦练习擒拿的技击与功力，在实践中反复体验和强化，掌握了典型技法，知其术，明其理，才可以举一反三，根据不同的场合、对手、不同的形式与环境，因时、因地、因物采用相应的技战术，运用自如达到"神明、神化之境"。

The techniques of Qinnashu are extensive, the moves are numerous, and the names and principles are complicated. However, as long as we master the basic forms and rules of each part and strengthen them repeatedly in practice, grasp the typical techniques, know the techniques and understand the reasons, we can draw inferences from one instance to another according to different occasions, opponent, different forms and environments, according to the time, the place and the things, adopt corresponding techniques and tactics, and use them freely to reach the "divine and deified state".

第二节　擒拿要害部位分类
6.2 The Key Parts of Qinna

一、擒拿部位分类 Classification of the Parts in Qinna

擒拿根据人体关节运动特征可以分为拿指、拿腕、拿肘、拿肩、拿头颈、拿腰、拿膝、拿足踝等人体重要部位，每个部位依据不同动作态势运用不同的拿法，上肢是擒拿攻击的主要部位。拿指分为折拇指、分指、拿掌；拿腕有缠腕、卷腕、扣腕、折腕、背腕、提腕等；拿肘有别肘、搬肘、扛肘、截肘、压肘、抬肘等；拿肩有锁肩、压肩、扣肩等；拿头颈有锁喉、扭头、推头颈等；拿腰有别腰、顶腰、跪腰等；拿膝有踩膝、跪膝、扳膝等；拿足有拧踝、托踝、踩足等。

According to the important parts of human body such as finger, wrist, elbow, shoulder, head and neck, waist, knee and ankle. Each part has different catching methods according to the various posture.The upper limbs are the main part of the capture For example, the fingers can be folded outside;the elbows can be broke outside; the shoulders can be pressed down; the neck can be squeezed and so on.

二、擒拿身体要害部位 The Key Parts of Qinna

（一）头部 Head

1. 耳部 ear

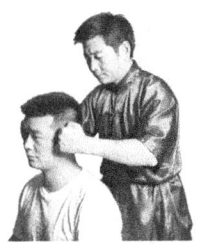

图Fig 6-2-1

两手同时拍击对方双耳。轻则击穿对方耳膜，使其神经受损丧失反抗力，重则可使敌人脑震荡。(图 6-2-1)

Clap on the opponent's ears simultaneously, which will break through the eardrum of the opponent or make him concussion. (Fig. 6-2-1)

2. 太阳穴 temple

用掌外侧、拳头或肘戳击太阳穴。(图 6-2-2)

Punch the temple with the outside of the palm, fist, or elbow. (Fig. 6-2-2)

图Fig 6-2-2

3. 眼睛 eye

食指和中指分开成"V"形挺直击刺对方双眼，也可以用相邻两个手指第二关节戳击眼窝。(图 6-2-3)

The index finger and the middle finger are separated into "V" shape and straightly stab into the enemy's eyes, or the second joint of two adjacent fingers can be used to stab the eye socket. (Fig. 6-2-3)

图Fig 6-2-3

4. 鼻 nose

以掌外侧或拳横击对方鼻梁，可击碎其鼻骨，使其疼痛难忍丧失反抗能力。近距可用掌跟向上顶击对方的鼻子。(图 6-2-4)

If you hit the other side of the nose with your palm or fist, you can break the nose bone and make the pain unbearable. (Fig. 6-2-4)

图Fig 6-2-4

5. 嘴唇 mouth

手掌或拳外侧砸击对方嘴唇，能使其昏厥。(图 6-2-5)

Hitting the lips with the outside of the hand or fist.(Fig. 6-2-5)

图Fig 6-2-5

6. 下巴 chin

用掌跟或定肘打击对方下巴。(图 6-2-6)

Hit the chin with the palm.(Fig. 6-2-6)

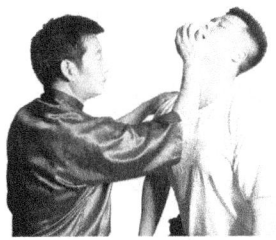

图Fig 6-2-6

7. 喉结 larynx

用手掌外侧、拳、脚、膝攻击对方喉结。(图 6-2-7)

Attack the opponent's larynx with the outside of the palm, fist, foot and knee.(Fig. 6-2-7)

图Fig 6-2-7

8. 咽喉 throat

手指直戳其咽喉下部凹处或手指卡抓喉结。(图 6-2-8)

Cut the concave part of the lower part of the throat with fingers or grasp the laryngeal knot.(Fig. 6-2-8)

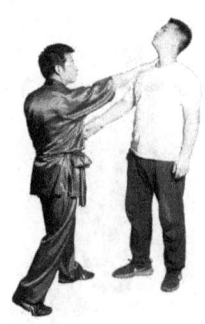

图Fig 6-2-8

9. 颈部 neck

图Fig 6-2-9

用手掌、拳、臂撞击对方颈外侧（耳下略靠前处），能使人颈静脉、颈动脉和迷走神经受到打击而昏迷。(图 6-2-9)

Hitting the other side of the neck with the palm, fist and arm (slightly in front of the lower ear) can strike the human jugular vein, carotid artery and vagus nerve and cause coma. (Fig. 6-2-9)

10. 扳锁头颈 lock head and neck

双手合力扮锁头，使其颈部拧结。(图 6-2-10)

Make two hands a lock and twist the neck. (Fig. 6-2-10)

图Fig 6-2-10

11. 擒锁颈部 lock neck

双手臂前后合力擒锁颈部。(图 6-2-11)

Both arms work together to lock the neck. (Fig. 6-2-11)

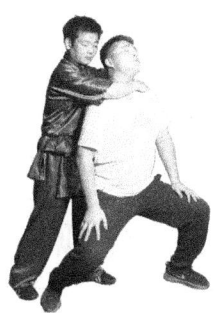

图Fig 6-2-11

(二) 躯干部位 Trunk Parts

1. 胸窝 chest

以拳、肘冲击对方胸窝剑突部位。(图 6-2-12)

Strike the xiphoid part of the chest with fist and elbow. (Fig. 6-2-12)

图Fig 6-2-12

2. 腹部 abdomen

用拳、肘、膝猛击对方腹部。(图 6-2-13)

Hit the opponent's abdomen with fist, elbow and knee. (Fig. 6-2-13)

图Fig 6-2-13

3. 腋窝 armpit

用拳、肘打击对方腋窝，可使其产生剧痛和短暂的局部瘫痪。（图 6-2-14）

Hitting the opponent's armpit with fist and elbow can cause severe pain and short-term local paralysis.(Fig. 6-2-14)

图Fig 6-2-14

4. 肋部 rib part

用拳、肘、拳指关节、脚或膝盖顶击对方肋部，可致其损伤。（图 6-2-15）

The injury can be caused by hitting the opponent's ribs with fist, elbow, foot or knee.(Fig. 6-2-15)

图Fig 6-2-15

5. 裆部 crotch

脚尖踢裆部。（图 6-2-16) 近距离以拳、膝击打裆部。（图 6-2-17）

Kick the crotch with the toe. (Fig. 6-2-16) Close fists and knees hit the crotch.(Fig. 6-2-17)

图Fig 6-2-16　　　　　图Fig 6-2-17

6. 脊椎 vertebra

图Fig 6-2-18

可用膝、肘、脚跟、脚尖击对方脊椎，配合双手控制。（图 6-2-18）

Use knee, elbow, heel, tiptoe to hit the enemy's spine, cooperate with hands control.(Fig. 6-2-18)

（三）肢节部位 Arthropod Parts

1. 指关节 knuckle

扣压、掰折、控制对方指和手掌关节。手关节多而小，指细而长，五指分散，单指力量薄弱，一旦被分开控制，则难于逃脱。

Buckle, break and control the knuckles of fingers and palms. the five fingers are scattered, and the strength of the single finger is weak. Once controlled separately, it is difficult to escape.

（1）折拇指：抓握对方拇指推反压。（图 6-2-19）

(1)Thumb fold : grasp the other thumb and push it back. (Fig. 6-2-19)

（2）折指：当对方在身后卡抱腰部时，按封其双手，用力背向掰搬一指，形成背向对折。（图 6-2-20）

(2) Finger fold: when the other side is clasping the waist behind, grasp his hands and lift one finger back folded. (Fig. 6-2-20)

图Fig 6-2-19　　　　图Fig 6-2-20

图Fig 6-2-21　　　　　　图Fig 6-2-22

（3）分指：双手抓握对方同一手的不同手指，使其伸直向两侧用力分掰。（图 6-2-21）

(3) Finger split: grasp different fingers of the same hand with both hands, and stretch them to the opposite sides. (Fig. 6-2-21)

（4）拿掌：用拇指的扣压力，抓握对方手掌四指扣压。（图 6-2-22）

(4) Take the palm: with the pressure of the thumb, grasp the other hand and press the four fingers. (Fig. 6-2-22)

2. 手腕关节 wrist joint

双手合力固定并扣握对方手掌背部，将其手腕掰向肘尖方向成直角折掰。（图 6-2-23）

Place the thumb of both hands on the back of the palm, and break the wrist at a right angle towards the elbow tip. (Fig. 6-2-23)

图Fig 6-2-23

3. 肘关节 elbow joint

图Fig 6-2-24　　　　　　图Fig 6-2-25　　　　　　图Fig 6-2-26

用手抓住敌人手腕或小臂并向后拉直其臂膀，以手掌后部、手掌外侧或臂肘击压肘关节，（图 6-2-24）或双手与臂内旋（外旋）对方手臂，合力反其肘关节。（图 6-2-25、图 6-2-26）

Grasp the wrist or forearm of the enemy with your hand and straighten the arm back. Press the elbow joint with the back of your hand, the outside of your hand, or the elbow, (Fig. 6-2-24) or both hands and arms rotate inside (outside) the other arm, and the resultant force is opposite to the elbow joint. (Fig. 6-2-25, Fig. 6-2-26)

4. 肩关节 shoulder joint

缠拿对方手臂内旋顶压其肩膀，将其手臂后掰，控制其肩关节。（图 6-2-27）

Twist the rival's arm and press it against the shoulder, break the arm back, and control the shoulder joint. (Fig. 6-2-27)

图Fig 6-2-27

5. 膝关节 knee joint

用脚侧踹对方膝关节外侧或膝盖骨，能踹裂其韧带和软骨，使其剧痛和行动不便。（图 6-2-28）

Kick the outside of the knee joint or the knee bone of the rival.(Fig. 6-2-28)

图Fig 6-2-28

6. 踝节部 ankle

脚踹蹬对方踝关节外侧或双手掰旋踝关节。（图 6-2-29）

Kick the outside of the ankle or turn the ankle with both hands. (Fig. 6-2-29)

7. 脚背 instep

以脚猛跺对方脚背，可使其脚背小骨断裂，造成剧痛和行动不便。（图 6-2-30）

Stamp on the rival's instep. (Fig. 6-2-30)

图Fig 6-2-29　　　　　图Fig 6-2-30

第三节　擒拿解脱方法举要
6.3 The Ways to Get away from the Capture (Jietuo)

（一）抓头解脱拿法 Escape from the control of the head

被对方正面抓头发时，（图 6-3-1）快速双手交叉盖压其手掌，（图 6-3-2）以双手和头形成夹击合力，屈膝弯腰下伏上体，使其手掌成外翻反关节受制而解脱并擒拿对方。（图 6-3-3）注意分清对方左右手，下压时向对方外侧旋拧，将其另一手置于身体最远端，防止对方另一手臂反击。

When the hair is grabbed by the opponent from the front, (Fig. 6-3-1) cross your hands quickly and press down on his palms, (Fig. 6-3-2) form a clamping force with your hands and head, bend the knees and the upper body, make his palms become an anti-joint and to release yourself and capture the opponent at the same time. (Fig. 6-3-3) Distinguish the left and right hands of the opponent, when pressing down, screw them to the outside of the opponent, and place his other hand at the farthest end of the body to prevent the opponent's other arm from counterattacking.

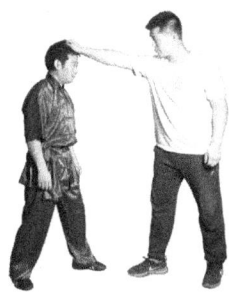  

图Fig 6-3-1　　　　　　　图Fig 6-3-2　　　　　　　图Fig 6-3-3

（二）卡喉解脱拿法 Escape from the clutching

1. 单手卡喉解脱法 one hand clutching

图Fig 6-3-4　　　　　　　图Fig 6-3-5　　　　　　　图Fig 6-3-6

图Fig 6-3-7　　　　　　　图Fig 6-3-8

对方右手卡自己喉部时，（图 6-3-4）以右手扣握对方右掌外侧，（图 6-3-5）配合左手助力扣压，（图 6-3-6）身体微右转，两脚分开站稳，以两臂合力使其腕内旋，从上向下以臂力和身体顶压其右腕，或以左臂压制对方右肘，（图 6-3-7）以右脚踩踏对方右膝侧。（图 6-3-8）

When the opponent uses his right hand to clutch your throat, (Fig. 6-3-4) hold the outside of the opponent's right palm with the right hand, (Fig. 6-3-5) cooperate with the left hand to assist the clasp, (Fig. 6-3-6) turn the body slightly to the right, stand on the feet separately, rotate the wrist inward with the joint force of the two arms, press the right wrist with the strength of the arms and the body from up to down, or press the right elbow of the opponent with the left arm, (Fig. 6-3-7) step the right knee of the opponent with the right foot. (Fig. 6-3-8)

2. 双手卡喉解脱法 two hands clutching

对方双手同时卡自己喉部时，(图 6-3-9) 以右手（左手）从对方两臂中间扣握对方右掌（左掌）外侧，(图 6-3-10) 配合左手（右手）助力扣压，身体微右转（左转），两脚分开站稳，以两臂合力使其腕内旋，从上向下以臂力和身体顶压其右腕（左腕），或臂肘压制对方肘关节，(图 6-3-11) 以膝盖顶压对方膝外侧。(图 6-3-12)

If the opponent uses two hands to clutch your throat, (Fig. 6-3-9) hold the outside of the opponent's right palm (left palm) with the right hand (left hand) from the middle, (Fig. 6-3-10) cooperate with the left hand (right hand) to assist in pressing, turn the body slightly to the right (left), stand on the feet separately, use the joint force of both arms to make his wrist turn inward, press his right wrist (left wrist) with the strength of arms and body from up to down, or press the elbow of the opponent with the elbow, (Fig. 6-3-11) press the outside of his knee with your knee top. (Fig. 6-3-12)

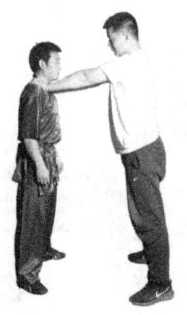
图Fig 6-3-9

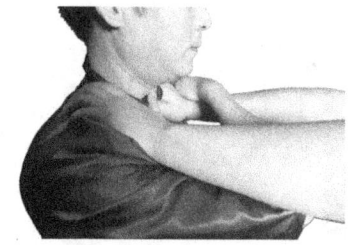
图Fig 6-3-10

图Fig 6-3-11

图Fig 6-3-12

（三）抓领解脱拿法 Escape from the collar-grasping

1. 正手抓衣领解脱拿法 front collar-grasping

（1）扣压腕解脱：对方右手（左手）正手抓自己衣领，（图 6-3-13）快速双手叠压其手掌，（图 6-3-14）以双手和胸部形成夹击合力，屈膝弯腰下伏上体，使其手掌成外翻反关节受制而解脱并擒拿对方。（图 6-3-15）

(1) press wrist: If the opponent grabs your collar with the right (or left) hand with thumb up, (Fig. 6-3-13) quickly press his palm with both hands, (Fig. 6-3-14) form a clamping force with both hands and chest, bend his knees and lean down to the upper body, make his palm become an eversion reverse joint subject. (Fig. 6-3-15)

图Fig 6-3-13　　　　图Fig 6-3-14　　　　图Fig 6-3-15

（2）别肘解脱：对方左手（右手）正手抓自己衣领，（图 6-3-16）以左手（右手）扣握对方左掌（右掌）外侧，（图 6-3-17）左手（右手）和胸部形成夹击合力，顶压使其腕成反关节，同时右肘（左肘）垂直横别或砸击对方左肘（右肘）。（图 6-3-18）

(2) press elbow: If the opponent grabs your collar with the left hand (or right hand) with thumd up, (Fig. 6-3-16) holds the outside of the left palm (right palm) of the other side with the left hand (right hand), (Fig. 6-3-17) forms a clamping force between the left hand (right hand) and the chest, presses the wrist component joint, and at the same time, the right elbow (left elbow) vertically crosses or hits his left elbow (right elbow). (Fig. 6-3-18)

图Fig 6-3-16　　　　图Fig 6-3-17　　　　图Fig 6-3-18

2. 反手抓衣领解脱拿法 back grasping

对方左手（右手）反手抓自己衣领，（图 6-3-19）自己左手（右手）按压其手，（图 6-3-20）左手（右手）和胸部形成夹击合力向下，右手（左手）上托对方左肘（右肘），左右手以旋拧力，使其肘外翻反关节受制。（图 6-3-21）托肘时若对方反方向力抵抗则借对方力量方向托肘反压。（图 6-3-22）可配合左脚踩踏对方膝外侧。（图 6-3-23）

If the opponent grabs your collar with the left hand (or right hand) with thumd down, (Fig. 6-3-19) press his hand with your left hand (or right hand), (Fig. 6-3-20) make the left (right) hand and the chest form a combined force downward, the right（left）hand hold on the opponent's left (right) elbow, use both hands to twist the opponent's elbow turn outside. (Fig. 6-3-21) If the opponent resists, you can make use of his force press the elbow against the counter pressure. (Fig. 6-3-22) At the same time, you can kick the outside of the knee of the opponent with your left foot. (Fig. 6-3-23)

图Fig 6-3-19

图Fig 6-3-20

图Fig 6-3-21

图Fig 6-3-22

图Fig 6-3-23

（四）抓肩解脱拿法 Escape from the shoulder-grasping

1. 砸肘解脱拿法 punch elbow

对方双手正面抓自己双肩，（图 6-3-24）双手握拳屈肘从两侧猛砸对方两肘外侧，使其肘反关节受强力解脱。（图 6-3-25）

If the opponent grasps your shoulders with both hands from the front of you, (Fig. 6-3-24) clench your fists and bend your elbows to punch the outside of the opponent's elbows. (Fig. 6-3-25)

图Fig 6-3-24　　　　　　　图Fig 6-3-25

2. 砸面解脱拿法 punch face

对方双手正面抓自己双肩，快速双手交叉握紧从对方两臂中间向上猛冲，以自己两臂撑扩开对方两臂，（图 6-3-26）双手交握拳下砸对方嘴唇面部。（图 6-3-27）

If the opponent grasps your shoulders with both hands from in front of you, quickly cross your hands and rushes up through the opponent's two arms, and expand the two arms, (Fig. 6-3-26) punch the face with your clenching fists. (Fig. 6-3-27)

图Fig 6-3-26　　　　　　　图Fig 6-3-27

3. 顶膝解脱法 ram chest

图Fig 6-3-28　　　　　图Fig 6-3-29　　　　　图Fig 6-3-30

对方双手正面抓自己双肩，(图6-3-28)快速双手交叉握紧从对方两臂中间上冲，双手勾搂对方脖颈，(图6-3-29)双手回搂对方上体，迅速以膝撞击对方胸腹。(图6-3-30)

If the opponent grasps your shoulders with both hands in the front of you, (Fig. 6-3-28) quickly rush your hands up through the opponent's arms, hook his neck, (Fig. 6-3-29) clench his upper body, and ram his chest with your knees. (Fig. 6-3-30)

4. 下潜解脱法 lower down

对方双手正面抓推自己双肩，(图6-3-31)快速下潜身体，缩肩低头从对方手臂下绕出，(图6-3-32)抬头顶项别对方手腕，(图6-3-33)以拳迅速撞击对方肋部。(图6-3-34)

If the opponent grasps your shoulders with both hands from the front of you, (Fig. 6-3-31) quickly lower down your body, shrinks your shoulders and out of the opponent's arms, (Fig. 6-3-32) raise your head and stuck his wrists, (Fig. 6-3-33) punch quickly the opponent's ribs. (Fig. 6-3-34)

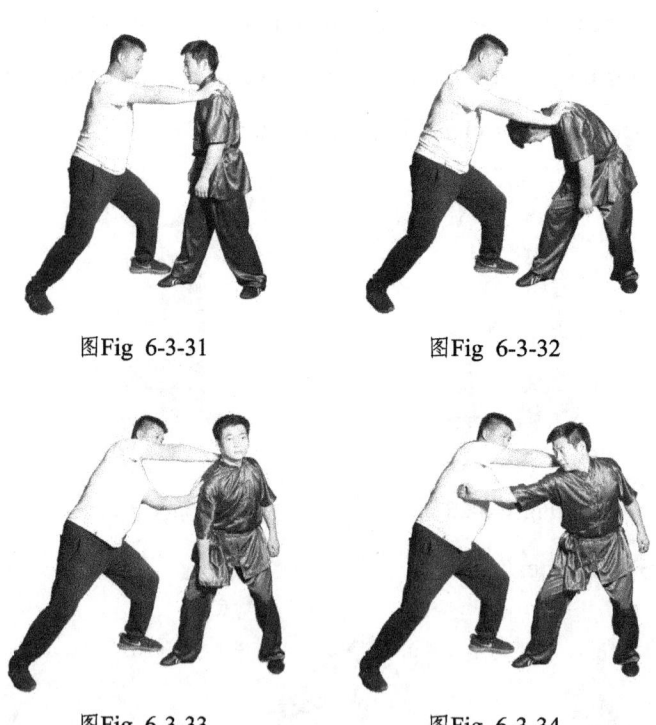

图Fig 6-3-31　　　　　　图Fig 6-3-32

图Fig 6-3-33　　　　　　图Fig 6-3-34

5. 扣腕解脱法 clasping wrist

对方双手正面抓推自己双肩，(图6-3-35)以左手(右手)扣握对方左掌(右掌)外侧，举旋右臂(左臂)，(图6-3-36)自己手、臂与肩合力旋压对方腕部。(图6-3-37)

If the opponent grasps your shoulders with both hands in front of you, (Fig. 6-3-35) hold the outside of the opponent's left (or right) palm with the left (or right) hand, lift and rotate the right (or) left arm, (Fig. 6-3-36) and rotate the opponent's wrists with your hands, arms and shoulders. (Fig. 6-3-37)

图Fig 6-3-35　　　　　图Fig 6-3-36　　　　　图Fig 6-3-37

6. 背后抓肩解脱拿法 grab shoulder

图Fig 6-3-38　　　　　图Fig 6-3-39

图Fig 6-3-40　　　　　图Fig 6-3-41

对方单手或双手背后抓自己肩，(图6-3-38)抓自己右肩（左肩）时以左手（右手）扣按对方手掌，(图6-3-39)举旋右臂（或转身左臂从对方两臂内上穿），(图6-3-40)以自己手、臂与肩合力旋压对方腕部。(图6-3-41)

If the opponent grabs your shoulder with one hand or both hands behind your, (Fig. 6-3-38) when he grabs your right shoulder (left shoulder), press the opponent's palm with your left hand (right hand), (Fig. 6-3-39) lift and rotate your right arm (or turn the body and make the left arm go through the opponent's two arms), (Fig.6-3-40) rotate the opponent's wrists with your hands, arms and shoulders. (Fig. 6-3-41)

（五）合抱解脱拿法 Escape from body holding

1. 正面臂上箍抱解脱拿法 front body holding

对方双手正前合围抱自己双臂与身体，（图 6-3-42) 以头撞击其面侧，快速双手交叉握掌挑打对方裆部，（图 6-3-43) 随后可脚踢其膝关节。

If the opponent holds your body and arms before you, (Fig. 6-3-42) hit one side of his face with your head, and quickly clench your hands and hit his crotch, (Fig. 6-3-43) then kick his knee joint.

图Fig 6-3-42　　　　图Fig 6-3-43

2. 正面合围抱腰解脱拿法 front waist holding

对方双手正前合围抱自己腰部，（图 6-3-44) 快速左右旋转身体扩充合围空间，以肘横击对方颈部。（图 6-3-45) 随后可脚绊对方支撑腿。

If the opponent holds your waist before you, (Fig. 6-3-44) quickly rotate your body left and right to expand the enclosure space, and hit his neck with elbows. (Fig. 6-3-45) Then stumble his supporting leg with your foot.

图Fig 6-3-44　　　　图Fig 6-3-45

3. 背后合围抱臂解脱拿法 back body holding

对方双手从背后合围抱自己双臂与身体，（图 6-3-46）自己身体下蹲，双臂屈肘上架，（图 6-3-47）左转身以左肘撞击对方左肋，（图 6-3-48）迅速右转身，以右肘撞击对方右肋，（图 6-3-49）随着对方臂力松散，左转身，以右拳击面。（图 6-3-50）

If the opponent holds your body and arms behind you, (Fig. 6-3-46) squat down and bend the arms to the upper place, (Fig. 6-3-47) turn left to hit his left rib with your left elbow, (Fig. 6-3-48) turn right quickly and hit the his right rib with your right elbow, (Fig. 6-3-49) turn left to beat his face. (Fig.6-3-50)

图Fig 6-3-46

图Fig 6-3-47

图Fig 6-3-48

图Fig 6-3-49

图Fig 6-3-50

4. 背后抱腰解脱拿法 back waist holding

（1）顶肘解脱法：对方双手从背后合围抱自己腰部，（图 6-3-51）双手掰扯对方手指得以解脱，（图 6-3-52）或继续右转身，以右肘击打对方右颈，（图 6-3-53）再左转身左肘击打对方左颈。（图 6-3-54）

If the opponent holds your waist behind you, (Fig. 6-3-51) break his fingers, (Fig. 6-3-52) or continue to turn right and hit his right neck with your right elbow, (Fig. 6-3-53) then turn left and hit his left neck with your left elbow. (Fig. 6-3-54)

（2）踩脚扳摔法：对方双手从背后合围抱自己腰部，（图 6-3-55）提膝震脚猛踩踩对方向前伸出的脚背，（图 6-3-56）继而以右转身肘击对方肋部，（图 6-3-57）再迅速左

转身以左手搂腿和右肘击胸扳摔对方。(图 6-3-58)

  If the opponent holds your waist behind you,(Fig. 6-3-55) lift your knees, and stamp heavily on this feet, (Fig. 6-3-56) then turn right and hit his rib, (Fig. 6-3-57) then turns left quickly and hold his leg with your left hand and hit his chest with your right elbow and throw him down. (Fig. 6-3-58)

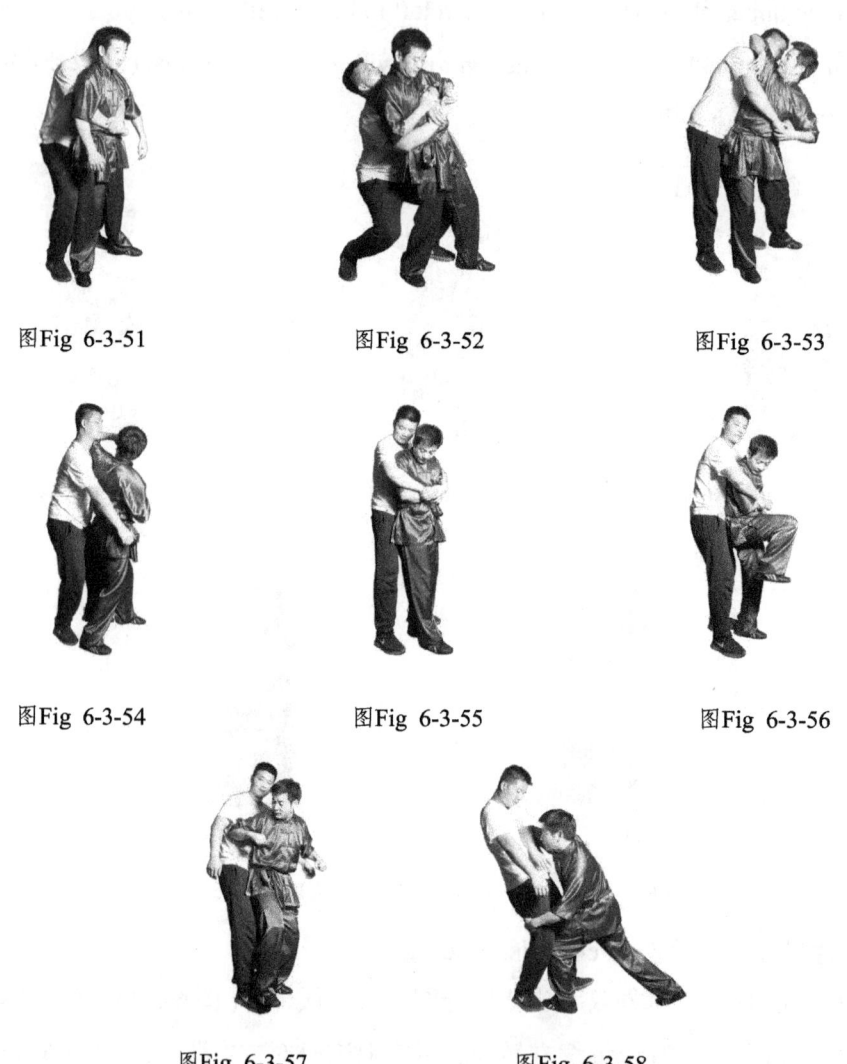

图Fig 6-3-51　　　　　图Fig 6-3-52　　　　　图Fig 6-3-53

图Fig 6-3-54　　　　　图Fig 6-3-55　　　　　图Fig 6-3-56

图Fig 6-3-57　　　　　图Fig 6-3-58

（3）抱腿坐压解脱法：对方双手从背后合围抱自己腰部，顶膝情况下，(图 6-3-59) 快速踩踩其脚背，双手抓抱对方脚踝上抬，身体弯腰向下猛坐压对方膝盖，身体与双手形成反向力使对方膝盖受损。(图 6-3-60)

  If the opponent holds your waist behind you, (Fig. 6-3-59) quickly stamp his feet, grasp the his ankles and lift them up, bend down and sit down on his knees, forming a reverse force between the body and hands to damage his knees. (Fig. 6-3-60)

图Fig 6-3-59　　　　　　图Fig 6-3-60

5. 背后抱颈肩解脱拿法 back holding neck and shoulder

对方从背后单臂抱锁自己颈肩，（图 6-3-61）快速踩跺其脚背，惊扰对方防范，左手抓其臂，右转身以右肘撞击对方右肋，（图 6-3-62）重心下蹲，一手拉对方手臂，一手搂其大腿，背摔对方。（图 6-3-63）

If the opponent holds your neck and shoulder behind you with one arm, (Fig. 6-3-61) quickly step on his foot to disturb his defense, grab his arm with your left hand, turn right to hit his right rib with your right elbow, (Fig. 6-3-62) squat down with lower gravity, pull his arm with one hand, hold his thigh with another hand, and throw him from your back. (Fig. 6-3-63)

图Fig 6-3-61　　　　　　图Fig 6-3-62　　　　　　图Fig 6-3-63

（六）抓腕解脱拿法 Grasping wrist

1. 缠腕解脱法 rotate wrist

对方右手抓拿自己右手，（图 6-3-64）左手快速扣压其右手背，（图 6-3-65）双手合拢，外旋右手掌，（图 6-3-66）右手抓握对方右腕，以右掌跟为支点杠杆式下压，使对方右臂内旋而形成腕肘反关节受制。（图 6-3-67）还可以用左肘压对方右肘，顺势膝盖顶压其膝。（图 6-3-68）

If the opponent grabs your right hand with his right hand, (Fig. 6-3-64) quickly press the back of his right hand with your left hand, (Fig. 6-3-65) the two hands are closed, and rotated outward the right palm, (Fig. 6-3-66) grab his right wrist with your right hand, and the root of your right palm as the fulcrum to press down his right hand, making his right arm rotate inward.(Fig. 6-3-67) You can also press the right elbow with your left elbow, and press his knee with your knee. (Fig. 6-3-68)

图Fig 6-3-64　　　图Fig 6-3-65　　　图Fig 6-3-66

图Fig 6-3-67　　　图Fig 6-3-68

2. 别腕解脱法 stuck wrists

对方右手抓拿自己右手，(图 6-3-69) 右手四指向上扣握对方右腕，手臂下沉，手指由下向上挑别其腕，(图 6-3-70) 右手拉直对方右臂，快速上左步于对方脚后，以左肘击对方右肋，(图 6-3-71) 还可伸直左臂横靠对方躯干，与右手扣握形成反向力靠摔对方。(图 6-3-72)

If the opponent grabs your right hand with his right hand, (Fig. 6-3-69) clasp his right wrist with your right hand, with fingers up, (Fig. 6-3-70) straighten his right arm with your right hand, quickly step up the left foot, and then hit his right rib with your left elbow, (Fig. 6-3-71) or stretch out the left arm close to his body, forming a reverse force with the right hand clasp. (Fig. 6-3-72)

图Fig 6-3-69　　　　　图Fig 6-3-70

图Fig 6-3-71　　　　　图Fig 6-3-72

3. 别肘解脱法 stuck elbow

对方右手抓拿自己右手，（图 6-3-73）上翘右手，以右手四指扣握对方右腕，身体右转，（图 6-3-74）若对方直臂，以左臂靠别对方右肘，若对方屈臂则左手托对方右肘，听其劲向上托别肘解脱，（图 6-3-75）或与右手配合，内旋下翻压对方右肘，使之受控。（图 6-3-76）

If the opponent grabs your right hand with his right hand,(Fig. 6-3-73) lift your right hand, clasp his right wrist with your right hand, and turn to the right. (Fig. 6-3-74)If the opponent's arm is straight, stuck his left arm with your right elbow. If his arm is bend, hold his right elbow, and lift it upward, (Fig. 6-3-75) or cooperate with your right hand, rotate inward and press his right elbow. (Fig. 6-3-76)

图Fig 6-3-73　　　　　图Fig 6-3-74

图Fig 6-3-75　　　　　图Fig 6-3-76

4. 肩靠解脱法 rock shoulder

对方右手抓拿自己右手，(图 6-3-77) 右臂绷劲快速向前杠杆力压制对方大拇指，使对方拇指受损伤放松抓握，(图 6-3-78) 继续向对方身后上步，右肩臂猛烈撞靠对方躯干，使之后摔解脱。(图 6-3-79)

If the opponent grabs your right hand with his right hand, (Fig. 6-3-77) press his thumb with your right arm fast. (Fig. 6-3-78) Step up behind the opponent, bump against his trunk with your right shoulder and arm.(Fig. 6-3-79)

图Fig 6-3-77　　　　　图Fig 6-3-78　　　　　图Fig 6-3-79

思考题： Questions for consideration

1. 擒拿术是什么？

1. What is Qinnashu?

2. 擒拿技法原理是什么？

2. What are the principles of Qinnashu?

3. 擒拿术手法主要有哪些？

3. What are the main techniques of Qinnashu?

4. 擒拿技法应用原则有哪些？

4. What are the application principles of Qinnashu?

5. 擒拿解脱时注意防范措施有哪些？

5. What precautions should be taken when escaping from the opponent's capture?

第七章 武术常用词汇汉英对照
Chapter 7 Chinese-English Wushu Terms

课程教学词汇汉英对照
Chinese-English Wushu Terms for Class Teaching

上课 [shàng kè] class begins

下课 [xià kè] class is over

休息 [xiū xi] have a rest/take a break

集合 [jí hé] fall in

立正 [lì zhèng] attention

稍息 [shāo xī] at ease

向右看齐 [xiàng yòu kàn qí] right dress

向左看齐 [xiàng zuǒ kàn qí] left dress

向前看 [xiàng qián kàn] eyes front

准备活动 [zhǔn bèi huó dòng] warm up

解散 [jiě sàn] dismiss

成二列队形 [chéng èr liè duì xíng] in two rows

二路纵队 [èr lù zòng duì] in two lines

第一组 / 队 [dì yī zǔ/duì] Group 1 / Team 1

注意 [zhù yì] attention

发力 [fā lì] generate/power

间距 [jiān jù] distance

伸直 [shēn zhí] stretch [arms]

平行 [píng xíng]parallel

规范 [guī fàn]norm

快速 [kuài sù]speedy

左 / 右转 [zuǒ/yòu zhuǎn]turn left/right

蹬直 [dēng zhí]stretch（legs）

继续练习 [jì xù liàn xí]go on practicing

准备 [zhǔn bèi]ready

跟我学（做）[gēn wǒ xúe(zuò)] follow me

课外练习 [kè wài liàn xí]exercises after class

国家级非物质文化遗产 [guó jiā jí fēi wù zhì wén huà yí chǎn]

national intangible cultural heritage

重心 [zhòng xīn]center of gravity

下沉 [xià chén]sink/go down

与肩同宽 [yǔ jiān tóng kuān]shoulder width apart

上下肢同时 [shàng xià zhī tóng shí] simultaneous upper and lower limbs' moves

两眼目视前方 [liǎng yǎn mù shì qián fāng]look ahead

摆头向左 / 右 [bǎi tóu xiàng zuǒ/yòu] swing head left / right

复习 [fù xí]review

学习新内容 [xué xí xīn nèi róng]learn new contents

顺肩 [shùn jiān] be along with the shoulder

转腰 [zhuǎn yāo]waist turn

压腿 [yā tuǐ] leg pressing

柔韧练习 [róu rèn liàn xí] flexibility exercise

踢腿 [tī tuǐ] leg kicking

拳术练习 [quán shù liàn xí]Quanshu practice

擒拿练习 [qín ná liàn xí]Qinna practice

模拟对抗练习 [mó nǐ dùi kàng liàn xí]simulated confrontation exercise

集体练习 [jí tǐ liàn xí]group exercises

分组练习 [fēn zǔ liàn xí]group practice

自己练习 [zì jǐ liàn xí]practice on one's own

两人一组 [liǎng rén yī zǔ]practice in pairs

放松 [fàng sōng]take ease/relax
跟上 [gēn shàng]follow up
抬头 [tái tóu]head up
挺胸 [tǐng xiōng]chest up

武术常用词汇汉英对照
Chinese-English Wushu Terms

一、基本动作 [jī běn dòng zuò]Basic Movements

基本功[jī běn gōng] Basic practice

（一）手型 [shǒu xíng]Hand Gesture

拳 [quán]fist

拳眼 [quán yǎn]eye of fist

拳心 [quán xīn]heart of fist

拳面 [quán miàn]face of fist

拳背 [quán bèi]back of fist

拳轮 [quán lún]curve of fist

瓦棱拳 [wǎ léng quán]Waleng fist

凤眼拳 [fèng yǎn quán]Fengyan fist

握杯拳 [wò bēi quán]cup-holding fist

掌 [zhǎng]palm

掌尖 [zhǎng jiān] palm tip

掌心 [zhǎng xīn]center of palm

掌背 [zhǎng bèi]back of palm

掌指 [zhǎng zhǐ]fingers of palm

掌根 [zhǎng gēn]root of palm

掌外沿 [zhǎng wài yán]external edge of palm

八字掌 [bā zì zhǎng]Bazi-palm

瓦面掌 [wǎ miàn zhǎng]Wamian-palm

九宫掌 [jiǔ gōng zhǎng]Jiugong-palm

扣掌 [kòu zhǎng]buckling palm

勾手 [gōu shǒu]hand hook

勾顶 [gōu dǐng] hook top

勾尖 [gōu jiān] hook tip

凤眼勾 [fèng yǎn gōu]phoenix-eye hook

螳螂勾手 [táng láng gōu shǒu]mantis hook hand

指 [zhǐ]finger

剪刀指 [jiǎn dāo zhǐ]scissor fingesr

剑指 [jiàn zhǐ]sword finger

爪 [zhǎo]claw

鹰爪 [yīng zhǎo]eagle-claw

猴爪 [hóu zhǎo]monkey-paw

虎爪 [hǔ zhǎo]tiger-paw

(二) 手法 [shǒu fǎ]Hand Techniques

拳法 [quán fǎ]fist techniques

平拳 [píng quán]horizontal fist

立拳 [lì quán] erect fist

抱拳 [bào quán] hold fist salute

摆拳 [bǎi quán]fist swing

栽拳 [zāi quán] fist punching downward

劈拳 [pī quán]chopping with fist

砸拳 [zá quán]hammering with fist

抄拳 [chāo quán]fist punching upward

贯拳 [guàn quán] fist goes vertically

架拳 [jià quán]fist uphold

冲拳 [chōng quán]beat forward horizontally with fist

横拳 [héng quán]horizontal punch

盖拳 [gài quán]covering with fist

撞拳 [zhuàng quán]fist goes up forward

钻拳 [zuān quán] drilling with fist

斩拳 [zhǎn quán] chopping with fist

截拳 [jié quán] block with fist

探拳 [tàn quán] probe with fist

崩拳 [bēng quán] bursting out with fist

挂拳 [guà quán] fist hanging

鞭拳 [biān quán] whip with fist

掌法 [zhǎng fǎ] Palm Techniques

掌型 [zhǎng xíng] palm form

推掌 [tuī zhǎng] palm pushing

架掌 [jià zhǎng] blocking with palm

亮掌 [liàng zhǎng] showing palm

挑掌 [tiǎo zhǎng] snap tilting

劈掌 [pī zhǎng] vertical chopping with palm

拍掌 [pāi zhǎng] palm clapping

穿掌 [chuān zhǎng] palm piercing

按掌 [àn zhǎng] palm downward pushing; palm downward thrusting

插掌 [chā zhǎng] palm thrusting

撩掌 [liáo zhǎng] palm swing

挂掌 [guà zhǎng] hanging palm

扑挂掌 [pū guà zhǎng] palm swirling

撩阴掌 [liáo yīn zhǎng] palm swinging down

摆掌 [bǎi zhǎng] palm swaying

阴掌 [yīn zhǎng] Yin palm

阳掌 [yáng zhǎng] Yang palm

切掌 [qiè zhǎng] palm cutting

托掌 [tuō zhǎng] palm holding

掖掌 [yè zhǎng] palm rib-attacking

双撞掌 [shuāng zhuàng zhǎng] palms double-bumping

迎面掌 [yíng miàn zhǎng] head-on palm

蹋掌 [tà zhǎng] palm pressing

盖掌 [gài zhǎng] pressing downward with palm

抡臂 [lún bì] arm blowing

顶肘 [dǐng zhǒu] elbow pushing

盘肘 [pán zhǒu] hook elbow

架肘 [jià zhǒu] carry with elbow

滚肘 [gǔn zhǒu] rotating elbow; rolling elbow

钉心肘 [dīng xīn zhǒu] striking the rival on the breast with elbow

靠肘 [kào zhǒu] bumping backward with elbow points

圈肘 [quān zhǒu] circling one's elbow inside

挑肘 [tiāo zhǒu] pushing elbow upward

砸肘 [zá zhǒu] smashing downward with elbow

格肘 [gé zhǒu] blocking with upward bending elbow spinning inward or outward

拐肘 [guǎi zhǒu] elbow butt

提肘 [tí zhǒu] elbow lifting

采手 [cǎi shǒu] hand grabbing

封手 [fēng shǒu] hand blocking

刁手 [diāo shǒu] hook grasp

缠手 [chán shǒu] twist grasp

搂手 [lǒu shǒu] hand grabbing; outward grasp

舞花手 [wǔ huā shǒu] hands twisting

金鸡独立 [jīn jī dú lì] golden rooster standing on one leg

野马分鬃 [yě mǎ fēn zōng] detach the wild horse's mane

白鹤亮翅 [bái hè liàng chì] white crane spreading its wings

搂膝拗步 [lóu xī ào bù] brushing knee on twisting step

单鞭 [dān biān] single whip

搬拦捶 [bān lán chuí] carrying and punching

海底针 [hái dǐ zhēn] needle in the bottom of the sea

揽雀尾 [lǎn què wěi] grasping the peacock's tail

双峰贯耳 [shuāng fēng guàn ěr] strike the opponent's ears with both fists

如风似闭 [rú fēng sì bì] pushing one's hands forward in defense

（三）步形 [bù xíng] Foot Stance/Step form

弓步 [gōng bù] bow stance

马步 [mǎ bù] horse-riding stance

虚步 [xū bù] empty stance

仆步 [pū bù] crouch stance

歇步 [xiē bù] cross-legged crouch stance

丁步 [dīng bù] T stance

并步 [bìng bù] feet-together stance; folding stance

坐盘 [zuò pán] cross-legged sitting stance

叉步 [chā bù] X stance

横裆步 [héng dāng bù] side bow stance

半马步 [bàn mǎ bù] semi-horse-riding stance

骑龙步 [qí lóng bù] dragon-riding stance

跪步 [guì bù] squatting stance; kneeling stance

高虚步 [gāo xū bù] high empty step

双弓步 [shuāng gōng bù] double bow stance

四平马 [sì píng mǎ] four-balance horse-riding stance

（四）步法 [bù fǎ] Foot techniques

击步 [jī bù] forward step

进步 [jìn bù] forward step

撤步 [chè bù] backward step; backward moving step

退步 [tuì bù] retreat step; stepping backward

盖步 [gài bù] forward crossover step

插步 [chā bù] back cross-step; backward crossover step

震脚 [zhèn jiǎo] stamping foot

垫步 [diàn bù] skipping step

纵步 [zòng bù] hopping step

行步 [xíng bù] walking step

趟泥步 [tāng ní bù] padding step in the mud

活步 [huó bù] loose step

闯步 [chuǎng bù] stepping out abruptly

麒麟步 [qí lín bù] Qilin Step

滑步 [huá bù] sliding step

上步 [shàng bù] advancing step; taking a step forward

跟步 [gēn bù] follow-up step

弧行步 [hú xíng bù] circular-walking steps or curved steps

跃步 [yuè bù] leaping step

（五）膝法 [xī fǎ] Techniques of the Knee

提膝 [tí xī] raising the knee; lifting the knee

顶膝 [dǐng xī] knee butting

扣膝 [kòu xī] knee clasping

（六）腿法练习 [tuǐ fǎ liàn xí] Exercise of leg techniques

直摆性腿法 [zhí bǎi xìng tuǐ fǎ] Straight Leg Swinging Techniques

正踢腿 [zhèng tī tuǐ] front kicking

侧踢腿 [cè tī tuǐ] side kicking

外摆腿 [wài bǎi tuǐ] outward swing

里合腿 [lǐ hé tuǐ] inward swing

后撩腿 [hòu liáo tuǐ] back arc kicking; back kicking

斜踢腿 [xié tī tuǐ] oblique kicking

倒踢腿 [dào tī tuǐ] inverse kicking

后摆腿 [hòu bǎi tuǐ] backward swing

单拍脚 [dān pāi jiǎo] single foot slapping

里合拍脚 [lǐ hé pāi jiǎo] inside foot slapping

屈伸性腿法 [qū shēn xìng tuǐ fǎ] Leg Techniques in Flexion and Extension

弹腿 [tán tuǐ] spring

侧踹腿 [cè chuài tuǐ] sideward striking

蹬腿 [dēng tuǐ] kicking

点腿 [diǎn tuǐ] pointing

铲腿 [chǎn tuǐ] shoveling

缠腿 [chán tuǐ] twisting

踩腿 [cǎi tuǐ] stamp

扫转性腿法 [sǎo zhuǎn xìng tuǐ fǎ] Leg Rotating and Sweeping Techniques

后扫腿 [hòu sǎo tuǐ] sweeping backward

前扫腿 [qián sǎo tuǐ] sweeping forward

劈叉性腿法 [pǐ chà xìng tuǐ fǎ] Leg Splitting Techniques

竖叉 [shù chà] front-back leg splitting

横叉 [héng chà] sidelong leg splitting

（七）平衡练习 [píng héng liàn xí] Balance Exercise

提膝平衡 [tí xī píng héng] knee-lifted balance; front knee-lifted balance

扣腿平衡 [kòu tuǐ píng héng] back leg-crossed balance

望月平衡 [wàng yuè píng héng] look-at-moon balance; moon-watching balance

探海平衡 [tàn hǎi píng héng] search-sea balance

燕式平衡 [yàn shì píng héng] swallow balance

朝天蹬 [cháo tiān dēng] skyward kick

盘腿平衡 [pán tuǐ píng héng] leg-crossed balance

侧身平衡 [cè shēn píng héng] side way balance

倒立 [dào lì] stand upside down

（八）跳跃练习 [tiào yuè liàn xí] Jumping Exercise

腾空飞脚 [téng kōng fēi jiǎo] jumping and kicking

腾空摆莲 [téng kōng bǎi lián] swinging in the air

腾空箭弹 [téng kōng jiàn tán] jumping and kicking

腾空侧踹 [téng kōng cè chuài] kicking in the air

旋子 [xuàn zi] spinning

旋子转体 [xuàn zi zhuǎn tǐ] twist in the air

旋风脚 [xuàn fēng jiǎo] whirl-wind foot

侧空翻 [cè kōng fān] side flip

鲤鱼打挺 [lǐ yú dǎ tǐng] kip up

大跃步前穿 [dà yuè bù qián chuān] forward in giant leap

盘腿跌 [pán tuǐ diē] leg-crossed drop

二、拳术与器械 [quán shù yǔ qì xiè]Quanshu and Instruments

（一）拳术 [quán shù]Quanshu

套路 [tào lù]set; routine; set pattern

规定套路 [guī dìng tào lù]required routine

规定拳 [guī dìng quán]Regular Quan

传统武术套路 [chuán tǒng wǔ shù tào lù]ancient Wushu routine

十路弹腿 [shí lù tán tuǐ]Shilutantui

长拳 [cháng quán]Chang Quan

南拳 [nán quán]Nan Quan

自选拳 [zì xuǎn quán]Optional Quanshu

查拳 [zhā/chá quán]Zha/Cha Quan

形意拳 [xíng yì quán]Xingyi Quan

华拳 [huá quán]Huá Quan

红拳 [hóng quán]Hong Quan

炮拳 [pào quán]Pao Quan

花拳 [huā quán] Huā Quan

绵拳 [mián quán]Mian Quan

八卦拳 [bā guà quán]Bagua Quan

八极拳 [bā jí quán]Baji Quan

五步拳 [wǔ bù quán]Wubu Quan

戳脚 [chuō jiǎo]Chuojiao Quan

翻子拳 [fān zǐ quán]Fanzi Quan

地趟拳 [dì tǎng quán]Ditang Quan

六合拳 [liù hé quán] Liuhe Quan

通背拳 [tōng bèi quán] Tongbei Quan

八门拳 [bā mén quán] Bamen Quan

太祖拳 [tài zǔ quán]Taizu Quan

梅花拳 [méi huā quán]Plum-Blossom Quan

劈挂拳 [pī guà quán]Pigua Quan

少林拳 [shào lín quán]Shaolin Quan

罗汉拳 [luó hàn quán] Luohan Quan

武当拳 [wǔ dāng quán] Wudang Quan

三皇炮锤 [sān huáng pào chuí] Sanhuangpaochui Quan

弹腿 [tán tuǐ] Tantui Quan

象形拳 [xiàng xíng quán] Imitation Quan

螳螂拳 [táng láng quán] Mantis Quan

鹤拳 [hè quán] Crane Quan

猴拳 [hóu quán] Monkey Quan

蛇拳 [shé quán] Snake Quan

虎拳 [hǔ quán] Tiger Quan

鹰爪拳 [yīng zhǎo quán] Eagle Claw Quan

梅花桩 [méi huā zhuāng] Plum Blossom Zhuang

燕青拳 [yàn qīng quán] Yanqing Quan

咏春拳 [yǒng chūn quán] Yongchun Quan

醉拳 [zuì quán] Drunken Quan

太极拳 [tài jí quán] Taiji Quan

二十四式太极拳 [èr shí sì shì tài jí quán] Twenty-Four Styles Taijiquan

陈式太极拳 [chén shì tài jí quán] Chen Style Taijiquan

杨式太极拳 [yáng shì tài jí quán] Yang Style Taijiquan

吴式太极拳 [wú shì tài jí quán] Wú Style Taijiquan

赵堡太极拳 [zhào bǔ tài jí quán] Zhaobu Style Taijiquan

武式太极拳 [wǔ shì tài jí quán] Wǔ Style Taijiquan

孙式太极拳 [sūn shì tài jí quán] Sun Style Taijiquan

（二）器械类 [qì xiè lèi] Instruments

刀 [dāo] broad sword

刀身 [dāo shēn] broadsword blade

刀刃 [dāo rèn] edge of broadsword

刀背 [dāo bèi] back of broadsword

刀尖 [dāo jiān] tip of broadsword

刀首 [dāo shǒu] head of broadsword

刀柄 [dāo bǐng] handle of broadsword

护手盘 [hù shǒu pán] hand guard of broadsword

刀彩 [dāo cǎi] broadsword banner; broadsword tassel

剑 [jiàn] straight sword

剑身 [jiàn shēn] sword blade

剑刃 [jiàn rèn] edge of sword

剑脊 [jiàn jǐ] spine of sword

剑锋 [jiàn fēng] sword blade

剑尖 [jiàn jiān] tip of sword

剑首 [jiàn shǒu] head of sword

剑柄 [jiàn bǐng] sword handle

剑格 [jiàn gé] hand guard of sword

剑穗 [jiàn suì] sword tassel

棍 [gùn] club/cudgel/stick

棍身 [gùn shēn] body of club

前段 [qián duàn] front section

中段 [zhōng duàn] middle section

后段 [hòu duàn] rear section

棍把 [gùn bǎ] butt of club

棍梢 [gùn shāo] tip of club

梢端 [shāo duān] top of club

把端 [bǎ duān] butt end

枪 [qiāng] spear

枪尖 [qiāng jiān] point of spear; spear point

枪头 [qiāng tóu] head of spear; spear head

枪缨 [qiāng yīng] tassel of spear; spear tassel

枪身 [qiāng shēn] shaft of spear; spear shaft

枪把 [qiāng bǎ] shaft of spear; spear shaft

大 枪 [dà qiāng] long spear (about 3.5 meters long with a spear head about 0.4 meters long)

双头枪(亦称双头蛇)[shuāng tóu qiāng (shuāng tóu shé)] double-headed spear

大刀 [dà dāo]broad sword

朴刀 [pǔ dāo]long-hilt broadsword

护手 [hù shǒu]hand guard of sword

苗刀 [miáo dāo]Miao broadsword

双刀 [shuāng dāo]double broadsword

鞭 [biān]whip

单鞭 [dān biān]single whip

双鞭 [shuāng biān]double whip

九节鞭 [jiǔ jié biān]nine-joint whip

鞭杆 [biān gān]Biangan

钩 [gōu]hook

单钩 [dān gōu]single hook

双钩 [shuāng gōu]double hook

护手钩 [hù shǒu gōu]hand-guarding hooks

钩尖 [gōu jiān]hook point

钩端 [gōu duān]hook top

钩锋 [gōu fēng] hook blade

背峰 [bèi fēng]blade back

月峰 [yuè fēng]new-moon-shaped blade

钩柄 [gōu bǐng]hook handle

横梗 [héng gěng]hook brace

钩钻 [gōu zuàn]hook drill

锤 [chuí]hammer

八棱锤 [bā léng chuí]eight-edged hammer

双锤 [shuāng chuí]double hammer

流星锤 [liú xīng chuí]meteor hammer

绳镖 [shéng biāo]rope-dart

双节棍 [shuāng jié gùn]two-section stick

三节棍 [sān jié gùn]three-section stick

小连枷 [xiǎo lián jiā] Xiao Lianjia

拐 [guǎi] Guai

扇 [shàn] fan

斧 [fǔ] axe

大斧 [dà fǔ] long-handled axe

戟 [jǐ] halberd

方天画戟 [fāng tiān huà jǐ] fangtianhuaji, double crescent spear-headed halberds

青龙戟 [qīng lóng jǐ] black dragon halberd

禅杖 [chán zhàng] monk-spade

铲 [chǎn] shovel

月牙铲 [yuè yá chǎn] crescent shovel

匕首 [bǐ shǒu] dagger

峨眉刺 [é méi cì] E-mei dagger

叉 [chā] fork

飞叉 [fēi chā] flying fork

杆子鞭 [gǎn zi biān] rod-handled whip

飞刀 [fēi dāo] flying dagger

飞镖 [fēi biāo] flying dart

弩 [nǔ] crossbow

盾 [dùn] shield

（三）对练类 [duì liàn lèi] Pair practice

徒手对练 [tú shǒu duì liàn] bare-handed pair exercises

器械对练 [qì xiè duì liàn] pair exercises with weapons

徒手与器械对练 [tú shǒu yǔ qì xiè duì liàn] bare-handed against armed

三、基本名称 [jī běn míng chēng] Basic Names

武术 [wǔ shù] Wushu/Gongfu/Kungfu/Martial Arts

民间武术 [mín jiān wǔ shù] folk Wushu

现代武术 [xiàn dài wǔ shù] modern Wushu

传统武术 [chuán tǒng wǔ shù] traditional Wushu

擒拿 [qín ná] Qinna

套子 [tào zi] routine/Taozi

拳术 [quán shù] Quanshu

格斗 [gé dòu] tussle/fighting

散打 [sǎn dǎ] Chinese boxing

功法 [gōng fǎ] practicing method

内家 [nèi jiā] Neijia Quan

外家 [wài jiā] Waijia Quan

器械 [qì xiè] weapon/instrument

长器械 [cháng qì xiè] long weapon/instrument

短器械 [duǎn qì xiè] short weapon/instrument

软器械 [ruǎn qì xiè] soft weapon/instrument

双器械 [shuāng qì xiè] double-weapon/instrument

短兵 [duǎn bīng] (1) short weapons; (2) combat

长兵 [cháng bīng] Changbing (1) weapons that can be shot in a long distance, for example a bow and an arrow; (2) weapons with long handles, such as a spear; (3) the combat with long weapons

三节 [sān jié] three sections

三尖 [sān jiān] three tips

四击 [sì jī] four attacks

八法 [bā fǎ] eight techniques or methods

十二型 [shí èr xíng] twelve forms of actions in Wushu

二十四要 [èr shí sì yào] twenty-four basic techniques in Wushu

起势 [qǐ shì] preparation form

收势 [shōu shì] closing form; end up

定势 [dìng shì] fixed postures; a still posture or position in routine techniques

分段 [fēn duàn] part of a whole set of Quan; also called "tang"

刚柔 [gāng róu] hardness and softness

刚柔相济 [gāng róu xiāng jì] coupling hardness with softness

功夫 [gōng fū] Gongfu

功架 [gōng jià] postures, or actions as the general designation of the hand forms, stances, body forms, hand techniques, footsteps and leg techniques

功力 [gōng lì] one's ability or achievement in a special field gained by long period of practicing.

国术 [guó shù]Guoshu; alter-name for Wushu

技法 [jì fǎ]techniques of Wushu or Quan in general.

技艺 [jì yì]craft

劲 [jìn]power

劲力 [jìn lì]power and force

诀窍 [jué qiào]essentials in practice

绝招 [jué zhāo]unique skills

亮相 [liàng xiàng] a pose in preparing form and closing form

南拳北腿 [nán quán běi tuǐ] Gongfu players in the South using more fist techniques, while those in the north using more leg techniques

内功 [nèi gōng]internal exercise, or works

外功 [wài gōng]external exercises or works, opposite to internal exercise

气功 [qì gōng] Qigong or internal breathing system for health and vitality

拳场 [quán chǎng]non-official place or organization for practicing Quan

拳诀 [quán jué]rhymed formula of Quan practicing

拳理 [quán lǐ] Quan Rules

拳派 [quán pài]schools of Quan

拳谱 [quán pǔ]records of Quan

拳势 [quán shì](1) movements of Quan; (2) momentum in practicing Quan, which shows the mental outlook and quality of the player

拳系 [quán xì]different branches in a school of Quan

拳谚 [quán yàn]proverbs of Quan

身架 [shēn jià]posture and intrinsic sublimity that is gained by a long period of good training

门派 [mén pài]schools of Wushu

门户 [mén hù](1) schools of Quan; (2) posture for protection; (3) parts being attacked in fighting

顺势 [shùn shì]take advantage of an opportunity at one's convenience

外家拳 [wài jiā quán]Waijia Quan

喂手 [wèi shǒu]giving your hand to the opponent and let him to punch it (a kind of match practicing way)

五行 [wǔ xíng]five basic elements in Chinese philosophy

武术图解 [wǔ shù tú jiě]illustration

武艺 [wǔ yì]skills or art of Wushu

虚实 [xū shí]emptiness and solidness

虚招 [xū zhāo]empty or false movements

阴阳 [yīn yáng]Yin and Yang

招法 [zhāo fǎ] craft

十八般武艺 [shí bā bān wǔ yì]skills in using 18 kinds of Chinese traditional Wushu weapons, though it has different versions, generally, they are broadsword, spear, sword, halberd, battle-axe, tomahawk, hook, fork and so on.

四、长拳主要动作术语 [cháng quán zhǔ yào dòng zuò shù yǔ]Main Action Terms of Chang Quan

并步抱拳 [bìng bù bào quán] step with feet close together and fists clenched

弓步冲拳 [gōng bù chōng quán]bow stance and thrust punch

弹腿冲拳 [tán tuǐ chōng quán]kick and thrust punch

转身马步架冲拳 [zhuǎn shēn mǎ bù jià chōng quán]turn the body, block and thrust fist with Horse-riding stance

弓步架推掌 [gōng bù jià tuī zhǎng]bow stance with palms upholding and pushing

提膝挑掌 [tí xī tiǎo zhǎng]knee uplift with palm raised

弓步连环冲拳 [gōng bù lián huán chōng quán]bow stance with double thrust punch

弓步顶肘 [gōng bù dǐng zhǒu]bow stance and elbowing

仆步穿手亮掌 [pū bù chuān shǒu liàng zhǎng]crouching stance with arm piercing and palm flashing

并步砸掌 [bìng bù zá zhǎng]feet together and fist pounding

虚步架栽掌 [xū bù jià zāi zhǎng]empty step with fist downward and arm uplifting

预备式 [yù bèi shì]preparation form

上步冲拳 [shàng bù chōng quán]step forward and punch fist

上步撑掌 [shàng bù chēng zhǎng]step forward and push palm

勾手上提 [gōu shǒu shàng tí] hook hand raising

弓步斜行 [gōng bù xié xíng]step forward in bow stance

仆步切掌 [pū bù qiē zhǎng]cut with palm in crouching stance

歇步冲拳 [xiē bù chōng quán] punch in leg-crossed stance

转身推掌 [zhuǎn shēn tuī zhǎng] turn body and push palm

进步左挑掌 [jìn bù zuǒ tiǎo zhǎng] step forward and snap left fist

提膝左冲拳 [tí xī zuǒ chōng quán] raise knee and punch with left fist

弓步右劈拳 [gōng bù yòu pī quán] chop with right fist in bow stance

虚步双勾手 [xū bù shuāng gōu shǒu] hook both hands in empty stance

身型 [shēn xíng] Body Forms

头正 [tóu zhèng] head straight

颈直 [jǐng zhí] neck-erecting

竖项 [shù xiàng] neck-erecting

挺胸 [tǐng xiōng] chest-erecting

含胸 [hán xiōng] chest-relaxing

圆胸 [yuán xiōng] drawing chest slightly in a circle, one basic technique in Nanquan

拔背 [bá bèi] back-erecting

团胛 [tuán jiǎ] cupping blade-bones

沉肩 [chén jiān] shoulders loosening.

坠肘 [zhuì zhǒu] elbow-down

立腰 [lì yāo] waist-erecting

收腰 [shōu yāo] waist straightening

实腹 [shí fù] abdomen erecting

敛臀 [liǎn tún] hip-lifting

收胯 [shōu kuà] hip-lifting

身法 [shēn fǎ] Body Techniques

伸缩开合 [shēn suō kāi hé] extending, contracting, opening and closing

冲撞挤靠 [chōng zhuàng jǐ kào] knocking rival suddenly with head, shoulder, elbow, knee, hip or crotch, the techniques for close wrestling

尾闾中正 [wěi lú zhōng zhèng] keeping body straight regardless of whatever action, a special term in Taijiquan

旋转拧裹 [xuán zhuǎn nǐng guǒ] spinning or twisting

以肩带手 [yǐ jiān dài shǒu] using shoulders as driving force for hands movement

手随步行 [shǒu suí bù xíng] hands- move-with steps

眼法 [yǎn fǎ]Eye Techniques

随视 [suí shì]watching along the movements

注视 [zhù shì]watch

呼吸 [hū xī]Exhalation & Inhalation

提气 [tí qì]Qi-inhale

托气 [tuō qì]Qi-holding

聚气 [jù qì]Qi-collecting

沉气 [chén qì] Qi-going- down

五、器械主要动作术语 [qì xiè zhǔ yào dòng zuò shù yǔ]Main Action Terms of Wushu weapons

刀法 [dāo fǎ]Broadsword Techniques

握刀 [wò dāo]broadsword-gripping

抱刀 [bào dāo]broadsword- holding

缠头刀 [chán tóu dāo]broadsword-twining

裹脑刀 [guǒ nǎo dāo] broadsword-wrapping-head

劈刀 [pī dāo]broadsword-chopping

截刀 [jié dāo]broadsword-crosscutting

撩刀 [liáo dāo]broadsword-cutting upward

挂刀 [guà dāo] broadsword-parrying upward

扎刀 [zhā dāo] broadsword-thrusting

扫刀 [sǎo dāo]broadsword-sweeping

云刀 [yún dāo]broadsword-rotating

点刀 [diǎn dāo]broadsword-pointing

挑刀 [tiǎo dāo]broadsword-raising

按刀 [àn dāo]broadsword-pressing

藏刀 [cáng dāo] broadsword-hiding

握剑 [wò jiàn]sword-holding

持剑 [chí jiàn] sword-holding-upright

立剑 [lì jiàn]sword-erecting

平剑 [píng jiàn]sword-leveling

刺剑 [cì jiàn] sword-stabbing

劈剑 [pī jiàn] sword-cleaving

挂剑 [guà jiàn] sword-hanging

撩剑 [liáo jiàn] sword wielding

云剑 [yún jiàn] sword-rotating

抹剑 [mǒ jiàn] sword-sliding

绞剑 [jiǎo jiàn] sword-twisting

架剑 [jià jiàn] sword-propping

挑剑 [tiǎo jiàn] sword-tilting

点剑 [diǎn jiàn] sword-pointing

崩剑 [bēng jiàn] sword-tilting

截剑 [jié jiàn] sword- cleaving

抱剑 [bào jiàn] sword-holding in front of chest.

带剑 [dài jiàn] sword-blowing

穿剑 [chuān jiàn] sword-piercing

腕花 [wàn huā] sword-spinning

压剑 [yā jiàn] sword-pressing

棍法 [gùn fǎ] Club Techniques

云棍 [yún gùn] spinning club overhead

扫棍 [sǎo gùn] club-sweeping

点棍 [diǎn gùn] club-striking

戳棍 [chuō gùn] club-poking

劈棍 [pī gùn] club-cleaving downward

撩棍 [liáo gùn] club-waving

推棍 [tuī gùn] club-pushing

压棍 [yā gùn] club-pressing

托棍 [tuō gùn] holding up club

挂棍 [guà gùn] club-hanging

拨棍 [bō gùn] club-blowing

崩棍 [bēng gùn] club-flipping

立舞花棍 [lì wǔ huā gùn] vertical club-swing

平舞花棍 [píng wǔ huā gùn]horizontal club- swing

枪法 [qiāng fǎ]Spear Techniques

持枪 [chí qiāng]spear-holding

背枪 [bēi qiāng]spear-shouldering

扎枪 [zhā qiāng]spear-thrusting

拦枪 [lán qiāng]spear-blocking

拿枪 [ná qiāng]spear-rotating

缠枪 [chán qiāng]spear-coiling

摆枪 [bǎi qiāng]spear-waving

崩枪 [bēng qiāng]spear-flipping

拨枪 [bō qiāng]spear-blowing

六、武术竞赛常用词汇 [wú shù jìng sài cháng yòng cí huì] Terms of Wushu Competition

(一)竞赛组织 [jìng sài zǔ zhī]Competition Organization

裁判委员会 [cái pàn wěi yuán huì]referee commission

仲裁委员会 [zhòng cái wěi yuán huì]arbitration board

竞赛委员会 [jìng sài wěi yuán huì]competition commission

竞赛办公室 [jìng sài bàn gōng shǐ]competition office

竞赛项目 [jìng sài xiàng mù]competition item

比赛地点 [bǐ sài dì diǎn]competition site

比赛场地 [bǐ sài chǎng dì]competition spot

比赛时间 [bǐ sài shí jiān]competition time

秩序册 [zhì xù cè]program brochure

报名表 [bào míng biǎo]application form

报名截止时间 [bào míng jié zhǐ shí jiān]deadline for registration

性别 [xìng bié]gender

男运动员 [nán yùn dòng yuán]sportsman

女运动员 [nǚ yùn dòng yuán]sportswoman

抽签 [chōu qiān]draw lots

评分表 [píng fēn biǎo]scoring form

第一类 [dì yī lèi] the first category

第一场地 [dì yī chǎng dì] the first court

第二场地 [dì èr chǎng dì] the second court

比赛记录表 [bǐ sài jì lù biǎo] game records

成绩统计 [chéng jì tǒng jì] calculation of results

成绩公布 [chéng jì gōng bù] announcement of results

授奖 [shòu jiǎng] award

纪念奖 [jì niàn jiǎng] memorial reward

中线 [zhōng xiàn] centre line

锦标赛 [jǐn biāo sài] championship

金牌 [jīn pái] gold medal

银牌 [yín pái] silver medal

铜牌 [tóng pái] bronze medal

全能 [quán néng] all-rounded

全能冠军 [quán néng guàn jūn] all-round champion

拳术冠军 [quán shù guàn jūn] Quanshu champion

器械冠军 [qì xiè guàn jūn] instrument champion

开幕式 [kāi mù shì] opening ceremony

闭幕式 [bì mù shì] closing ceremony

（二）裁判组成员 [cái pàn zǔ chéng yuán] referee group member

总裁判长 [zǒng cái pàn zhǎng] chief referee

裁判长 [cái pàn zhǎng] chief referee

评分裁判员 [píng fēn cái pàn yuán] rating referee

套路检查员 [tào lù jiǎn chá yuán] routine inspectors

计时员 [jì shí yuán] timer

检录长 [jiǎn lù zhǎng] head registrar

宣告员 [xuān gào yuán] announcer

（三）竞赛项目 [jìng sài xiàng mù] Competition Items

规定套路 [guī dìng tào lù] regular routines

自选套路 [zì xuǎn tào lù]optional routine

传统套路 [chuán tǒng tào lù]traditional routine

个人项目 [gè rén xiàng mù]individual event

全能项目 [quán néng xiàng mù]combined events

集体项目 [jí tǐ xiàng mù]group event

表演项目 [biǎo yǎn xiàng mù]exhibition event

（四）竞赛规则 [jìng sài guī zé]Competiton Rules

点名 [diǎn míng]call the roll

预备 [yù bei]ready

开始 [kāi shǐ]start

上场、出场 [shàng chǎng、chū chǎng]enter the court

进场、入场 [jìn chǎng、rù chǎng]entrance

抱拳礼 [bào quán lǐ]salute with fist

比赛 [bǐ sài]competition

决赛 [jué sài]finals

退场 [tuì chǎng]exit

（五）评分标准 [píng fēn biāo zhǔn]Grading Standards

动作规格 [dòng zuò guī gé]standard of movements

演练水平 [yǎn liàn shuǐ píng] performance level

姿势 [zī shì]posture

劲力 [jìn lì]strength;power

节奏 [jié zòu]rhythm;rhythm

速度 [sù dù]speed

精神 [jīng shén]spirit

风格 [fēng gé]style

协调 [xié tiáo]coordination

内容 [nèi róng]content

布局 [bù jú]arrangement

结构 [jié gòu]structure

准确 [zhǔn què]accuracy

熟练 [shú liàn]proficiency

沉稳 [chén wěn]stability

发声 [fā shēng]sound-making

分段 [fēn duàn]section

动作组合 [dòng zuò zǔ hé] moves combination

训练 [xùn liàn]training

起伏 [qǐ fú] up and down

定势 [dìng shì]fixed posture

编排内容 [biān pái nèi róng]content

创新难度 [chuàng xīn nán dù]degree of difficulty of movements innovation

现场演练 [xiàn chǎng yǎn liàn] on- the-spot demonstration

（六）扣分内容 [kòu fēn nèi róng]Defuction

没有完成套路 [méi yǒu wán chéng tào lù]unfinished routine

器械、服装影响动作 [qì xiè、fú zhuāng yíng xiǎng dòng zuò]movement affected by appliances and costumes

碰身 [pèng shēn]touch the body

器械折断 [qì xiè zhé duàn]appliance broken

器械掉地 [qì xiè diào dì]appliance fall on the carpet

弯曲变形 [wān qū biàn xíng]apparatus deformed

上体晃动 [shàng tǐ huàng dòng]body shaking

脚移动 [jiǎo yí dòng]foot moving

脚跳动 [jiǎo tiào dòng]foot jumping

倒地 [dǎo dì]fall onto the carpet

附加动作 [fù jiā dòng zuò]additional movement

附加支撑 [fù jiā zhī chēng]additional support; extra support

弃权 [qì quán]quit

出界 [chū jiè]outside boundary

遗忘 [yí wàng]forget

失去平衡 [shī qù píng héng]lose balance

重做 [chóng zuò]re-perform

时间不符合规定 [shí jiān bù fú hé guī dìng]time violation

服装（开纽）[fú zhuāng [kāi niǔ]](costume) unbuttoned

击打落空 [jī dǎ luò kōng]miss in attack

误中对方 [wù zhòng duì fāng]hitting the partner by mistake

队形不整齐 [duì xíng bù zhěng qí]unclear-cut movements during team performance

轻微不符 [qīng wēi bù fú]slight inconformity

显著不符 [xiǎn zhù bù fú]apparent inconformity

严重不符 [yán zhòng bù fú]serious inconformity

扣分 [kòu fēn]deduction of points

加分 [jiā fēn]bonus

取消比赛资格 [qǔ xiāo bǐ sài zī gé]disqualify

示分 [shì fēn]display points

得分相等 [dé fēn xiāng děng]same score

最后得分 [zuì hòu dé fēn]final score

最高分 [zuì gāo fēn]highest score

最低分 [zuì dī fēn]lowest score

总分 [zǒng fēn]total points

七、武术组织制度术语 [wǔ shù zǔ zhī zhì dù shù yǔ]Organizations and Hierarchy

组织机构 [zǔ zhī jī gòu]Organizations

中央国术馆 [zhōng yāng guó shù guǎn]Chinese Central Wushu Gymnasium

中国武术协会 [zhōng guó wǔ shù xié huì]Chinese Wushu Association

国家体育总局武术研究院 [guó jiā tǐ yù zǒng jú wǔ shù yán jiū yuàn]Wushu Research Institute of Chinese General Bureau of Sports

中国体育科学学会武术分会 [zhōng guó tǐ yù kē xué xué huì wǔ shù fēn huì]Wushu Branch of Chinese Academy of Sports Science

国际武术联合会 [guó jì wǔ shù lián hé huì]International Wushu Federation

亚洲武术联合会 [yà zhōu wǔ shù lián hé huì]Asian Wushu Federation

武术教练员技术等级 [wǔ shù jiào liàn yuán jì shù děng jí]Technical Hierarchy of Wushu Coaches

国家级教练员 [guó jiā jí jiào liàn yuán] national coach

高级教练员 [gāo jí jiào liàn yuán] senior coach

武术运动员技术等级 [wǔ shù yùn dòng yuán jì shù děng jí] Technical Hierarchy of Wushu Athletes

武英级 [wǔ yīng jí] Wushu Master (or Wushu athletes of master grade)

一级武士 [yī jí wǔ shì] Wushu athletes of first grade

二级武士 [èr jí wǔ shì] Wushu athletes of second grade

三级武士 [sān jí wǔ shì] Wushu athletes of third grade

武术裁判员技术等级 [wǔ shù cái pàn yuán jì shù děng jí] Technical Hierarchy of Wushu Referees

国际级裁判员 [guó jì jí cái pàn yuán] international referee

国家级裁判员 [guó jiā jí cái pàn yuán] state (or national) referee

一级裁判员 [yī jí cái pàn yuán] referee of first grade

二级裁判员 [èr jí cái pàn yuán] referee of second grade

中国武术段位制 [zhōng guó wǔ shù duàn wèi zhì] Grading System of Chinese Wushu

初段位 [chū duàn wèi] Junior Grades

一段 [yī duàn] the first grade

二段 [èr duàn] the second grade

三段 [sān duàn] the third grade

中段位 [zhōng duàn wèi] Middle Grades

四段 [sì duàn] the fourth grade

五段 [wǔ duàn] the fifth grade

六段 [liù duàn] the sixth grade

高段位 [gāo duàn wèi] Senior Grades

七段 [qī duàn] the seventh grade

八段 [bā duàn] the eighth grade

九段 [jiǔ duàn] the ninth grade

八、歌诀、谚语 [gē jué、yàn yǔ] Verses and Proverbs

未曾学艺先识礼，未曾习武先明德 [wèi céng xué yì xiān shi lǐ, wèi céng xí wǔ xiān míng dé]

Know courtesy before learning skill; cultivate one's virtues before learning Wushu.

中节不明，全身悬空 [zhōng jié bù míng, quán shēn xuán kōng]

(of practicing and fighting) If one doesn't know his mid-section, the gravity of the whole body he will lose his balance.

不怕千招会，就怕一招熟 [bù pà qiān zhāo huì, jiù pà yī zhāo shú]

Being good at one special movement is better than merely superficially learning a thousand.

手是两扇门，全凭脚打人 [shǒu shì liǎng shàn mén, quán píng jiǎo dǎ rén]

The hands are like two doors for protection and the legs are mainly used for attacking.

行家一伸手，便知有没有 [háng jiā yī shēn shǒu, biàn zhī yǒu méi yǒu]

A master shows ability at the very beginning.

练拳不练功，到老一场空 [liàn quán bù liàn gōng, dào lǎo yī chǎng kōng]

One who practices Quan without basic training will eventually make vain attempts.

练拳不活腰，终究艺不高 [liàn quán bù huó yāo, zhōng jiū yì bù gāo]

One who practices Quan without being able to wiggle the waist freely will never be skillful.

剑走青，刀走黑 [jiàn zǒu qīng, dāo zǒu hēi]

The key for practicing sword is being smart, and the key for practicing broadsword is being strong.

一日练，一日功，一日不练十日空 [yī rì liàn, yī rì gōng, yī rì bù liàn shí rì kōng]

One day's practice leads to one day's attainment. Without practice for even one day, all is in vain.

拳打千遍，身法自然 [quán dǎ qiān biàn, shēn fǎ zì rán]

Practicing thousands of times helps create natural body technique.

力要顺达，功宜纯 [lì yào shùn dá, gōng yí chún]

The force should be smooth and the skills should be highly proficient.

无拳无勇，职为乱阶 [wú quán wú yǒng, zhí wéi luàn jiē]

If one has no fighting skills nor courage, then he is not a good Wushu player.

手似流星眼似电 [shǒu sì liú xīng yǎn sì diàn]

The hands should be quick as shooting stars and the eyes as electric current.

外练手眼身法步，内修精神气力功 [wài liàn shǒu yǎn shēn fǎ bù, nèi xiū jīng shén qì lì gong]

External training concerns the hands, eyes, and foot pace. Internal cultivation concerns spirit, Qi, force, and Gong.

习武贵在得法，求功尚在持久 [xí wǔ guì zài dé fǎ, qiú gōng shàng zài chí jiǔ]

The most important thing in practicing Wushu is to grasp the methods, and the pursuit of achievements is to stick up long enough.

尊师要像长流水，爱徒要如鸟哺雏 [zūn shī yào xiàng cháng liú shuǐ, ài tú yào rú niǎo bǔ chú]

Respecting your master is like long-lasting flowing water, and caring your disciples is like birds feeding their babies.

枪为百兵之王，剑为百兵之君 [qiāng wéi bǎi bīng zhī wáng, jiàn wéi bǎi bīng zhī jun]

The spear is the king of all weapons, and the sword is the lord of all weapons.

四两拨千斤，一力降十会 [sì liǎng bō qiān jīn, yī lì xiáng shí huì]

The tiny force can move the thousand tons, and the great force can beat ten skillful tricks

冬练三九，夏练三伏 [dōng liàn sān jiǔ, xià liàn sān fú]

Practice in the bitterest cold winter and the hottest summer.

无前后，能者为师 [wú qián hòu, néng zhě wéi shī]

In Wushu learning, there is no old nor young, the one who does better can be the teacher.

拳如流星臂如鞭，腰走龙蛇眼似电 [quán rú liú xīng bì rú biān, yāo zǒu lóng shé yǎn sì diàn]

The fist is as fast as a meteor, the arm goes as fast as a whip, the waist is as flexible as a dragon and the snake and the eyes are like electric current.

百看不如一练，百练不如一专 [bǎi kàn bú rú yī liàn, bǎi liàn bú rú yī zhuān]

It's better to practice once than to watch thousand times.It is better to focus on one thing than learning hundred things.

师傅领进门，修行在个人 [shī fu lǐng jìn mén, xiū xíng zài gè rén]

The master will lead you in Wushu world, but the learning totally depends on yourself.

内练一口气，外练筋骨皮 [nèi liàn yī kǒu qì, wài liàn jīn gǔ pí]

Practice breathing inside and muscles and bones outside.

强中自有强中手，莫在人前自夸口 [qiáng zhōng zì yǒu qiáng zhōng shǒu, mò zài rén qián zì kuā kǒu]

You can never be good enough in Wushu practice, so never show off in public.

发于根，顺于中，达于梢 [fā yú gēn, shùn yú zhōng, dá yú shāo]

(of the club practicing)generated from the root, smooth in the middle, all the force reaches to the end.

刀如猛虎，剑似飞凤 [dāo rú měng hǔ, jiàn sì fēi fèng]

The broadsword is like a tiger, and the sword is like a phoenix.

单刀看手，双刀看走 [dān dāo kàn shǒu, shuāng dāo kàn zǒu]

Single broadsword playing focuses on hands movements, and double broadsword playing focuses on feet movements.

主要参考文献

Bibliography

中国武术大辞典编辑委员会. 中国武术大辞典 [M]. 北京：人民体育出版社，1990.9

Chinese Wushu Dictionary Editorial Board. *Dictionary of Chinese* Wushu [M]. Beijing: People's Sports Press, 1990.9

中国武术拳械录编纂组. 中国武术拳械录 [M]. 北京：人民体育出版社，1993.6

Chinese Wushu Weapons Records Compilation Committee.*Chinese Wushu* Weapons R*ecords* [M]. Beijing: people's sports press,1993.6

中国武术百科全书编撰委员会. 中国武术百科全书 [M]. 北京：中国大百科全书出版社，1998.10

Chinese Wushu Encyclopedia Compilation Committee. *Encyclopedia of Chinese* W*ushu* [M].Beijing: Encyclopedia of China Publishing House, 1998.10

全国体育院校教材委员会. 武术理论基础 [M]. 北京：人民体育出版社，1997.7

National Sports Teaching Materials Committee of Physical Education Institutions. *Basis of* Wushu T*heory* [M]. Beijing: People's Sports Press, 1997.7

陕西省文化厅. 红拳 [M]. 西安：陕西人民美术出版社，2014.11

Cultural Department of Shaanxi Province.Hong Quan[M].Xi'an: Shaanxi People's Fine Arts Publishing House, 2014.10

全国体育院校教材委员会. 中国武术教程（上册）[M]. 北京：人民体育出版社，2004.1

National Sports Teaching Materials Committee of Physical Education Institutions. *Chinese* Wushu C*ourse* (volume 1) [M]. Beijing: People's Sports Publishing House, 2004.1

全国体育院校教材委员会. 体育学院专修通用教材《武术》（上册）[M]. 北京：人民体育出版社，1991.6

National Sports Teaching Materials Committee of Physical Education Institutions. Wushu (volume1) [M].Beijing: People's Sports Publishing House, 1991.6

温搏. 中国武术中英双语教程 [M]. 北京：北京师范大学出版社，2014.2

Wen Bo.*Chinese and English Bilingual Course of* Wushu [M].Beijing: Beijing Normal University Press, February, 2014

张大为. 武术谚语释义 [M]. 北京：红旗出版社，1988

Zhang Dawei. Interpretation *of* Wushu P*roverb*s [M]. Beijing: Red flag Publishing House, 1988

赵大元. 实用擒拿学 [M]. 北京：人民体育出版社，2008.1

Zhao Dayuan. *Practical* Qinna. Beijing: People's Sports Publishing House, 2008.1

李天骥，李德印. 形意拳术 [M]. 北京：人民体育出版社，1981.12

Li Tianji, Li Deyin, Xingyi Quan, Beijing: People's Sports Publishing House, 1981.12

后 记

中国武术有着神奇的魅力，无形之中让热爱追求的修炼者总想为它做些什么。我出生于关中文武圣地，从小接受关中红拳熏陶、洗礼，其传统古典的练习手段、方法、思路、理念在我脑海里生根发芽，一直影响着我对武术的认知与修悟。结合武术专业学习、训练和武术教学工作积淀，理论学习、实践和思考让我思维更加清晰，认识变得明锐，越发想为传统武术做些力所能及的挖掘工作，希望从肤浅的技能动作上能有所传承，由此为基，才好更大地奢望传统武术技法实战的拓展发掘。所以，有了这本传统武术教程，希望从武术文化、基本技能、功法等传承与弘扬进行探究，培养学生传统文化的习得与弘扬，有效推动传统武术文化传承与国际化发展，助力中国文化"走出去"，以公共外交发挥传统武术文化价值与功能。

书中难免有观点和认识上的错误，不足之处敬请批评指正，我们将虚心接受和学习。

最后，以后记的惯例衷心诚意地抒发感谢一番。

感谢我的武术师父王镇邦、王辉、韦志平、张开来、张林等老师，本科学习阶段的白鸿顺老师，李正恩老师，通备拳艺师父、硕士导师刘宝禄教授，博士导师董尚文教授，有了他们的无私奉献与时常指导，才有了我开展武术工作的滴滴进步，感谢各个学习阶段帮助我的老师们，以及书中引用文献资料的学者老师们。感谢好友杜林哲为动作拍照，好友崔晓峰和周勇强提供场地和帮助，李磊为擒拿术陪练，感谢我的学生靳鑫和介耀辉处理图片，感谢黄淮学院教务处和体育学院领导及同事们，正是有了您们的帮助，才有了我学术研究上的进步。感谢为拙作出版进行审查、修正以及出版事宜联系的朋友和编辑。

肖亚康

2022 年 11 月

Acknowledgments

Chinese Wushu has magical charm, which attracts the practitioners who have fallen in love with it to do something for it. I was born in Guanzhong (Shaanxi Province) and influenced deeply by Guanzhong Hong Quan since I was a child. Its traditional and classical practice means, methods, ideas and concepts have taken root in my mind, which has always affected my cognition and cultivation of Wushu. With the accumulation of professional Wushu learning, training and teaching, I have built up a systematic understanding of Wushu theory, practice, learning and teaching, which makes me have much desire to do something for the inheritance and development of Wushu. Therefore, with this bilingual course of traditional Wushu, we hope to explore the inheritance, cultivate students' acquisition and communicate Chinese culture. That will also help Chinese culture "go out", and give full play to the value of traditional Wushu culture through public diplomacy. If there is any deficiency, don't hesitate to tell us and we will be very grateful.

At last, I would like to thank my Wushu masters Wang Zhenbang, Wang Hui, Wei Zhiping, Zhang Kailai, Zhang Lin and other famous masters. Pro. Bai Hongshun, Pro. Li Zhengen in my BA learning, Pro. Liu Baolu in my MA learning, and Pro. Dong Shangwen in my Ph.D learning and other professors and colleagues due to their selfless dedication and guidance, I have made great progress in my academic work. I would like to thank all the teachers who helped me in every learning stage, as well as the scholars and teachers who cited the literature in the book. My thanks also go to Du Linzhe, the photographer, Cui Xiaofeng and Zhou Yongqiang, who arranged the photostudio, and Li Lei, my training partner in the pictures. Jin Xin and Jie Yaohui, my students, who made the photos, and to the leaders and colleagues of the Physical Education School of Huanghuai University, whose help has made my academic research and personal progress possible. I would like to thank my friends and editors for the revision and the publication of this book.

Xiao Yakang
November 2022